W9-BVG-823

14. 12. ﬔ

To my wonderful Lots- family
with the best wishes for the days
to come
        your
            most grateful Garry

Christmas 1951.

THE
BOOK OF
AUSTRIA

PUBLISHED BY ÖSTERREICHISCHE
STAATSDRUCKEREI·VIENNA

Compiled
and issued by

Ernst Marboe

Translated by

G·E·R·Gedye

English versions
of songs and poems by
Patricia de Ferro

ILLUSTRATIONS

**Architectural sketches,
maps and plans,**

Eugenie Pippal-Kottnig

**Pictorial maps
and decorative illustrations,**

Hans Robert Pippal

**Fashions, national costumes,
decorative illustrations,**

Elli Rolf

**Illuminated lettering,
general arrangement of text
and illustrations,**

Epi Schlüsselberger

The following persons have together been responsible for about a third of the text;

Dr. Egid Filek

Arthur Fischer-Colbrie

Karl Emmerich Gasser

Dr. Franz Gschnitzer

Dr. Franz Hadamowsky

Dr. Fritz Heer

Dr. Hanns Koren

Dr. Hans M. Loew

Dr. Alfred Micholitsch

Dr. Hans Nusko

Hans Riemer

Bernhard Scheichelbauer

Alois Schiferl

Dr. Edwin Vysloncil

Erik G. Wickenburg

Dr. Fritz Zimmermann

MARGINAL NOTES TO
"THE BOOK OF AUSTRIA".

There is a gap in the world's knowledge of Austria. Perhaps we ourselves are to blame. There is another gap in the literature concerning Austria. Let us hasten to bridge them both.

In contrast to other books, the Book of Austria does not wait until you encounter it by chance. It comes to you, approaches you in word and picture—and in many another way.

Learn to know Austria, for it is a lovely part of the world. Get to know Austria through yourself, for it is a large part of you.

Negative declarations—what the "Book of Austria" does not attempt to be:—Neither a Baedeker nor an encyclopedia, neither a history of the country nor an art history, neither a festival issue nor an almanach. And yet—take it for all in all, it is a book.

A warning against misunderstanding: the reproductions are described as plates, the other pictures are most of them illustrations of the text. These latter are modern; the Book of Austria is intended mainly for contemporary readers.

Austria is made up of nine different provinces, and for this reason the various parts of the country have been presented in nine widely diverging monographs. The way in which heterogenous chapters have been collected side by side corresponds to the contrasts of the country and its life. Unfortunately a book is no library.

The Book of Austria is indebted to the Fine Arts and Natural History Museums, the Municipal Collections of Vienna, the House, Court and State Archives, and in particular to the Austrian National Library, more especially to its Picture Archives, for their very valuable assistance.

The Österreichische Staatsdruckerei (Austrian State Publishing Office) has had a major share in the production of the Book of Austria, in editing, printing and publishing, showing great consideration and full understanding in the difficult question of arrangement. The graphic staff deserve special mention for their willing and enthusiastic co-operation, whereby they have given fresh proof, not only of their exceptional technical skill but also of their devotion to their profession.

Ernst Marboe

CONTENTS.

PART I

ILLUSTRATED
FEUILLETON
AUSTRIA

UNBORN
AUSTRIA

HE WHO WOULD FIND AUSTRIA ON THE GLOBE MUST TURN THE ROUND BALL OF THE EARTH SLOWLY ON ITS SLANTING AXIS, OTHERWISE HE MIGHT EASILY OVERLOOK THE AUSTRIA OF THE 20TH CENTURY.

The "Venus" of Willendorf, (approximately 15,000 years B.C.)

WHERE IS THIS MUCH-TALKED-OF AUSTRIA? WHAT IS HER PLACE IN SPACE AND TIME, IN HISTORY AND CULTURE?

3

I f, as Hercules set forth to pluck the golden apple of the Hesperides, he had asked the giant Atlas who supported the arch of the heavens upon his shoulders, whether the weight of Austria seemed an especial burden to his neck, the latter would have wonderingly denied it.

Or he might have answered: "Austria, is there such a thing?" In this he would not have been entirely in the wrong, for in those times, as the giant Atlas and Hercules, son of the gods, were each cunningly seeking to lay the burden of the heavens upon the others' shoulders, the world did not extend beyond the confines of the Mediterranean. The part of the earth where Austria lies was unknown to the Greeks. Never would they have planned expeditions to it—the cattle of the Sun God did not graze there, no Golden Fleece could be won there, and King Eurystheus would at most have been able to give Hercules a thirteenth task for the winning of immortality; that of clearing vast forests, and the uniting in a single stream of a great malachite-green river with its many arteries stretching across boundless steppes.

For this reason, that part of the earth which lay to the North-East behind Olympus was for long presumed by the Greeks to be a realm of the dead. A secret. Impenetrable darkness, the mystery of birth and death in the magic mists of creation and mythology.

4

The secret of all origins, of all creation, is to be found in the territories through which flows a mighty river out of the heart of Europe eastward, parallel to the towering chain of the snow-capped Alps.

Regarded from that historical distance which is the present, with all that it has brought us as evidence of the past, we see the coming and going of peoples intermingling, pairing off, becoming fruitful and multiplying. Biological selection works among tribes and races during their centuries of migration.

3500 to 2000 B.C. Stone-Age. Indogermanic tribes.

2000 to 1000 B.C. Illyrians.

776 B.C. The first Greek Olympiad.

753 B.C. The founding of Rome.

Driven by vast forces—storms and floods, famine and drought at their heels, living now in nomads' tents, now in the lake-dwellings of the New Stone Age, or in straw-huts, gradually learning to know Celtic walls, Roman boundary walls of stone and the wooden forts of the Huns, widely differentiated races moved across that part of Europe which was later to become Austria—primitive peoples, Illyrians, Celts, Cimbrians, Teutons, Marcomanians, Vandals, Allemanians, Huns, Goths, Avars, Slavs, Magyars and perhaps other nameless, uncounted hordes.

1700 B.C. The Bronce Age.

1100 B.C. The Hallstatt Period.

All these tribes wandered through the areas which are watered by this river, or lie at the foot of the Alps. It became a bridge for the migrating peoples, who by their passage through it merged their individual histories into the pattern of a still undiscernible future.

600 B.C. The Celts pass through Europe.

594 B.C. Solon in Athens.

The bartering of the primitive necessities of daily life and work began; wax, honey, pine-torches and cheese were given in exchange for tools, for pins to fasten garments, for battle-axes and urns.

Two highways traversed these territories. Along the one, the River Danube, the timid natives paddled their barques eastwards, laden with rocksalt. Down the other, the "Road of Amber", the golden-yellow trinkets from the coasts of Jutland and from the virgin, white-shell-covered shores of the Baltic passed down through Bohemia, skirting the Alps, to the warmer seas of the South. In Rome and in

Alexandria the amber found a ready market for use as ornaments.

The hub of the great wheel of trade and commerce gradually centered on Carnuntum, east of Vienna. The Roman genius for spreading civilisation was quick to appreciate the importance of the lands of the Alps and the Danube. Before long, the Consul of the Roman Empire was bargaining with the chieftains of Celtic tribes for the right to exploit iron-fields in Upper Krain.

399 B.C. Death of Socrates.

La Tene-Period.

Following on the mining prospectors from Rome, over the Alps came the merchants of Northern Italy, their waggons laden with heady and intoxicating wines. Close on their heels followed civilisation, with its strange, new conception of luxury in life. The doctrines of Epicurus taught that life's aim should be pleasure. ... A little later, gold was mined for Rome in the Tauern Mountains and in the valley of Gastein.

146 B.C. Greece becomes a Roman province.

150 B.C. Celtic Federal State in the Danube Alpine lands.

Roman Coach, Maria Saal.

Just at the time that the Celtic tribes of the Alps were coming under the sway of Roman colonists, and the advance guards of the Roman Legions were approaching the Danube, strange races burst out of the mysterious forests beyond the Elbe and overran the lands of the Bojars and thrust down into the South-East. First came the Cimbrians, then the Teutons, blond-headed, blue-eyed giants, accompanied by their well-grown women-folk.

113 B.C. The Romans defeated at Noreia.

101 B.C. Marius defeats the Cimbrians.

When this invading torrent from the North had been flung back, the Alpine valleys were open to Roman expansion. Along the

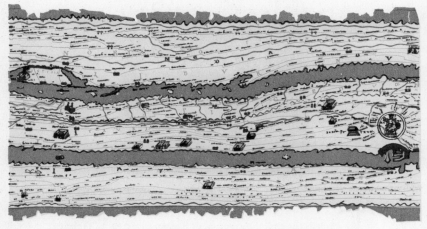

Tabula Peutingeriana, Roman Road Map.

magnificent new military and trading routes marched the Roman Legions, protected by their stout stone walls, towards the River Danube. Behind the protecting frontiers of the Roman Empire, the Legionary was at once the guardian of an empire and the pioneer of a highly developed civilisation. Wheat and the vine, cherries and peaches, flourished along the Danube.

After the Legionaries came civil administrators, Roman citizenship and the law, architects and tax-gatherers. Along the line of the river grew up a network of fortifications and citadels stretching from Regensburg and Passau through Linz, Enns and Mautern right up to the foot of the Alps, closing in on the Rhine in the West and spreading out in search of yet more territory to the South-West.

7

The Tassilo Cup, Kremsmünster.

12 to 9 B.C.

9 A.D. Battle of
the Teutoburg
Forest.

64 A.D. Nero,
the Burning of
Rome.

70 A.D. The De-
struction of Jeru-
salem.

The Birth of
Christ.

19 A.D.

Towards the end of the period of Roman supremacy, Tiberius, wishing to consolidate the rule of Rome up to the Danube against attack from the North, built a fortress at Carnuntum which was at one and the same time a key-position and centre of communications. Simultaneously he made it the seat of the Governor of the Province of Pannonia, which included the Vienna Forest and stretched from it to the spot where Budapest stands to-day. Alongside the military fortifications a civilian settlement came into existence, inhabited at first by traders and merchants. Soon there were added to this settlement decorative and comfortable noble houses, and holy shrines decorated with reliefs.

This was a strange facet of Rome's Empire, this on the Danube: a garrison made up of Syrian troops, moved hither in case of trouble during the siege of Jerusalem, the cult of Mythras, a temple to Jupiter Dolichenus. Here was the base and the harbour of the Danube flotilla, an amphitheatre holding 8,000 persons and extensive thermal baths, doubly valued by the Romans in the damp climate of the northern forests—a brilliant epoch under the aegis of provincial Governors and a philosophic Emperor.

115 A.D. Persecution of the Christians under Trajan.

With the death of Marcus Aurelius, the shadow of approaching disintegration spread over the far-flung Roman Empire. And just at this time, a new star which had risen in the Eastern provinces ascended out of the depths of the catacombs. Gentle-mannered men traversed the countryside with strange and wonderful tidings. Their talk was of a supreme God, of triumph over death, and of the equality of all mankind. From the shores of the Black Sea to the far-off island of Britain they carried their doctrine of love. They preached that a new empery was at hand, not of this world, and different from the Roman Empire of the Praetorians and of Caesar.

180 A.D. Marcus Aurelius dies at Vindobona.

300 to 400 A.D. Christianity appeares on the shores of the Danube.

300 A.D. Persecution of Christians under Diocletian.

A new empery—did, then, the peoples of Europe desire this? Suddenly, without warning, vast tribes of men were seen on the move. Deserting their homelands, they formed themselves into great moving columns which migrated across the whole continent of Europe. Uninvited, unexpected, they surged forwards from the North and the East. From the shores of the Baltic Sea they came, from Holstein and Jutland, from the broad plains of the Vistula, from the vast steppes of Russia. And in their wake, leaving behind them the plains of Mongolia, came the Huns.

375 A.D. The Migration of Peoples sets in.

Soon Austria was submerged beneath the wild and uncontrollable flood of migrating peoples. Sullenly the Celto-Roman peasantry clung to the soil of the Danube lands, where before long they found themselves without the protection of the walled citadels. Vandals, West Goths and Huns approached from the East. At Attila's Court on the river Theiss, Hun chieftains and Germanic and Slavonic hostages, the children of kings, intermingled with the Asiatic women. The ominous tramping of the marching columns—Slavs, Teutons, Syrians and Samarians, Burgundians, Franks, Goths and Thuringians, Celto-Romans and Vandals, shook the soil of the Danube country, while its inhabitants could only suffer in silence. All the highways used by the migrating hordes came together on this territory, which from the beginning had formed a turntable between North and South, East and West.

In Celtic times there arose on a terrace whose cliffs ran down in the North-East towards the former main channel of the Danube (today the Danube Canal) the old Vindobona, still plainly recognisable above the Salzgries near the Church of St. Maria am Gestade.

The strategic advantages of this situation were utilised in the permanent Roman camp under Claudius, who retained the name of Vindobona. In the North-West the camp was bounded by the deep channel of the Otta-kring brook, the "Tiefe Graben" of today. In the East also, along the line of what is now the Rotenturmstrasse, there was a ditch which turned to the South-West by the Stock-im-Eisen Square, forming, as a natural moat, the "Graben", which constituted the defence against the West. The walls, which were still visible in the middle of the 13th century, formed a square, with rounded corners, and were set about with towers. One of them near the old Freisingerhof, long remained standing on the site of the present Graben Café. Within the camp the main road, the "Via Principalis", ran across the settle-ment in the direction of the Lichtensteg and the Wipplinger-strasse. Outside the camp walls lay the civilian town, a conglomeration of traders' booths, stretching out towards the road leading southwards, the Heeresstrasse.

11

394 A.D.

Silently the darkened soil swallowed up lamentation and mourning, hopes and horrors.

Meanwhile, in the arenas of the Roman Empire, Christianity had progressed after an age of suffering from being a religion of martyrs into becoming a State religion. Out of the catacombs the liberated Christians had emerged into the light of day. Their priests had penetrated across the frontiers and through the passes of the Alps, setting up at first hermit's cells, and later, monasteries. While Odoaker, Prince of the Herulans, was establishing himself as King in Rome, St. Severin was converting the people to Christianity.

Carnuntum was still to experience the glories of the meeting of the four Emperors—Diocletian, Galerius, Maximinian and Licinius—in the year 307 A.D. A century later its very name was obliterated in the storm of migrating races. Vindobona, on the other hand, we find noted in the records of the Goths (under the name of Vindomina) in the year 493 as being the most important place in Western Pannonia. The city is first mentioned under the name of Vienna about 880 A.D., during the struggles between the Franks and Magyars.

The tribe of the Bajuvars (Bavarians) made good its footing in Southern Germany in the sixth century Christianising and Germanising influences pushed slowly but surely towards the East, until at last the Empire of the Franks was established under Charlemagne. The new polity assumed, during decades of bloody warfare, the task of securing the Danube territories against the onslaughts of Avars and Magyars.

Armed with the mandates of their overlord, king or bishop, and, for the rest, relying on their personal faith and courage, dukes with their retinues, abbots with their monks, rode forward

476 A.D. End of the West-Roman Empire.

529 A.D. Founding of the Benedictine Monastery at Monte Cassino.

590 to 604 A.D. Pope Gregory the Great.

488 A.D. Withdrawal of the Roman troops of occupation from Austria.

568 A.D. The Avars in the Danube Area.

700 A.D. Saint Ruprecht in Salzburg.

739 A.D. Bonifacius founds the Bishopric of Salzburg.

816 A.D. Salzburg receives the right of jurisdiction.

955 A.D. The Magyars defeated at Lechfeld. End of the migration of peoples.

Nibelung Song.

Then spake the Tronje Hagen:
"Stand ye at the wall!
Let not the glowing ashes
Fall on your helmet straps.
With your feet stamp them deeper
Into the bloody mass
This was a sorry wedding
To which the queen
bade us."

Amidst such scenes and anguish
The night at last passed by
And still before the threshold
The minstrel stood on guard
And Hagen his brave comrade,
Stood resting on his shield,
Still greater woe awaiting
From them of
Etzel's Land.

into the forbidding wilderness of vast territories, their faces set towards the rising sun. As they moved, they cleared the forests, ploughed up the land, fighting, colonising, establishing villages and monasteries and writing their names on the scrolls of history.

Under the rule of the Ottonians there came a turning point in the history of Europe. In 962 A.D. Otto the Great received the Imperial Crown of Rome at the hands of the Pope. With that act there came into being, through the intimate union of Church and Throne, that "Holy Roman Empire" which was to be dissolved only during the Napoleonic era in 1806. But Otto's only son, Otto II had to fight within the Empire to maintain its existence. Count Luitpold of Babenberg proved himself a loyal henchman of the Emperor in the crushing of the revolt of the Bavarians. As a reward he was endowed — moment of historic importance for Austria—with the Eastern Province of the Reich.

976 A.D. House of Babenberg begins to rule in Austria.

THE
DUCAL RESIDENCE
WANDERS

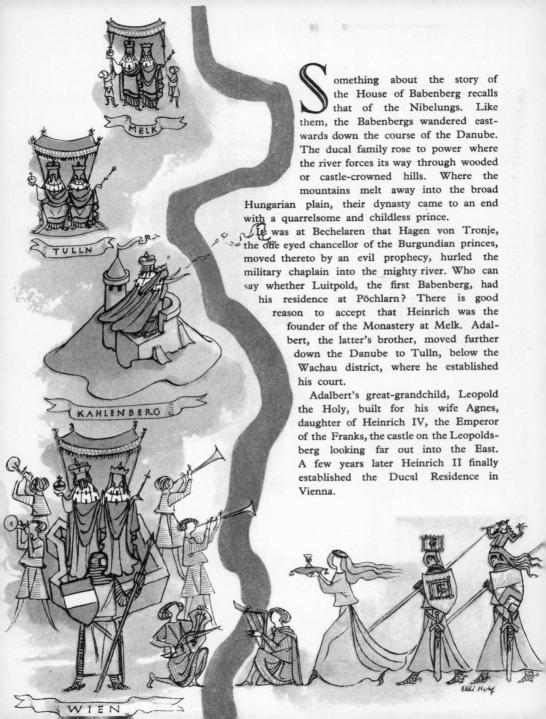

Something about the story of the House of Babenberg recalls that of the Nibelungs. Like them, the Babenbergs wandered eastwards down the course of the Danube. The ducal family rose to power where the river forces its way through wooded or castle-crowned hills. Where the mountains melt away into the broad Hungarian plain, their dynasty came to an end with a quarrelsome and childless prince.

It was at Bechelaren that Hagen von Tronje, the one eyed chancellor of the Burgundian princes, moved thereto by an evil prophecy, hurled the military chaplain into the mighty river. Who can say whether Luitpold, the first Babenberg, had his residence at Pöchlarn? There is good reason to accept that Heinrich was the founder of the Monastery at Melk. Adalbert, the latter's brother, moved further down the Danube to Tulln, below the Wachau district, where he established his court.

Adalbert's great-grandchild, Leopold the Holy, built for his wife Agnes, daughter of Heinrich IV, the Emperor of the Franks, the castle on the Leopoldsberg looking far out into the East. A few years later Heinrich II finally established the Ducal Residence in Vienna.

MELK

TULLN

KAHLENBERG

WIEN

Plate I

Erhard Altdorfer; St. Leopold Finding the Veil. Klosterneuburg Museum.

Plate II

Enamel Panel; The Master of Verdun, about 1181. Klosterneuburg Monastery.

How wise was the House of Babenberg! Frequently dragged into the dangerous feud between Pope and Emperor, forced to keep always a wary eye on the Bohemians and Magyars, joining in Crusades to the Holy Land, it never ceased its efforts, tenaciously and purposefully to consolidate its rule over its own domains.

In Austria, crafts and trade grew apace. Gold was washed from the sands of the Danube and the Inn, and mining developed. They found silver. They shipped salt down the Danube. Cities were named and became known — Enns, Krems, Graz and Judenburg. Wagons, heavily loaded with the goods of commerce, rumbled down the highways in all directions. Where the goods were handled, especially in Vienna, regular trading centres grew up which encouraged the circulation and the lending of money. Records of market dues and customs regulations, of bridge-tolls, river-dues and toll-gate-charges point to the growth of trade in the Danube valley.

Vienna, first mentioned as the scene of battles between Germans and Hungarians in 881 A.D. and again in 1030, blossomed forth as a centre of politics and trade soon after Heinrich Jasomirgott set up his ducal court at "Am Hof" in Vienna. Mentioned first as a fortified city in 1137, Vienna soon outstripped Krems and Enns as a market place and trading centre. As the furthest-flung Germanic centre for the deposit and storage of goods on the Danube, the Crusades acted as a spur to its activities. Under Heinrich II, a new settlement grew up around the Stephanskirche which was situated beyond the city walls, where foreign traders may well have had their settlement.

Under the rule of Leopold III, the Holy, the monasteries of Klosterneuburg and Heiligenkreuz were founded. In these places, as in Vienna, Leopold, the patron saint of Lower Austria, is still a popular name. *1095 to 1136.*

Heinrich Jasomirgott marks a milestone in Austrian history. It was under him that Austria was raised in 1156 to a duchy, with rights of succession through both male and female lines, and its own jurisdiction. From this date the Babenbergs were freed from the obligation to do duty at the Imperial Court or to do military service in distant parts. *1141 to 1177.*

This charter of independence, the "Privilegium Minus", which the Emperor Friedrich Barbarossa was constrained to grant in return for the renunciation of all claims to the ducal coronet of Bavaria, gave Austria a specially privileged

Ducal Crown.

position within the Roman-German Empire which led to its establishment as an independent state.

Leopold, known as "The Virtuous", never forgot his grievance against the English King Richard the Lionhearted, who had deeply wounded Leopold's honour and *1177 to 1194.*

reputation at the storming of the fortress of Acre, in the Holy Land. The Englishman, making his way home after having been ship-wrecked in the Adriatic, decided to proceed by way of Austria disguised as a merchant. This proved fateful to him in Vienna, where he was recognised. His captivity in Dürnstein Castle and his discovery by the faithful Blondel are recorded in contemporary ballads.

From the ransom paid for the English King, fortifications as protection against the East were built at Hainburg, Wiener Neustadt, and Bruck-on-the-Leitha. The virtuous but vindictive Babenberg was excommunicated by the Pope and died tortured by the pains of conscience.

Leopold the Glorious, married like Heinrich Jasomirgott to a Princess of Byzantium, was a visionary. He invaded the Holy Land to conquer Jerusalem for Christendom. On failing to realise this dream, he turned towards Egypt, where the fortunes of war went against him once more at Damiate.

In the country of his heritage he proved a friend of the peasants and of the townspeople. Under his rule, Vienna not only achieved the status of a city, but expanded to nearly nine times its former area. The Stephanskirche, in its original romanesque form already one of the greatest of basilicas, became the centre of the circular, walled-in city area. Within the mighty walls which with their 19 towers and six gates formed a ring round the city stood, even in the days of the Babenbergs, 21 churches and chapels. Houses were several stories high; below them lay two or more tiers of cellars.

Under the Babenbergs, Austria began to make its weight felt in the world—and not only in political affairs. Remote from the centre of Imperial power on the Rhine, the Babenbergs developed a ruling system which was backed by the loyalty of contented citizens and a well-to-do peasant class. Threatened sometimes by revolts of nobles, it was never overthrown by them.

Scattered throughout the land there arose stately monasteries—Kremsmünster, St. Florian, Melk, Göttweig, Klosterneuburg, Heiligenkreuz, Seitenstetten, Zwettl and Lilienfeld. Most remarkable was the rapid growth of prosperity in Vienna, By the end of the 12th century it had become the most important German city after Cologne. From the articles of its municipal charter we get a vivid picture of an industrious trading class and flourishing commerce. Soon the "Hausgenossen" (who struck the coinage) and the "Laubenherren" (the masters of the textile trade)

18

formed the beginnings of a well-to-do patrician middle class. Even apart from the existence of the House of Babenberg, it seemed that a proud future as a "Free Town" of the Reich awaited this city, which after 1237 was declared independent on numerous occasions.

The Song of the Nibelungs tells how Etzel and Kriemhild held their nuptials in Vienna. The "Wonniglicher Hof" (the "Blissful Court") at Vienna and the "Artushof" ("Arthur's Court") on the Danube drew the knights errant. "As the bees hasten to their hive, so do the mournful to the virtuous Prince of the House of Babenberg, there to lose their sorrows."

It was in the days of St. Leopold that the nun Ava composed the first German poetry. A generation later we hear of one Heinrich, of Reichersberg Monastery, and of one Heinrich, of Melk; Kürnberger, the Upper Austrian, first of the minstrels, made ballads of the folksongs.

At the court of Leopold V, Reinmar the Ancient, the Duke's Poet Laureate, and his pupil, Walther von der Vogelweide, broke through the trammels of fashionable romantic verse to pour forth an abundant richness of poetic art and verse forms.

Walther, who in his own words had learned "reciting and singing" in Austria, lived for twenty years at the Court of Vienna. Many of his phrases, particularly those of a political turn, fired his hearers like the words of popular orators. A powerful rhythm lent force to the simple language, the dialogue was richly dramatic. The fine, tenderly intimate forms of his lovesongs and lyrics place these at the head of all his compositions.

It was in Austria, too, that the moving legends of the migration of nations drawn from the subconscious memories of the peoples and given creative poetic form, found their ultimate and unique expression in the Song of the Nibelungs and the Song of Gudrun.

With Walther von der Vogelweide the brilliant epoch of poetry backed by the patronage of courts came to an end. Meantime, the destruction of the mediaeval corporations had become complete. The clashes between Empire and Papacy had weakened the conception of authority. The revolutionary movement of the Crusades brought to those who joined them equality,

There where we twain have sat together,
Under the linden on the wold,
Canst thou yet plain see where forever
The flowers are crushed in grassy mould.
Hard by a forest in a broad vale, tandaradei!
Sweetly sang the nightingale.

I came a-fleeting to sward shadye
But my darling was before!
Such was the greeting, Merciful Ladye!
That I am joyous evermore.
Oft must he have bent to kiss, tandara-
See how red my mouth still is   dei!

And flowers bringing me my lover
Did make for us a fragrant bed.
Any would have to laugh to see it,
If any should the same path tread.
By the roses he may see, tandaradei!
Where has lain the head of me.

And how we lay there, if one guessed,
Thou Gracious Lord, of shame I'd die!
What he dared do, and how he caressed,
Knoweth only he and I —
And a little birdielie, tandaradei!
It will surely silent be.

Walther von der Vogelweide um 1200

Gri
Schlüsselberger

Elli Rolf

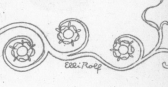

freedom and advancement in rank, on the sole condition that they took the Cross. The burghers came to the front in the towns. The chivalric order supported now the nobility, now the peasantry.

As the order of chivalry lost its meaning as a social institution with the decline of the thirteenth century, as poetry dependent on Court patronage degenerated into a parade of modes and mannerisms, Austria found a figure to characterise this period in Ulrich von Lichtenstein, the Don Quixote of chivalry.

Now the conception of money fell into bad odour. The granting of credits and the collection of interest came to dominate all aspects of trade and industry. To check the growth of usury, Leopold put up 30,000 silver marks to establish a municipal bank of credit. He lost the money, as the Church intensified its strictures on the taking of interest, so that money dealings passed more and more into the hands of the Jews. Sometimes a debtor found himself paying 200 per cent interest. The Church ordained spiritual penalties; under the threat of exclusion from the Sacrament and Christian burial, it was forbidden to charge interest in any form. The mere defence of money-lending and financial transactions was branded as heresy. By these means an attempt was made effectively to check the impoverishment of the masses and their reduction to a proletarian level.

1230 to 1246. Of the last Babenberg, Friedrich the Quarrelsome, Sassmann writes: "The Prince had the faculty of adding together his illusions and treating the totals as facts, even if they had not the remotest connection with reality." His reign was marked by a series of romantic experiments which from that time on became an essential part of Austrian history. A dozen times his fantastic warlike expeditions would meet with failure, on another occasion unexpected success would be his lot. It was in the middle of the 13th century that the vast Mongolian hordes swept on to Hungary after overrunning Russia and Poland. Europe was in a panic. The Pope preached a Crusade against the Yellow Peril. The German Emperor himself shrank from the struggle. Duke Friedrich ignored the fact that he stood alone against the onrush of 500,000 Mongols. With a few centuries of indifferent troops he occupied the fortified castles of Western Hungary and held them

Vienna Pfennig.

The Dukes of Babenberg appeared with their usual aimiability at the "Feast of Violets" with which the Viennese used to celebrate the approach of spring. From the dark and narrow streets of the city the women hurried out into the countryside where the meadows made a popular dance-floor for spritely measures. The man who found the first violet laid his hat over it and ran to the Duke at Vienna to tell him of the event. On receiving the news the latter left his affairs to come to the dance with all the ladies and gentlemen of his court. The lucky finder of the violet was allowed to choose the most beautiful or distinguished maiden as his dancing partner for the whole year.

Section of Vienna, Meister des Wiener Schottenstiftes.

until the Tartar flood receded. In the course of a subsequent dispute he made plans to seize the Crown from the King of Hungary, but fell fighting the Magyars at the Battle of Leitha. He left no heir, and with him the House of Babenberg became extinct. The country lapsed into chaos; prosperity had vanished as a result of wars and taxes. And yet this ruler on whom fortune so rarely smiled was one of the most popular of his race.

Despite everything, in the days of this last and cantankerous Babenberg and the collapse which followed his reign, people must have lived tolerably well. Perhaps

24

they did so anticipating the phrase which was later coined to characterise the Austrian attitude — "Live and let live". For the Poet Laureate of the last Friedrich declared that between Rhine and Danube, Elbe and Po, he found nowhere such happy peasants as in Austria.

As the House of Babenberg died out and the period called "the time of Terror, when no Emperor was" set in, the national characteristics of the Austrian people were formed. In the fertile soil of a conglomeration of races brought together by outside circumstances in the Austrian countryside, there lay, buried and dormant but ready to germinate, instincts and talents of diametrically opposed races. Gothic imagination, Hellenic vitality, Celtic sense of form and Slavonic intensity of feeling, bound together by the visions of the East and embodied now in the Austrian character, were ready to grow and to bear artistic fruit.

The *Genius loci*, Austria's oldest spiritual aristocracy, had been born.

WORLD HISTORY
BETWEEN
TWO GRILLPARZER
DRAMAS

Playbill of the First Performance of Grillparzer's "King Ottokar, His Rise and Fall".

1241. The Mongols invade Europe under Batu, son of Genghis Khan.

With Friedrich II a glorious epoch of Austrian history came to an end. The princely throne from which were governed two countries, Austria and Styria, whose confines stretched from the wild forests of Bohemia to the southern vineyards of the Adriatic, with prosperous cities, monasteries and markets, dotted with castles and populated by a contented, industrious and song-loving people, was left vacant after 270 years. Grillparzer depicts this period in the oft-quoted lines:

Walther von der Vogelweide, greatest of Austrian minstrels at the Court of Vienna.

> Look round about you! Where your eyes may rest,
> It laughs as when a bride goes to her bridegroom.
> Its meadows living green, its harvests gold,
> Broidered with flax and saffron blue and yellow,
> Sweet spiced with flowers and many a fragrant fruit,
> It sweeps beyond the verge in spacious valley —
> A rich bouquet of blossoms everywhere,
> Tied with the Danube's bow of silver ribbon.
> Higher it climbs to hills all clad in vines

Where up and up the golden cluster hang
And swell and ripen in God's sparkling sunshine,
While capping all, dark woods rejoice our hunters.
And over it God's breath is mild and soft,
Warming and ripening, making our pulses beat
As never a pulse beats on the chilly plains.
That's what the Austrian is, blithe and frank,
And wears both faults and pleasures in the open.
He envies none, preferring to be envied;
And what he does is done with cheerful heart.

(King Ottocar, His Rise and Fall, Ottocar Horneck, Act III)

The peaceful development of Austria was now interrupted by an uneasy period of indecisive struggles for the heritage of the Babenbergs. There was no one qualified to inherit under the "Privilegium Minus" of 1156. In consequence the Emperor Friedrich II, namesake of the last Babenberg, was tempted to seize the rich provinces as a vacant fief for the Reich. But this extension of Imperial power met with the energetic opposition of the Pope, who was just at this time engaged in a violent conflict with Friedrich II and had even pronounced a sentence of excommunication on him. Thus began the struggle between the papal and the imperial claimant for the Danube heritage. When the rival King, Wilhelm of Holland, acting on Papal orders, conferred Austria and Styria on the Margrave Hermann von Baden (who was married to a niece of the last Babenberg), the Emperor made the Duke of Bavaria ruler over Austria and installed the Count of Meran as Governor of Styria.

1248. Thomas Aquinas starts to teach in Cologne. Scholastic philosophy nears its climax.

1250. Death of the Staufen Emperor Friedrich II.

Founding of the Sorbonne in Paris.

The death of the Emperor Friedrich changed the situation. The Emperor left behind him a realm which was breaking up in chaos. Despotism and injustice flourished unchecked, while the weakness of men who were rulers in name only undermined the authority of the Imperial writ.

Wenceslaus I, Přemysl Ottokar, the ambitious son of the King of Bohemia, seized the opportunity thus presented to get possession of the heritage of the

Rudalfus Archidux Austrie tertii

Rudolf IV, the Endower.

The Italian Sculptor, Nicola Pisano, produces his famous reliefs in Pisa, Sienna and Bologna.

Babenbergs with the acquiescence of the Austrian nobles. Advancing through Linz and Enns, he entered Vienna on December 12th, 1251. At the Battle of Kroissenbrunn, Wenceslaus blocked a simultaneous effort made by Bela, King of Hungary, to extend his domains in the same way.

Pure aggrandisement of this type, making no pretence of legal justification, was obviously bound to end in conflict with a resuscitated Imperial power. It was at once apparent that such a disturbance of the political balance in Central Europe as the annexation of Austria was bound to have serious repercussions throughout the continent.

By adding Carinthia and Krain to his dominions, Ottokar secured a powerful position. He was successful in combining this with the pursuit of a wise policy at home.

> From the Baltic to the Adriatic Gulf,
> From Inn to Vistula with its cold shores
> There's none whom Ottocar does not command.
> The world since Charlemagne has never seen
> A realm as wide and great as that I rule.

(Ottocar, Act I)

1265. Dante Alighieri born in Florence.

The first general Parliament meets in London.

Middle of the 13th century. The Turks establish themselves in Asia Minor.

In the Austrian provinces Ottokar granted increased powers to the nobles and promoted the development of cities. Under his orders a feudal register was compiled in which land holdings and the concomitant services were recorded. Vienna was especially singled out for royal favours.

Behind Ottokar Přemysl's establishment of his kingdom was the idea of making Bohemia the centre of government from which to carry out the political organization of the Danube area. Very likely the King came later to realize that the position of his country was too near the periphery of that area, and his subjects too primitive, for him to be able to fulfill his self-imposed mission. Perhaps that is why we find a tendency on his part to

30

move the centre of gravity to the Southern part of his realm and as far as possible to encourage the Teutonic elements. Grillparzer interpreted this tendency with perhaps more psychological than historical accuracy when he made his Ottokar tell the Bohemians:

> I'll put the Germans where your fur is thick
> To nip and pinch till smart and anger rouse you
> From your dull torpor and you kick out
> Like a roweled horse.

(Ottocar, Act I)

When the Electors assembled in 1273 to select the new King, they were determined to choose an energetic personality who would be prepared to combat existing abuses, yet not such a mighty prince as, for example, Ottokar, who with his extensive power might seriously threaten German liberty. So their choice fell on Count Rudolf of Hapsburg, whose estates lay in the south-western part of the Empire. Only King Ottokar of Bohemia refused his agreement. The strong arm of the new German ruler soon made itself felt. His immediate object was to move against his dangerous rivals in the south-eastern areas of the Empire and restore law and order there. His enforcement of Imperial rights in Austria opened up for him a personally pleasant prospect, that of establishing extended powers for his own House, without which a strong German kingdom would be unimaginable.

1273 to 1291. Rudolf of Hapsburg.

1271. The Venetian Marco Polo sets out on his great voyage to Eastern Asia.

1276. Giotto di Bondone born. First appearance of Renaissance painting.

Vienna Hofburg, Schweizertor.

Ottokar was summoned to answer for his acts, first to Würzburg and later to Augsburg. When he failed on each occasion to put in an appearance, the Reichstag pronounced the forfeiture of all his fiefs and his own outlawry from the Empire. Thus a conflict became inevitable. In the autumn of the year 1276, Rudolf marched with his troops into Austria, where he was hailed as the bearer of Imperial authority and the guardian of the law.

Throughout the German lands peace now prevails;
The robber barons punished; feuds allayed;
Through prudent marriages, by use of force,
The Princes are at one and leagued with him;
The Pope supports him; with one common voice
All praise and bless him who has saved their lives.
Just recently, when he sailed down the Danube
With all his troops amid much noisy clamour,
The sound of bells rang out from either shore;
On either shore the shouts of joyful praise
From crowds who came and gaped amazed and knelt.

(Ottocar, Chancellor, Act III)

While the nobility, especially in Styria, rallied to his banner, Vienna closed her gates against him. The situation of Ottokar, who was camping in the Marchfeld, steadily deteriorated. Ladislaus, King of Hungary, who was allied to Rudolf, drew on with his forces, while disunity and desertion spread through Ottokar's ranks. Thereupon the Bohemian King decided to renounce all his acquisitions and to content himself with his hereditary domains, Bohemia and Moravia.

End of the 13th century.

North German towns of the Hanseatic League achieve a mono- poly position in European mari- time trade.

The peace, however, proved to be of short duration. The proud spirit of the "Golden King" could not swallow these humiliations. Spurred on by his ambitious consort, Kunigunde, he began accumulating arms for a new campaign which should re-establish his wider dominions. But Ottokar had already passed his zenith. In alliance with the Hungarians, Rudolf decisively defeated the Bohemians at Marchfeld in 1278. Ottokar himself fell in the battle.

You lie here stripped of royal show, great King,
Your head supported on your servant's lap.
And now of all your splendid robes and riches
You 've not a single scanty cover left
To use for shroud to wrap your body in.
The Imperial mantle you aspired to wear
See, I'll take off and spread it over you
That you be buried like an emperor,
Who died a poor and lonely beggar's death.

1280. In East Asia, Kubilai sets up the Great Mongolian Em- pire embracing the whole of China, Korea, Mongolia, Manchuria and Tibet.

(Ottocar, Rudolf of Hapsburg, Act V)

Few military events in the history of the world can compare in importance with this Hapsburgian victory. It settled the fate of South Eastern Europe

Plate III

Maximilian of Austria; From the Statute Book of the Order of
the Golden Fleece. Vienna, National Library.

Plate IV

Schoolbook of Maximilian I; Vienna, National Library.

for many centuries. The drawing of the political map of the Danubian territories fell, not to Bohemia, but to Austria. This development was bound up with the family which now assumed power in Austria. In 1282 Rudolf conferred Austria, Styria and Krain on his two sons, Albrecht and Rudolf. A year later, at the instance of the Estates, he decreed that Albrecht alone should hold the duchies of Austria and Styria, while Carinthia and Krain were allotted to Meinhard II of Tyrol.

> And now, my son...
> I will invest you with the fief of Austria.
> Be great and strong; increase your race and line
> Until it dwells in lands both near and far
> And Hapsburg's name shines glorious as a star.
> I hail you as the sovereign of this land.
> Come everyone, come loud your welcome cry,
> Until it rolls like thunder through the sky.
> Hail! The first Hapsburg hail in Austria!
>
> (Ottocar, Rudolf of Hapsburg, Act V)

But the Hapsburgs were not secured in their new position of power in the South-East. Internal and external enemies were soon on the scene to challenge the new ducal House. Rudolf's son, Albrecht I, proved himself the right man to master these troubles and to anchor the power of his family. Personally courageous and energetic, yet by nature conciliatory, he combined considerable strategic qualities with those of delicate diplomacy. Albrecht was as successful in foiling the intrigues of the nobles as in gaining the upper hand over a powerful coalition of princes which embraced the Archbishop of Salzburg, the Duke of Bavaria, Ottokar's son, King Wenceslaus of Bohemia and the German King, Adolf of Nassau. This coalition wanted to depose the Hapsburgs in Austria as well, after the death of Rudolf. Having secured his position in his own domains by these successes, Albrecht was free to develop his policy in other directions. In 1298 he even secured the Imperial Crown of Germany. His indomitable attitude, his caution and energy were good omens for his reign. But it was not long before he was assassinated by his own nephew Johann, who received the appellation of "Parricida".

Friedrich the Handsome, who lost the prospect of succeeding to the throne at the Battle of Mühldorf, was followed by Albrecht II. This ruler took no interest in Imperial politics, but concentrated his energies on his own domains with considerable success. In 1335 he acquired Carinthia and Krain.

1295. The Model Parliament, the first full representation of the Estates, meets in London. Parliament secures the right to control taxation.

1309. The Holy See moves to Avignon.

1315. Battle in the Morgarten Defile. Victory of the Swiss over Leopold of Hapsburg. Dawn of Swiss independence.

1335. Austria acquires Carinthia and Krain.

St. Maria am Gestade, Vienna.

With Rudolf IV, called "the Endower", once again an unusual personality came to power. He succeeded to the throne at the age of 19, and reigned only eight years, yet with such energy and ambition that his reign constitutes a milestone in Austrian history. His proud nature quickly found it intolerable that the "Golden Bull" of the Emperor Karl IV should not have accorded to his House the Elector's vote to which both his position and his possessions entitled him. It was at this juncture that the forged document known as the "Privilegium Majus" made its appearance in Rudolf's chancellery. This document purported to establish for Austria her independence from the Empire, and for her princes, full sovereignty from the days of Caesar and Nero to those of Friedrich II. The mere fact that this Privilegium was at first accepted as genuine shows how far Austria had already progressed towards being regarded as independent. It was the Italian poet and humanist Petrarca who first demolished this audacious effort on the part of the young Duke.

Between Rudolf and Karl IV of Luxembourg (who had his Residence in Prague), relations were strained. The rivalry often proved advantageous to Austria. Duke Rudolf, for example, unwilling to be outdone by his father-in-law who had established a University in Prague, founded Vienna University, which soon grew into a centre of science and art. In 1363 Rudolf succeeded in making an important acquisition to his domains. After the death of Meinhard III of Tyrol, he managed by the exercise of skilfull diplomacy to persuade the latter's heiress, Margareta, to cede this beautiful and valuable Alpine province to the Hapsburgs. By this means he secured a bridge to the Hapsburgs possessions in South-West Germany and Switzerland. Proudly, Rudolf found himself able to write: Omnes stratae et transitus de Germania ad partes Italiae porrectae nostrae dominationi subsunt—

1339. The Hundred Years' War begins between France and England.

1340 to 1400. With Geoffrey Chaucer, England takes a place in world literature.

1348. Foundation of Prague University under Karl IV.

Foundation Document, 1365.

1363. Austria secures Tyrol.

34

"All roads leading from Germany to Italy are subject to Us." Rudolf was able to conclude other agreements affecting rights of succession which proved of considerable importance later.

The population of the towns grew rapidly and a prosperous middle class developed. The administrative and judicial systems were extended, and rapid progress was made in building. The beginnings of the gothic additions to St. Stephen's Cathedral are inseparably linked with the name of the Endower. When Rudolf died, still a young man, he left behind him a rich country which had developed along its own lines. Ahead of it lay unique possibilities as a bridge between the Teutonic North and the Latin South, as a political factor in the development of South-Eastern Europe, and as a centre of culture. Engraved in Rudolf's seal are the words: "Felix Austria"— "Happy Austria".

1366. The Englishman John Wycliffe, the most outstanding forerunner of the Reformation, begins his campaign against Rome.

Twixt the child
That's Italy and Germany the man
You stand, a gallant lad with warm red checks.
May God preserve the heart of youth in you;
May he make good what others have destroyed.

(Ottocar, Horneck, Act III)

But the hopes which might justly have been entertained concerning Austria's development were not immediately realized. Rudolf's brothers, Albrecht III and Leopold III, agreed in 1379 on a partition of the country which had the most unhappy consequences. Albrecht received Upper and

1369 to 1415. John Hus, the great Bohemian Reformer.

Lower Austria and founded the Leopoldian Line with Styria, Carinthia, Krain, Tyrol—and also Istria, which had in the meantime become part of the family's domains. Leopold was able to add the important city of Trieste to his possessions and to form a link with Swabia through his acquisition of the province of Vorarlberg, but the power of the Throne was on the decline. The Swiss territories began to fall away and there were growing signs of a financial crisis. Progress in the Austrian Lands practically ceased when, following the

1374. Austria acquires parts of Istria and Lower Krain.

1382. The Mediterranian port of Trieste falls to the Leopoldian line of the House of Hapsburg.

TU FELIX AUSTRIA

1477
BURGUNDIAN MARRIAGE

*Maximilian I
Maria of Burgundy*

NUBE

1 4 9 6
SPANISH MARRIAGE

Philip of Hapsburg
Johanna of Castile
and Aragon

1 5 1 5
BOHEMIAN-
HUNGARIAN MARRIAGE

Ferdinand I of Hapsburg
Anna of Hungary and Bohemia
Louis II of Hungary and Bohemia
Maria of Hapsburg

death of these two Dukes, they were actually split in 1396 into three parts. Rule by regents, family quarrels, banditry and a devastated countryside brought grave internal disorders to these states. The ruling House, divided against itself, failed to produce a personality with the strength to abolish these evils.

So many arms, but who can be the head?

(Family Strife in Hapsburg, Rudolf, Act I)

Even the wiser policy of Albrecht V failed to bring stability. The critical period continued through the long reign of Friedrich III into that of Maximilian I, under whom peace was re-established in the Duchies and their frontiers made secure. Through his marriage with the only daughter of the Hungarian King Sigismund, Albrecht V came into possession of the Crown of St. Stephen's. In 1438 he was elected German King and in 1439 he won the day against a Polish rival in Bohemia. But in the same year Albrecht died on his way back from a warlike expedition against the Turks, who were already at the gates of Hungary. He was the first Hapsburg to establish his rule over the vast area which stretches from the River Theiss to the Rhine, and from Silesia to the Adriatic.

Ladislaus ("the Posthumous") came into the world after the death of his father. Friedrich of Inner Austria governed his realms as regent. Ladislaus failed to subdue either the Jagellone Wladislaw or John Hunyadi. He was deprived of all say in the affairs of Bohemia by its Governor, who later became King George Podiebrad. On the death of Ladislaus in 1457, the bond holding the Danubian Reich together dissolved and it broke up into its component parts, each ruled by its own Prince.

Meantime, Friedrich III had been crowned German King, and in 1452 he was crowned Emperor in Rome. He was the first Austrian ruler to wear the Imperial Crown, which henceforth remained with the House of Austria— with a single break during the reign of Karl VII (1742 to 1745)—until 1806, when the Holy Roman Empire fell.

Lucas Cranach : Tournament.

In Friedrich III we meet with one of those strange characters which are so frequently found in the history of the Imperial representatives of the House of Hapsburg. He was a man of such a patient and dispassionate spirit as to suggest at times a complete lack of interest in political affairs. Sluggish and indifferent to good or ill fortune, he was yet a man of unusual dignity, conscious of his royal attributes, and imbued with an inner feeling of superiority. His reign cannot be considered a happy one. It was marked by family quarrels, the insubordination of the Estates, factional struggles among the nobles, loss of territory in the West and East, invasions by the Turks and peasant discontent. Unable on every occasion when decisive action was called for to make up his mind, the figure of this Emperor comes down to us enveloped in a strange haze of depression and indifference.

1450. John Gutenberg sets up the first printing press in Mainz.

1452. Leonardo da Vinci, world-genius of the Renaissance, is born.

1453. The Turks capture Constantinople.

> This is the curse of Hapsburg's noble house:
> Halfway to halt, and doubtfully to aim
> At half a deed, with half considered means.
>
> (Family Strife, Matthias, Act II)

But despite harsh blows of fortune and the persistence of abuses, a development started under Friedrich which was shortly to make it possible for the House of Austria to take its place among the leading powers of the world. This rise in status was initiated by and founded on—a marriage. Between Switzerland and the North Sea there had risen a wealthy Duchy having an extensive commerce. Burgundy, which had expanded and had strengthened its economic position under Charles the Bold, had risen to a position of European importance. Through the marriage of Maximilian, son of the Emperor Friedrich, with Charles' only daughter, this rich inheritance fell to the Hapsburgs. Maximilian, last of the knights, had to defend this inheritance in long wars against France. And now began the century-long conflict born of this inheritance between France and the "Maison d'Autriche". Meantime Matthias Corvinus, King of Hungary, had occupied Lower Austria and captured Vienna, which city, like Ottokar before him, he wished to turn into the capital of a great Empire of South-Eastern Europe under Hungarian domination. But after the death of Matthias his plans came to nothing and Maximilian, now wearing the Roman Crown, succeeded in restoring Vienna and Austria to the sway of their legitimate ruler.

When the Emperor Friedrich III died in 1493, he was succeeded by a person of very different character, Maximilian, a man of action with easily aroused enthusiasms. For 125 years the whole of the Hapsburg possessions had been united under a single ruler. Maximilian made this heritage secure in a seriesa of daring military campaigns in Carinthia and Tyrol, to which he paid especial attention because they were the gateway to Italy. He established a well organized royal administration. Peace and order returned to the country and the sense of unity among its peoples was strengthened.

1471. Albrecht Dürer born in Nuremberg.

1477. The Burgundian marriage of Maximilian. Flanders, Artois and the Franche Comté of Burgundy pass to the House of Hapsburg. Titian born.

1485. End of the Wars of the Roses in England. The House of Tudor comes to power.

1492. Christopher Columbus discovers the New World, crossing the ocean four times.

1494. Charles VIII of France marches into Italy.

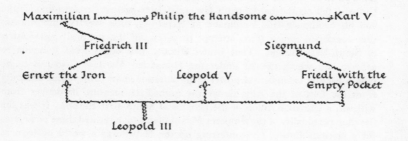

The Family Tree of the Hapsburgs, after Josephus Grünbeck, Historia Friderici III et Maximiliani I (unknown master, Altdorf School).

Observe the world your eyes can plainly see,
How hill and dale and brook and meadow stand.
The heights, though bare themselves, attract the clouds
And send them down as rain into the vale.
The wood holds off the wild, destructive storm.
A spring does not bear fruit, yet nurtures fruits.
And from such interchange of high and low,
If fruit and shelter, comes an ordered whole
That earns the right to live, because it is.

(Family Strife, Rudolf, Act III)

The Burgundian marriage of Maximilian had brought the House of Hapsburg on to the stage of world politics. The marriage of his son Philipp and Johanna, daughter of Ferdinand of Aragon and Isabella of Castile, soon showed itself as the foundation on which this family was to build up a unique preponderance among world Powers. Through the death of the heiress, the Spanish Infanta, and a second, elder Spanish Princess, the children of Philipp and Johanna inherited United Spain together with Sicily and Naples, as well as the still uncharted territories overseas which embraced almost the whole continent of America.

1498. Vasco da Gama discovers the sea route to India.

1503 to 1521. The Pontifical Years of the two great Renaissance Popes, Julius II and Leo X. (Bramante, Michelangelo and Raphael in Rome).

1517. Martin Luther posts his 95 Theses at Wittenberg.

A marriage celebrated in Vienna in 1515 between the grandchildren of Maximilian, Ferdinand and Maria, and Ludwig and Anna, children of the King of Bohemia and Hungary, proved of vital importance to the future of Austria. This act of political wisdom united the countries of the Danube basin at the moment when the Turks were preparing their advance into the heart of Europe. These lands were welded together, not by an act of dynastic caprice, but as the result of a real political necessity which at the same time involved a fundamental European interest. When the Jagellone, Ludwig, fell on the battlefield a few years later against the invading Turks and his brother-in-law, Ferdinand of Hapsburg, took over the inheritance, this developed into a third attempt to carry out the political organization of South-East-Europe. That which Ottocar had failed from Bohemia to achieve and which proved under the Hungarian Matthias Corvinus to be only a passing extension of power of no duration, now came about naturally from the foot of the Alps under the immediate pressure of danger from without, a Christian union of the peoples of South-East-Europe. It was the dazzling personality of the Emperor Maximilian which created these postulates for a glorious future, for conferring on the Hapsburgs a world position as rulers of an Empire on which the sun would never set, and for the creation of a super-national Danubian Empire. Aside from world politics, the arts

1517. The Spaniard Ferdinand Cortez sets out to conquer Mexico.

42

and sciences found in this gifted ruler, himself a talented writer and thinker, an understanding patron. Albrecht Dürer and Peter Fischer enjoyed his favours and humanism found a home in Vienna.

> The peasant walks behind his plough in peace,
> While in the towns the workmen ply their trades
> And industries and guilds lift up their heads.

(Ottocar, Rudolf, Act III)

After the death of Maximilian, his grandchild Karl V took over a vast empire. He inherited Spain, Burgundy and the old Hapsburg possession; he was elected King in Germany and later crowned Emperor at Bologna. In 1521 he divided his Empire with his brother Ferdinand, to whom he gave the Austrian Duchies. From this time onwards one finds references to an Austrian and to a Spanish line of the House of Hapsburg. The reign of Karl V was filled with internal German conflicts arising out of the start of the reformation. Constant wars with France and Turkey left him no peace. Karl V was another of the strange, gloomy and apathetic figures to be found among the Hapsburg rulers. His plans to win back for the Imperial Crown its ancient power and splendour and to preserve the unity of the old Catholic faith were brought to naught, partly on account of the egotism of the Lutheran Princes but also because of their devotion to their faith. Karl thereupon renounced the crown and retired to the monastery of San Yuste in Spain. A lonesome and frustrated figure, he turned his back on that life which would have made him ruler of a world Empire.

1519 to 1521. The Portuguese Ferdinand Magellan first circumnavigates the world.

1526. Bohemia and Hungary pass legally into the possession of Austria.

1528. Under Henry VIII, the first steps are taken which led up to the separation of the English Church from Rome.

1536. Death of Erasmus of Rotterdam.

> There order dwells, there order has its home
> While here confusion lives and vain caprice.

(Family Strife, Rudolf, Act I)

In the meantime Ferdinand was ruling prudently and ably in Austria. The new doctrines from Wittenberg quickly penetrated to Austria, where they spread rapidly. Soon appeared the first signs of a clash of beliefs which was to prove particularly significant for Austria. Efforts to bring about religious reforms brought with them social discontent, which manifested itself particularly in peasant revolts, and in the formation of the sect of the Baptists.

In 1526, Ludwig II, King of Hungary and Bohemia, lost the day and his life as well in the battle of Mohacs against the Turks. Under the Treaties

1540. Foundation of the order of Jesuits.

1545 to 1563. Council of Trient. The Catholic Church grows more powerful and the Counter-Reformation begins.

OCCIDENS

Ptolomaic Map of the World

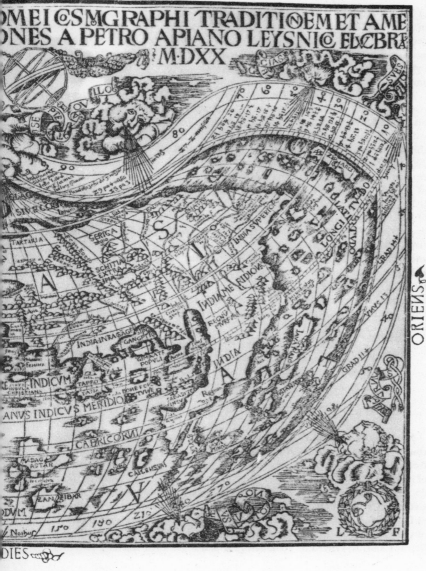

OMEI COSMGRAPHI TRADITIOEM ET AME
ONES A PETRO APIANO LEYSNIC ELCBRÆ
·M·DXX

ORIENS

of 1515 Ferdinand should have succeeded to the inheritance. But while in Bohemia he was able to secure his rights after signing an agreement concerning the Elections, in Hungary he had to gain them by force of arms against John Zapolya, the Voivode of Transylvania. The latter, hotly pursued by Ferdinand, fell back into Transylvania where, prompted by short-sighted ambition, he entered into an alliance with the Turks.

1520 to 1566. The Ottoman Empire flourishes under Suleiman the Magnificent. Turkey stretches from Budapest to Bagdad.

At this period the Ottoman Empire was ruled by the warlike Sultan Suleiman the Magnificent, who eagerly seized this opportunity of putting into practice his long-cherished plans for Europe. In the summer of 1529 he marched with his forces into Hungary. Before long it became evident that this was a thrust into the heart of Europe. His army of 270,000 men equipped with 300 canons moved through Ofen, Gran and Raab towards the Austrian frontier. Only fortified Vienna stood between the Turks and the conquest of Central Europe. The defence of the city was assumed by Niklas, Count Salm. He had only 18,000 men with whom to repel the furious onslaught of the mighty army. On October 14th the beginning of bad weather, the decimation of his forces and shortage of food forced the Sultan to raise the siege. But the defence was in no position to follow up the retreating army and inflict on it a decisive defeat. In 1532 the Turks again violated the soil of Austria. On this occasion they were halted at the small fortress of Güns, which was defended by the Croat, Jurishitsh. On the approach of a formidable Imperial army to relieve him, the Turks hastily decamped. Once again the opportunity of effecting a decision by a counter-thrust was lost.

1530. Nicholas Copernicus, founder of modern astronomy, completes his revolutionary work "De revolutionibus orbium coelestium".

1532. Francis Pizaro and Diego di Almagro overthrow the Empire of the Incas in Peru and Chile.

> Not only does the Emperor's purpose waver;
> The Turks, as heathens, are a faithless folk,
> And prospects of the distant future hold
> A goodly share of danger and of doubt.

> (Family Strife, Klesel, Act II)

1553. Queen Mary tries to recatholicise England.

1555. The "Religious Peace" of Augsburg, regulating differences between Catholics and Protestants.

Now set in a decade of continuous frontier warfare for the exhausted country, keeping it in a state of constant uneasiness. The confusion resulting from the division in the Church extended to Austria. The standing threat of invasion by the Turks in itself sufficed to prevent Ferdinand from embarking on stern measures against heresy, but he did his utmost to strenghten the Catholic Church from within. In December, 1550, he requested Ignatius of Loyola, founder and first General of the Order of Jesuits, to send members of the Order to Vienna. The first Jesuits, among them the famous Father Petrus Canisius, arrived in Vienna in 1551 and began their teaching activities.

Very soon this Order, spreading throughout Austria, was working towards that revival of Catholicism which proved of such fundamental importance to the intellectual and cultural development of the country.

When his brother Karl V renounced the throne, Ferdinand was elected Roman Emperor. The inclination towards the Protestant faith shown by his son and heir, Maximilian II, was a source of great pain to the new Emperor. It seemed that all his efforts to dissuade his son from the path towards which he was inclining were doomed to failure.

But when Maximilian ascended the throne on the death of his father, he did not himself adopt the Lutheran creed, as might have been expected, but contented himself with according a wide measure of tolerance to its disciples. Ferdinand had made a grave mistake in once again dividing the Austrian territories. Upper and Lower Austria, Tyrol and the "Fore-Lands", and Styria, Carinthia, Krain and Istria were seperately administered by his three sons. Three Courts and three Governments wasted much-needed money. There was no unity of military and political leadership, even at this time when the danger from the Turks made a full concentration of forces essential. It was under the Emperor's brothers, Ferdinand and Karl, that those harsh measures of the Counter-Reformation were applied which drove into exile large numbers of those who were determined to remain true to their Protestant belief.

1558 to 1603. The Elizabethan Period in England.

1562. Beginning of the Wars of the Huguenots in France.

1564. Death of Michelangelo and birth of Shakespeare.

1571. Battle of Lepanto. Victory of Don Juan d'Austria over the Turks.

1572. St. Bartholomew's Eve.

> Not merely said, but done.
> In Styria, all Inner Austria,
> The seed of heresy is rooted out.
> One day alone, on orders from their Prince,
> Some sixty thousand souls embraced the Faith
> And twenty thousand fled to foreign lands.

(Family Strife, Ferdinand, Act I)

The re-Catholicisation of Austria is a landmark in the country's history. It was during this period of the Counter-Reformation that Austria acquired its Catholic imprint. The whole art and culture of the country, drawing their strength from the spirit of Catholicism, became rooted in the historic events of this century. From the days of Fischer von Erlach onwards we see the traditions of this period being constantly renewed and sustained by such figures as Haydn, Mozart and Grillparzer, right down to Hugo von Hofmannsthal.

End of the 16th Century. Start of the great overseas expeditions of England under the daring seamen Francis Drake, Walter Raleigh, Thomas Cavendish and Martin Frobisher.

The Funeral Procession of Karl V,

1581. The Nether-
lands declare
their independ-
ence,

1587. Execution
of Mary, Queen
of Scots.

1588. Destruc-
tion of the
Spanish Armada.
English supre-
macy at sea is
established.

1600. The great
Spanish drama-
tist, Calderon,
born.

After the death of Maximilian II, Rudolf, eldest of his five sons, became successor in the German Empire, in Hungary and in Bohemia, inheriting further an undivided Upper and Lower Austria. The other two branches of the Hapsburgs ruled over the rest of the Austrian territories. The constant frontier fighting against the Turks gradually became an intolerable burden. We find records of 188 invasions over a period of seven years of nominal peace. Guarding the frontiers swallowed up one million gulden a year. When war broke out openly in 1592, no decision was secured, but the exhausting battles continued with varying fortunes for years.

A new rebellion of the Hungarians under Stephan Bocskay and religious strife in the hereditary territories resulted in increasing disorders before which Rudolf remained powerless and inactive. In this monarch we find again that strange shrinking from action, that gloomy tendency towards inner withdrawal and the morbid fear of taking any decision.

> For what seems resolution to the men of state
> Is mostly lack of conscience as a guide,
> Frivolity and arrogance that seek
> Their selfish ends and disregard all else;
> Whereas a good man in control of men
> Is fearful of results his acts may bring,
> When one stroke of his pen bequeaths to those
> As yet unborn, disaster or good luck.

(Family Strife, Rudolf, Act III)

48

Bruxelles, 1559.

In the hope of averting the worst, the Archdukes met in conference in Linz. Their object was to open the eyes of the Emperor to the danger threatening him and to concert measures of salvation. Command of the forces in Hungary was entrusted to the King's brother, Matthias, who concluded peace with the Magyars and the Turks.

1603. The House of Stuart succeeds to the Throne of England.

When the Emperor sought to breach this peace again, and when his weak and indecisive policy proved incapable of dealing with the realities of these troubled times, the Archdukes conferred a Regency over Hungary and Austria on Matthias. Thus came fraternal strife to the House of Hapsburg. Filled with distrust of his ambitious brother, the Emperor would not yield. Despite his inability even at this juncture to make up his mind to any decisive step, he was so convinced of the justice of his cause and of the rights conferred by his position that he found the strength to keep up a tenacious struggle against his brother and the nobles who supported him.

1605. Miguel de Cervantes begins his work on Don Quixote.

> I am the bond that ties and holds this sheaf,
> Unfruitful, yes, but needed, since it binds.

(Family Strife, Rudolf, Act III)

Before long the nobility of Bohemia also ranged themselves on the side of Matthias. When Rudolf II attempted to deprive his brother of the right of succession in Bohemia, the latter dethroned him there also. Helpless and deserted, Rudolf II died shortly afterwards.

But his successor Matthias, who accepted the guidance in affairs of state of that skilled politician, Bishop Melchior Klesel, now showed himself

1609. The Protestant Union and the Catholic League established in Germany.

4

incapable of dispersing the approaching storms. Religious differences became even more acute. The counter-strokes of the "Catholic Revival" grew more and more powerful and the attitude of both parties more uncompromising. Brought to power by the nobles, Matthias soon found himself obliged to rule in defiance of them. He soon proved a disappointment to the Protestants who had supported him against his brother. And now in Prague there occurred the "Defenestration" of Matthias' Counsellors. With it broke out the conflict which soon changed its character from that of a war between religions to that of a struggle for political power which devastated the heart of Europe for 30 years — the Thirty Years' War.

1618. The De-fenestration in Prague. Begin-ning of the Thirty Years' War.

Playbill of the First Performance of Grillparzer's "Family Strife in Hapsburg".

50

THE JESUIT
THEATRE

t the time when, in 1540, the Pope formally sanctioned the Society of Jesus which had been founded by the Spanish aristocrat, Ignatius of Loyola, Catholicism in Austria was in a bad way. Luther's doctrines had gained a host of adherents whose numbers were steadily growing in all classes of society; a considerable section of the aristocracy and of the middle classes already adhered to the new faith.

It cannot be disputed that many abuses had grown up in the Church during the 15th century, and their existence gave fresh impulse to the Protestant movement. Starting on a purely religious basis, the latter soon became linked up with political and social interests. Just at this time, the Catholic Church in Austria was without men who by quality of leadership and example might have called a halt to the changes with which it was threatened. The Church found its main support in the Monarch. Ferdinand I left no doubt about the fact that he stood behind the Catholic Church. It cannot be denied that it was in part political motives which led him to adopt this course; his most powerful antagonists, the nobles, had in the main embraced the Protestant faith.

But all Ferdinand's efforts were of little avail so long as he had nobody within the Church on whom he could rely to support his endeavours. The number of priests was steadily declining. In 1542, the whole Diocese of St. Stephen's in Vienna could master only four priests. Of 13 parishes, ten were without incumbents. The monasteries were suffering similarly. The total number of Dominican monks sank from 86 to ten.

Faced with such conditions, in December 1550 Ferdinand made an urgent appeal to Ignatius of Loyola to send him instructors capable of training priests who could be depended on to work on the masses. It was in April and May 1551 that the first Jesuits arrived in Austria—actually in Vienna. Ferdinand allotted part of the Dominican Monastery to them as residence. They promptly took over the cure of souls and assumed control of the theological faculty at the University. In 1553 they established the first public school. In 1554 they moved to the abandoned Carmelite Monastery at "Am Hof", which then became their first permanent headquarters in Vienna. Three hundred pupils attended their classes, which in this year, 1554, already numbered five. By 1556 they had 400 pupils attending six classes, with ten teachers to instruct them. By such means the Jesuits built up a powerful cadre of persons who could be relied on to spread the doctrines to which they adhered.

Whatever one may think of the Order of the Society of Jesus, the fact remains that, particulary through their schools, the Jesuits dominated the mentality of Austria from the middle of the 16th century up to Rousseau's "Age of Enlightenment", and to a considerable degree controlled cultural development.

In the Jesuit schools, a system of study was devised which obtained its effect from the uniformity of its application. The first principal of education was belief in God. There were two clear-cut divisions of the curriculum. The lower corresponded to the education furnished in the middle schools, the higher to that of the universities. In contrast to the middle schools, which aimed at developing the mind by means of a general classical education, the Jesuit schools sought to attain this end by giving their pupils the most perfect command possible of the Latin language. For nearly half a century the curriculum was studied and tested before, in 1599, it was introduced into the Jesuit schools generally. Perfection in Latin, extending to oratorical efforts which had to include the arts of poetry and declamation, paved the way to higher scholarship in the natural sciences, philosophy and theology.

Starting with the elementary classes, pupils were trained in extempore speaking and were taught how to make their words effective by the cultivation of a self-confident manner and quickness in repartee. This result was achieved in the first place through rehearsals which were often of a theatrical character. These gradually expanded from monologues and controversial debates to full theatrical performances, with many participants and elaborate scenery. From the small world of the class-room, students could progress to making an appearance before the Emperor in famous dramas, with a house made up of distinguished figures from both the lay and clerical worlds. Skilfully the Jesuits directed this training towards their objective, of turning out an impressive, confident and convincing speaker who could hold his own in wordly and spiritual controversies, in philosophical as well as in theological disputes and achieve success in all. After thorough preparation in class, the first four classes appeared on the stage once a year before a limited public, while in the fifth and sixth classes each individual pupil had to give proof of his ability in declamation and controversy. Apart from minor theatrical productions, once a year at the end of term there was a grand performance, the *"Actio Major"*, at which the students had to prove in public that they were worthy of the prizes which they were subsequently to receive.

It was in accordance with the militant spirit of the Jesuits that training for spiritual conflict should have been among the most important subjects that their schools sought to inculcate. From the elementary grammar classes onwards the boy was taught to be critical of the work of his fellow-pupils. He had to be quick to spot

Vienna. Old University and Jesuit Church.

the mistakes of others, to criticise and to correct them. Ambition was made the spur. The best scholars were publicly commended at the end of the school year, were awarded prizes, and amidst the sound of drums and trumpets, their names were announced with great ceremony to the assembled visitors present at the end of term performance. Their names were inscribed on a list of the successful which was distributed to the guests. Rivalry between the aristocracy and middle classes also encouraged the spirit of competition the former believing that their superior rank obliged them to secure a similar superiority in learning, in which endeavour they frequently met with the competition of sons of middle class parents.

Vienna was the oldest Jesuit stronghold (after Cologne) in the German-speaking countries. Ten years later, in 1561, a second branch of the Order was established within the frontiers of present-day Austria, the college at Innsbruck, and was soon followed by another, that of Hall-in-Tyrol, in 1569. A year later, in 1570, a branch was established in Graz, in the year 1600 the Jesuits settled in Linz, in 1604 in Klagenfurt, in 1613 in Leoben, 1616 in Krems, 1621 in Judenburg and in 1632 in Steyr. Protestantism at this time was practically unchallenged in the places where these centres were established. In each of them schools were promptly opened and plays were staged in all; the Faith was spread, not only by the ear but also through the receptive medium of the eye.

Many conversions, many changes of outlook must be attributed to the emotional effects of these dramatic representations. Records often refer to the pleasure which Catholics and others found in these performances.

About the middle of the 18th century, 53 Jesuit colleges and settlements existed in the Jesuit "Province" of Austria, in addition to a number of resident and travelling missions. In almost all these 53 centres there were middle-schools and at almost all of them plays were produced, between two and three in a year, unless school, as was often the case in Hungary, had to be broken up on account of the dreaded plague or of danger from the Turks. These usually scattered the pupils to the four winds.

The growth of the Jesuit Theatre continued from 1558 to 1773 in two major stages. During the first, which lasted until about 1650, the main objective was the inculcation of the Faith; during the second period, education played the greater role. The Jesuit Theatre took over from the mediaeval theatre the pattern of the ecclesiastical year, culminating in the festivals of Christmas and Easter. It also adopted the traditions of the "school-theatre". The Order of Jesuits was not alone in introducing its pupils to the stage, but no other Order did so on such a scale, with such perseverance and with such remarkable results.

To appreciate the significance of the Jesuit Theatre, one must remember that with its amateur actors, it was a means to an end and not, like the professional theatre, an end in itself.

The first stage performance in Vienna was given in 1555. The Jesuits had made barely habitable the building of the Carmelite Monastery, which during the recent years when it had been left almost unoccupied had become a ruin, and had just established their schools there. They repeated their performances every year, increasing their number. Scenery and costumes were added. By the second half of the 17th century the productions easily bore comparison with the elaborate set-up of those at the Imperial Court Theatre. The stage-struck Leopold I was the most enthusiastic patron, and at the end of the performance he distributed prizes to those pupils who had most distinguished themselves.

There were primarily three occasions in the year on which plays were regularly produced. On Good Friday, a play with religious content was put on, corresponding to the mediaeval Good Friday drama in St. Stephen's Cathedral, which was kept up until the 19th century. On the second occasion, that of Corpus Christi, the performance was closely linked with the religious procession from altar to altar which from time immemorial had been carried out with great pomp in Vienna. The play then performed also had mediaeval characteristics. The religious story was divided into acts which were produced in turn before one or other of the street altars at which the Corpus Christi procession halted. In 1579, for example, the "Tragic Story of the Prodigal Son" was produced. Two acts were played before the High Altar, and another act before each of the other three altars at which the procession halted. The third regular date when plays were produced was the occasion of the distribution of prizes at the end of the school year, usually in September, which was turned into an impressive theatrical spectacle, with elaborate scenery.

e Great with the Ruler of the Underworld.

Besides this, plays were sometimes performed at Christmas time which had been cleverly adapted from the traditional Christmas plays, performances of a lighter type at Carnival time, such as, for instance, a play about drunkenness in the year 1579, as well as plays on the festival days of the Order (the day of St. Ignatius and of Francis Xaver, the missionary to India), then performances occasioned by the visits of highly-placed persons or special festivals of the Imperial family. The originally simple dialogue plays soon developed into regular theatrical performances, the visual effect being increased by minor theatrical devices. Thus, for instance, when in the year 1610 the story of the Jewish boy who was thrown alive into the fire was played during the Passion procession, it "was pleasing and moving"—this double effect being the main object—that the Virgin Mary aided the boy in the flames. A preliminary to the great theatrical performances of the Baroque period was the imposing stage background which the Congregations began to construct in the first half of the 17th century. The Congregation of the Most Holy Virgin Mary constructed in the year 1618 a *mis-en-scène* consisting of five pyramids with the Sacrament as central point, brilliantly lit by 600 lamps, and, in the year 1629, one of an enormous pyramid with the inscription: "The Wounds of Christ". At the impressive Good Friday procession of the same year, allegorical pictures from the Middle Ages were mingled with motivs of the approaching Baroque period. Side by side with tableaux depicting mourning and

sorrow occasioned by the suffering of Christ, actual personalities were put on the stage, for instance, that of Christ, from whose side blood was flowing.

Soon after the beginning of the theatrical performances we find mention of the first noble visitors; from 1570 onwards the Archdukes were present at the Good Friday services and processions, which were always accompanied by short plays. Later the Emperor and his Consort also attended. The presentation before the Archdukes Ernest and Max in the year 1587 of the drama of Scilius, King of Chaeronea, who admonished his sons to live in brotherly agreement, was certainly a broad hint. When the Emperor Matthias visited the College in the year 1604 and dismounted from his horse, nine fauns sprang towards him from the various sectors of the gardens, greeting him with verses, songs and dancing and accompanying him to the doors of the College; there he was received by a pupil as emissary of his patron saint, St. Matthias who, bidding the Emperor welcome, also bade the fauns begone from the threshold of the sacred College. Matthias then took the evening meal together with the Jesuits in the garden to the sounds of music, afterwards watching from a window of the building the drama of St. Matthias which was presented on a stage in the garden. Here he took his leave. One can believe that he spoke the truth when he said that he was very pleased with everything. In 1695, Prince Liechtenstein was ceremoneously received at the College and greeted by speeches in seventeen languages; among these Latin, Greek and Hebrew were naturally foremost, but English, French and Italian as well as Bohemian, Hungarian, Croatian, Furlanian and Danish were also used; German too, of course, although it is mentioned as eleventh on the list.

In 1620 the troops of the Emperor defeated the soldiers of Friedrich, King of the Pfalz, at the Battle of the White Mountain near Prague, thereby deciding the struggle between Reformation and Counter-Reformation in Austria in favour of the latter, even though it was a long time before it was brought to a conclusion. Thereafter sterner treatment was meted out to the Protestants, first of all in the towns. The followers of Martin Luther were confronted with the choice of returning to the Catholic religion or leaving the country.

In Vienna the Jesuits took over the University in 1662, moving from the building at Am Hof, thereafter called "Bei den oberen Jesuiten"—"Upper-Jesuit-House"— together with their pupils, to the University—thereafter called "Bei den unteren Jesuiten"—"Lower-Jesuit-House"—in the Bäckerstrasse. This was soon found to afford insufficient space. In 1625, the construction of a Jesuit College with school attached was begun on the site of the present Universitätsplatz; the church was started in 1627. The boys' school was built on to the college, separated from it only by a big door which stood in the present Bäckerstrasse. According to a report of Testarello, Canon of Vienna during the last ten years of the 17th century, the school was "of no mean elegance, very properly and comfortably built. Above it is to be found a large and handsome lecture hall with theatre attached for the performance of plays such as cannot find its equal in any other centre of the Jesuit Fathers. This lecture hall has many windows on either side, with a great choir for the musicians at the back. The upper hall is panelled with fine woodwork, gilded horses, landscape paintings, foliage and so forth. In the front there is a fine façade with sculptures, various decorations and beautiful architecture. The theatre, which has a stage larger and longer than the lecture hall, adjoins it; so big is it that its scenery can be changed in an instant as often as twelve times. The above-mentioned lecture hall is so large that it seats about 3000 persons. In the lower half of the building there is another, smaller hall which has also its well-built theatre, decorated with various scenes; the lower schools use this for their private plays and declamations". The upper as well as the lower theatres have undergone many changes in course of time; the upper hall received a new ceiling painting in the year 1736, depicting the Virgin Mary floating among angels in a baroque heaven, by the artist Anton Hertzog, who is also responsible for the frescoes in the library of the College buildings.

In this stately hall, the oldest auditorium of Austria and, in fact, one of the oldest in the world, the Jesuits acted plays with their pupils from the middle of the 17th century onwards at least five times a year. In each year there were four minor performances and one major one. In the year 1650 a boys' school with six classes was established in the Professhaus Am Hof, from which the young men had been transferred to the Bäckerstrasse, which soon numbered 600 pupils; like the Collegium Academicum in the Bäckerstrasse, it presented four minor plays and one full drama at the end of every school year. Thus there were nearly always ten theatrical performances sponsored by the Jesuit schools every year until 1761. In 1760, the four lower classes still acted their plays as usual in the Professhaus Am Hof as well as in the Bäckerstrasse College; the subjects were taken from religious history, such as "Martyr Hermagen" or "Joseph" (who was sold by his brothers) or were based on the classics, for example "Epaminondas", "Perseus" and "Midas".

The finished school performances of the Jesuits which lasted for over a hundred years created a demand in the Austrian section of the Order for about 80 to 90 plays a year—roughly, 9,000 during the whole period. Among them were masterpieces by Avancinus, Adolph, Bidermann and others.

The soul of school productions was the form-master. He not only wrote the play, but also produced it. In the 16th century the Professor of Eloquence at the Vienna College, Bartholomaeus Vuastonianus, was appointed as "the present instructor in dialogue and acting". If the form-master fell ill or died, the work of a whole year went for nothing. Thus, for instance, in 1738, the master of the third form at the Grammar School of Görz had rehearsed his pupils for the play when a "tragicus casus" brought all plans to nought. The son of a cobbler had been expelled from school for brawling, arriving late (the report termed it "theft of minutes") and similar misbehaviour, but had been reinstated at request of his parents. As he failed to mend his ways, he was finally expelled, whereupon he determined to avenge himself on his master by murdering him. He went to the place where the play was being studied at the school with a stone, two pounds in weight, concealed in the folds of his cloak and asked that his teacher should come out to him. As he was not able to secure readmission to the school either by persuasion or threats, he struck the master with such force on the head that "it was almost a wonder that he did not drop dead on the spot". The man afterwards recovered, but the play had to be cancelled for that year.

Preparations lasted throughout the school year, and if, for any reason—usually it was the dreaded plague—the schools could only be opened later, in February or

March of the school year instead of in September, that year's performance had to be abandoned.

Of the thousands of plays which in course of time were presented in the Austrian "Province", only a few have been preserved. The contents of a number of them are known to us, the so-called "Periochen" which were printed for and distributed among those of the audience who were deficient in Latin. The oldest known Viennese "Perioche" dates from the year 1610—the tragedy of "Jephte".

All plays were based on a definite theme, an article of faith or a moral lesson, the argument being driven home by the dramatic presentation of the story of some event. At first the subjects were religious stories of sacred history taken from the Gospels, the Old Testament or the writings of the Fathers of the Church. The fate of the Martyrs was a favourite theme chosen to exemplify religious faith and courage in confessing it. Later, moral themes were also made use of, at first in connection with religious stories; subsequently we find stories taken from history, especially after the beginning of historical studies early in the 18th century. From the rulers of antiquity by way of the ancient German and Lombard kings up to the reigning House of Hapsburg, all with high rank or well-known names which might serve either as an example or a warning to youth were brought into these plays. It is noteworthy that a number of subjects reappeared in the literature of subsequent decades, especially in the period of classicism. In the Jesuit Theatre we find, to mention only a few examples, a forerunner of Schiller's "The Robbers", as well as of the "Iphigenie" of Goethe and Körners' "Zriny". Thus the Jesuit Theatre was of value in preparing the way for the literature of later times, as well as because it was in itself the most comprehensive theatre organisation known to history. Far and wide it cleared the ground for the professional stage by making the cultured classes acquainted with the theatre from their earliest youth. In many towns of the Jesuit "Province" of Austria—for example in Hungary—it was the immediate forerunner of the professional theatre. The value of this Jesuit Theatre lay not so much in the grandiose stage presentation at some particular place such as Vienna or Graz, nor in the literary value of the works of such a man as Avancinus, but rather in its achievements for the general development of culture. Its mission once fulfilled, it faded away.

With Rousseau's "Age of Enlightenment" there began a conflict about the Jesuit schools which for two centuries had supplied the Emperor with his leading statesmen and to which the Counter-Reformation in Austria owed its success. The main argument against them was that they were in themselves reactionary and their methods old-fashioned. Yet it was just the Jesuit schools which in the first half of the 18th century proved themselves to be thoroughly progressive, for it was they who introduced the teaching of history and encouraged study of the natural sciences. In Vienna they founded a "*Musaeum Mathematicum*", the first institute of its kind in Austria and a precursor of the modern museums, and pursued definite educational aims through its collection of physical and astronomical instruments. The Jesuits were also the first in this part of the world to make serious experiments in physics and chemistry and to demonstrate them in public. The Emperor Franz, Consort of Maria Theresia, even called the Brothers to Schönbrunn Palace to make such demonstrations.

Until the latter half of the 18th century the students in the Jesuit schools of the Austrian Province numbered more than 16,000 and although thereafter their numbers began to decrease slowly, the abolition of the Order put an end to an educational system which was still flourishing.

The final performance at the theatre in the Bäckerstrasse was given in the year 1760 by the sixth class, that of rhetoric, which acted "Menaeus"—actually the last play produced by the Jesuit Theatre in Vienna. The beauty of the play, the acting of the boys and the fine scenery was much admired, and no one guessed that they were acting for the last time. Soon afterwards an Imperial decree was issued totally forbidding this type of training in the schools, and in the year 1761 "nobody set foot again in the theatre". The stage fell into decay; not until 1766 was the tangle of rafters and the disorder in the hall removed to prepare the auditorium for lectures, but the old glory had departed; seven years later the entire activities of the *Societas Jesu* were forbidden (1773).

The "Age of Enlightenment" had finally reached Vienna. A clear-cut difference of intellectual attitude divided the city, and slowly the Jesuit Theatre had to yield place to the professional theatre with its literary basis.

The Order of Jesuits left the country in obedience to the Emperor's command, its mission fulfilled. Embattled Catholicism in conjunction with Imperial Power had weathered the storm of Turkish invasion. The age of Baroque blossomed forth in glory.

Since the days of the Jesuit schools the word "theatre" has formed an inseparable part of the thoughts and imagination of the Austrian people—the theatre as a stage for free discussion, as a means for acquiring knowledge, as a method for the exchange of ideas among men. For seven generations youth had been taught to link up and to compare the theatre with the surrounding world, seeing the one in the other and through the one understanding the other.

Placed amid that outside world which often put might before right, the theatre became increasingly a home for daring ideas, and the stage developed into an open platform for free speech. Thus in Austria, not only for the professionals, the authors and actors, but also for the public, the idea of the theatre has become one of the most cherished features of life, that great world-theatre where life is a dream, a play by and for every man.

THE
TURKS·1683

A PAGE FROM HISTORY'S CALENDAR

1453	The Turks capture Constantinople.
1521	The Turks capture Belgrade.
1526	The Turks conquer Hungary. Battle of Mohacs.
1529	Vienna drives back the Turks after the first siege.
1532	The Turks besiege Güns on the Austrian frontier.
1554	The Turks acquire Algiers. Tunis and Tripoli.
1541	The Hungarian capital and the fortress of Ofen are captured by the Turks.
1565	The Knights of the Order of St. John hold Malta against Turkish attacks.
1566	Fresh invasion of the Turks in Hungary.
1570	The Turks seize Cyprus from the Venetians.
1571	Don Juan of Austria destroys the Turkish fleet in the sea battle of Lepanto.
1663	Fresh declaration of war by the Turks against Austria. The Turks are victorious in Hungary.
1664	The Turks at St. Gotthard ‹Burgenland› beaten back by the army of the Emperor.
1667	Beginning of Louis XIV's wars of expansion.
1669	Crete is conquered by the Turks.
1678	Poland loses Podolien to the Turks.
1679	The Plague in Vienna.
1683	Second Siege of Vienna. The Turks driven back.
1686	Ofen is libareted after 145 years of Turkish rule.
1697	Prince Eugene defeats the Turks at Zenta.
1699	The Treaty of Karlowitz.

When Turkey had recovered from the grave internal disorders in which she was involved during the first half of the 17th century and, under the capable Grand Viziers, Mohammed and Achmed Köprülü, began to revive the great tradition of Suleiman the Magnificent, the Holy Roman Empire of German Nations, in the words of the great satirist Voltaire, was neither holy, nor Roman, nor an empire. Bled white by the murderous campaigns of plunder of the Thirty Years' War, ravaged by a hostile soldiery which carried fire and sword through the land, or by wandering bands of plundering mercenaries, it had become a helpless tool of foreign Powers in the pursuit of their own interests. The north was under Swedish control, in the west "Le Roi Soleil", Louis XIV, was preparing to realise his boundless ambitions and in the south-east, powerful thrusts of Ottoman imperialism against the Republic of Venice, Poland and Russia were paving the way for a main attack on the heart of Europe. While the German princes were not able to free themselves from the cramping effects of their particularist policy, Austria kept watch on the Rhine and the Danube. To her Emperor, Leopold I of Hapsburg, a quiet and peace-loving man, fell the historic task, not only of damming in a series of glorious campaigns the French efforts towards expansion, but also of facing in the south-east the danger from the Turks which had been weighing on Europe for almost two hundred years. Austria's oldest and gravest responsibility, that of guarding the centre of Europe, now entered on a culminating phase of deadly peril.

In the year 1664 a Turkish army under Achmed Köprülü was prevented from invading Austrian territory by the resourceful General Raimund Montecuccoli. But the Austrian statesmen of the day must have already been filled with grave anxiety. The Crescent had planted its sacred banner before the gateways of Lower Austria, France was reaching out, in the "Réunions" (a portion of Alsace-Lorraine claimed by Louis XIV), for the Rhine, in Hungary the Kuruzzas were in rebellion and the Army Paymaster of the Court reported that he had not even a hundred gulden in his treasury. In the meantime, indications of extensive Turkish preparations had so increased as to amount to an alarming certainty.

In March 1683, the Ottoman forces set out with a great train of artillery from Adrianople, where they had assembled, towards the north. The Sultan Mohammed IV, himself no soldier, had insisted together with his entire Court on accompanying his army as far as Belgrade. Over a hundred carriages were required for the harem alone. Herds of cattle were driven along with the columns. Contingents of many races of the Orient and Occident, Turkish Spahis, Janissaries, Bosnians, Slavs and Tartars lent brilliant colour to the train. The Turks, over 300,000 strong, together with the Hungarian Tököly troops and the long columns of artillery, led by the ambitious Grand Vizier, Kara Mustafa, moved forwards behind the billowing green flag of the Prophet over the Belgrade Bridge towards the West. Their watchword was: Vienna, Prague, then the Rhine. The Turkish Chancellor, Köprölü, had taken an oath to stable the horses beneath the vaulted dome of St. Peter's in Rome. To face this situation, Europe presented anything but a firm and united front. On the contrary, the diplomats of the "Roi Soleil" were everywhere doing their best to assist the Turks against the House of Austria. When the Emperor Leopold looked around for allies, he found only a few prepared to help him. The Pope was the first to give his assistance in the form of generous subsidies which brought some peace of mind to the desperate Paymaster to the Forces. Spain, Portugal and the Italien City-States followed his example. Poland, which was ruled by King Sobieski, exchanged guarantees of mutual assistance with Austria. A number of German princes, in the forefront those of Bavaria, Saxony and Franconia joined the Emperor. But many others, headed by the great Elector of Brandenburg, stood resolutely aside from the conflict.

The coordination of the many auxiliary services of an army which it was planned should amount to 80,000 men demanded, among a hundred other things, time above all. Precisely this was lacking. Thus, for example, the Marshal to the Emperor, Duke Karl of Lorraine, was faced with the impossible task of holding, with only 24,000 operational effectives, the advance on the capital and chief residential city of the Empire of an enemy ten times his strength. To confront the enemy in open battle was out of the question; he decided to fall back with his army behind fortified Vienna and wait for the approach of his allies from the north and west. Not until the Tartar hordes had penetrated into the Vienna Forest, on July 7th, did the Emperor together with his court leave the city, which now hastily began preparations to stand a siege. The Turkish army pressed forward towards the Leitha frontier,

TURKISH PAMPHLET, ANNO 1683.

"We Mola Mohammed, Glorious and Absolute Sovereign Emperor of Babylon and Judea, of the Orient and the Occident, King of all Earthly and Heavenly kings, Sovereign King of Holy Arabia and Mauretania, heir and fame-crowned King of Jerusalem, Lord and Master of the grave of the crucified god of the Unbelievers, pledge to thee, Emperor of Rome, and to thee, King of Poland, as well as to all thy followers, Our Holy Word by the mercy of God who rules in Heaven, that We are about to plunge your little countries into war. We have with Us thirteen kings with 1,300,000 warriors, infantry and cavalry. With this army, the like of which thou and thy followers have never seen, we will crush thy little country without mercy or compassion beneath the hooves

of Our horses, delivering it up to fire and sword. Firstly, We command thee to await Us in thy capital, Vienna, so that We may behead thee, and thou also, little Kinglet of Poland, do likewise. We will exterminate thee as well as all thy followers, causing that very lowest creation of God, which is a giaur, to disappear from the earth. We shall first expose great and small to the most terrible tortures and then hand them over to the most ignominious death. I will take thy little Empire from thee and sweep away the entire population, allowing thee and the King of Poland to live only so long that ye may satisfy yourselves that We have carried out everything We promised. This, with due respect.

Given in Our 40th year of life and in the 26th year of Our all-powerful Reign."

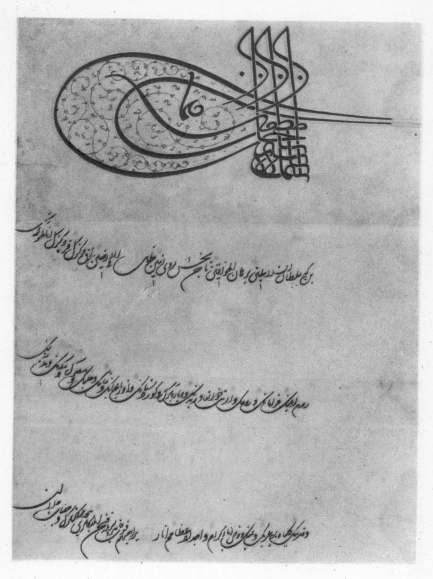

Report of the Victory of Sultan Suleiman I, 1534.

The Turkish Siege.

crushing everything in its path. Village after village went up in flames. Enveloping the capital, the savage hordes swept onwards, ravaging and laying waste the countryside. With breathless anxiety all Europe watched to see what would be Austria's fate.

Even at that time Vienna had the reputation of being a gay and genial city, but frivolity and gaiety alike vanished before such imminent danger. A new and admirable spirit of determination seized the population. The fortifications which had been sadly neglected were feverishly put in order. The tireless and courageous Burgomaster Liebenberg set an example to all. Rüdiger, Graf Starhemberg, assumed command of the defences with about 16,000 men at his disposal, including the corps of citizen volunteers. The students joined up under the Rector of the University, the guilds set up "Free Companies" and women flung themselves energetically into the construction of defence works.

The Victorious Commanders after the Relief of Vienna.

On July 14th the main body of the Turkish army appeared before Vienna and began its preparations for a siege. By the following day a city of tents had spread out in a semicircle extending from Laaerberg to Heiligenstadt. The main front of the attack was directed towards the Burgtor and the Schottentor, where Janissaries and other Turkish elite troops were encamped. The contingents from the auxiliary and tributary Balkan countries were posted on the North-West, near Heiligenstadt, the Asiatic and African troops at Laaerberg. On July the 16th, Duke Karl of Lorraine, who until that time had held out in the Leopoldstadt, crossed the Danube with his small force of cavalry—the infantry he handed over to Starhemberg—destroying the bridge behind him. Then the Turks crossed the Canal and completed the encirclement of Vienna from the North.

Right at the start of the siege the Grand Vizier realized that the city could not be taken by a sudden assault. An attempt to reduce it by constant artillery bombardement proved hopeless in face of the effective opposition which the Viennese were able to put up with the 312 pieces of artillery mounted on the walls. The only hope of victory for the Turks obviously lay in the slow and methodical processes of a siege. Dysentry and many other diseases considerable weakened the besieged garrison in its defence. The city was kept under almost continual bombardment and was

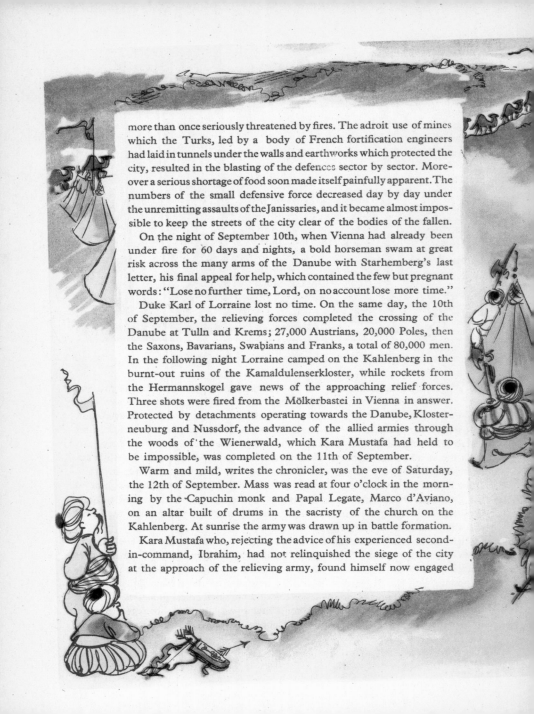

more than once seriously threatened by fires. The adroit use of mines which the Turks, led by a body of French fortification engineers had laid in tunnels under the walls and earthworks which protected the city, resulted in the blasting of the defences sector by sector. Moreover a serious shortage of food soon made itself painfully apparent. The numbers of the small defensive force decreased day by day under the unremitting assaults of the Janissaries, and it became almost impossible to keep the streets of the city clear of the bodies of the fallen.

On the night of September 10th, when Vienna had already been under fire for 60 days and nights, a bold horseman swam at great risk across the many arms of the Danube with Starhemberg's last letter, his final appeal for help, which contained the few but pregnant words: "Lose no further time, Lord, on no account lose more time."

Duke Karl of Lorraine lost no time. On the same day, the 10th of September, the relieving forces completed the crossing of the Danube at Tulln and Krems; 27,000 Austrians, 20,000 Poles, then the Saxons, Bavarians, Swabians and Franks, a total of 80,000 men. In the following night Lorraine camped on the Kahlenberg in the burnt-out ruins of the Kamaldulenserkloster, while rockets from the Hermannskogel gave news of the approaching relief forces. Three shots were fired from the Mölkerbastei in Vienna in answer. Protected by detachments operating towards the Danube, Klosterneuburg and Nussdorf, the advance of the allied armies through the woods of the Wienerwald, which Kara Mustafa had held to be impossible, was completed on the 11th of September.

Warm and mild, writes the chronicler, was the eve of Saturday, the 12th of September. Mass was read at four o'clock in the morning by the Capuchin monk and Papal Legate, Marco d'Aviano, on an altar built of drums in the sacristy of the church on the Kahlenberg. At sunrise the army was drawn up in battle formation.

Kara Mustafa who, rejecting the advice of his experienced second-in-command, Ibrahim, had not relinquished the siege of the city at the approach of the relieving army, found himself now engaged

in a fight on two fronts which soon put him in a very unenviable position. The left wing of Karl of Lorraine was the first to be markedly successful. Despite a desperate defence by the Turks, Nussdorf was stormed and Heiligenstadt threatened. Soon the main body reached Grinzing. When the left wing of his forces had pressed forward far beyond Döbling, Karl determined on a swerve to the right which rolled up the Turkish front from the flank. After an attack of the Turkish cavalry on the left flank designed to relieve the pressure on their forces which was broken on the resistance of the Polish armoured cavalry, the Turks were forced despite their obstinate resistance to abandon the lost battle. Their troops now fled in such disorder that it was not until they had reached Raab, in Hungary, that it was possible to reform their ranks. The treasure of the Grand Vizier and the rich plunder of the oriental camp fell into the hands of the victors. Vienna, however, King Sobieski wrote to his wife, was a place of wretchedness. Only very slowly was the heavily stricken city able to recover.

The victory of Kahlenberg made an overpowering impression throughout the whole of the West. Among the many congratulations sent to Austria were, in accordance with the rules of etiquette, even those of the King of France. For the unexpected and incredible relief of Vienna, Louis XIV used the word "miracle".

Among the Imperial Troops a slender young officer, Prince Eugene of Savoy, distinguished himself by his courage.

In the year 1684 a book appeared by P. W. Hörnigkh, which its author introduced with the words: "Austria over all, if she but desires it."

The great decision had fallen. The defeated Porte had no longer the power to cling to its possessions.

BAROQUE IN
AUSTRIA

Austrian Baroque is not just an art style. It is not a matter for museum collections and it is not just a phase which is dead and gone, to be docketed and laid aside with the past. Austrian Baroque is a mystery, a wonder, which is alive to-day. Like every mystery which is real and has a message, it will yield its secret only to those who live and feel with it.

To the friends of our country, especially to the friends of our capital, Vienna, the ancient "Haupt- und Residenzstadt", we would say: —

If you wish truly to understand and to appreciate this curious country, to unravel the living mystery which is Austria, you must learn how to experience the most intimate and most glorious manifestation of her spirit, as it exists in legend and song, in literature and painting, in architecture and in the great festivals of the country. It is in our Baroque that you must seek it.

"Our" Baroque! There is, of course, a magnificent Italian Baroque whose illustrious ancestors were Borromini and Bernini, and which reaches back even to Michelangelo. There are magnificent French and Dutch styles of baroque architecture. There are the widely diverging forms of Franconian and Bohemian Baroque. Each has its own importance for us as an "art form". But how do they help us? Hardly at all. For Austrian Baroque is not merely a certain form of art. It is the secret of one of the hours when fortune smiled on Austria, born of the triumph over threatening doom, over the terror which had gripped the souls of her people and the peril of being overwhelmed by alien force.

Baroque Theatre, Burnacini; Il fuoco eterno.

In those days, in 1679, the Plague was rampant in Vienna. The city was fast vanishing beneath hecatombs of the dead. Four years later, in 1683, she was attacked by the Turks. The preceding century had witnessed the hard-won triumph of the "Catholic Revival" over the Protestant movement, a process which was accompanied by great suffering, sorrow, hardship, and at times by brute force. Now the people yearned with heart and soul for liberation. When it came, it was with the effect of sudden intoxication for the city. That city had only just reduced its fine suburbs to ruins and ashes to prevent them from falling into the hands of the enemy. Its citizens' homes had been filled until just previously with unburied dead. Almost at the end, on September 4th, 1683, 4,000 Janissaries had struck at the city's exposed flank and had forced their way into the Burg bastion, only to be beaten back after hours of some of the most bloody fighting of the war.

And at last it was there, Victory! If ever in the world's history there had been a true victory, then this was it. It cannot be dismissed with mere accounts of the expeditions of Prince Eugene of Savoy, of the Peace Treaties of Karlowitz (1699) and Passarowitz (1718), which made of Austria a great Western power extending

77

The Karlskirche, Vienna.

far into the Balkans—to Belgrade, Bosnia and Wallachia. What happened in Vienna, in the heart of Austria, under the three great Baroque Emperors Leopold (d. 1705), Joseph I (d. 1711) and Karl VI (d. 1740) has a far deeper significance than the military-political pageant which brought the people, as usual, much shouting, sorrow and echoes of war, but not the sweet miracle for which they were longing. Their dream was of hearts and minds flung open before the fullness of life, the ready and joyous acceptance of all things good, lovely and strong—yes, and of contrasting elements from East and West, North and South, making up the harmony of contrasts.

This the Baroque gave to Austria—to be a clear mirror of the West and of Europe, to unite and reconcile their contrasts in a concert of many voices, many tones. What was amazing and unique about this victory was that the country did not stand aside in arrogant isolation as victorious countries are apt to do after a hard and painfully-won triumph. Our country, on the contrary, threw wide her portals to the world, growing and expanding. She offered hospitality to everyone—the Italians and French, the Spanish and Dutch, the Germans, Hungarians, Bohemians and Southern Slavs. They came—as simple bricklayers' labourers, as technicians to the Court Theatre, as doctors and builders, as poets of the Court, as composers and preachers; they came as makers of fine textiles and objects of art, as soldiers and actors, as singers and painters, as hard-working peasants and as great nobles.

Now the production could be put on—the transformation of the world into a mighty stage, into a festival theatre. For this is the heart and soul of our Baroque— from beginning to end it is theatrical, from the pompous funeral of Joseph I in 1711 (it was Fischer von Erlach who built the Castrum Doloris, that ornate catafalque designed to honour the exalted figure of the late Emperor) down to the "Wurstel-prater", Vienna's "Fun City".

Yes, the profusion of side-shows in the Peoples Prater, that amusement centre for the ordinary people, for the Little Man, with its roundabouts, its trips through grottos, with "the Great Chinese, Kalafatti", and the dance of the ghosts (to be seen in pantomime inside one of the booths), all this, too, is really Baroque, even though but its swan song. We have here the old themes—joy and sorrow, anxiety, horror, mortal fear, major and minor alarms—all overcome in their presentation, in the artistic mastery of the last and most secret, most tragic emotional tension which can affect the heart of man.

Let us pause here for a moment to consider the extent, the grandeur and the radiant force of this Austrian miracle. Not only did palaces and castles, churches and monasteries and the lords spiritual and temporal, in Vienna and far away in the North-East—Poland and Volhynia, and in the South-East—Hungary and the Banat—don the garb of this new world fashion from Austria. Soon it dominated

everyday life. Cribs and cradles, roundabouts, dinner-plates—the simplest household articles—songs, words and figures of speech among the common people took on the colour and form, sound and symphony of that great victor over all contrasting elements, our Baroque Age.

Who thinks to-day when he hears the easy and graceful "Küß die Hand" from the simple lips of some "alter Wiener", some Viennese of the old school, that this expression dates from the Spanish court ceremonial of our baroque Emperor?

Who remembers nowadays in the Wurstelprater, among the fairies and dwarfs of these side-shows for the Little Man, that they derive from the "Cabinet of Magic" of the Imperial Court Theatre, from the festivals of the Great Man on whose realm the sun never set ...

The setting sun! When to-day in the Schwarzenberg Gardens or in Schönbrunn, the sun's rays softly and playfully caress the stone cupids, the pairs of lovers, the nymphs, goddesses and human beings—then, surely that sun remembers in gentle affection his most brilliant hour in Austria.

Our Baroque was born as an Imperial art form. Life and the drama of life were all centred on the Emperor and his Reich. Glance at the famous original design of J. B. Fischer von Erlach (1695) for Schönbrunn. We see a vast expanse of gardens, row upon row of subsidiary buildings enclosing large areas for festive occasions, processions and the great spectacles of the court and of society. These were so designed as to lead on the guest to the mighty, sweeping facade of the Palace itself. Here stands revealed the extent—and the extravagance, the measure and the profusion of Baroque. Nature is transformed into trimmed and clipped French parks, the arts dance a measure round the new "Roi Soleil". This planned Schönbrunn was to have been a super-Versailles.

It remained a project only. In that, too lies Austria and her Baroque. As a contrast, take that other project of Fischer von Erlach, that baroque symbol of Vienna, the Karlskirche. This is reality—a monumental, imperious realisation of the urge to include everything in a single concept. In 1713, when the Plague came to Vienna for the second time, the Emperor Karl VI had taken a vow to build such a church. It was fulfilled between 1716 and 1737. There is a story that the idea which was realised in this wonderful harmony of pillars, outer hall and cupola was given to Fischer von Erlach by a glimpse of the view from the Pincio, Rome's most familiar hill. He is said to have seen St. Peter's and Trajan's Column as one whole in the light of the evening sun—the Rome of antiquity combined with the Rome of Christendom. Actually this would have been in accord with the forceful inner aims of Imperial Baroque; the Karlskirche seeks a synthesis of Roman Forum and Christian-Imperial majesty. The harmony of contrasts, of the eras of antiquity and of Christianity, of the Clerical and the Secular, of East and West, of North and South. The Benedictine Monasteries of Melk and Göttweig—radiant mon-

The Academy of Sciences: Maulpertsch. The Baptism of Christ (Section).

Schönbrunn Castle: the Great Gallery.

The Academy of Sciences: Maulpertsch. The Baptism of Christ (Section).

strances set on the delicately shaded, conical hills of the country round Vienna—endeavour to glorify such an exalted and sacred unison in buildings which embody a winged and festive happiness. Classical and religious education, art, the Stage and science were to find here an enchanting and sumptuous home. In these baroque monastery buildings are combined church, monastery, imperial hall, library, theatre, art collection and natural history museum, to form the indivisible unit of a single jewel. Once again, the splendour of the whole is designed to serve the cult of the ruling Monarch. Thus, for example, at Göttweig we see the Emperor enthroned as the Sun God in the sky, surrounded by allegorical figures taken from the arts and sciences. To this stairway-fresco corresponds and responds in the vast, many-voiced choir of great baroque edifices, Daniel Gran's famous fresco in the Vienna

National Library, depicting Karl VI as ruler over heaven and earth, as Roman Emperor, as Hercules, as Lord of war and peace! In hymnal dance, a chorus of the Virtues, of the Arts and of the Sciences surrounds him. As the "School of Athens", Vienna experiences here its glorification as a world-centre of culture!

Once again, this is the art born of a great victory. On the fringe of the sphere of light, the Vices are depicted here falling into the depths in wild confusion; they stand, of course, for the political and religious enemies of the Empire.

Such festive adulation of the imperial idea, if one so regards it, may seem to assume almost overwhelming, overpowering forms. In the old monastery of Kloster-neuburg, closely connected with the history of Austria ever since its foundation in 1106, it was planned to have nine cupolas for Donato d'Allio's baroque renovations of the Imperial tract alone. Of these, only the central pavilion with the Imperial crown, and the cupola at the north-east corner with the Austrian Ducal crown were actually constructed. The whole was intended to be, indeed it is, the "Escorial" of Austria.

Once again we pause for a moment, almost overawed. The vibrant majesty, the imperious and magnificent opulence of these imposing edifices robs one of breath. It inspires not only the buildings of the Emperor. It displays its proud countenance in a stately galaxy of castles, country seats and town houses of the nobility, and even to-day is the dominant note of many a street and square in Vienna.

There are the castles and palaces of Prince Eugene (the Belvedere), of the Schwarzenbergs, Liechtensteins, Kinskys (Daun), Schönborns—of the whole of the Austrian aristocracy in and near Vienna. Let us glance at the changes in the baroque style itself: the Palais Starhemberg (the modern Ministry of Education),

built in 1670, may serve as an example of the still severe and massive Early Baroque, while for an example of High and Late Baroque we may take the town residence of Prince Eugene in the Himmelpfortgasse (the modern Ministry of Finance), built partly by Fischer von Erlach and partly by Lukas von Hildebrandt.

These facades of the Vienna *palais*! Cold and reserved, how often they serve quietly to conceal from the outer world a beautiful interior. Above their staircases play strange mythological creatures born of some artist's capricious mood, yet forming a deliberate part of the plans of both the builder and the architect. They lead us on to interior apartments, to a succession of halls and chambers, panelled in silk and damask, in costly inlay work, in white and gold mouldings, which were once peopled by an elegant aristocracy amusing itself with cards and dancing, minuettes and chamber music.

Here in the haunts of music and frivolity, where soft colours and sweet melodies soothed the spirit, one feels more at ease. This Baroque, this Austrian Baroque, is not just a sumptuous display of the power, the riches and the love of ostentation of lordly courtiers and arrogant aristocrats. It is something more than the attempt to celebrate proud festivals of personal luxury and indulgence at the cost of the whole world beyond. This fashion which Austria gave the world, this Baroque, had to spread its light abroad. They could not hold it captive in the Hofburg or in the Vienna *palais* of the aristocrats. Gleefully, swiftly, bursting its bonds, filled with the spirit of colourful and uncontrollable youth, it spread outwards—first to the population of the cities, to the makers of gingerbread, the little shop keepers, the burghers and merchants. Merrily it transforms sober handicraft products into art—a simple candlestick, wrought-iron bars, a door-hasp or a wooden mould

Palais Schwarzenberg.

for cake-making. It set its victorious and unmistakable seal on great chests, on simple dinner plates. Nothing was exempt from the magic of its touch. It came to the baby in the cradle, ornamenting it with cherubs, it leaped laughing on to the boards of the Volkstheater, to furnish to the "Wurstel", the Viennese clown, that peculiar vein of humour in which tears season the laughter that not even the tragic experiences of two centuries right down to the present day have been able to kill. Baroque is no respecter of persons or places. It entered the pulpit, storming and blustering in speach and in song, admonishing and—rarely—praising the Viennese. Through the mouth of the famous preacher, Father Abraham a Sancta Clara, it gave its message—"Behold it, Vienna" and "Rise up, rise up, ye Christians".

The swelling bells, like wet-nurses of the heavens, with their broad scrolls inscribed with mottoes, carried its message abroad. It was perhaps in some small village church or solitary chapel, in a wayside cross, a column to the Trinity, or a statue of the Virgin, that it revealed itself most fully to a sympathetic onlooker. At such times it was all voice to disclose its inmost secret, that of the soul of Austria.

Light and glitter, games and dancing, magical splendour and melody—but what is fame, what is the glory of this world? A strange drama, the presentation of a play before God and man in which everyone can take up his allotted role. Emperor and beggar, prince and peasant, each has been given his part in this Great

Vienna; Belvedere.

The National Library : State Hall.

World Theatre. In this idea of the World Theatre is rooted the moral lesson which Baroque would teach—that each should do his utmost to play his part to the best of his ability. To escape from the stage, to dance outside the ranks, to break away from this other world, which is all God's and all mankind's, is impossible. Everyone must dance, act and sing in cooperation with the rest of the caste. In this lies the great and fundamental force of Austrian Baroque. The fact that so many thousands of willing assistants had played their roles as workers in stucco, masons, wood carvers, handicraftsmen of the arts, house-painters, musicians, poets of the court and of noblemen, alone made possible the penetration of Austrian Baroque to the most remote village.

In its essence there lay the comforting assurance that joy and pain, suffering and gaiety, life and death, man and nature, belief and knowledge, art and science, God and the world, were in tune with each other. The one was linked to the other and all belonged together, from the "Krampus" to the angel, from the Styrian "Kripperlspiel" to the Imperial Court Theatre in Vienna and to the theatre of high politics, with its great political and military figures.

Nations, empires, success and glory of this world? A pretty and amusing musical play, very beautiful, really beautiful, which called for careful study of its roles, constant rehearsal, for distinguished and worthy artists to set it to music, to direct and produce it festively. The proud castles and palaces, the churches and monasteries sought to dominate and imprison the surrounding countryside and cities with their glittering façades. In its boundless ambition, each new building sought to tower above and eclipse its neighbour.

But this is not the final note struck by Baroque. It concludes in impressive modesty and humility. To quote a phrase of Leibniz, the great writer of the baroque time, Baroque is the harmony of pleasing tones, colours and contrasts, all blended together to serve a high ideal.

In Baroque Austria the "Holy Empire" of the West found its last realisation.

METTERNICH'S
POLICY
OF A BALANCED
EUROPE

Rudolf von Alt, Ballhausplatz.

Since the break-up of the mediaeval system, two political principles both of which aimed at the control of the Continent of Europe had been in conflict. The one had been that of predominating force, the other that of the balance of power. The principles of the dominant force, usually based on a strong nationalistic or ideological impulse, sought to subject European state systems to the political and sometimes to the ideological dictatorship of a single nation. It involved an attempt to standardise and to regiment the diverse forms of Western thought. In the 16th century it was Spain which had made a bid to dominate the Continent. During the second half of the 17th century, a European coalition was required to put an end to the imperialistic demands of the France of Louis XIV. The turn of the 18th century brought with it the dictatorship of Napoleon Bonaparte. After him, it was Bismarck's Germany which was seized with the drive to dominate the world, that reached its climax in the "Third Reich". Contrasted with such ideas of violence is that of balance of power, which aims at a well-balanced system, an equilibrium of forces, and in principle is opposed to attempts by any one State to secure predominance at the expense of the liberty and independence of another. This is the policy which England usually and at decisive moments also Austria has pursued.

THE VIENNA CONGRESS—
WHAT THEY SAID.

When the witty Prince de Ligne coined the much-quoted bon mot: «Le Congrès danse, mais il ne marche pas», he must have been thinking chiefly of the pleasure-loving Czar Alexander, for the worthy Emperor Franz of Austria always preferred his bed to evening festivities. Friedrich Wilhelm, King of Prussia, who achieved the feat of sitting for hours at the side of his charming but unfortunate partner at a ball in silent adoration, was certainly no social lion, and the King of Württemberg was prevented by his monstrous girth which earned him the nickname of "le monstre wurtembergeois" from joining in such active arrangements. The Czar of Russia, however, missed no chance of tripping on the light fantastic toe. He even appeared at a children's dance given by the Schwarzenbergs, enjoying himself enormously among the little dancers. No wonder that His Russian Majesty was able to establish the unusual record of having danced through 40 nights in a few weeks. The temptation was certainly great, for Vienna was in gala attire. The alluring city sparkled like champagne with charm, brilliance and hospitality. For these few months it was for more than the Capital of the Danube Monarchy—it was Europe.

There is perhaps a touch of exaggeration in the claim of the contemporary Comte de la Garde that a hundred thousand visitors from all over Europe had come to a rendez-vous in Vienna. But what a vast train must have come with the Courts of St. Petersburg, Berlin and Copenhagen alone, apart from those who accompanied the Kings of Bavaria and Württemberg and the other reigning German princes. To them must be added the huge staffs of the diplomatic missions from nearly

Europe at the beginning of the 19th century was confronted, not only with the remarkable growth of the power of revolutionary France, but also with the advance of two other States to the status of Powers which had to be taken into account, Prussia and Russia. The European balance of power seemed to be threatened from various quarters. There was need of a personality who could not only unite the available but discordant opposition to Napoleon and prove himself the equal of the Corsican in diplomacy, but could also restore as far as might prove feasible the political system which had been overthrown, take its measure and maintain it for the future. In Clemence Lothar Metternich both these requisites were united.

When the young Metternich began his diplomatic career with his appointment as Ambassador in Dresden, two wars against Napoleon had already been lost. Two years later (Metternich had by then been advanced to the position of Austrian Ambassador in Berlin), William Pitt the Younger, the great English predecessor of Metternich, formed the third coalition against a Napoleon who was seeking to conquer Italy and North Germany. In 1805 followed the catastrophe of Austerlitz and the Treaty of Pressburg, by which Austria lost Tyrol and the frontier territories as well as her Venetian possessions. Thereby she also lost her power in Germany and Italy, where the influence of the Corsican now became absolute. In 1806, Metternich walked into the lion's den with his appointment as Ambassador in Paris. It looked as though nothing could check Napoleon's victorious progress. During 1806-1807 he subdued Prussia and introduced his "Continental System" which forbade all trade with England. At Tilsit he made an agreement with the unreliable Czar

Alexander I, by which Europe was divided into an Eastern and a Western block. In 1807 Portugal was occupied by the French, and one year later Joseph, the brother of Napoleon, was placed on the throne of Spain.

Against this intolerable pressure the nations began to revolt. A rebellion broke out in Spain, the English landed on the Peninsula, and in Austria preparations were made to strike a decisive blow. The great rising of 1809, the battles of Aspern and Wagram and the revolt of the Tyrolese peasants under Andreas Hofer belong to the finest pages of Austrian history. The final defeat of Austria after she had thrown her last reserves into the breach against not only the overweening power of the French but also against Napoleon's ally, Russia, caused the collapse of such resistance as still continued to France's predominance on the Continent. Under the Treaty of Vienna, Austria was forced to cede Salzburg, Dalmatia, Istria, Western —and a part of Eastern—Galicia, thus losing an area of over 113,000 square kilometres, and her access to the sea.

In this dark hour, when Metternich took over from Count Stadion the direction of Austrian foreign policy, the situation might well have been called hopeless. In material and in moral the country was completely exhausted. Prussia was enchained, Russia an ally of the Dictator, England blockaded from all access to the Continent, while Italy, Spain and the Germanic States had been degraded to the position of Napoleon's satellites. Concurrently, Austrian interests were being seriously threatened from another angle through the aggressive Balkan policy of Russia. Even had Austria been in possession of her full strength, to pursue a policy directed simultaneously against East and West would have been impossible. Metternich therefore decided to form a temporary alliance with France. The new relationship was confirmed by the marriage of Napoleon with the Austrian princess Marie Louise. The new Austrian Minister of State was starting on his special diplomatic tricks, his *"Finesses"* as he called them. The first of these was undoubtedly his courting of the victor of yesterday, which was hardly taken seriously. Even before the signing of the Vienna Treaty which imposed so many losses on Austria, Metternich explained this policy of his to the Emperor in a statement on his political objectives : —

"Whatever the conditions of peace, in the end we shall have to seek our security only by

all the countries of Europe, and the many who were drawn by sheer curiosity to Vienna.

Political intrigue was everywhere in progress, during the morning corso on the bastions, in the afternoon rides or excursions to the Prater, at brilliant redoutes as in the quiet apartments of the countless ladies of the world—and of the half-world—who were magnetically drawn to the exciting atmosphere of the Congress. In the Palais Palm, in the Schenkenstrasse, lived the gay and lovely Princess Bagration, who, once a close friend of Metternich, later seemed to have lost her heart completely to the Czar. This did not deter her from consoling the hearts of other princes, so that her salon was thus characterised by Schiller in the hardly flattering lines : —

"Who counts the races, knows the names,

Of those who there together came?"

attaching ourselves to the triumphant French system. How little we really belong with the system, which is opposed to all the principles of sound policy and to every strong union of States, I do not need to remind Your Majesty. My principles are unchangeable, but necessity knows no law." If it be remembered that two years later, Russian troops marched into Belgrade, one can gain an idea of how difficult must have been the diplomatic manoeuvres of the State between two power groups which on the one hand threatened its existence and on the other hand courted it. History must pay tribute to Metternich's statesmanlike gifts in that he succeeded in freeing Austria from this situation and restoring the old balance of power in Europe.

The cooling off of relations between Napoleon and the Czar did nothing to improve the situation, but brought nearer a decision which in any case was bound to be unfavourable for Austria. When the break finally occured and the last great struggle began, Austria, together with a small auxiliary corps under Prince Schwarzenberg, was indeed found on the side of Napoleon. But there are proofs that at the same time Metternich had secret connections with the Russian Court. Even after the catastrophe which befell the "Grande Armee" in Russia, the Austrian Chancellor was in no undue hurry to show his hand. He had first to secure full freedom of movement; the political reactions of the defeat could not yet be calculated. On the one hand it was necessary to see that Napoleon never recovered his former position of supremacy in Europe, but on the other, Russia's tendency to expansion, as well as certain Prussian ambitions, could not be viewed with equanimity. Here was a chance to head a coalition which should deliver the decisive blow against Napoleon. In the meantime,

Spanish Court Riding School, 1805, Carousel.

the opposing Powers were once again attacking one another. Russia and Prussia signed a treaty of alliance at Kalisch, and there was a French army 300,000 strong in Saxony. Metternich's procrastinating policy was designed to await a favourable political and military situation in which an intervention to restore a peace which should be based on a re-establishment of the old European balance of power might have a prospect of success. The favourable outcome of several clashes had given Napoleon renewed self confidence, but the attitude of Metternich remained unchanged. Even such a tempting offer as the return of the unforgotten province of Silesia was not enough to persuade him to join France. At last a suitable arrangement was made with the allies, Russia and Prussia. A mutual guarantee of the possessions of the States concerned was to secure the balance of power against any attack of an imperialist tendency. Napoleon, however, rejected this compromise. Once again the sword was unsheathed.

It cannot be overlooked that even after the "Battle of Nations" at Leipzig, when the war was carried by the victorious allied armies across Germany into the interior of France, Metternich did not favour the deposition of Napoleon. The sudden

Isabey: The Vienna Congress.

In the same house lived also the Duchess of Sagan, who was a mistress of Metternich, while her sister, Countess Perigord, sweetened the days of the dignified Talleyrand. When political tension between Russia and Austria concerning the fate of Poland had reached its height and the Czar was for weeks not on speaking terms with Metternich, the former permitted himself to extend their rivalry in politics to their private affairs, intriguing with the Duchess of Sagan against the Austrian statesman.

Major official entertainments such as the routs in the Court Riding School, with orange groves and three rows of silver candelabra in which burned 10,000 candles, were less popular than the more intimate house-balls in

lust for action shown by the advancing Czar showed the need of caution. Apart from consideration for the son-in-law and grandson of the Austrian Emperor, it was chiefly the principle of the balance of power which caused Metternich to adopt this policy. The complete subjection of France would have created a dangerous vacuum in Europe which might have endangered a stable peace. The man who had mastered the French Revolution was still, in Metternich's eyes, the most suitable guarantor of a France which should keep the peace at home and be strong abroad. It was necessary only to limit his Caesarian ambitions by a well-thought-out system of security. It was a fatal mistake in Bonaparte's diplomacy not to have

99

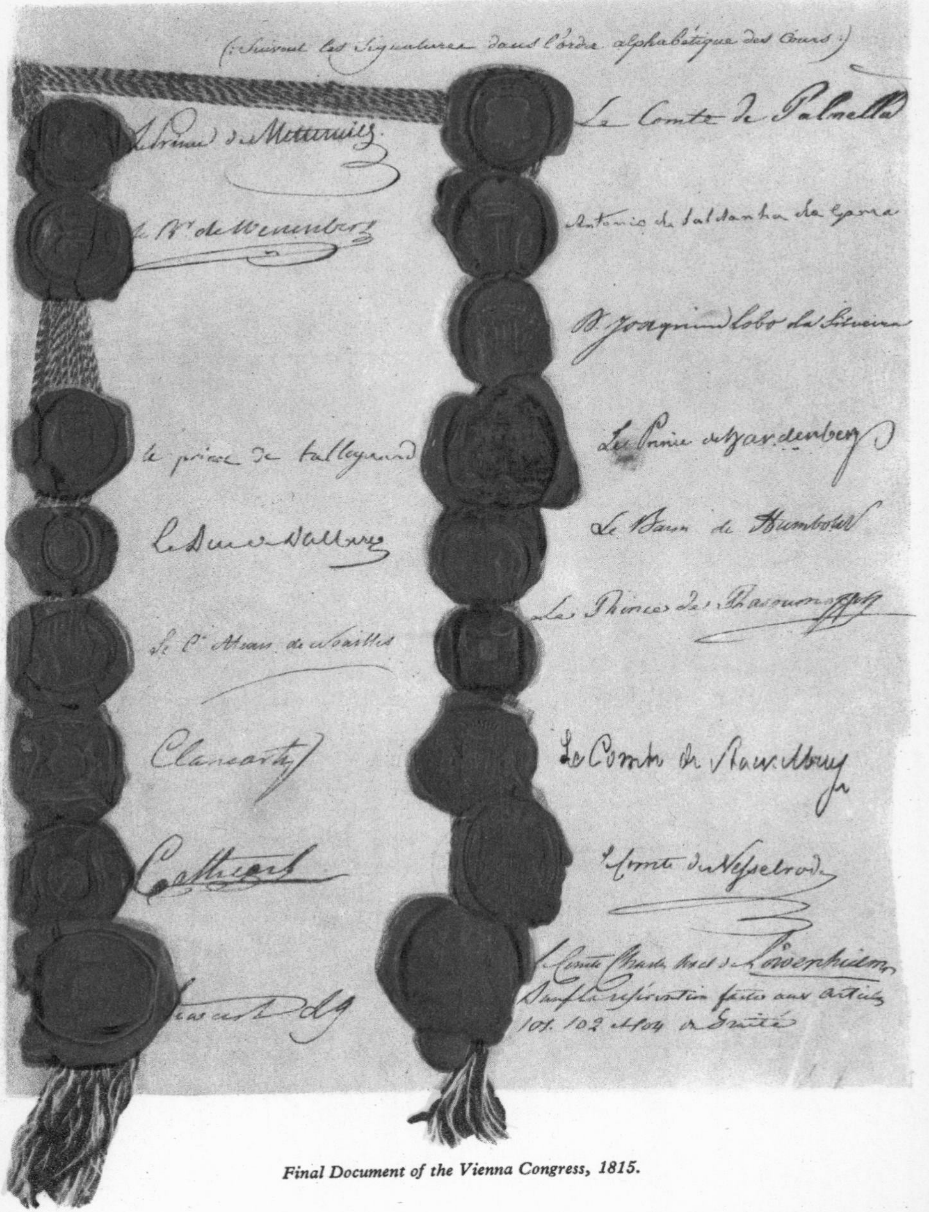
(Suivent les Signatures dans l'ordre alphabétique des Cours.)

Le Prince de Metternich

Le Bn de Wessenberg

le prince de talleyrand

Le Duc de Dalberg

Le Cte Alexis de Noailles

Clancarty

Cathcart

Stewart L.G.

Le Comte de Palmella

Antonio de Saldanha da Gama

D. Joaquim Lobo da Silveira

Le Prince de Hardenberg

Le Baron de Humboldt

Le Prince de Rasoumoffsky

Le Comte de Stackelberg

Le Comte de Nesselrode

Le Comte Charles Axel de Löwenhielm
Sauf la réservation faite aux articles 101. 102 et 104 du Traité

Final Document of the Vienna Congress, 1815.

the private residences of the Austrian aristocracy. Imposing military parades were always a draw. The biggest display of this sort coincided with the first anniversary of the Battle of Leipzig. Less pleasant was the great wild boar hunt held in the autumn in the Tiergarten at Lainz. The beasts were herded together in the smallest possible space and driven towards the gentlemen of quality who had posted themselves in order of precedence. When the Emperors missed, the kings got the chance of a shot. If they also missed, the mere princes could be relied upon to finish off the luckless boar.

During the winter months, pleasant excursions by sleigh to Schönbrunn gave the Viennese populace something to stare at.

The weaknesses of the prominent figures attending the Congress were naturally soon noised abroad. The gluttony of the King of Württemberg, for whom a semicircular opening had to be cut out of the table to accomodate his swollen belly, was a current joke. Everyone had some story to tell of the amorous exploits of the Czar and the former Viceroy of Italy, Eugène de Beauharnais, in the humbler suburbs of Vienna, or of the parsimony of Lord and Lady Castlereagh. Attendance at the many masked balls naturally cost money, and the clos.-fisted Lady Castlereagh is said on one occasion to have tired her hair with her husband's Order of the Garter, thus unwittingly causing general amusement. The "enfant terrible" of the Congress was Castlereagh's brother, Lord Charles Stewart, who, when mildly intoxicated, challenged a Vienna fiacre-driver to a bout of fisticuffs in the street. The cabby apparently got the best of it, for Lord Charles had subsequently to receive medical attention. The violent temper and the irritability of Don Pedro Gomez Labrador, the Spanish delegate, was another source of malicious stories,

made use of this attitude of the Austrian Minister of State at the right moment. The peace negotiations of Chatillon ended abortively. The allies renewed their pact and decided to conclude no separate treaties, but to fight on until their united forces had overthrown the adversary. On March 31st, 1814, Friedrich Wilhelm III of Prussia and the Czar Alexander entered Paris by the Porte St. Martin, and on April the 11th Napoleon signed a document of unconditional abdication at Fontainebleau.

The first Treaty of Paris is a rare example of wise moderation on the part of the victors. France, which had disturbed the peace of the Continent through two centuries, holding it in thrall and repeatedly making war in its territories, retained her possessions, which had been increased, since the outbreak of the Revolution by 5000 square kilometres, with a million inhabitants. The allies demanded no reparations and even allowed the French galleries and museums to retain all the art treasures which had found their way to Paris in the course of the Napoleonic Wars. This peace was the result of the Anglo-Austrian policy of the balance of power which sprang from the wise and statesmanlike recognition that the stripping of such a political factor as France of her rights and her power would not bring pacification, but would only give rise to new crises. When, therefore, the great Congress was summoned, the French delegate, Talleyrand, came to Vienna as a member with the same rights as those of the victors. The fruits of this attitude were soon visible when Russia demanded the whole of Poland and Prussia attempted to assimilate the Kingdom of Saxony. England, France and Austria stood together to oppose this. As a result, a counter-balance was established which was capable of hindering any undue expansion of the two Eastern states.

At one time it was almost the fashion to criticise the Vienna Congress. There was condemnation, not only of the apparent frivolity with which such a great problem as the re-modelling of Europe had been treated in the light-hearted city on the Danube, but also of the results of the Congress, in which, it was considered, too little attention had been paid to national aspirations. In the light of the experiences of the past century, one is obliged to revise one's judgement of an agreement among the Powers which secured peace for 30 years—in essence its decisions remained valid for 100 years, until 1914—and introduced an era of remarkable cultural and intellectual progress.

The principles underlying Metternich's political ideas which guided the Congress in its decisions remain valid to-day. The security and prosperity of the European continent can still be guaranteed only by a union of States among whom power is evenly distributed, which can set a limit to such consequences of nationalism as arrogance, intolerance and imperialism. It was not a pure accident that it was in Vienna that the leading statesmen of the day began to talk of universalism, of Europe as an indivisible whole. The Danube Monarchy, not unjustly, was regarded as the last relic of the Holy

Roman Empire, a relic which lasted on into the 20th century, preserving in many respects the spiritual traditions of mediaeval universalism. In addition, considerations of practical politics were taken into account. No second state of Europe could be so dangerous to the rising tide of nationalism as Austria. A hundred years before Geneva, the Danube Monarchy was a League of Nations, based on national tolerance and limitations imposed in the name of a super-national common weal. This truly civilised state concept sought to extend itself through the general system of States throughout Europe. Friedrich von Gentz, the faithful right hand of Metternich and one of the most important publicists of the "*Vormärz*" epoch which preceeded the Revolutionary period in Austria, sums up this Austrian conception of a communal life for the European States in a few concise sentences: —

"Through their geographical position, through the uniformity of their customs, their laws, their needs, their mode of life and culture, all the States of this part of the world constitute a great political league which has been called with some reason the European Republic. The various components of this League of Nations form such a close and continuous community that no important change which is carried out in any one of them can be a matter of indifference to the others."

These mellow sentences show how the European problem was regarded in Austria. In the Europe of those times, there was no better guarantee for this much-needed cooperation than Austria herself, a State in the heart of the Continent, with interests in the German areas, on the Apennine Peninsula, in the Balkans and in East Europe. Her mere existence was a barrier to a possible predominance of power in either as were the exaggeratedly simple tastes of Frederick VI of Denmark, who earned the nickname of "King of the Tandelmarkt" (the well-known second-hand market of Vienna).

Apart from a round of unbridled pleasures and entertainments, Vienna also offered rich artistic fare to her guests. The Imperial and privately-owned art-galleries, whose "inexhaustible riches" are enthusiastically described by Varnhagen von Ense, were widely praised. "It is unbelievable", wrote the Archduke of Weimar, Karl August, to Goethe, "what quantities of treasures have been accumulated here from every branch of art and science, and how many persons of distinction one meets here who take their possessions very seriously".

It is hard to believe that the concert at which 20 pianos were played each by two persons simultaneously, so that no less than 80 hands were pounding the keys at the same time, proved a pure musical treat. But the concerts of chamber music were of a very high standard. The gala concert given by Beethoven personally must have been an unforgettable experience. The Maestro's "Fidelio" met with the most enthusiastic applause from the international audience.

The Danube City, with its gay atmosphere, its light-heartedness and sense of humour, its human virtues and failings and its love of beauty, offered an auspicious background to this unique Peace Conference. One can question whether it would have ended so satisfactorily in any other metropolis.

Western or Eastern Europe and set a limit to sudden and exaggerated imperialist or nationalist demands.

The tragedy was that in the person of Metternich the conception of the balance of power had become petrified as a political doctrine which was combined with an obstinate adherence to the social system of the "ancien régime" that stifled the vital need of the masses to expand and develop. The intellectual trends of the "Age of Enlightenment", together with new romantic conceptions, had begun to penetrate political life with ever-increasing strength. Social, liberal and national forces were crying out for recognition and attempting to change the structure of state and society in accordance with the new theories and the requirements of the age. These influences which, struggling for expression, seized popular imagination with elemental force, could not long be successfully opposed even by the most carefully devised system. The outmoded past found itself confronted by the youthful aspirations of a new-born century. The deep insight and the skill which England in particular has always shown in a sound blending of progress and tradition was not to be accorded to the Austria of Metternich. His rigid adherence to the formulas of a dead and irrevocable past brought about a stifling inner-political stagnation from which the forces of the age were only able to liberate themselves in eruptive fashion. This rigidity and inability to change, the panic fear of revolutions and revolutionary movements, had the further result of hindering the natural development of the European state system. Such a policy of intervention in favour of "legitimate" regimes as soon made itself evident in Italy and Spain could bring no permanent solution. The President of the United States, Monroe, made an energetic protest during the War of Independence of the Spanish Colonies in South and Central America against any intervention of European Powers in questions which concerned the American Continent. England under Canning also distanced herself from a policy which, under a pretence of preserving the balance of power, set bounds to the internal independence and freedom of the peoples. Even Russia, whose Czar Alexander had been the creator of the three-power-pact of the "Holy Alliance", after some initial hesitation allowed considerations of practical politics to rule, and gave her support to the revolt of the Greeks against Turkish rule. The revolution of 1830 which placed the "Citizen King", Louis Philippe of Orleans, on the throne of France, led to the independence of Belgium and occasioned the great Polish uprising. It might have served as a warning that it is impossible, to rule in defiance of the vital forces of the age. But the "*Vormärz*" system of government was no longer capable in itself instituting the necessary reforms. The Revolution of 1848 was the inevitable outcome of internal necessity.

What calls for admiration in Metternich is his conception of a pan-European policy, his idea of a league of nations and his intellectual universalism. In him the policy of a European balance of power experienced its last triumphs. After his fall, national passions were let loose. An unbridled reaching out for power and unchecked national egoism replaced well-thought-out cooperation and a workable balance of forces. The age of imperialism had set in which was to find its continuation in the bloody world wars of the 20th century.

LAND
OF MUSIC

The music of Austria is born of her scenery and is deeply rooted in the people. When Grillparzer says: "If you from Kahlenberg have seen the verdant land, so you will know myself, my works, and understand", these words convey not only the thoughts of the poet, but are at the same time an expression of that indescribable charm which affects the composer even more than the poet.

The way was prepared for Austrian music by centuries of development. As early as the 12th century, Reimar von Hagenau tells us that "poor and rich dance and fiddle". At the Ducal Court, Walther von der Vogelweide sang his loveliest songs and Neidhart von Reuenthal played for the people, and for their dances.

During the 15th and 16th centuries when the Dutch were fixing the trend of music in Europe, the best composers from the Netherlands were making a name for themselves at the Austrian Court. After the establishment of the *Wiener Hofmusikkapelle* by the Emperor Maximilian I, Austria had gravitated steadily towards the centre of the musical world of those times. Men of note such as Heinrich Isaac, Ludwig Senfl, Paul Hofhaimer of Salzburg (said to be one of the greatest organists of his day), Jakobus Gallus and Philipp de Monte produced compositions of merit in Vienna, contributing in no small measure to the development of sacred music in Austria to a degree which was unequalled to any other country.

The aristocracy as well as the middle classes found pleasure in this church music, which has been enthusiastically cultivated up to the present day. All the great figures in the musical world who were connected with the Catholic Church served the *Musica Sacra*. Instrumental church music is an integral part of Austrian music in the truest sense of the word, and is hardly challenged by the opposite tendency of Cäcilianism.

With the coming of the opera and similar forms of art such as the oratorium and cantata in Italy in the 17th century, the supremacy of the Dutch was ended in the world of melody. The Austrian Monarchy favoured the new fashions in music, and summoned to the Court Italian composers who were accorded a brilliant reception. Famous men such as Bertali, Cesti, Draghi and Caldara made the Imperial Court a centre of music in Europe. The Vienna Court set value on elaborate scenery in opera productions. In 1667, for the marriage of Leopold I with Margaret of Spain, Cesti's ceremonial play "Il Pomo d'Oro" was enacted with such a display of splendour that it was still talked about forty years afterwards.

Among the leading composers of this epoch, the Austrian-born Court-Composer and Court-Orchestra-Leader of Leopold I, Johann Joseph Fux, made a special name for himself. His works include eighteen operas and ten oratorios, as well as church music; they paved the way for Gluck and subsequent Vienna classics.

The Hapsburgs, who had always been fond of art and music, not only patronised the latter generously, but had themselves composers as well as musicians in their family. The works of Ferdinand III, Leopold I, Joseph I, and Karl VI occupy no mean position in the history of baroque music.

Apart from the baroque drama, which was especially favoured by the upper classes, popular items such as ballets and light musical interludes were introduced into the performances. The composing of these provided local musicians with respectable employment.

The death of Karl VI proved a turning point in the history of music in Austria. Maria Theresia, who succeeded her father on the throne, inherited great financial burdens which she could only overcome through strict economy at court. This put an end to the splendour and versatility of the baroque opera in Vienna. The Court Theatre was transformed into a National Theatre which —managed by a private person—was open to everybody. In it, Italian and German operas were alternately performed, as well as French comedies with music and ballets. Contemporaneous with these developments in Austria, a new trend of thought was dawning in Europe which aimed at the introduction of popular sentiment and simplicity into poetry, music and art. The Italian tendency in music, which was deeply rooted in the soil of Austria and to which, after the fashion of the

times, even composers of Austrian origin were faithful, had gradually to be ousted before the new ideas could take effect. Keen competition developed between the composers and musicians of the two nations of which Vienna had again become a focus. Apart from the Italians Scarlatti and Salieri, there were already famous Austrians at work such as Wagenseil, Gassmann, Dittersdorf and Monn, who had won special recognition for their part in the development of instrumental music. Their work was a foundation for the new forms of sonata and symphony which later became perfected in the Vienna classics.

Maria Theresia's accession to the throne meant the gradual disappearance of Italian grand opera in Austria. But at the same time the great theatre, the Opera, became a national heritage, enabling the public to influence the selection of the pieces which should be produced. Thus the comedy with music, which had previously been confined to small suburban stages, won wider recognition and developed in these new surroundings into an important form of art, based on popular support.

At this period of change in the baroque form of music and the gradual tendency to seek new types of musical expression, a musician appeared whose mission it was to revolutionise opera, and at the same time to link baroque with classical music. His name was CHRISTOPH WILLIBALD GLUCK. At this time the intellectual world was absorbed in the controversy as to which was the most important factor, the author or the composer and musician. Until then the author had ruled dictatorially over the spoken word, while the arias had been purely the affair of the composer and his melodies—as well, of course, of the singers.

To this Gluck opposed his own vigorously presented conception, that the only thing that mattered was the musical-dramatic work of art as a single and indivisible unit.

On the occasion of his meeting with Händel in London and with Rameau in Paris, where he learnt the harmonious combination of ballet and choir, and from the various countries he visited during his journeys as an orchestra conductor, Gluck received many inspirations. As a mature person of wide culture—the Vienna Court had long before conferred on him the appointment of Composer for Theatre and Chamber Music, while the Pope had decorated him with the Order of the Golden Spur—he began his work of reform, after having composed a series of charming musical plays and ballets. Turning his back on the plots based on intrigues which were the fashion of the day, he took as his pattern the drama of antiquity, with its human passions, its spiritual conflicts and its great heroes. His music takes on an elevating character, the Italian coloraturas give place to simple songs better attuned to the spirit of the libretto, the chorus taking an active part in the performance. His first work was the "Orpheus", followed by "Alceste" and "Paris and Helen". Gluck's great successes in Vienna were soon heard of in Paris, from which city he received commissions to write several works. Despite intrigues and theatre scandals, his important and daring compositions "Iphigenia in Aulis", "Armide" and "Iphigenia auf Tauris" were triumphant in the French capital. Gluck returned covered with honours to Vienna, the city to which he owed his decisive musical success. At the close of his busy life, the musical trinity of Haydn, Mozart, and Beethoven was moving gradually to the front and a new era of music was born which led Austria to olympic dominance in the world of melody.

During the early classical period, the musical life of Austria was mainly limited to private circles. It was the aristocracy rather than the middle classes which became the patron of music, and almost every feudal family retained an orchestra for which new compositions were constantly required. The best musicians of the day formed part of these orchestras, where they found abundant opportunity to put their creative talents to the test.

Thus we find JOSEPH HAYDN, the oldest of the Vienna classicists, spending most of his creative period at the court of a prince. In him we had a musician of genuinely Austrian character. His life was outwardly uneventful, and his fame grew but slowly. At a time when Haydn was at the height of his success, when the whole world honoured him, he retired, quietly and unassumingly, to his country seat at Gumpendorf on the outskirts of Vienna to wait peacefully for the death which overtook him at a historic moment, that of Napoleon's sojourn in Vienna and the Battle of Aspern.

Haydn had come to Vienna at the age of eight, as a "Sängerknabe" and even then knew how to play the violin and piano. But when his voice began to break, the choirmaster abruptly turned him on to the street. On a November morning, Haydn was found by one Spangler, a church vocalist, half-starved and half-perished, on a bench in the open where he had spent the night.

"When I at last lost my voice, I had to eke out a miserable existence for eight whole years by teaching the young. Many geniuses are ruined by this wretched

Esterházy Castle ; The Haydn Orchestra.

means of gaining a livelihood which leaves them no time for study. I would never have made what little progress I have, had I not been driven by my enthusiasm for composing to work on into the night."

Haydn's first string quartettes were formed in the hospitable house of Baron Fürnberg, born of private musical evenings. After a temporary position as orchestra leader at Count Morzin's, Haydn at barely thirty years of age became in 1761 conductor in Prince Esterházy's private chapel in Eisenstadt. With an orchestra and theatre at his disposal, his musical talent there blossomed forth during almost thirty years of activity into genius. He was the creator of the classical string quartette and the early-classic symphony.

After the Esterházy Orchestra in Eisenstadt had been dissolved, Haydn returned to Vienna, relieved of anxiety for the evening of his days. As an ageing man he made two journeys to England, writing for this purpose his twelve most beautiful symphonies, among which was the "Surprise". Accorded a great reception in London, he was given an honorary degree at Oxford. The outcome of the journey to England, where he heard Händel's Oratorium, was "Die Schöpfung" and "Die Jahreszeiten".

In 1809, on May 26th, Haydn assembled his staff of servants, had himself carried to the piano, and played the Austrian National Anthem (his own composition) three times. This was his last musical effort. Five days later he died.

Haydn's tireless creative urge resulted in 120 symphonies, a countless number of pieces of chamber music, piano concertos, sonatas, and *divertimenti*, as well as 24 operas and masses which in their simplicity and popular character all display inspiration and grandeur. Sonata, chamber music, and symphony are born of Haydn. With them he created a new world of melody. Through his instrumental music Haydn became the creator of the classic style which Mozart and Beethoven were to bring to perfection.

WOLFGANG AMADEUS MOZART was born in Salzburg in 1756 as the son of Leopold Mozart, himself a musician of note.

Unusual phenomena marked his career from the outset. At four years of age Mozart tried to write a piano concerto and in his fifth year he was composing minu-

Franz Schubert

Hedge Roses

On his way a boy espied
Pretty blushing roses,
Fresh and bright the hedgerow's pride:
To admire he turns aside
And to pluck proposes.

Roses·roses·roses red·pretty blushing roses.

Thus he speaks:·"I gather thee
Gayest of the roses!"
Rose says:·"Better let me be,
Or you will get stung by me–"
Then her spines discloses.
Roses·roses·roses red,
Pretty blushing roses.

Still the rude boy pulls away
This fair queen of roses.
With a wound he has to pay,
But in vain the rose does pray,
Him in vain opposes.
Roses·roses·roses red,
Pretty blushing roses.

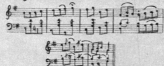

GERMAN TEXT BY JOH·WOLFG·GOETHE

ENGLISH VERSION BY H·STEVENS

SILENT NIGHT
HOLY NIGHT

SILENT NIGHT, HOLY NIGHT! ALL IS CALM,

ALL IS BRIGHT, 'ROUND YON VIRGIN MOTHER AND

CHILD, HOLY INFANT SO TENDER AND MILD,

SLEEP IN HEAVENLY PEACE, SLEEP
IN HEAVENLY PEACE!

SILENT NIGHT · HOLY NIGHT!

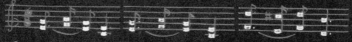

SHEPHERDS QUAKE AT THE SIGHT · GLORIES

STREAM FROM HEAVEN AFAR · HEAV'NLY HOSTS

SING ALLELUIA · CHRIST THE SAVIOUR

IS BORN · CHRIST · THE SAVIOUR ·
IS BORN ·

MELODY BY FRANZ GRUBER
TEXT BY JOSEPH MOHR

FROM THE
HEILIGENSTADT
TESTAMENT
OF LUDWIG VAN BEETHOVEN

OH YOU PEOPLE WHO HOLD
ME OR DECLARE ME TO BE
HOSTILE, OBSTINATE OR
MISANTHROPIC, HOW GREATLY
YOU WRONG ME! YOU DO NOT
KNOW THE SECRET CAUSE OF THAT WHICH
GIVES YOU THIS IMPRESSION. FROM CHILDHOOD
UPWARDS MY HEART AND MY SPIRIT
WERE INSPIRED BY GENTLE FEELINGS OF
BENEVOLENCE AND WERE ALWAYS READY FOR
GREAT ACTIONS. BUT ONLY CONSIDER
THAT FOR SIX YEARS I HAVE BEEN AFFECTED BY AN
INCURABLE CONDITION ··· BORN WITH A FIERY
AND LIVELY TEMPERAMENT, VERY SUSCEPTIBLE
TO SOCIAL PLEASURES, I WAS EARLY FORCED
TO SEGREGATE MYSELF AND TO SPEND MY
LIFE IN SOLITUDE. WHAT HUMILIATION, WHEN
SOMEONE IS STANDING NEAR ME AND
HEARS A FAR OFF FLUTE AND I CANNOT HEAR IT.
OR WHEN SOMEONE HEARS THE SHEPHERD
SINGING AND I CAN HEAR NOTHING.
SUCH EXPERIENCES NEARLY DROVE ME TO
DESPAIR, AND IT WOULD HAVE TAKEN LITTLE TO
MAKE ME END MY OWN LIFE. ONE
THING ALONE, THE ART OF MUSIC,
RESTRAINED ME

ettes. One day he was found to be playing the violin, and nobody knew exactly when he had started to play, or even when he had tried to for the first time. His father, Leopold, went on long concert tours with the six-year-old boy and his highly talented sister Nannerl, visiting Germany, England, Austria and Italy over a period of ten years. Everywhere there was the same wild enthusiasm over the "wonder child". Mozart's first sonata was played in public in Paris when he was seven years old, soon to be followed by his first symphony. Joseph II entrusted the twelve-year-old boy with the composing of an opera, and "Bastien and Bastienne" was the outcome. At fourteen, Mozart was appointed concert director of the archiepiscopal orchestra in Salzburg and received the Order of the Golden Spur from the Pope. Medals and decorations accumulated, the number of orders for orchestral compositions kept increasing. But all attempts to secure a better position were fruitless.

In his fourteenth year Mozart became a member of the Philharmonic Society of Bologna. He displayed inconceivable virtuosity in his mastery of violin, piano and organ.

A journey to Vienna in the train of the ruling prince brought a decisive change. Young Mozart, whose work had aroused great admiration at the Court of Vienna on his very first visit to that city, was one of the first of the great masters to sever connection with the ruling prince, thus bringing to an end a position of dependence in which he was regarded rather as a subject than as a musician and a free creative artist. He left Salzburg to reside in Vienna. From then on there was no trace of the popular to be found in his compositions, no further concessions. The characteristic and inimitable Mozart style was born. He had set foot on the path leading to the "Unique Musician", even if Beethoven was the first to tread it.

Now set in a new and pain-filled phase. Did the world lose interest in Mozart or did he turn his interest away from the world? Even his appointment as "Composer to the Imperial Court", did not save his family from being continually in want. Even though "Il Seraglio", which was first performed in the year 1782, proved a promising beginning for his work in Vienna, the immortal works which he created in the course of the next few years, "The Marriage of Figaro", "Don Juan", "Cosi fan tutte", "Titus", "The Magic Flute", and his wonderful compositions for string quartettes and piano concertos did not bring the eagerly awaited pecuniary success. Mozart, however, did not deviate from the lines on which he had planned his works. It was during the three summer months of 1788 that he created the three great symphonies, the E-flat-major Symphony with its strongly contrasting moods through which the idyll tries to continue, the Symphony in G-minor which might be called Mozart's "Tragic Symphony", and the Jupiter Symphony, characterised by brilliance and triumphant force.

Mozart at the Spinet.

The urge to create became a drain on Mozart's vital forces which burned themselves out prematurely. The Requiem became one for the genius himself; in the middle of November he fell seriously ill. Splendid offers from all over the world now came too late. On December 4th, Mozart wanted to hear the "Magic Flute" once again. In the afternoon he sang the Requiem with friends. He died that same night.

The body was blessed at the catacomb entrance to St. Stephen's Cathedral. Only a few friends were present. They followed the coffin as far as the Stubentor, but there, because it was raining and snowing, they turned back. Nobody was present as Mozart was buried in a common grave at St. Marx Cemetery, and when his widow visited the cemetery after some time, the new grave-diggers could not say where the body was lying.

Can posterity ever make good the neglect of contemporaries towards their great brothers?

LUDWIG VAN BEETHOVEN. When the sixteen-year-old Beethoven came to Vienna to become a pupil of Mozart, the latter, on hearing his improvisations, said: "Take heed of that one. One day he will make the whole world talk of him."

Born in 1770 as the son of a drunkard, the boy grew up to want and hardship. When twelve years old he composed his first piano variations and sonatas. He confronted the miseries of life—the courts took him out of the hands of his father, and his mother died of consumption—with his tempestuous will: "I will thrust my hand into the jaws of fate. I will not let it bow me down entirely".

When twenty years old he made another journey to Vienna, his patron, Count Waldstein, writing in his autograph album on parting: "Through unremitting zeal you have received the spirit of Mozart from the hands of Haydn".

The landscape and atmosphere of Vienna may be proud of the fact that they satisfied this intellectual Titan throughout his life. The slopes of the Wienerwald knew him as he hastened through them, the quiet paths climbing to the hills, the

114

villages dreaming among their vines, the pastoral atmosphere of the green country-side and the wide vistas of the Imperial City.

Anything which is said about the work of Beethoven can only have an approximate meaning. Within the bounds of such inadequacy it is possible to say: Beethoven's music is one single confession of faith, a single recognition. It is a passage from Heaven to Hell. It is a constant restoration of order to chaos, a turning back from an apostate creation.

One can cite certain high-notes of what we feel in his works—the heroic, the radiant quality in the first movement of the Eroica, the gloomy, uncanny force of the Fifth, of the Symphony in C-Minor, the sweetness of the Sixth, the Pastorale. In the Ninth, Nature's instrument, the choir of human voices, has to come to the rescue in order to express the joy of overcoming, prevailing.

The name of no other composer is glorified by similar achievements—"Coriolan", "Egmont", the third "Leonora Ouverture", piano and violin concertos and "Fidelio", the great anthem of true marital love. The "Missa Solemnis", breaking through the framework of devotional music, the "Moonlight", "Kreutzer", and "Waldstein" Sonatas, the "Pathétique", the "Appassionata".

Beethoven moved as an equal among princes and rulers. After a few years of work there were no longer any difficulties with publishers: "For one thing, I also have six or seven publishers and even more. People no longer bargain with me—I demand and they pay".

In spite of this, the talented man was not spared the necessity of saying "*Miser et pauper sum*" — "poor and wretched am I".

In his twenty-sixth year an atrophy of the acoustic nerves began. Everywhere a constant buzzing in the ears went with him. It led in the end to complete deafness. At thirty-two years of age he drew up the "Heiligenstadt Testament": "Oh you people who hold me or declare me to be hostile, obstinate or misanthropic, how greatly you wrong me! You do not know the secret cause of that which gives you that impression. From childhood upwards my heart and my spirit were inspired by gentle feelings of benevolence and were always ready for great actions. But only consider that for six years I have been affected by an incurable condition ..... Born with a fiery and lively temperament, very susceptible to social pleasures, I was early forced to segregate myself and to spend my life in solitude. What humiliation, when someone is standing near me and hears a far off flute and I cannot hear it, or when someone hears the shepherd singing and I can hear nothing. Such experiences nearly drove me to despair, and it would have taken little to make me end my own life. One thing alone, the art of music, restrained me".

Soon it became necessary to write on scraps of paper everything which was to be communicated to Beethoven. He himself refused to recognise the disease, and although he could not hear a sound, he insisted on conducting in person. When he conducted a performance of the Ninth Symphony in 1824, he did so in appearance only, for the orchestra paid attention solely to the signs given by the concert director. After the second movement there was thunderous applause, but Beethoven did not hear it, and the singer Unger had to turn him round so that he could see the clapping hands and acknowledge the ovation.

When Beethoven breathed his last in the midst of a thunderstorm on March 26th, 1827, he was mourned by the whole world.

FRANZ SCHUBERT. — Among the vast crowd of mourners present at the funeral of Beethoven was Franz Schubert. The eulogy at the graveside written by Grillparzer was delivered by Anschütz, a famous actor of the Burgtheater. The earth began to cover the coffin and the mourners left the cemetery.

Schubert retired with his friends to an inn and, lifting his glass, toasted "To him whom we have buried"! At the second glass he said "To him who will be the next"!

Nineteen months later he himself, the great prince of song, was also dead, barely thirty years old.

Schubert the dreamer! Small was the world in which he spent his too short life. It was the Vienna of the Biedermeier period, in which a happy, light-hearted man composed for a circle of good friends songs of the most varied types, masses, and symphonies in the style of the "Hausmusik" of the Biedermeier period.

Born in 1797, Schubert learnt singing from the choirmaster of Lichtental. When he was eleven he was accepted into the "Konvikt der Sängerknaben" (Choristers). About this time he committed his first notes to paper—at that time against the will of his father. As an assistant schoolmaster and later as teacher at Himmelpfortgrund he was exempted from many years of military service.

At twenty-one years of age Schubert gave up teaching in order to devote himself for the future solely to the writing of music. He enjoyed the most moving support of his friends. They found him lodgings, bargained with publishers, presented him to wealthy middle-class families, provided him with inspiration and amusement and were loyal to him.

In course of time musical evenings among women and music lovers grew into the famous "*Schubertiaden*". There were hours of pure enjoyment when Schubert played his new compositions. A source from which sprang the joy of life, of untiring creation, had come into being. Vienna in the Biedermeier age had found its most perfect form of expression.

Gustav Klimt; Beethoven Frieze; Music.

Schubert's works, which reveal the whole delicacy of feeling of his times, are very numerous. They include more than 600 songs, 6 masses, 30 pieces of chamber music and 450 piano pieces, as well as 17 stage compositions and 9 symphonies.

Side by side with Beethoven, the instrumental dramatist, Schubert had become the instrumental lyric writer with his "Erlkönig", "Gretchen am Spinnrad", "Forellen-Quintette", "D-minor-Quartette", "Der Tod und das Mädchen", and "Wandererphantasie". To him was it allotted to achieve perfection in song-writing. In his 26th year Schubert was attacked by a severe illness. A letter to a friend expresses deep resignation: "Imagine a person whose health simply refuses to mend".

He understood nothing of dealing with publishers, giving away his compositions for laughable sums. Modest and shy, he gave his first concert in 1828 which was also the year of his death. Barely 31 years of age, he was carried off by typhoid fever.

Of his works the "Unfinished Symphony" remained lost for more than half a century. This wonderful composition was first found in 1875, this music in which nature herself seems to raise her voice in song, in music telling of joy and sorrow in life.

"Unfinished"—this word is symbolical of Schubert's early demise. In a higher sense it could be applied to Austria: The heart is moved when Schubert is played. One recalls the memory of all those whose lives have been spent in the devotion to high ideals. Never has Austria been sparing with her sons in this respect.

With the death of Beethoven and Schubert the long process by which music ceased to depend for its encouragement on the patronage of courts in favour of that of the middle-classes was completed. Apart from the "House Music" of the aristocracy, there now arose musical societies among well-to-do circles in the cities which gradually paved the way for public concerts. At the beginning of the 19th century musical societies were formed in Vienna and in Austria generally for the purpose of encouraging music in all its branches. One of the most famous is the "Gesellschaft der Musikfreunde", founded in 1812, followed later by the great Vienna choral associations, the "Singverein" and the "Singakademie". Together with the "Vienna Philharmonic" (founded in 1842), they remain today outstanding centres of Austrian musical culture. Through the male voice choral societies which gained a footing in Austria in the last half of the past century, Austria's heritage of folk song and the male choir literature then established found a permanent home. It is also to the credit of these societies that they have awakened and kept alive a love of singing and music-making among the broad masses of the population.

Lighter music had not until this time been prominent among musical developments in Austria. But with JOSEF LANNER and JOHANN STRAUSS there now

Moritz von Schwind: A Schubert Evening.

began an epoch which gained Austria—and especially Vienna—a name in the world for such music of this type also. Their waltzes, minuettes, polkas and marches fired the music-loving city with enthusiasm, and in all the countries which were visited by the elder Strauss, his melodies were enthusiastically welcomed. Still greater fame was reached by his son, JOHANN STRAUSS, born in Vienna in 1825, whom the world has dubbed "The Waltz King".

The elder Strauss apprenticed the boy to a book-binder, but he was not to be kept down, and one day he ran away, straight into the arms of a musician. When only 15 he was playing the violin in the famous Lanner Quartette. At 19 Strauss the younger conducted his own orchestra in public for the first time in the Dommayer Casino in Hietzing, playing his own compositions, openly competing with his famous father, and with striking success. His waltzes preceded him throughout the whole world. "Morgenblätter", "Künstlerleben", "Wiener Blut", "G'schichten aus dem Wienerwald", "Wein, Weib, Gesang", "Frühlingsstimmen", "Seid umschlungen Millionen", "Freut euch des Lebens", "An der schönen blauen Donau", "Der Kaiserwalzer". In Germany and Paris, in London and St. Petersburg, everywhere the same enthusiasm was aroused. The famous orchestra of Johann Strauss played a part in Queen Victoria's marriage festivities. In Boston, on the occasion of the hundredth anniversary celebration of the Declaration of Independence, Strauss conducted a crowd of several thousands included in the choir and orchestra. "As we

had begun more or less simultaneously, my whole attention was concentrated on seeing that we also stopped at the same time" he declared.

In Vienna Strauss ran an orchestra of 300, which was split up night after night among various restaurants, or provided ball-room music. He himself tore from one restaurant or ball-room to another, conducting every night at five or ten different places.

He wrote over 500 compositions, including 14 operettas; "Indigo", "Die Fledermaus", "Prinz Methusalem", "Eine Nacht in Venedig", "Das Spitzentuch der Königin", and "Der Zigeunerbaron" among them. The songs of Schubert and the waltzes of Strauss were the favourite offspring of the Vienna Biedermeier period. Few other countries can boast of having made equivalent contributions towards the gaiety and pleasure of mankind.

Apart from Johann Strauss there were a whole series of successful composers of modern music,—to begin with, JOSEF and EDUARD STRAUSS, the brothers of Johann; then MILLÖCKER and ZIEHRER, ZELLER and HEUBERGER. Their numbers continued to be added to in the twentieth century, the most prominent among the late-comers being FRANZ LEHÁR.

In the latter half of the 19th century, and then almost at the same time that the Viennese waltz and the Vienna operetta were at their best, three new stars arose in the firmament of music: Brahms, Bruckner and Hugo Wolf.

Like Beethoven, the young JOHANNES BRAHMS, born in 1833, was attracted to the music-capital of Vienna in order to show his talent there. Like Beethoven, he was never again able to escape from the city's charm. It was in 1862 that he came to Vienna, where he was received as a successor to Beethoven. The reception accorded to his artistic talents was shown in his selection to be choirmaster of the Vienna *Singakademie*, which occurred when he had been in Vienna only one year. After one single departure from the capital, he returned to it in 1869, to remain true to it as an independent composer until his death. His longing for the beauties of nature found complete satisfaction in Austria. Thus we find that his most famous works were written by the lakes of Carinthia, in Styria, in the Salzkammergut and in the Wienerwald, which has its charms at all seasons of the year. He found inspiration of many kinds for his creative labours in folk songs and Viennese waltzes. Basing his efforts on those of Beethoven and Schubert, he left behind him four symphonies, the "German Requiem", a great amount of choral and orchestral music, chamber music and about two hundred songs. His death in 1897 left a painfully felt gap in the Austrian world of music.

The second great musician who achieved outstanding fame shortly after 1890 is ANTON BRUCKNER, the great symphonist and mystic of music. He first saw the light of day in the year 1824 as the son of a village schoolteacher in Ansfelden, Upper Austria. The boy received his first impressions of music in church through the organ, which he loved whole-heartedly all his life. After losing his father when 13 years old, he became a choirboy in St. Florian Monastery, where he became acquainted with the devotional masterpieces of the Vienna classicists. There followed bitter years of wandering as assistant in various small village schools until he finally succeeded, in 1845, in getting an appointment as teacher to his beloved St. Florian. There he was made monastery organist. The great knowledge of organ playing and compositions which he acquired through untiring perseverence (his "Missa Solemnis" was completed during these years), he owed to his appointment at Linz as Cathedral Organist. During his twelve years there he studied the theory of music untiringly, learnt to know the world of opera and concerts and occasionally sat in Vienna for examinations by musicians of note. A decisive experience for Bruckner which proved a turning-point in his creative work was his discovery of Richard Wagner's music. He, who until then had kept strictly to the classic, found in Wagner's work the path which he was himself to tread in future, and the technical equipment wherewith to do so. This change from the classic to the romantic school is noticeable even in his D-minor Mass, composed in 1864. In the year 1868 he accepted a call to Vienna to become Professor at the Conservatorium. Here he wrote his great symphonies which were little understood by his contemporaries. Bruckner's music does not philosophise and does not seek to express ideas, but is content to be just music, the music of a profound, simple and devout heart. At times it approaches the mystery and the solemn splendours of the Catholic Church.

For a time this man of a rustic devotion found enemies on all sides who belittled him wherever he achieved any success. Of modest character, he felt bewildered by the wickedness of the world. None the less he continued on his chosen path, sustained by his unshakeable faith in God, although often filled with melancholy. Success and honour came to him toward the end of his life; he received them with childlike gratitude. The Master was especially delighted at receiving the honorary degree of doctor of Vienna University.

"I, the Rector Magnificus of the Vienna University, bow to the former Assistant-Teacher of Windhaag."

And the Emperor granted Bruckner an apartment in the Belvedere Palace.

Deeply mourned, yet only fully understood by a later generation, he departed this life in the year 1896. With the monumental Nine Symphonies, the mighty "Te Deum", the three great masses and his remarkable choral works, Bruckner has assured himself a permanent place in the history of music.

HUGO WOLF. For days and weeks he was simply not able to put the fullness of his conceptions on paper, so prolifically did they flow to and beat over him.

Hugo Wolf was the creator of a new art of song-writing. He himself was like a fine, over-sensitive instrument. He understood how to reproduce moods of unsuspected delicacy. His nerves were alert to every impulse, sensing and preserving each vibration and burdening themselves with them all. Hugo Wolf was always tense, always a prey to changing emotions, rarely calm and never at peace. Thus this musician also burnt himself up at the age of 37. In 1897 his creative powers and his life itself were eclipsed by insanity.

Fanny Elssler as one of the Three Graces.

Dismissed as a boy from school, put on the street after holding a position as leader of the orchestra at the Salzburg Municipal Theatre, Hugo Wolf long carried his finished compositions about with him in his pocket, unable to find a publisher for them. At 28 his life was decided for him. He began to compose songs, ideas and melodies crowding into his brain. Within 6 months he had written the music for 350 poems. Then his creative powers ceased abruptly. Years, fruitless years were to follow, in which all he wrote was four acts of the opera "Corregidor", a few pieces of choral music and the poetic symphony, "Penthesilea". At 36 fortune smiled on him once more. Again songs came to him. Now his songs were being played everywhere and there were even publishers for them. A year later he became a victim of the illusion that he was Director of the Vienna Court Opera. This was followed by an anxious period of ups and downs which ended in an asylum. Hugo Wolf lost all memory of his own identity: "Yes, if I were Hugo Wolf . . .".

There was scarcely a concert programme which did not bear his name. But the wandering mind of Hugo Wolf was occupied with other matters.

The spring from which music has flowed through Austria throughout the centuries did not by any means dry up with these three famous names in the world of melody. GUSTAV MAHLER, the great director of the Court Opera in Vienna who brought

The Bruckner Organ in St. Florian.

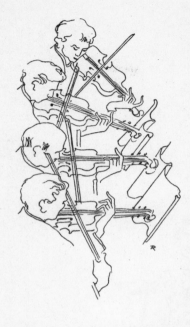

himself to an early grave, the unforgettable creator of moving symphonies such as the "Lied von der Erde", and the talented FRANZ SCHMIDT who was born in the twentieth century gave a new impulse to Austria's heritage of symphony. RICHARD STRAUSS, although not an Austrian by birth, has the closest spiritual ties with this country and its music. What is his "Rosenkavalier" but a public declaration of faith in Vienna?

WILHELM KIENZL, JULIUS BITTNER and FRANZ SCHREKER have scored notable achievements in operatic music. JOSEPH MARX, following the lead of Schubert and Hugo Wolf in song, has enriched the literature of music with costly gems of true Austrian workmanship. ARNOLD SCHÖNBERG, ANTON WEBERN, ALBAN BERG, EGON WELLESZ, ERNST KRENEK and others are among the representatives of the new—and newest—musical trend in Austria, the musical-historical value of which it must be left to the future to judge.

THE RINGSTRASSE

Vienna, 1609.

Etching by Hufnagel.

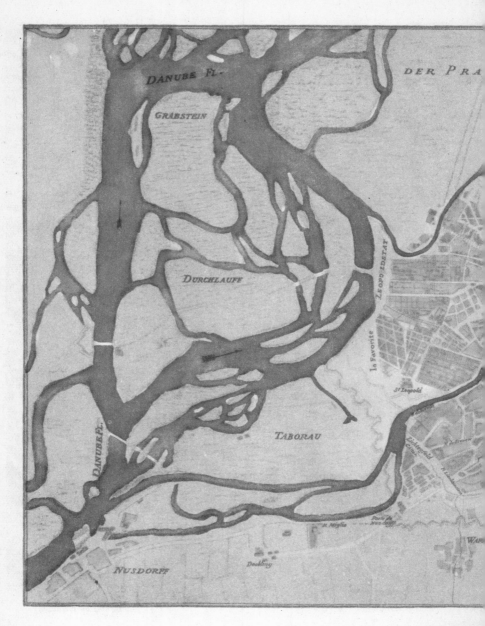

Baroque Vienna

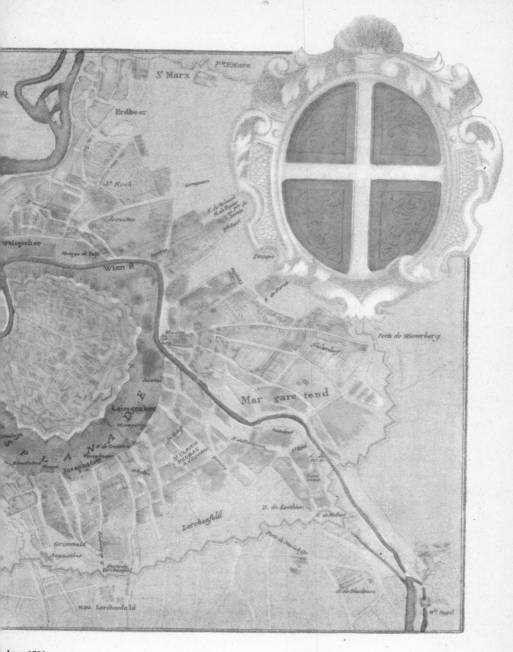

about 1730.

THE VIENNA RING-
STRASSE.

A wide green belt with parks and stately buildings, it is the pride of the country and perhaps of a whole continent. It can be compared only with the Paris boulevards.

Foreigners and visitors stand beneath the trees on the broad and well-kept avenues admiring the great buildings, or wander around the squares which branch off from them, abandoning themselves to the festive spirit invoked by this great roadway and enjoying the stimulus of its light-hearted magnificence. Untrammeled by thoughts of time the crowds stroll by, glancing idly now at their immediate surroundings, now at some more distant prospect, now surveying the bustle in the streets of the Inner City, now catching a glimpse of the needle spire of St. Stephen's as it appears above some ancient, narrow alley. Left and right lie enticing parks, clumps of flowering bushes. The disconcerting smiles of Viennese girls strolling among the crowds lend a special quality to the whole scene.

But pause a while in pensive mood before the Dominikanerbastei and imagine that you can detect among the blocks of modern houses traces of an old gateway, or find in the embankment of the bastion the remains of a defensive wall. Or let some one point put to you the traditional Beethoven House on the Mölkerbastei; from there it was at one time possible to look out across the glacis, then unencumbered by buildings, into the countryside as far as the Schneeberg and the Semmering Pass. Surely you will then want to know just how the former fortified Imperial residential city came to exchange its walls and ramparts, its bastions with their flanking sentry-beats, the deep city moats with their lively frog population and massive gates with barrier and draw-bridge, for the sunny splendour of the buildings on the modern Ringstrasse.

In Hufnagel's famous etching, mediaeval Vienna rises again before us almost in plastic form. There, side by side, yet clearly distinguishable, are the homes of nobles and burghers, the church and the cemetery. Some of the buildings date back to the Babenberg period, to Leopold the Glorious. Lack of space compelled the builders to pile as best they could story upon story, and to construct below these deep cellars and catacombs. Many churches grow up amid the streets of the city, the arcades where the drapers sold their goods and the market-places. Some of these churches are Romanesque but most are Gothic. Rarely does one find specimens of Renaissance, for in the 16th century the Turkish foe stood menacingly on the frontiers.

When after two centuries the threat of the Janissaries subsided and they were forced to evacuate Austria, Hungary and Transylvania, with Prince Eugene thrusting them far back into Wallachia and the Balkans, and the nightmare of the threat from the East had vanished, city and countryside heaved a sigh of relief. Unexpected, undreamt-of prosperity sprang from the blood-drenched soil of Austria. Baroque, breaking through the old forms with elemental force with hardly a transitional period, transformed the whole appearance of the city. The Imperial Residence was still enclosed by bastions and still an armed fortress. But in response to the passionate impulse of Baroque, new buildings were everywhere springing up. Soon there was no street so narrow that it had not its distinguished portal or delightful façade, behind which a daringly conceived stairway led to halls richly decorated with frescoes. The damage inflicted on the city by the prolonged and stubborn siege soon disappeared from view among the many new palais and winter residences of the aristocracy, the churches and secular edifices.

But the builders of this period were not to be restricted within the existing city boundaries. Surmounting bastions and glacis, their daring plans created a baroque landscape immediately beyond the gates of the city, with gardens, parks and the summer residence of the nobility. Soon the Viennese saw grand façades arising, the palais of the Schwarzenbergs, the Trautsohns, the Rofrano-Auerspergs, the magnificent Palace of Prinz Eugene, the Belvedere, and the cupola of the Karlskirche.

Nor were these great buildings the whole story. New districts housing the citizenry soon became new suburbs—Leopoldstadt, Josefstadt and other areas of prosperity. Beyond the new suburbs another line of fortifications, the "Linienwall" was constructed. Beyond that again, on the slopes of the Wienerwald, lay amidst vines a girdle of shady villages, tempting the city dwellers to excursions in their leisure hours.

Thus in the 18th century Vienna consisted of three separate zones. Plans enough were drawn up to unite them. But the early death of the Emperor Joseph II, enthusiast for

The Kärntnertor with a View over the City.

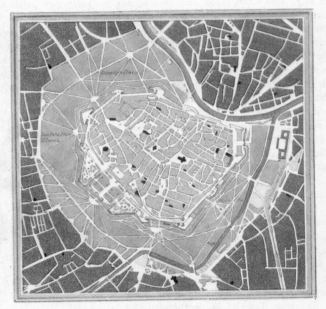

The Heart of the City, with Fortifications and Glacis.

The Newly-Finished Ringstrasse.

Connections of the centre of the City and the Outlying Districts with the Ringstrasse.

135

reforms, and events in France, caused history to take a different course. The Napoleonic age had dawned, bringing with it decades of struggle and wars. Just as generations before the taxes imposed to enable the Turks to be fought had robbed the country of prosperity, so now the constant levies and expenditure on armaments prevented the realisation of more peaceful aims.

Although by 1814 Metternich's policy had brought external perils to an end, the Crown Lands had been bled white. The wounds inflicted during the era of "Glorious Imperialism" had cut too deeply into the flesh of Europe for it to be possible to take up the threads where the masters of the Baroque had been forced to let them drop.

And there was something else. Not only had the peoples once again changed their rulers, the war period had altered their sense of values. Life had come to have a new aim—a happiness whose keynote was modesty and simplicity. So was born the age of Biedermeier.

Biedermeier! This meant the reverse of all that had been before. "Gloire" and "Victoire" had lost their demonic power. The people were sick of the unfurling of banners and of resounding phrases. The career of hero, militarism as an ideal, had become a memory of bitterness experienced, stripped of all illusions. Even the roughest and most brutal could no longer find attraction in the eternal round of levies and billeting, leave-taking and the whole paraphernalia of soldiering. The brave music of a distant drum had lost its power to attract; now was the time for the loaf of bread beneath the bough. A flower from the hand of some fair maiden meant more than a breast full of medals, good talk among friends more than the resounding word of command. Popular interest turned to the everyday things of the new age—a house, a garden, a song, a serenade; a store in the market, nosegays and miniatures, the sweet notes of an old spinet, the gentle gestures of love and all the forms in which unpretentious happiness expresses itself. Biedermeier is a reaction of mind and soul turning its back on the heroic age of marching and slaughter. Biedermeier stood for the right which the Little Man had wrung from the world to seek peace and happiness—the Little Man who, it was implied, must be regarded as a human being, as a decent human individual.

For a whole generation Austria lived in this, her idyll. Yet at the same time a tragic development was in progress. Metternich's peace, at first a benevolent godfather of Biedermeier, had hardened into the rigid system of a ruling class which had petrified from the head downwards. Bohemian artists enjoying a riotous evening's amusement, lovers beneath the garden wall, were questioned by the prying police as suspected enemies of the State. Freedom of speech was once again suppressed. Grillparzer committed to paper his embittered petition on the freedom of the press.

The first shots of the 1848 Revolution rang out. Prince Metternich, now an old man, left the city in a hurry; troops were called out, there were sharp commands to fire and blood flowed in the streets. The idyllic episode was over and history ad resumed its course.

When the young Emperor, Francis Joseph, ascended the throne at the age of 18 and everyday life gradually took on the colour of the new order, people in Vienna began to realise that the heart of the city was still ringed round by ancient fortifications. On the last day but one of the year 1857 came the historic moment when Francis Joseph put his signature to an Imperial document ordering that the bastions should be razed and the glacis levelled. There had been much controversy on the subject before this decision was taken. Artists of note, among them the painter Amerling, had gone on their knees to the Emperor, begging him to let the historic fortified area stand as it was.

Now a period of feverish activity set in. Vast building projects were initiated which were to keep excitement alive in Vienna for years, almost for decades. Great spaces were now available for the erection of new buildings, for the bastions and the glacis had formed a ring around the Inner City many kilometres long and hundred of metres wide. Enormous sums were realised by the sale of these great building plots. More ambitious and comprehensive planning was called for. It was not just a question of conjuring the Ringstrasse into existence; the surrounding areas had to be opened up by the construction of new roads and linked with one other by harmoniously conceived blocks of buildings. Apart from the Ringstrasse and its surroundings, over 90 new streets and squares and over 500 buildings were added to the city at this juncture.

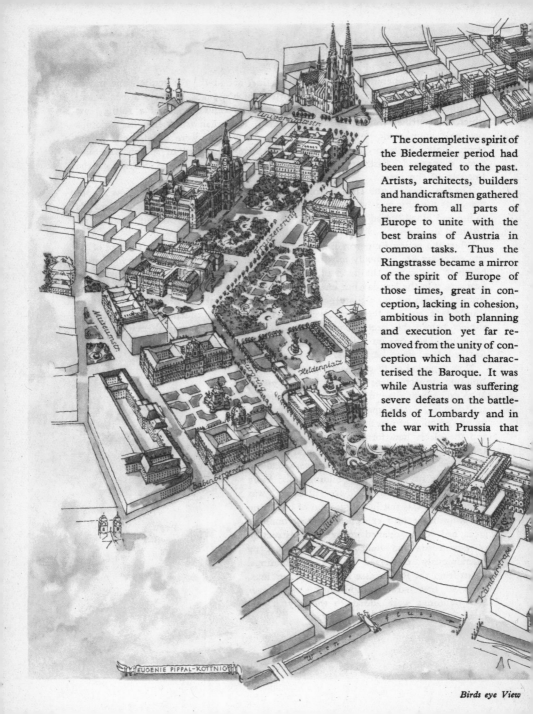

The contempletive spirit of the Biedermeier period had been relegated to the past. Artists, architects, builders and handicraftsmen gathered here from all parts of Europe to unite with the best brains of Austria in common tasks. Thus the Ringstrasse became a mirror of the spirit of Europe of those times, great in conception, lacking in cohesion, ambitious in both planning and execution yet far removed from the unity of conception which had characterised the Baroque. It was while Austria was suffering severe defeats on the battlefields of Lombardy and in the war with Prussia that

Birds eye View

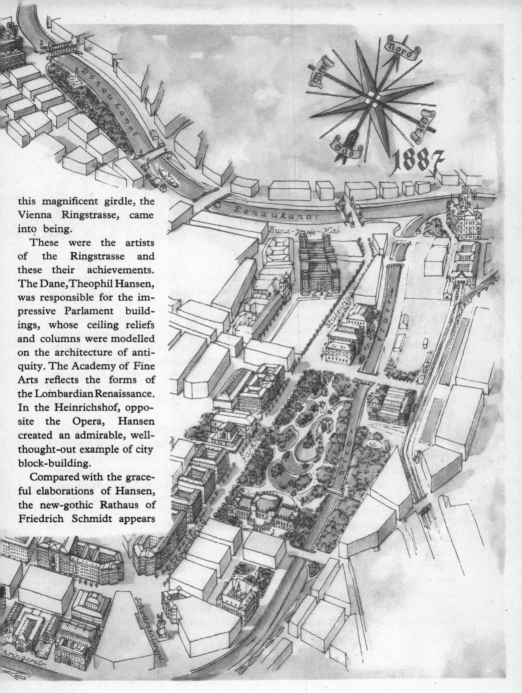

this magnificent girdle, the Vienna Ringstrasse, came into being.

These were the artists of the Ringstrasse and these their achievements. The Dane, Theophil Hansen, was responsible for the impressive Parlament buildings, whose ceiling reliefs and columns were modelled on the architecture of antiquity. The Academy of Fine Arts reflects the forms of the Lombardian Renaissance. In the Heinrichshof, opposite the Opera, Hansen created an admirable, well-thought-out example of city block-building.

Compared with the graceful elaborations of Hansen, the new-gothic Rathaus of Friedrich Schmidt appears

of the Ringstrasse.

severe and cold. Even though late-gothic city halls in Belgium may have served as a pattern for the imposing splendour of the edifice, the sober horizontal lines and the buoyancy of the structure betray native genius.

The Votivkirche was built by Ferstel, a Viennese with wide education, in his 27th year. Later he built the new University, in which there is an arcaded courtyard of exceptional beauty. His stairways, however, are not to be compared with Hasenauer's wonderful flights of stone in the two Museums (the Museums of Natural History and Art) and in the Burgtheater. Van der Nüll and Siccardsburg were the brilliant and ill-fated builders of the Opera. When the new Opera House was solemnly opened with Mozart's Don Giovanni, in 1869, both of them were already dead.

Between the two Museums, Zumbusch placed the great monument to the Empress Maria Theresia, while opposite, on the Heldenplatz, Fernkorn created the bold equestrian statue of the Archduke Karl and Prince Eugene. Feuerbach painted the colossal "Fall of the Titans" for the Academy of Fine Arts, and Gasser ornamented the Stadtpark with the delightfully Viennese "Donauweibchen". Among many other masters of their crafts who might be mentioned are Semper, Kundmann, Tilgner, Hellmer, Weyr and Bitterlich.

The Ringstrasse was thrown open to the public in 1865, before the magnificent Ringstrasse buildings had arisen. The Viennese looked with critical eyes and reserved comment. They mourned what they had lost, without being able to form a proper judgment of the innovations, which were still only fragmentary. The whole city now went through a transitional period of change and expansion. Somewhere about 1870, something gradually came back which the Viennese will never willingly dispense with—"atmosphere". Then, when it was possible to stroll along the Ringstrasse as once on the bastions, when bands began to play in the newly-laid-out

parks and the trees in the avenues for the first time cast their shade, then the ice of prejudice began to melt; the Ringstrasse and Vienna belonged one to the other.

In the outside world great events were taking place. Bismarck had the triumph of the entry into Paris and shortly afterwards the shock of the great bank failures made itself felt in every country.

In Vienna everything unpleasant was nonchalantly disregarded. People got more and more accustomed to the Ringstrasse. New builders came before the public eye, first Otto Wagner and later Adolf Loos. Vienna was on the way to becoming a great capital. New districts were planned on a grand scale, mansions sprang up in the heart of the city, the zone between the Ring and the Gürtel, and the settle-

ments on the far side of the former Linienwall had now grown together. The contours of further municipal building projects became visible.

Then for a time, Vienna gave itself up to the dizzy magnificence of the Makart period. The name Makart had become a symbol. Among the Makart fashions there was the "Makart Red", the "Makart Collar", and the "Makart Rose". Above the pompous coiffure an enormous cartwheel hat was worn, with flowers and swaying feathers—the "Makart Hat". The styles of a bygone century were revived in a bombastic new baroque mode which dominated the middle classes of the city for 20 years and was adopted above all by the new rich and the recently en nobled in a pompous display of magnificence.

A memorable event of those years was the Makart Procession, which took place on the occasion of the Emperor's Silver Wedding in the year 1879. It was a brilliant parade of national costumes, peasant-groups, arts, crafts and allegoric scenes. The Emperor Francis Joseph accepted the homage of the paraders beneath a giant canopy which had been designed by Otto Wagner. At the side of the Emperor stood the fabulously beautiful Elisabeth, dressed in crimson and wearing a Makart white feathered hat with a gold-embroidered mantilla. Among the onlookers were those artists who at the turn of the century joined in founding a new movement which bore the name of "Sezession".

Vienna, still the brilliant metropolis of a happy Empire, was preparing for its next task. The City had need of a progressive municipal administration, and certain public undertakings were to be socialised. There arose a man in the Imperial City during the last decade of the Monarchy who became its greatest Burgomaster, a man of genius and a burning patriot, Dr. Karl Lueger.

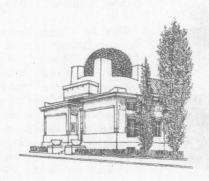

THE VIENNA
SCHOOL
OF MEDICINE

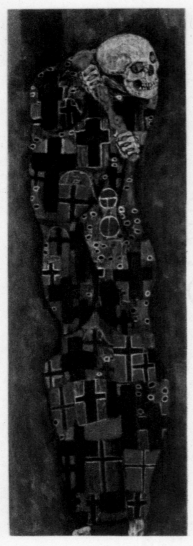

Gustav Klimt: Death and Life (Section).

Between two eternities, prior to birth and after death, mankind, rising out of darkness, has a glimpse of the golden light which means life, and at the same time is forced to realise the terror of a never-ending night. Against this vague, primitive fear of man wars that faithful servant of the body, and even of the soul, medicine. Here we would speak of Austria's share in this radiant force and its fight for life against death, of the Vienna school of medicine.

Even at the Rudolfine University of Vienna, in 1365, there was a medical faculty. When compared with what had been achieved in the fields of theology and philosophy, achievements in that of medicine can, indeed, only be regarded as a forerunner of what the Vienna School of Medicine was later to bring forth, an academic stump on to which the green twig was to be grafted by a later age. Medical-scientific thought, not especially kindly to those bygone centuries, alternated between a rigid adherence to ancient theories and the un-challenging tolerance of medievalism.

One name, however, must be remembered with honour. It is that of the great doctor of the middle ages, the excellent physician who cured leprosy, gout and dropsy with great skill, Philippus Theophrastus Bombastus Hohenheim, known as Paracelsus (1493—1541).

He pointed to five sources of illness: the stars, poisons, heredity, the mind, and the afflictions of God. He said

Gustav Klimt : Death and Life (Section).

"There is a cure for all sicknesses, without exception, but there are some which still defy our knowledge". He discovered hidden relations between forms and colours, learning not lost or forgotten. He believed that heart-shaped leaves were of assistance in cases of heart trouble, and for jaundice he prescribed yellow chellidonium,—the Greater Celandine—but his medicines took effect!

His extensive theory of medicine was a mixture of deep philosophical insight and the magical superstitions of his time. To this experienced master great credit is due for having introduced chemistry to medicine. His words formed the basis of medical studies for centuries.

When the wise Empress Maria Theresia ascended the throne and began to rule and care for her empire and people as a great family, the *alma mater* Rudolfina had been in existence for almost four hundred years. The Empress' attention was soon attracted to the school of medicine of her capital. But the University was far removed from her modern far-sighted ideas. A State within a State, ruled in many cases by mediaeval privileges and ordinances, the University proved unable to grapple with the great task of becoming the mental nursery-garden of the Reich. Maria Theresia found in the Dutchman van Swieten a man with sufficient personality to reform the University. With him began what is now known as the First Vienna School of Medicine. It was a collaboration planned in the modern spirit between teacher and pupil, based on a knowledge of research work which had been handed down through generations, and a self-sacrificing devotion to suffering humanity. Van Swieten got rid of the musty, old-fashioned staff of teachers, summoning the best brains to Vienna from far and near. Among them were the botanist Jacquin, the gynaecologist Crantz, de Haën as professor of practical medicine, and, later, Stoll, the famous clinical worker.

The work of van Swieten and his contemporaries is marked less by new discoveries than by great organisational achievements. The whole subject of medical science was examined and catalogued and a well-thought-out system of research and teaching instituted. The teaching methods of the faculty have in the main remained unaltered until the present day.

One detail of the developments during this period must be mentioned—percussion, that form of examination in which a doctor sounds the body of his patient from the outside. It was discovered by Leopold Auenbrugger, the son of an innkeeper in Graz, who is said to have been given the idea of examining patients in this fashion through the winegrower's practice of ascertaining the state of a barrel's contents by knocking on it.

The Emperor Joseph II, "the People's Friend", was specially interested in medicine, but from another point of view. Within a short time he founded the Allgemeine Krankenhaus and the Medizinisch-Chirurgische Akademie. With the Allgemeine Krankenhaus, Vienna was given a general hospital for public assistance and for the furthering of science; few cities of Europe had so large an institution. It was able to take in over 2000 patients, the number of beds in all the other Vienna hospitals put together being only 1400. Through this gift the Vienna School of Medicine found its historic sphere of activity.

By founding the Medizinisch-Chirurgische Akademie Joseph II wished to combat another evil. The death-rate among soldiers in the Seven Years' War, for instance, was shockingly high. Even in times of peace infectious diseases took a heavy toll, but in wartime the slightest wound often led to gangrene and fever. The Emperor sought a remedy by the founding of a special school for the thorough training of military surgeons and their assistants. The Garnisonsspital, with a capacity of 2000 beds, was established near the Josephinum, and at the same time an excellent system of military doctoring was extended over the far-flung territories of the old Monarchy. The more important garrison towns received well-equipped military hospitals, and medical attention spread until it was soon more concerned with the civilian population than with the Army.

A man of versatile personality was needed to take charge of and to develop the great institution of the Allgemeine Krankenhaus. In 1795 this task was entrusted to Peter Frank. His life's work was the establishment of a corps of police surgeons, but he made improvements in all directions. He modernised the curriculum, performed operations in an operating theatre of his own and developed a system of pathological anatomy.

Frank brought about radical changes in the treatment of the insane. Until the turn of the 18th century the mentally unbalanced were quite simply labelled fools. They were locked up in a tower called the "Tower of Fools" (Narrenturm), where the population could take delight in the strange picture they presented. Frank did away with the Narrenturm, transforming it into a branch of the hospital where sick people might be cared for. Under this far-sighted physician—who, by the way, refused to wear the customary wig—Vienna became the first city on the continent to introduce Jenner's inoculation against smallpox. One of his personal friends was the aged Haydn.

The Second School of Medicine became famous through the names of Rokitansky, Skoda and Hebra. It is still interesting to examine the pictures of the pre-revolution doctors in the yellowed pages of the biedermeier period. When these men started work in their youth there was little common stock of medical knowledge resulting from research, experiment and exact post-mortem. But by the time the names of these men had appeared on the faded leaves of the biedermeier age at the end of their life's work, the foundations of modern medicine had been laid and clinical practice as well as methods of examination and treatment had been developed. If the doctor of today is able to make a correct diagnosis without any special technical means, but only through putting questions and by the observation of his eyes

The Plague Hospital, Vienna, 1679.

and by his exploring and tapping hand, he has to thank the praiseworthy research of the men who belonged to the Vienna School of Medicine of pre-Revolution times, that is, to the Second Vienna School of Medicine.

The man who overcame the mental limitations of his age, passing beyond "Enlightenment" and scepticism to empirical medicine was Rokitansky. Post-mortems —he is said to have carried out more than 80,000 of them—combined with the study of clinical reports, resulted in the evolution of a great new body of doctrine. Rokitansky's work in the Pathological Institute and his collaboration with the internal specialist, Skoda, the dermatologist Hebra, the progressive surgeon Schuh, and Kolletschka, the unfortunate friend of Semmelweis, were of essential importance to practical medicine.

Not all those who battled within the venerable walls of the Allgemeine Krankenhaus to preserve life saw their efforts crowned with success. The fate of Semmelweis, for instance, rings in our ears like a ballad of devotion and despair. About the middle of the century the gynaecological authorities in Vienna were concerned with the burning question of why three times as many mothers of new-born children died in the clinic where students were being trained who also worked in the dissecting room, as in the adjacent section in which midwives were trained.

The historic hour of Semmelweis struck when he read the post-mortem diagnosis on his friend Kolletschka, who had cut himself while dissecting a corpse, and realised that this diagnosis was identical with the post-mortem diagnoses of the dead women. In both it was a case of infection, carried to the birth clinic by the hand of the doctor from the dissecting table.

Semmelweis now began his fight, but however convincing the evidence he brought forward may seem to us today, his contemporaries wished neither to see nor to believe it. He was destroyed by his discovery of this evil, and by the inertia of his contemporaries. But posterity had been saved from the scourge of puerperal fever.

New knowledge was being gained in many other fields. Schuh was the first to make use of chloroform in surgery. Türck, a pioneer in the field of neurology, became by his introduction of the laryngoscope the founder of laryngology, the science of affections of the throat.

Side by side with the first clinical specialists must be placed other distinguished personalities among the pre-clinical workers. Foremost of these was Josef Hyrtl, the son of an oboe player in Haydn's orchestra. He put together the entire anatomical knowledge of his times, exploring, often by methods of his own, the last unknown regions of the human body. Half a world clamoured for his book on anatomy, his scientific writings and his preparations. Doctors came from all the capitals of the continent to hear his lectures; he spoke the language of a poet and his sparkling humour was matchless. The medical faculty of Vienna University had now become world-famous.

The second pillar of pre-clinical teaching, physiology, continually received fresh impulse through the many discoveries in physical chemistry. Brücke, whose works on the subject broke into new fields of knowledge, was its most conspicuous representative from the Vienna School.

During the second half of the 19th century physics, optics and chemistry competed with each other to find new possibilities of development for medicine. Surgery based on narcosis led to undreamed-of progress. More and more special fields were opened up through internal medicine and surgery. The microscope and the discoveries of bacteriology revolutionized medical thought, to which, at the end of the century, further wonderful opportunities were presented through the discovery of the X-rays. In this general situation the Vienna School of Medicine gained a lead in its third phase, which made it for a long time a leading school in very important fields. Here the name of Billroth has become historic. This great surgeon, son of a North-German pastor, became one of the medical men of Vienna in 1867. He was a doctor with all-round experience, bold, and original in his methods and technique. Through his operations—he specialised in the larynx, oesophagus, stomach and genital organs—he paved the way for a new epoch. He chose his students with uncanny instinct and developed his methods into a new medical school. His favourite pupil, Eiselsberg (involuntarily one recalls the time of van Swieten), was summoned to practise in Holland.

The Josephinum, Vienna.

From the almost uncountable number of doctors who in those days were the pride and glory of medical Vienna, only a few are mentioned here in conclusion:—

Albert, a brilliant teacher of comprehensive knowledge; the surgeons Gussenbauer, Winiwarter, Eiselsberg, Hochenegg, and Nothnagel, the masters of diagnosis, Bamberger, Neusser, Noorden, Herschl, Pirquet, Paltauf, and Weichselbaum. Each of these names meant new discoveries, each of them is world-famous. Meinert and Obersteiner devoted their lives to the study of the nervous system and the brain. Laryngology was greatly developed by Chiari and Schrötter, while Politzer and Urbantschitsch became pioneers in the study of diseases of the ear, a branch for whose work in which Barany, a Viennese, was awarded the Nobel Prize. The significance of the X-rays was early recognised in Vienna. Holzknecht, the leading expert of these times, fell a victim to his own research work.

The little Austria of the year 1918 saw its highest duty to lie in the preservation and extension of the cultural values of the greater Austria. Poverty-stricken and sadly restricted in their field of work, the Austrian people did not fold their hands in idleness. The lecture halls of the colleges were just as full as in better times. Scientists and doctors worked for starvation salaries for the sake of the sick at the great task of research. The reputation of the Vienna School was not only not lost, but won fresh laurels. Billroth's inheritance, the schools of Eiselsberg and Hochenegg, became important to the whole world, and orthopaedics and accident surgery received

150

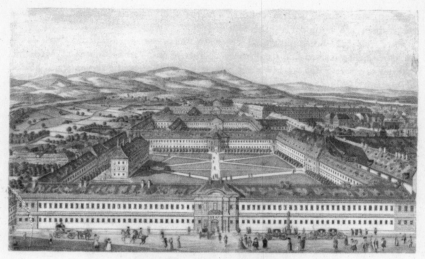

The Allgemeine Krankenhaus, Vienna.

fresh impulse through Albert Lorenz and Böhler. Internal clinical science found such excellent men as Quostek, Ortner and Jagić. In Eppinger a man came to the fore who made use of every refinement of chemical and technical methods in his researches, and whose reputation soon spread beyond the confines of Europe. The pharmacologist and physiologist Loewi discovered the heart hormone and was rewarded with the Nobel Prize. The same was the case with Wagner-Jauregg, who succeeded in banning the demon of paralysis by the induction of a curative fever. And where else could Siegmund Freud have gained his deep insight into the hidden places of the human soul than here in Vienna, where the most varied types of humanity meet and reveal their innermost thoughts? In Vienna the organising genius of Leopold Arzt continued the work of Hebra, Economo added to the knowledge of cerebral pathology, and Landsteiner, another Nobel prize-winner, worked out the scientific and practical basis on which blood-transfusion could be carried out.

Even in the pre-clinical field the old record has been maintained. Fürth played an authoritative part in the adrenalin synthesis, and the talented physiologist Exner was succeeded by Durig, whose Institute is among the most active in existence. Tandler, a pupil of Zuckerkandl, and himself an anatomist with a world-wide reputation, found insufficient outlet in his own branch and devoted himself to providing Vienna with hygienic and social welfare organisations, tuberculosis centres, mothers' instructional centres, children's homes and sanatoria, school dental clinics, etc., which are a model to the world.

Here we would honour them all, those who have been mentioned, as well as the unnamed. Thanks are due to all these doctors of the Vienna School of Medicine, for they are part of the world's great body of medical men, the servants and healers of humanity. Across frontiers and the trenches of wartime comes their appeal—to keep the peace and to love one's neighbour.

Gustav Klimt : Medicine (Section).

THE CAPUCHIN
CRYPT

B eneath an overcast sky in the midday hours of November 30th, 1916, the late Emperor Francis Joseph was driven over the Vienna Ringstrasse to the Crypt of the Capuchins (the Kapuzinergruft), the resting place of his forbears, where the Hapsburg rulers in ancient and venerable halls, in crypt and tomb, await their resurrection. Since the early morning, a vast assemblage of mourners had been collecting behind the ranks of the troops lining the streets. The closed windows of the surrounding houses were filled with onlookers and the crêpe-covered pavement-lamps and arc lamps burned in the daylight, creating a strange atmosphere of gloom. This fateful day meant more than the end of a 68 year reign, much more than the close of an epoch, for the last hour of the Austro-Hungarian Monarchy had struck.

Long before the end, the coming collapse had cast its shadows before. Among these were the tragedy of the Crown Prince Rudolf at Mayerling, the fatal attack by an anarchist on the Empress Elisabeth, the murderous shots fired at Francis Ferdinand, the heir to the throne, and his wife at Sarayevo in 1914. The Emperor was fated to stand beside all the biers and to see those around him dying off, one after the other.

Once again the Ringstrasse echoed the hoof-beats of horses sharply checked by the bearing-rein, the rumbling of funeral coaches drawn by caparisoned steeds, the rolling of muffled drums and the funeral march of the Trabant- and Arcières-Bodyguards. It was that same Ringstrasse which the Emperor had ordered to be built two generations earlier, the growth of which he had watched from the windows of his palace; he had seen its beauty as a unique monument to all that had been achieved during the francisco-josephinian era for Vienna and the Empire.

The summons had gone forth to assemble the funeral cortège of the Emperor. It was at the same time the funeral cortège of his Empire. On this last occasion, the Dual Monarchy paraded its might before the world. But with mourning for the deceased Monarch was mingled anxiety and fear of the inexorable decrees which Fate might be about to pronounce. Just once more the venerable Monarchy called its colourful mixture of peoples and nations to march past, formed up the hierarchy of its social order—aristocracy and parliamentary deputies, guilds and citizens, in accordance with the well-established formulas of age-old ceremony and with effortless ease. For one last occasion its army, rich in honour and tradition, was summoned to march past in sombre, funereal array.

On the outskirts of this silent zone, where boys were climbing street lamps to get an unhindered view of the procession, and where newsboys were shouting the headlines of extra editions, the situation was characterised by different slogans —"Przemysl", "Battle of the Isonzo", "Representation for the People", "Wilson"—and "the Republic".

The historic scene at which half Europe had its princely ambassadors and special envoys was nearing its close. Starting from the Stephansdom and traversing part of the Kärntnerstrasse, the funeral procession turned off at right angles to the Neuer Markt, to the quiet church of the Capuchin Brothers. Swords flashed in the air, commands rang out, the escorting troops froze to attention and the coffin of the Emperor was carried into the church for its last benediction.

On the right-hand side of the hall of mourning a space had been cleared. There the "Steps of the Dead" lead down to the Emperor's Crypt, last resting place of the Hapsburg Monarchs since the time of the Thirty Years' War. The folk of Vienna who filled the great square outside, pushing their way on to steps and stairways, and craning their necks to catch a better glimpse of what is going on, ask to be told—of course, it happened long ago—how it was in the days of "Franz the Kaiser".

"Before the closed doors", they tell one another, "the coffin was placed on the ground. The Master of Ceremonies lifted his baton—heavy black tassels hung from it—and knocked three times on the door.

"It had been locked from the inside by the Monastery folk and behind it stood the Pater Guardian with a lighted candle. He is in no hurry to open, and first asks: 'Who demands entry?'

"The Master of Ceremonies—the same one who times out of number, in the long gallery at Schönbrunn, had announced the coming of his Liege to invited guests—gives answer: 'His Apostolic Majesty, the Kaiser Franz.'

"The Church, however, sees a coffin before it in which a dead man lies and rejects any idea of majesty. Therefore the monk answers: 'I do not know him.'

"The Master of Ceremonies then lifts his mace again and knocks on the door with a triple rap. 'The Sovereign Kaiser Franz wishes to be admitted.'

"Unshaken and grave comes the answer: 'I do not know him.'

"And once again the voice of the monk questions: 'In the Name of God, who wishes to enter?'

"Quite simply the Master of Ceremonies returns: 'Your brother Franz, a poor sinner.'

"Only now is the door to the crypt opened and the new guest received into the realm of his forebears with that reverence of spirit which the pious monks accord to all men who believe in the resurrection of the dead."...

Waiting, whispering and conjecturing, the masses fill the square. In the meantime the monks have carried the coffin down to the crypt, where it is once again set down and the Master of Ceremonies asks: "Do you recognise the Emperor Francis Joseph?"

He is answered by the Pater Guardian "I know him. He will rest securely here."

Now the dead ruler is carried past his predecessors—twelve emperors, sixteen empresses and over a hundred archdukes lie here. The tombs of the founders of the crypt, Matthias and Anna, are simple and humble, plain four-sided leaden caskets. The coffins stand side by side in long rows, bearing coats of arms, or the heads of lions beside the metal carrying rings.

Surprisingly magnificent sarcophagi stand beside them. Baroque, with its determination that one should live with every atom of one's force—and so die—has descended into the realm of the dead. Eagles about to soar in flight and couchant lions support massive coffins. Heads of veiled women, their faces wrung with grief, ornament the corners.

Maria Theresia and Franz von Lothringen! This monumental sarcophagus is a memorial of love on which the Empress and her husband are artistically depicted facing one another in lifelike fashion. At their heads waits an angel with a trumpet to arouse them on Judgment Day. Eleven of her children are grouped around the Empress, Joseph II in a simple coffin of copper.

Now Francis Joseph, after doing his duty like a soldier up to his last breath, has joined the ranks of his ancestors.

In October 1918 came the collapse of the Central Powers. English officers, standing in front of the Hotel Imperial, held in their hands newspapers with the headlines: "The War is Over."

For Austria it was much more than a war which was over. If the essential Austria had been no more than what was then laid to rest under the insignia of the Double Eagle, the country would then—in 1918—have certainly come to an end.

Instead, there occurred something entirely unexpected, something unique. The little Austria which remained after the destruction of the Monarchy, a severely mutilated torso to which in widespread circles in Europe it was sought to deny not only all rights, but even its ability to exist, this fragment of the heart of a continent defied the blows of fate and arose again, re-establishing its sovereignty as built up on and supported by the labours and solidarity of its workmen, peasants, and middle classes.

Eternal, indestructible, resurrected Austria!

156

PART II
LAND·PEOPLE AND NATIONAL COSTUMES

ÖSTERREICHISCHE BUNDESHYMNE

Land der Berge·Land am Strome·Land der Äcker·
Land der Dome·Land der Hämmer·zukunftsreich! Heimat bist du
großer Söhne·Volk begnadet für das Schöne·vielgerühmtes
Österreich·Vielgerühmtes Österreich·

Heiß umfehdet·wild umstritten·liegst dem Erdteil du
inmitten·einem starken Herzen gleich·Hast seit frühen Ahnentagen
hoher Sendung Last getragen·vielgeprüftes Österreich·
Vielgeprüftes Österreich·

Mutig in die neuen Zeiten·frei und gläubig sieh uns schreiten·
arbeitsfroh und hoffnungsreich·Einig laß in
Brüderchören·Vaterland dir Treue schwören·vielgeliebtes
Österreich·Vielgeliebtes Österreich·

MELODIE VON W·A·MOZART
TEXT VON PAULA PRERADOVIĆ

THE AUSTRIAN
NATIONAL ANTHEM ·

Land of mountains, land on river,
Land of ploughed fields, land of churches,
Land of hammer, land of future,
Motherland of mighty sons,
People blessed with beauty's crown,
Austria of proud renown!
Austria of proud renown!

Scene of feuds and bitter strife,
Still you lie amidst this region
Like a heart with courage high,
Since your earliest ancestors
You have borne a mission's burden,
Sorely tested Austria,
Sorely tested Austria.

Courageously towards a new age,
Strong in faith, and free we march
Joy in work and hope is ours,
Our word as brothers thus united
To thee, oh Fatherland, is plighted,
Much beloved Austria,
Much beloved Austria.

BE-
TWEEN
RHINE

VORARLBERG

AND
ARL-
BERG

WORD-PALETTE
VORARLBERG

Alpine gateway·Europe's great watershed·
East-West·West-East Express·
Formerly portals 'gainst Alsace and Burgundy·
Austria's Rhine Province now·
Sharply defined in landscape·customs and its people·
Shepherds' pastures·pine-fragrant valleys·
Schesaplana·deep blue Silvretta·distant prospects·
The moving shadows of cable-railway cabins across verdant
green slopes·Promontories jutting out into
Lake Constance·valley of the Rhine·
Garlanded breeding cattle·"Maisäss"·peasants' seasonal treks·
"Ländle" not "Land"·"townlet" not "town"·freedom on every pathway·
Sparing·deliberate gestures·practical·consequent minds·
Industry freed from smoke and soot·"white coal"
from her native mountains·
Production without proletariat·rising birth-rate in the towns·
Gay-coloured textiles·ball and chain shot·exquisite
hand-made lace·
Ski-lifts·swaying passenger-conveyors·thrill of
lightning descent·
Blue shadows of ski-tracks on the snow·
Silently whispering legends of wintertime·
White springtime in Austria·

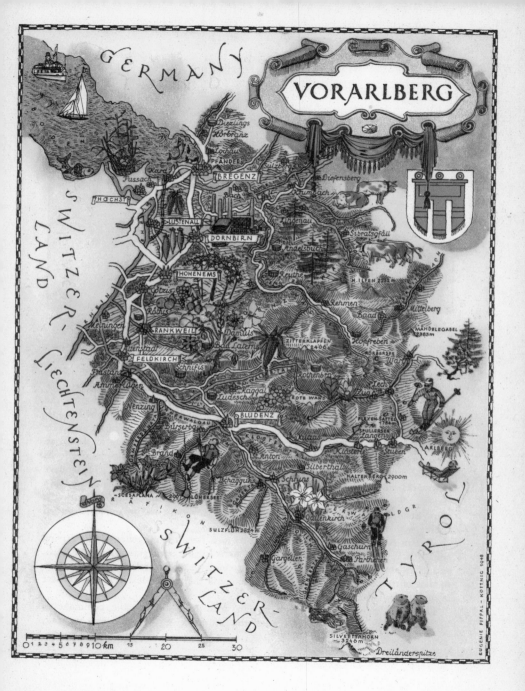

Bregenz in 1799.

BREGENZ AND LAKE CONSTANCE. Old and venerable Bregenz, Austria's gateway to the West, has maintained its leading position in the life of Vorarlberg throughout the centuries and today it is still the capital. It has been favoured in its situation. On one side it nestles beneath the protecting spurs of the Northern Alps; on the other it stands astride the route which traffic has followed from the earliest times along the banks of the Rhine, one of the natural highways of Europe. These factors have made of it a little town with a charm which is all its own. Its strategic importance was proved again and again during the chaos of barbarian invasion by the Saracens or from the East, during the quarrels of feudal overlords and the inroads of the Appenzell folk and the Thirty Years' War. These have left marks on its countenance which, do it honour and give it a claim on one's respect. These lines are not the wrinkles of age, but an indication that the spirit behind them has learnt how to overcome adversity and to pursue a settled course with courage and consistency.

Modern Bregenz is once again proving by its actions the existence of this driving spirit. It is fully aware of its importance as Austria's open gateway to the West, and from this realisation has come the strength to begin reconstruction, which in view of the Motherland's difficult position after the second destructive world-war is doubly important.

The cable railway which leads straight from the town to the commanding heights of the Pfänder reveals that the attraction of Bregenz lies not only

IT ALL BEGAN WITH THE FLOOD.

When Noah first set foot from the ark on dry land, he found himself not on Mount Ararat, as is generally believed, but in Vorarlberg, at the summit of the Widderstein. It is true that the venerable mountain mentioned in the Old Testament is not the only one which claims to have been the landing place of the Ark after the flood. But the attempts of other places to steal the glory of having been the second cradle of mankind must be disregarded in view of the claims which Vorarlberg can advance. When the first ascent of the Widderstein was made, remains of the bulworks of the Ark — or at least of some of them — were still lying on the summit. This discovery, the Vorarlberg people claim, of course put an end for all time to the controversy as to which country Noah first set foot on. The second patriarch of the human race was thus the first inhabitant of Vorarlberg.

Alas that efforts to continue the history of Vorarlberg from this point onwards should oblige one to admit that the descendants of the Old Testament hero must have remained an alphabets through several thousands of years, at least until the birth of Christ, for they have left to posterity no record that they ever existed.

Otherwise, Vorarlberg's first inhabitants seem to have known a very elementary form of civilisation. There are few traces of their activities, other than a few primitive hearths sheltered behind rough walls. Much ingenuity was called for to find even these.

In fact, the first tidings of Vorarlberg come to us from one of the many branches of the family of Noah, those who called themselves Romans. They selected the fifteenth year after the Emperor Augustus ascended the

in its historic importance and cultural activity, but also in its geographical position. This overhead railway is one of the oldest and most popular in Austria. Certainly the view from the Pfänder over Lake Constance and the ⁄ Swabian Plain which lie below, spread out like a map framed by the Swiss and Vorarlberg mountains, can hardly find its equal. And the lake itself! In its manifold beauty, whether it presents a limpid surface ruffled by tiny sparkling waves which caress the swimmer, or some masterpiece of colouring by nature which takes one's breath away, with the tinted curtains of the sunset changing from minute to minute, or the threat and fury of unleashed elements, lies a magic attraction from which few are immune and which tempt the poet to take up his pen in their praise.

THE AUSTRIAN GEOGRAPHY OF THE RHINE.

As the whole world knows, the question of the left bank of the Rhine has been the starting point of many bloody European wars, even of the world wars.

Strange how the most complex questions change their whole character when treated in Austrian fashion. The left bank of the Rhine! Who knows that Austria possesses a left bank of the Rhine, or that the river is crossed by two Austrian bridges? That the Vorarlberg parishes of Höchst, Fussach and Rheinau belong to the left bank? (It may be

View of the Town of Bregenz.

mentioned here that Goethe crossed Lake Constance from Fussach when he returned from Italy in 1811.)

The landscape which extends on either side of the Rhine's artificial channel is a peculiar one. Suddenly transported there, one would not believe oneself to be in a mountain district any longer. Swamps, in part made fertile through drainage, spread out for miles. Looking north, one has the illusion of being in a sunken plain. A colony of many varieties of birds inhabits this stretch of land. Few can withstand the charm of the softly waving reeds. The broad expanse of country, the rustling and whispering of the brittle stalks and slender foliage of the reed-banks seem to liberate the spirit. Unconsciously one breathes more deeply, the eye drinking in greedily the distant blue, the ear attuned to the voice of nature. The heart is soothed by the spirit of the moors in the all-pervading stillness, broken only by the harsh cry and the beat of the wings of some startled bird.

The largest Rhineside market town in Vorarlberg is Lustenau, celebrated like all Rhine settlements for its rich harvests of carefully tended fruit. As a settlement the big market town presents a singular picture. The houses, scattered over an area which is wide in comparison with the number of its inhabitants, are often hidden behind the dense foliage of fruit trees which entirely conceal them from the road. Lustenau is more or less of an enclave. Both in language and physiology, its inhabitants differ considerably from those of the rest of the Province, who

166

*throne to pay a visit to their very
distant relatives in Vorarlberg (who
had remained on their patriarchal
inheritance) to teach them new and
more modern ways of living and, as
opportunity offered, to batter in their
skulls.*

*These drastic methods of instruction
seem to have taught the ancient Vorarlbergers within a remarkably short
space of time how to build streets and
houses, indeed even regular settlements.
They served their apprenticeship in
this new art by setting up a fortified
castle with its dependent courts and
buildings which their distant relatives
from the South named "Brigantium",
or Bregenz, perhaps in honour of the
family of Brigantius which lived there.
As at the moment it was the thing to
engage in trade, and to give their
Vorarlberg connections a concrete
example of what trade meant—chiefly,
taking what one wanted from
others and giving them in exchange
what one found useless—the Romans
founded a Brigantium branch of their
world-wide exchange system. As this
town on Lake Constance was at the
crossroads of some of the most important
highways of the time, it soon became
well-known to the civilised world.*

*Thanks to the attentions of their
Roman relatives, the people of Vorarlberg and their province soon began
to play a part in history.*

*A trace of special worldly wisdom
confronts one on the wall of a house
on the outskirts of Montafon:*

*An honest mind and dealings fair,
Result in nought but wretched care.*

A BRAVE PEASANT FOLK.

*Until the end of the Middle Ages
many of the upper valleys of Vorarlberg
were very sparsely populated or
totally uninhabited. About this time
began the exodus of Germanic races*

jokingly accuse them of being descended from
"gipsies". That is, of course, an exaggeration,
but it contains a small grain of truth, for
while other parts of Vorarlberg were subject
to some feudal lord or other during the Middle
Ages, Lustenau was a "freier Reichshof",
meaning that anyone might take up residence
there without special permission. It was small
wonder that all kinds of wandering folk made
use of this freedom, though not to the disadvantage of the present day inhabitants! Their
vivacity and ready wit have been in part
responsible for the prominent part which the
people of Lustenau played and still play in
Vorarlberg intellectual, more especially musical
life and sport.

"HERE STUDIO DORNBIRN!" This call-
signal coming over the ether a dozen times
a day has made familiar the name of a town in
Vorarlberg which until recently, despite the
fact that it has the largest population of the
province, led something of the existence of a
sleeping beauty. Only in textile-trading circles
has its name been famous for many years
beyond the frontiers.
Dornbirn is Vorarlberg's
industrial centre. Such
a description is usually
in itself sufficient to
condemn a place, con-
juring up as it does a
vision of tenements, soot-
laden air and a forest
of smoking factory
chimneys. All who can-
not picture an industrial
town otherwise are re-
commended to visit
Dornbirn, which has
the additional appelation

Sample of Peasant Weaving from the XVII Century.

of "Garden City". The social problem is solved here in noteworthy fashion, for although more than half the population is dependent on industry, it has no proletariat.

In grappling with its problems, the town has, of course, been helped by its favourable geographical position. The winter sport resort of Bödele which is easily reached by a picturesque road brings life to Dornbirn as soon as the white carpet covers the ground. In summer its chief attraction is a beautiful and sinister gorge which is reached by a romantic artificial flight of steps—the Rappenlochschlucht. Closed in by walls of rock which tower vertically to a height of several hundred feet, crossed far above by a bridge, the turbulent mountain waters far below foam and roar through the gorge. The spectacle is well calculated to awaken a wholesome respect for the might of those forces which give shape and form to surrounding nature, and through her to our own lives.

From the tree-covered summit the hoary keep of Neu-Ems Castle overlooks the valley of the Rhine. The steep crag commanding the town bears the ruins of Alt-Ems, before its destruction in the Appenzeller War one of the greatest castles of the German Reich, equal in size to the famous Wartburg. The palace built by Count Kaspar still stands today at the foot of the Castle Rock. A number of other buildings and historic names lend to Dornbirn that magic of departed grandeur which always lingers around historic walls and ancient monuments.

THE GARDEN OF VORARLBERG. In the midst of the plain through which flows the Rhine rises the Kummenberg, a witness to the activity of the Rhine Valley Glacier in the Ice Age. To the south its tree-covered

from the canton of le Valais, in Switzer-
land. At the beginning of the 15th
century the number of these peasants
who came to settle in Graubünden
and Vorarlberg was steadily on the
increase. These new arrivals seeking
employment were readily welcomed by
the land-owners, and the uninhabited
upper valleys were allotted them to
build new homes. In order to persuade
them to settle permanently the gift of
land was accompanied by various
privileges. In this manner the uncultivated
part of the Tannberg, in the Upper
Bregenzerwald, and especially the two
Walser valleys which have taken their
name from it, developed into the home of
a sturdy peasant race which has become a
permanent factor of the national and
economic structure of the Province.

Anyone who wants to form a picture
of the strenuous way in which these
descendants of the old inhabitants of
the Valais who have retained much
of the peculiarities of their former
country in their speech, dress and
customs gain a bare existence from a
grudging nature, needs only to observe
how they live in the Grosse Walsertal.
Generations of bitter struggle for daily
bread have produced a sturdy and
weather-beaten folk whose existence is
deeply rooted in the soil.

The people of Vorarlberg are not
uniform in character, but form rather
a mosaic of various sturdy elements
welded together by historical develop-
ments.

slopes rise gradually, but to the north it falls away steeply. It is well worth the trouble of climbing, for looking down from its heights one has a delightful outlook over the entire Vorarlberg part of the Rhine Valley. In the east the pictu-resque houses of the market town of Götzis combine their greetings with those of the massive ruins of Neu-Montfort. The chief picture to the north and south is that of innumerable tiny rectangles of grass alternating with arable land, a clue to the agricultural structure of the countryside. An unusual trick of nature affords amusement to visitors to the summit of the Kummenberg: pieces of paper or material which are thrown out over the yawning depths are returned to their owner by the air currents. Even hats which have been tossed over are said to come back of their own accord, but not everyone cares to put this to the test.

To the south of the Kummenberg a vale branches off from the main Rhine valley which is called the "Garden of Vorarlberg". About a dozen pleasant villages cling to the foot of the mountain or have found themselves a sunny place half way up it, and in blossom-time the whole countryside is one fragrant bridal bouquet. On the sunny slopes flourish delicious grapes; Fraxern, hidden in a hollow between the green hills, is famous for its wonderful black cherries, which attract crowds of visitors who arrive with baskets and carts. Viktorsberg, looking

The Parish Church in Bregenz.

Vorarlberg is Austria's estate on the Rhine. Between the eastwards-flowing Danube and the westwards-flowing Rhine, between the one which finds its outlet in the Black Sea and the other which flows into the Atlantic Ocean, lies Austria, the bridge and watershed of Europe. In 1363 the House of Austria acquired its first possession in Vorarlberg in the shape of a small estate near Götzis. This was the start of a long process which led to the unification of a Province. As military leaders under the Emperors Karl V and Philipp II, the Counts of Hohenems embodied large numbers of serfs from their estates in their armed forces. From then onwards, Vorarlbergers have constantly emigrated from the Province, as labourers, stucco-workers and carpenters, selling grind-stones or herbs from Montafon, or in the employment of Bregenzerwald builders of the Baroque. It was not until industrialisation set in that this industrious race had the chance of finding work and a home in its native country.

It is characteristic of the Vorarlberger to dislike and avoid ostentation and exaggeration. In accordance with this reserve, he is sparing of gesture and words. These \ characteristics help to a clean-cut political sense and a natural feeling for democracy.

The people of Vorarlberg prefer their four small or medium-sized towns to one large one. They do not mind having to go sometimes to Bregenz and Feldkirch, sometimes to Dornbirn and Bludenz, for these towns after all lie close together. The Province is thus spared many a problem which may arise out of having a single large town in an alpine area.

The "Ländle" ("Little Province") has its characteristic industrial character.

down from the lofty Warte, is one of the oldest recorded settlements of Vorarlberg; even Karl der Dicke (Charles the Fat) is said to have toiled up there on a visit to the pious hermit Eusebius. Röthis, however, the heart of the Vorarlberg vineyards, lures one with many a sparkling drop, golden-yellow and ruby-red, down into the valley.

The chief town of the Vorarlberg Garden is Rankweil, which played a prominent and decisive role in the history of the Province throughout the whole of the Middle Ages and on into modern times. At one time the whole population used to congregate for the trial of criminals there. Today, as one of the greatest pilgrimage centres of this Catholic province, it has again become a meeting place for crowds in holiday mood. Its symbolic building is the double-towered Liebfrauenkirche, built on the remains of a former fortress, which confronts the stately Felsenwarte.

THE STUDIERSTÄDTLEIN (the "Students' Township"). Feldkirch has not always been called the "Studierstädtlein". Like Bregenz, it has had one of the most colourful histories of any place in Vorarlberg. In earlier centuries it was with equal justice called the "Officers' Township", but today both terms are inapplicable. It is noteworthy that in each case its municipal character was emphasized. Even today this is the most noticeable thing about it. Of all towns in Vorarlberg it has best preserved the character of the mediaeval burgher settlement. Like Bregenz, Feldkirch formed part of the Montfort property. Through repeated partitions of the estate among members of the family, which weakened all its powers of resistance, Feldkirch came at an early date into the possession of the Hapsburgs, thereby gaining in comparison with other areas which had remained under the rule

of local feudal lords, special privileges which ensured it unusual opportunities for development.

The picture of a mediaeval townlet which Feldkirch presents today is furnished mainly by the streets of the inner town, consisting of solid and impressive buildings in which merchants have carried on their affairs for many generations. Such evidence as survives of former defensive constructions like the Churer Tor, the Katzenturm and Schattenburg Castle, which towers over the town, conjure up visions of scenes long past to attract a stranger's attention.

Feldkirch was called "Studierstädtlein" in bygone days when it was of great importance—one might almost say of unparalleled importance—in educational affairs. It had a grammar school, a college for teachers which attracted students from all over the country, and the famous Jesuit college "Stella Matutina", well-known throughout Europe.

It could with almost equal justice have been called the "Township of Bureaucrats", although it was never a centre of government. But the majority of the other administrative bodies of the province are established in Feldkirch. The cosmopolitan character of the bureaucracy of the Austro-Hungarian Monarchy has affected the racial composition of the local population.

Feldkirch, as a junction on the only direct East-West route, is of importance to the Austrian traffic system. It is the main railway station on the frontiers of Austria with Switzerland and Liechtenstein, and thus a connecting-link in the West European transport organization.

DO YOU KNOW THE LEGEND OF THE THREE SISTERS? No? Then wander from Feldkirch through the Ill Ravine, the "Felsenau", that deep channel which the river has for centuries been cutting through the imprisoning rocks and which is still so narrow that there is only just room for the railway leading to the Walgau to run beside it. A feat of engineering was called for to carry the road over river and railway on a precarious bridge. Once one emerges from this narrow gorge, the character of the countryside is seen to have completely changed. Even the air is cooler, and the natives say that east of the Felsenau (i. e. in Walgau) it is "a jacket cooler" than in the Rhine Valley. You walk all

With only four factories employing over 500 persons, it is the smaller and medium sized specialised industries which are typical. First comes the textile trade. The Vorarlberg cotton industry, which enjoys an international reputation, produces not only the finest multi-coloured woven cloth in Austria, but also high class printed goods. Woven silk and specialised woollen and knitted goods are also typical of local industry. Vorarlberg's reputation for embroidery and hand-made lace has spread far beyond the confines of Europe. Other Vorarlberg industries concern themselves with refining and specialised finishing processes, for the Province is lacking in almost all raw materials. Cogwheels, gears, pumps and watches, sliding scales and specialised tools are all made here. The factories for the construction of elevators and cable-railways are based on "White Coal", on the natural water-power of the Province, the exploitation of which has been developed to a high degree.

the more easily and vigorously and you are quickly in Frastanz.

Here it was that three sisters once lived—at a happy period, no doubt, for, according to an accepted legend, a spring of pure gold flowed at the foot of the Garsellaspitze. One sunny Sunday these three sisters, instead of going to church as custom and piety dictated, started out towards the Garsellaspitze. Who knows whether it was the flowing gold which led them astray or whether they simply wanted to gather berries? In vain did the church bells call them once more to mass. The three sisters, their heads filled with mundane matters, ignored the summons. Soon they found a place where berries grew so thickly that they were able to fill basket after basket in a short time. As a last reminder of neglected religious duties came the faint tinkle of the transubstantiation bell. When they ignored this final warning, they met their fate. Unable to move, their bodies froze and turned to stone. When the faithful left the church after mass they stood and stared, for at the foot of the Garsellaspitze rose up side by side three tall rocks. The three sisters, however, were never seen again. Their baskets full of berries were found there on the following day. So came the three rocks by the name of "The Three Sisters".

WHERE THE UNICORN HAS ITS HOME. Yes, indeed, the mythical unicorn still exists in Vorarlberg, in the above-mentioned Walgau—in the coat-of-arms of Bludenz, its chief town. Here the landscape is sunny and smiling and the people vivacious and cheerful.

Despite the dominance of the unicorn in the Walgau, or

Rankweil.

Tisis.

rather in Bludenz, it is not dangerous to live there. On the contrary, this little town on the Ill with its romantic past and its industrious present offers many attractions and opportunities to visitors. To begin with there is the picturesque centre of the town with its narrow streets and mediaeval avenues. The Obere Tor is decorated with a fresco of Friedrich of the Empty Pocket which recalls how the people of Bludenz afforded their liege lord sanctuary and loyalty after he had been outlawed by the Emperor. There is a parish church built on a dominating cliff, and the more massive than beautiful Castle Gaienhofen, which has been put to various uses in the course of the years. As far back as the Celts and the Romans there were settlements on this site. The attractive and charming surroundings of Bludenz have earned it the name of "Gateway of the Alps". For one who wishes to get to know all the passes from the valley level to the snow-capped mountains of the main Alpine range it would be hard to find a more favourable centre than this little town of the Walgau.

Arriving at Bludenz by train, every traveller is struck by a snow-capped mountain of bare rock rising sheer out of the green valley. This is the Panüler Schrofen, the western "shoulder" of the Scesaplana, queen of the Rätikons. As the culminating point of a whole chain of mountains this giant is not only an attraction for local tourists, but is one of those peaks which have made history in the opening up of the Eastern Alps. Thanks to its commanding height, it offers an almost unrestricted view of the countryside, including a charming glimpse of Swiss Prätigau in the depths below.

THE VALLEY OF WHITE COAL. The Montafon valley played a part in national transport centuries ago, for it is the gateway to southern Europe, and more immediately to Veltlin. Today it is a power centre for countless industries scattered over a considerable part of Central Europe.

On the way from Bludenz to Montafon one passes through Vandans, a village which is threatened as no other by the primitive forces of the mountains. Millions of cubic metres of rubble and boulders lie waiting in clefts of the Vandanser Rock Wall, like a wild beast crouched to spring, ready to hurl itself down at a given moment on to the peaceful human community, carrying death and devastation. An attempt has indeed

Feldkirch; Churer Gate.

174

been made to guard against such an occurrence by the construction of mighty barricades. Whether man will be found to have succeeded in banning such elemental natural violence, the future will show.

Further up the Ill lies Schruns, the chief town of the Montafon, nestling picturesquely in an arm of the valley. Few places in Vorarlberg have been so fitted by climate and surroundings to become a health resort as this pretty market town.

Stuben on the Arlberg.

It is indisputable that the people of the Montafon are very different from the rest of the population of Vorarlberg, as their customs, temperament and language plainly show. Montafon has withstood germanisation longer than any other part of Vorarlberg, and has thus preserved certain characteristics of its original Romanic population.

Opposite Schruns lies Tschagguns, once much visited by pilgrims but nowadays more of a centre for winter-sport. Tschagguns has particularly good ski-ing facilities and is also the starting-point for trips to the Rätikon, the excursion being facilitated by a cable railway to Grabs, 4,800 feet above sea level. In the area accessible from Tschagguns, the exacting mountain climber will find the same satisfaction as the tourist who wants only to discover and meditate on the beauties of nature. The way to the Gauertal, which is widely known for its beautiful scenery, the end of the valley with the Lindau Hut rising from the last scrubby pines in the foreground, backed by the Three Towers in the distance, has been characterised by the most experienced and best-known Alpine climbers as unique and incomparable.

Bregenz Tower.

A few miles beyond Schruns, on the slopes of the mighty Kapelljoch, which is to be made accessible by a cable railway, in a narrow part of the Montafon Valley lies the district of the "Fratte", which divides the valley into Outer and Inner Montafon, or, as the inhabitants say, "Outer and Inner Fratte". The first hamlet of the Inner Fratte is St. Gallenkirch, whence the valley of the Suggadin river stretches away in the south to the mountain health-resort of Gargellen. Surrounded by the most bizarre of mountain scenery, the latter is, perhaps, artistically considered, the most attractive place in the entire Province. What makes of it a health-resort is the fact that of all places in the Province, it has the record for sunshine, and that it has the same wonderful climate as the Swiss health-resort of Davos, only 18 kilometres distant as the crow flies.

That the Montafon, particularly the Inner Fratte, has lost its original character of a mountain farming area is immediately evident when one comes to Parthenen, last of the valley settlements. At first glance it is recognised as an industrial township. Montafon's name of the "Valley of White Coal" is here justified, for the district in which Parthenen is situated is devoted to the production of electrical power. Cable-railways, elevators, narrow-gauge railways running at a height of over 5,000 and 6,000 feet, extensive plants and tunnels several kilometres in length show at first glance with what energy technical knowledge is striving to render the forces of nature of service to man. The source of these forces is the glaciers of the main range, the "Blue Silvretta", famous as a ski-resort in spring. It is easy to repeat without giving the matter further thought that the beauty and natural charm of the mountains are destroyed when their useful potentialities are exploited by mechanical means. It is far wiser and more just to go oneself (and how much simpler the many inventions of the much abused mechanical developments have made such a trip), to ascertain with one's own eyes that the two enormous artificial lakes at Vermunt and Obervermunt have lent a touch of beauty to the picture which was lacking in the monotonous valley which they have superseded. For the mountain lover there still remain the combs and peaks of the monarch of the Vorarlberg Alps, the 9,892 foot high Piz Buin, which he can approach with untroubled heart and a determination to dare its perils, without any risk that his ideal picture will be found marred by the spirit of a profit-seeking age.

THE LOFTY CASTLE OF THE WHITE ART. It is not so very many years ago that winter was regarded as a visitation of God. More especially was this the attitude of the mountain folk whose means of livelihood were drastically curtailed during the cold months by the many feet of snow. This attitude only underwent a change when human ingenuity succeeded in making use of two strips of wood bound to the feet with one end bent upwards, which brought with them greater freedom of movement even over deep snow. This happened in Austria towards the end of the last century. One of the areas in which this now widespread

Old Montafon National Costume (Woman).

"White Art" was developed and cultivated is the Arlberg, which takes its name from the pass which was well-known as a connecting-link between Tyrol and Vorarlberg even in mediaeval times.

The name Arlberg is a magic word which arouses echoes in the heart of every skier, of whom there are hundreds of thousands today. There is scarcely another part of Europe which satisfies so many demands of modern ski-ing as this mountain-world on the borders of Tyrol and Vorarlberg. It gave its name to a well-known ski-ing style, and the name of Hannes Schneider is inseparably connected with the conception of ski-ing. You will quickly get an inkling of the Arlberg district's meaning for the sporting side of modern ski-ing if, at the end of winter, you glance down the lists of winners of the great international races; again and again you find Arlberg names at the head of them. The importance of the Arlberg from a ski-ing as well as from a tourist point of view will be understood and never forgotten by anyone who has ever spent a week there at the height of the season.

The line of approach to this eldorado of the "White Art" is the Arlberg railway, which ascends from the Vorarlberg side of Bludenz in daring curves, overcoming the natural barriers of the narrow Klostertal by many a viaduct and tunnel to reach Langen-on-the-Arlberg, nearly 4000 feet above sea level.

On arriving in Langen one is at once confronted by a scene of activity. Motor-sleighs and innumerable horse-drawn sleighs, vast piles of luggage and a crowd of shouting and excitedly gesticulating people—a gathering of many nations— fill the square in front of the station. Within a few minutes this confusion resolves itself into an orderly line of vehicles which sets out over the Arlbergstrasse and Flexenstrasse with a rattling and tinkling of bells towards Stuben, Zürs and Lech, well-known winter-sport resorts. The drive over the Flexenstrasse, especially in winter, is an unforgettable experience. No one can fail to be impressed by the manner in which this important highroad has been built in defiance of natural obstacles, with a vast expenditure of time and money, but with a due regard for the beauties of nature.

The less attractive the Arlberg scenery around Zürs is in summer, the more appeal the treeless white slopes have in winter when they are softly blanketted in deep snow sown with glittering crystals. When a blue sky rises in an arch above, it is enough to make every heart beat more quickly. One feels an irresistible urge to set forth on skis, to plough a shadowy blue track in the virgin white, to hear the crackling and whispering of the myriad shining snow crystals, to abandon one's body and spirit to a purity and freedom which is only to be found in the alpine heights in wintertime. And the experience of the whirlwind descent, the snow flying up like clouds of star-dust! Here there is enjoyment for everyone, even though their numbers run into thousands. There is room enough for each one to get away from the others and to make a track of his own. The great hotels are ready to furnish proof that city dwellers who cling to their standard of comfort are also catered for. A first class ski-school provides individual and successful instruction in the White Art, and the ski-lifts enable those setting out on a ski-tour to reach attractive areas without effort.

Lech-on-the-Arlberg is even more beautiful scenically than Zürs, although it does not lie so high and is less fashionable. Perhaps just for this reason it is more intimate and cosy. Lech attracts many guests in summer as well, although it is chiefly a winter-sport resort, furnished with all the necessary modern equipment.

Before we say good bye to the Arlberg, let us take a glance at one of its wild and romantic beauties—the avalanches. Many readers may be surprised to hear avalanches numbered among the beauties of nature, but their surprise betrays that they have never experienced the grandiose spectacle of this wintery force on the Arlberg. When on fine days towards the end of March and in April the modestly blooming violet begins to oust the snow in the valleys, high up amidst the peaks, still in full winter costume, an ominous rolling and a muttering begin which strike a chill into one's very bones. Lying in the sun in a safe corner, one can watch this drama of nature for hours without wearying. Again and again one looks up as one catches the rumbling sound, and in a few seconds gigantic masses of snow like a great white river throwing up showers of spray cascade down over black rocks into the ravine below. Long

after the avalanche has subsided to the view, the accompanying thunderous roar continues, itself gradually subsiding into a silence which leaves the ear keyed up for the next demonstration.

The Walser villages are interesting, in character easily distinguishable from other places in Vorarlberg. Every farm is built at least a stone's throw away from the next, according to Walser custom, and isolated houses are to be found as high up as the last slopes which it is at all possible to reach by vehicle.

The picture of the Great Walser Valley reminds the observer that it is not always man who rules nature, but that sometimes it is nature who forces man to acknowledge her imperious rule. The impression left by a visit to the Small Walser Valley is a much friendlier one. This district, which economically is an enclave not only within Vorarlberg but also within Austria, has an individual note due to the highly developed tourist trade which is everywhere in evidence. The natural traffic routes of the Small Walser Valley connect it with the adjacent Allgäu, but it has no direct connections with Vorarlberg or Tyrol. This valley, which offers many opportunities for winter sport, but is also attractive in summer on account of its beautiful scenery, has built up a remarkable tourist connection. It can boast of a very large number of comfortable inns and hotels. You will find them all along the only road, which links up the market towns of Riezlern, Hirschegg and Mittelberg, and on the slopes above. Obviously such developments have an influence on the way of life of the native population. But it is surprising to learn that in the Lesser Walser Valley even simple peasant's farms are furnished with many of the comforts of civilisation. Most of them have central heating, running hot and cold water, mechanical washers and modern kitchen conveniences run by electricity.

MODERN NOMADS. The Upper Bregenzerwald, that is, the country above the Bregenzer Ache from the Bezau onwards, is chiefly mountainous in character, declining to hill country in the Lower Bregenzerwald. Populous settlements are scattered through the vales which branch off from the wide valley; solitary, sun-scorched farms reach far up into the green heights, to the scene of activity of a nomadic race. This exists here today in the heart of Europe, for the peasant of the Bregenz forests has remained a wandering shepherd despite all the developments of civilisation. He spends the winter in close companionship with his neighbours in the village, but as soon as the snow is finally gone from the mountains and the pastures on their slopes are beginning to turn green again, he moves off with family, goods and chattels to the "Maisäss", or "May residence", a

solitary farm which is situated halfway between the valley and the Alps. In summer the peasant drives his flocks and herds up the Alps, most of the other members of his family returning to the valley to work in the fields and harvest the hay. If, at the end of summer, pasture at the highest levels becomes too scanty, he and his family return to the Maisäss until here also the approach of cold weather makes the pasturage too meagre. Only then does the family occupy its quarters in the valley. With such a system it is not surprising that even large villages present an almost lifeless appearance at certain times of the year.

The church at Schwarzenberg well repays the art lover for a visit. The village, which has nowadays made a name for itself as a winter-sport and holiday centre was the second home of the well-known painter Angelika Kauffmann.

In conclusion, among the notable peculiarities of the Bregenzerwald the so-called "Bezegg Column" must not be forgotten, that symbolic monument which recalls the former council-house of the staunchly independent and democratic peasants and artisans of the Bregenzerwald. This building could only be

entered by a ladder which was removed as soon as the councillors had assembled and was not put back until the questions to be discussed had all been cleared up. This steadfast democratic spirit together with the commercial activity of its population is Vorarlberg's most valuable contribution to its great Austrian homeland.

181

LAND IN THE

TYROL

MOUNT-AINS

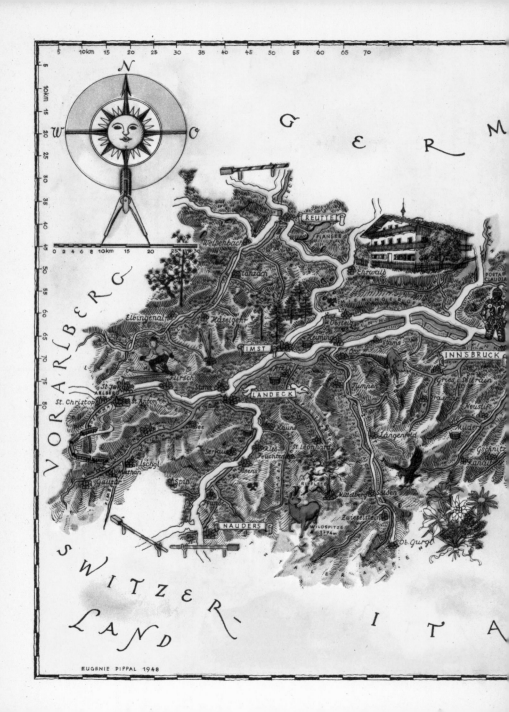

EUGENIE PIPPAL 1948

WORD-PALETTE
TYROL

Country of earliest-known mountain passes,
mules following Alpine tracks,
The rolling echo of stone-avalanches in the mountains
From afar going farther to Pope or the Emperor,
winds the column.
The earth with a hundred towers, peak above ridge,
ranges of sheer cliffs, meadows, pastures, south wind and
prevailing winds across the mountain ridges.
Fir-trees, stone pines, black cock and chamois, poachers in
the coverts. – By sparkling rivers,
Shining white townlets, markets and farms.
Decorative gables and oriel windows, gently sloping roof,
weighted with stones.
Hand-painted chests, rustling ribbons, broad brimmed hat.
Wood-carvers of saints, weavers, smouldering charcoal
in pine-fragrant woodlands.
Watchfully circling eagle, a man climbing after the starry edelweiss.
A solitary Christ on the wayside wooden cross
For the sins of the world, for the turbulent blood.
Ghosts, proverbs, curious customs.
Frank glances, frank words, open and free as in 1809.
Dance of Death, the last rally,
At Mantua in chains: "Adieu, thou cruel world!"
Homeland, beloved soil – Holy Province of Tyrol

Innsbruck, Goldenes Dachl.

Europe is distinguished from the other continents by its combination of the maximum number of diversities in the minimum space. Austria is similarly singled out among the other European countries. And within Austria, the same distinction applies to Tyrol. The strong feeling of unity found in this province, contrasted with the diversities of its population, landscape and climate make it as strange yet alluring as its own name—Tyrol . . . .

THE FORMATION OF THE PROVINCE. North Tyrol can be said to be divided into two by the axis of the Brenner line and to be evenly balanced on either side of it. Taking Innsbruck as lying on the axis itself, we have Hall and Zirl, Telfs and Schwaz, Imst and Jenbach, balancing one another. The two great valleys on either side, the Ötztal and the Zillertal, have the Silltal between them. The curve of the Inn near Landeck is counterbalanced by its bend near Wörgl; there its upper branch runs south, as here its lower branch runs north; there the railway leaves the river and climbs to the snowy Arlberg, here it branches off to the ski-ers' paradise on the heights between Kitzbühel and Hochfilzen.

In the Alps the Seefelder Sattel forms a continuation of the north-south axis. On the one side stretch the Mieminger and the Wetterstein, on the other the chain of the Karwendel. The pass and lakes of the Fern lead from the Upper Inn Valley, the lake and pass of Achen from the Lower Inn Valley towards Bavaria.

187

Ötztal Costume.

Beyond this territorial formation lies, in the north-west of the Province, the Außerfern, with intervening gateways—the district of Reutte through which flow the rivers Lech and Loisach, and in the south-east of the province of East Tyrol, the district of Lienz, watered by the Isel and the Drau.

The formation of Tyrol is regular —not rigidly symmetrical, but harmonious. The features which offset one another have both similarity and differences. The Ziller Valley, for example, at first broad and almost devoid of interesting features, rises a bare 300 feet at Mayrhofen. There it splits up into the "Gründe", like the fingers of a hand, and suddenly reveals its whole beauty; only the "thumb" has extended earlier at Zell in the Gerlos. In contrast, the valley of the Ötz rises by the "steps" of Ötz, Umhausen, Längenfeld and Sölden through delightfully contrasting gorges and basins until, after passing Zwieselstein, at Gurgl and Vent, it reaches the highest farmhouse, which lies at a height of over 6000 feet. The Sill Valley is unlike both. Starting from Innsbruck, the capital of the Province, it carries the main railway line and the main road up to a deeply cut pass with glaciers left and right. The Upper and the Lower Inn Valleys are equally important, but as different from one another as night from day, as are the chalk formations from the primary rocks south of the Inn.

The wanderer—in Tyrol one has to wander—comes across sudden changes in scenery as well as sudden changes of weather. North and south contest one against the other. The Föhn (south wind) forces the snow to retreat high up into the mountains in winter—the temperature may rise 70 degrees Fahrenheit in twelve hours—and in August a cold spell may cause a very sharp fall. Mountain and valley intensify the contrasts. He who freezes at midday in the eternal winter

A PAGE OF HISTORY.

Meinhart the Second (of Görz) who was Meinhart the First of Tyrol, the man who formed the Province into a political unit in the thirteenth century, giving it the name of his castle near Meran, Schloss Tirol, is little remembered today. His wife, Elizabeth, on the other hand, still lives in the memory of the people. The widow of the Emperor Conrad the Fourth and mother of Conradin, she gave Tyrol the impressive background of the Staufer Empire. She set up a permanent memorial to her unhappy son in the Monastery of Stams. Meinhart, through the marriage of his daughter with the son of the Emperor Rudolf I, established the first connection with the House of Hapsburg.

Popular interest concentrates much more on the stirring story of Meinhart's grandchild Margarethe Maultasch ("Pocket-Mouthed Meg"), who drove out her first husband to marry her own cousin. She was excommunicated by the Church on the grounds that this marriage involved a double sin. It was long years before the ban was lifted. She survived her second husband and only son; in 1363 she made over "the land on the Etsch and the Inn Valley with Schloss Tirol and all else appertaining · thereto" to Rudolf the Endower. Fourteen gentlemen of Tyrol put their seals to the deed in the name of all inhabitants of the Duchy, of the "clergy and laymen, nobles and commoners, wether living in the towns or in the country". With this impressive voluntary deed Tyrol began its life in the federation of Austrian Provinces. It soon found an opportunity to prove its loyalty.

Friedl with the Empty Pocket, popular despite his outlawry and excommunication, confirmed the freedom of the Province at the Diet of Meran in 1423, when for the first time burghers

of the ice world of the Ötztal may enjoy eternal spring the same evening 9000 feet below amid vines and chestnut trees. The modern mountain railways make the contrast even more unbelievable.

THE TYROLESE. You will find among the people of Tyrol as many contrasts as those which characterise its landscape. To Tyrol the Bavarians came from the north and north-east, from the west and north-west the Allemanians, and from the south, Latin races infiltrated. The remnants of an aboriginal population whose source is obscure sought refuge from the invaders among the crags and crannies of the mountains where their descendants are to be found to this day. Throughout the length and breadth of the country you will come across curious names of village and pasture which recall these various races. Tyrol, which resembles Switzerland in this respect, managed to weld these various tribes—and later the people of German, Italian and Ladinian race—together, to live peacefully in a small area. Today these elements have overcome the limitations of nationalism and feel themselves to be above all Tyrolese. Once again the forces making for unity proved stronger than those tending towards separation, and the passes, as the word implies, have become links, not barriers.

In Tyrol, inhabitants, dialect, costume, methods of building houses and of agriculture

Egger-Lienz : Dance of Death.

differ from valley to valley and often from village to village. Strong, blond giants are to be found side by side with dark-haired, slender, agile men. In a few disproportionately-built men and women lives on the race of the giants of legend.

As the peasant, so his cattle. In the valley of the Lower Inn the cattle are heavily built and piebald; in the Upper Inn Valley there is a lightly built, grey type, rich in milk, growing in grace and agility as the pasturage becomes more scanty and difficult of access. In the mountain villages and remote enclaves there still survive many individual specimens of breeds which are otherwise becoming extinct.

The inhabitant of the valley of the Upper Inn builds his house of stone, he of Lower of wood. The one keeps house and farm undivided, the other divides up the farm and even the house, so that not only may several families live under one roof, but in the four corners of a large kitchen there are sometimes four ranges, each belonging to a different person who is expected to keep within the imaginary lines which mark out his own share of the floor. The Lower Inn rings with laughter and song and no one is ashamed of an illegitimate child. The inhabitant of the Upper Inn is reserved and sparing of speech; with him, the smouldering of no less violent passions is not easily to be detected.

There are many varieties of dialect. The people of the Ötztal call "Ferner" what those of the Zillertal name "Kees" and which are called "Gletscher" —glaciers—only by the town-dwellers. The drawling and slurred vowel sounds, the clipped nasal consonants of the mountain dwellers, recall the speech of Latin races. The accent of the lowlander, in contrast, is graceful and often almost affected. In the broad valleys branching off from the main Inn Valley the inhabitants of the inner and outer valleys have little in common. In the Gschnitztal, for instance, Trins is a Romanish settlement, whereas Gschnitz at the foot of the valley is of German origin. One consequence of all this is that anyone who moves from his own parish, even if only to a neighbouring one, is regarded all his lifetime as an "immigrant".

Innsbruck ; Grave of Maximilian.

Volders.

But if one asks what, in view of its many contradictions, Tyrol really is, one is again confronted by something strange and mysterious. It is a fact that, looked at from outside—for instance from Salzburg or from Vorarlberg, Bavaria or Italy—Tyrol presents the picture of a close-knit unit. Is it the mountains which hold together the Province (which in all documents is referred to as the "Land in the Mountains" because it is entirely dominated by mountains and because from north to south the whole territory consists of mountainous country which never descends to the level of the plains)? Is it a gift conferred by the gods for good or ill fortune; is there some idea of sacred mountains behind the song which tells of the "Holy Province" of Tyrol? ...

The peculiarly pious devotion of the mountain dweller to his homeland and his liberty has done as much to create the feeling of unity as has the great history of Tyrol which people keep alive today in many customs and many forms.

THE ARTS. In Tyrol, art belongs to the soil. The supreme period of its architecture is reflected not only in venerable abbeys, stately mansions, churches and the houses of the nobility, but also in many a farm-house and its outbuildings, in wayside crucifixes, chapels and shrines.

Apart from the imposing buildings and monuments which served the interests of the aristocracy and the well-to-do citizens—the most important example of these is the Tomb of Maximilian beneath the lofty vault of the Hofkirche in Innsbruck—the simpler output of native craftsmen is often impressive and singularly moving as, for instance, that gem of art, the little rococo church in the dreamy hamlet of Gschnitz. Built in the spirit of devotion, its existence threatened on all sides—from avalanches and landslides from the mountain above, from the torrential river below in the valley—it seems amid the forces of nature to do honour to God in the Highest, man upon Earth, and to act as a gracious mediator between the two.

The artistic sense of the people is most apparent in the national costumes and

Stams ; Cistercian Monastery.

192

Imster Phantom Procession.

Rattenberg.

implements. Wood-carving is as native to Ladinian Gröden as to the Allemanian Lechtal. Represented by Michael Pacher of Bruneck (d. 1498), Joseph Koch of Lechtal (1768—1839), the Italian-Tyrolese Giovanni Segantini (1858—1899) the East Tyrolese Franz Defregger (1835—1921) and Egger-Lienz (1868—1926), Tyrol has distinguished herself honorably in plastic art.

The Tyrolese folk drama is renowned. The theatre, good and bad, false and true to life, plays a large part in the life of the Province. The old Pradler-Bauern-Theater is a joy to the people of Innsbruck, with its plays of chivalry composed of a blend of moving pathos and coarse jokes. The passion plays of Erl and Thiersee keep up the Roman Catholic tradition, while the carnivals, among which the Imster Phantom Carnival is fairly well-known, although not so much so as it deserves, have heathen origins. The customs and legends connected with these are similarly rooted in heathen superstitions, such as the magic of the "Rauhnächte" or the "Expulsion of Winter" or the "Ringing in the Grass". They tell of the "Perchte" (benevolent spirits) and the "Saligen Fräuleins" ("Happy Ladies"), the "Alm Dwarf", the "Venediger Gnome" and the "Ice Mannikin". Mountain and forest, water and air, cattle, trees and bushes—all are full of spirits. To compose and to think, to say and to sing, is all one.

Music is cultivated chiefly in the lowlands. From there came the violin maker, Jakob Stainer (d. 1621), the father of the German violin. The harp and trombone, like, of course, the zither, are played at home. In this country of mocking ballads, he earns praise who can devise humorous couplets on the spur of the moment. Ribald practical jokes and dry humour are likewise typical of the Tyrolese. The mountain dweller is apt to ponder more over the next world. Sometimes he developes into a rustic philosopher or scholar in remote districts, such as the map-maker Peter Anich and Blasius Huber from Oberperfuss.

194

and peasants were able to appear on a footing of equality with the nobility. Friedl's action conferred on Tyrol a democratic constitution, the like of which was not seen elsewhere on the Continent for many centuries.

With this Duke Friedrich ("Friedl") began Tyrol's period of greatness. The then very important North-South line —from Augsburg and Nürnberg to Venice—and the protection afforded by its mountains, made it the treasure store of the Empire. Bozen Market became famous throughout Europe. On the mines of Schwaz was founded the power of the Fuggers.

Friedrich's son, Siegmund the "Münz-reiche" ("the Rich in Coin"), was considered to be the richest prince of his day. The Münzerturm ("Mint Tower") in Hall, the castles of Sieg-mundslust near Schwaz and Siegmunds-kron near Bozen are mementos both of his name and of his jovial extravagance.

Tyrol reached its zenith during the reign of Maximilian I. The Emperor loved the Province above all else ; he formally gave it the proud des-cription "Heart and Shield of our Empire"—the Empire on which, his follower, Karl the Fifth, could boast, the sun never set.

It is not as the last of the knights of Europe that he will always be remem-bered by the people of Tyrol, but as one of themselves, a bold hunter, mountaineer and courteous gentleman. Tyrolese legend has the Emperor Max rescued from peril in the mountains on the Martinswand by an angel in the guise of a Tyrolese peasant. The cave in the sheer cliff is still shown from which he could have found no way out save for divine assistance.

By the Goldene Dachl which he built—legend attributes it to Friedl of the Empty Pocket—and by his tomb in the Hofkirche, Maximilian has ensured that for all time Innsbruck will be held in honour as his residential

Münzturm in Hall-in-Tyrol.

VILLAGE AND FARM. The Tyrolese mountains are impressive, but Switzerland has these too, still more impressive ones (with the exception of the Dolomites in South Tyrol, which cannot be compared with any other range). Tyrolese towns and villages have a character which is all their own, showing a strong community feeling. Note for example the varied and original treatment of the dormer window. Nothing is more typical and characteristic than the Tyrolese village and the Tyrolese farm.

Sometimes huddled together, sometimes loosely scattered, the farmhouses are grouped about the church whose slender tower with gothic spire or baroque dome seems to gather together the sur-rounding buildings, directing them towards the heavens. Even more closely than the living do the dead crowd about the church. Honourable

Hall-in-Tyrol.

men, all of them, as the inscriptions on the crosses of iron or wood testify, yet as in life grouped according to rank and precedence.

For the living it is a comfort to have the dead among them; for the dead, to continue to play a part in life. The sound of church bells calling to early mass starts the day; only the goatherd's horn has summoned the herds even earlier. At eleven in the morning the bell calls to dinner, and with the vesper bell the day is ended. The tolling of the bell marks out each working week, and marks out the year according to the festivals of the Church.

Public affairs centre on the church square. There official announcements concerning the parish are posted. Similar information is given out there after the service on Sundays. The cattle drink at the village well, and the men at the village inn. The women take no part in public life.

Every farm, whether it stands apart amidst its own fields, or whether it keeps good neighbourly company with others in the village, has an orchard and a small garden near the house. The garden grows vegetables and spices. Its many-hued flowers, pinks and lilies, asters and phlox, crown-imperial, mignonette, sweet-smelling herbs,

Wooden Mould.

city. The bronze Guards of Honour who, it was planned, should watch over him in the grave, belong to the many great conceptions which are perhaps most impressive in their unfulfillment.

With Maximilian, whose body actually lies buried in his native town of Wiener Neustadt, the star of Tyrol began to wane. Under Ferdinand I the Province became affected by the religious and social unrest of the Reformation, which was embodied in the person of Michel Gaismair ; at the same time, however, the Council of Trent met in the south of the Province.

It was this ruler who divided his provinces into three, and for a hundred years Tyrol had its own regents. The very first one, the Archduke Ferdinand, won the heart of the Tyrolese through his love match with Philippine Welser, of Augsburg, as well as through his encouragement of the arts and sciences, which found lasting expression in the collection of Schloss Amras, near Innsbruck.

Next it was a princess, Claudia of Medici, whose memory was enshrined in Tyrolese hearts, above all through the courageous rule of her Chancellor, Wilhelm Biener, who lived at Büchsenhausen near Innsbruck and who fell a victim to the executioner's sword in the fortress of Rattenberg. It was at this time that the Porta Claudia was set up at Scharnitz as a protection against the Swedes. Tyrol indeed escaped the Thirty Years' War, but

borage and rosemary and the coloured glass balls on sticks are the pride of the farmer's wife.

On entering the house it is easy to find one's way round. The living room and kitchen are on the ground floor, the sleeping quarters on the first story. The living room is panelled. In a darker corner away from the window stands the cosy, tiled stove, and in the window-nook the large table. A small bench runs the length of the walls, spreading out to form a comfortable chimney corner behind the stove. The cupboards are built into the walls and the tall grandfather-clock is built into the panelling. A font of holy-water is always to be found at the right hand side of the door, and a crucifix, decorated with a red and a yellow ear of maize, gives its blessing to the daily bread from the window corner overlooking

Weaving Pattern, XVII Century.

the table. Potted plants fill the tiny window; alone the electric light with its wiring disturbs the picture.

In the kitchen the covered range has almost completely banished the open fire, but the chimney-place is still often vaulted. It is called the "heaven", although covered with oily, shining soot and black as hell. But this heaven does not "hang full of violins", but full of sides of smoked bacon and sausages. In the dairy the wooden cream dishes have given place to the centrifugal separator and metal utensils. But the butter-tub, in which the butter is made by churning or pounding, still remains.

Except on feast days the peasants' diet is sparingly supplied with meat but rich in fat. *Knödel* (dumplings), small cakes, dough-nuts, stewed fruit and *Schmarrn* (a sort of broken-up pancake), thick soup and potatoes make up the simple, healthy fare. All eat from one dish. Grace is said before and after meals. Occasionally there will be butter and bacon to eat with the black bread which the true peasant bakes himself.

Much more could be told of the peasantry of Tyrol, of cowsheds, haylofts and threshing floors, of the ricks of hay and corn, of forestry and hunting, of mountain pastures, cow pastures and hay-fields, of sheep-pens and shearing, of fences, gates and stiles. How many townfolk know that a proper fence, like a peasant house built in the old manner, needs no nails and no scrap of iron? What do they know of the customs at weddings and baptisms?

For the farmer, his "*loden*" cape of coarse, woollen cloth is sufficient even when the weather is coldest. He must be able to move his arms freely, and at work in the open he does not feel the cold. In the house he goes about in shirt-sleeves. When he is abroad he carries an enormous gamp to protect him from the rain.

The farmer's wife wears long dresses almost suggesting a nun's habit, covered on weekdays by a blue working apron. On Sundays she dons her special finery—

the terrible danger with which it threatened them bit deeply into the minds of the people ; in such old customs as the "Schwedenritt" the memory of this lives on.

With the extinction of the Tyrolese branch of the ruling house, Tyrol lost its political eminence in 1665.

At the turn of the seventeenth and eighteenth centuries, after nearly a hundred and fifty years of peace, it became one of the battlefields of the War of the Spanish Succession. At first Prince Eugene was successful in the south of the country, but later it was occupied by the Bavarians. The Tyrolese rising, the merciless battle at the Pontlatz Bridge in the depths of the Upper Inn Valley, and the Battle of Lueg below the Brenner Pass, put an end to the "Bavarian Rowdies" and showed for the first time the almost unconquerable strength of a mountain people when it allies itself with the powerful natural defences of its native soil.

Peace returned to the Province and once again a great princess left her mark on the capital. Maria Theresia had come to Innsbruck to celebrate the marriage of her son Leopold ; a triumphal arch was to commemorate the event. Five weeks later the beloved husband of the Empress died in the Hofburg at Innsbruck. Thus it came about that, to remind one of the inconstancy of fate, the arch shows on the side through which the bridal pair entered the city, scenes of joy and of life. On the other, which faces the town, are scenes of mourning illustrating the transitory nature of human fortune. To this day it is called the Arch of Triumph. The triumph of life over death, or of death over life ?

The Napoleonic Wars brought to Tyrol its heroic epoch which culminated in the year 1809. Its tragedy was that Tyrol was important enough to be overrun, but not of sufficient importance

Andreas Hofer.

a shot-silk apron, and a kerchief over the short laced bodice; from the small, hard hat with gold braid and tassels hang long satin or velvet ribbons down her back; in her hair is a silver pin and she wears an old fashioned necklace of garnets. In winter-time she wears in addition a black shawl with long fringes. The children are movingly solemn duplications of their elders.

OF MOUNTAINS, TREES, MOUNTAIN PASTURES AND ANIMALS. Eagle and ibex, chamois and marmot, black-cock and capercailzie are all symbolic of the mountains, as are also almrausch and edelweiss, gentian and auricula, nigritella and artemesia. But as is often the case with symbols, the more frequently they are employed in old coats-of-arms and modern posters, praised in word and song, displayed stuffed, pressed and dried in museums, or grown and cultivated in gardens, the more legendary they become.

Many of them have long ceased to be representative. The eagle and the ibex have been forced by the greed of man to flee to sheltering heights, the edelweiss and artemesia to withdraw to inaccessible crags. Other alpine fauna are rarely seen by the tourist, since they avoid the times and places of his choice. Equally invisible are the mountain flowers which cannot flee from man.

Schwaz.

When the townsman takes his holiday, they have often ceased to blossom, or have fallen to the sweep of the scythe. In July and August the mountain is dead, and May and June, when its flowers blossom, is not the time for most tourists. So it should be for those who are only looking for mountain peaks, precipices and ice-fields and to whom flowers are no more than trophies! But anyone who really loves flowers, and is not simply out to collect rare specimens should be less ambitious, and should ascend the gently rounded hills which are despised by the alpinist and labelled cow mountains, cow-pastures, high hillocks or sheep mountains.

Starting out from the valley, he will soon reach terraces on which lie villages and isolated farms. Above these, yet before the hardly penetrable undergrowth of young trees is reached, begins the belt of larch wood, or larch meadows. These trees, the noblest and jolliest of all those whose needles turn yellow and carpet the earth in autumn, and which put forth indescribably delicate and tender shoots in May, love light and air. They grow in broad coverts, often intermingled with birches, and casting delicate shadows. Sometimes it seems as though it was not the wind which moves their branches, but that it is these softly waving branches themselves which set gentle currents

Kufstein.

of air in motion when one reverently enters their lofty precincts. Even the ground at their feet is soft and gaily be-decked. In May the gentians blossom here, in June the orchids of countless knightly orders; the columbine nods and the lilies-of-the-valley spread perfume, the field tragopogon turns its yellow wheel, the dark-blue devil's claw threatens.

How delightful to wander through this park! Behind the intertwined fence, to which the larches have contributed their hard, reddish wood—a silky silver-grey in winter, which withstands the weather and does not rot—begins the steep, thick-set mountain forest and the tiring climb. One hears the ringing blows of the axe, as the felled trees crash down

Kitzbühel.

to be able to effect a decision. Tragedy has accompanied the country up to this very day. Despite the courage of its people it was for the first time split into three parts. This only lent more importance to the heroic stand of the small mountain population against the foreign emperor as an example of a national uprising which was soon to be reflected on a much greater scale. For this reason also the names of Andreas Hofer, Haspinger and Speckbacher, the second battle at Pontlatz Bridge, and the three battles of Berg Isel have become history. The last words of the "Sand Innkeeper" of Passeier before his execution "at Mantua, in chains" rang out like the tolling of a bell to awaken the slumbering consciences of his contemporaries,—"Adieu, thou despicable world". Through his tragic fate and self-sought heroism, Andreas Hofer has become a symbol of the unity and freedom of the Province.

For the same reason the heroic defence of the southern frontier of the Province in the first World War by the "Standschützen" (Tyrolese peasant riflemen) which is for ever linked to the name of Innerkofler, will never be forgotten, all the more so because they were tragically unable to save South Tyrol from its fate. But even the attempt made from Tyrol during March 1938 to offer a last resistance to the threatened occupation of Austria which was condemned to failure will be preserved in the living history of Tyrol as often as the events of 1934 to 1938 are recalled. Over the struggle for South Tyrol, for its right to self-determination and to its national existence since 1918, it is best to be silent here. But whoever has scanned the history of Tyrol, however casually, will not be surprised that that lives on in the hearts of its people which history and culture have created in the course of centuries, and which frontiers have now divided.

Carol Singers.

into the runways which go down from mountain to valley. Here is the realm of the huntsman—and the poacher's kingdom.

On the fringe of the tree-clad zone, where the forest begins to dissolve, there are new features. The trees are not at all stunted—indeed, they were more so in the crowded spaces of the wood. Here each one stands alone, perfected in strength, beauty and individuality.

The stone pine, the mightiest of native conifers, first makes its appearance at this height. Its growth is slow and deliberate. After fifty years it is no taller than a man, and the giants have lived through the Napoleonic Wars and even the Peasant Revolts. Unlike the other conifers, every stone pine is an independent individual, broadly spreading or rising to a slender top, sometimes regular, sometimes fantastic in shape. Its needles are double the length of those of the pine tree, of softest blue-green, sometimes black-green, in contrast to the blue-grey of the pine. The cones of the stone pine are the largest of any. If one breaks a twig, a pleasant-scented resin oozes out.

As soft and delicate as is the impression conveyed by the larch, so is that given by the pine dark and sturdy. No fields lie below it, only rocks, the leaves of christmas roses and juniper.

The last of the firs and larches which have thrust their way up into the higher altitudes are of a different type. The larch has become bearded, fissured and gigantic, retaining few of its more delicate charms. The great weight of snow has pressed the branches of the mountain fir close to the trunk and crushed them downwards towards the ground. In winter wild creatures seek refuge from the elements in the warm tents provided by the down-bent branches. What appears in the distance to be the well-formed crown of a single fir-tree is revealed on nearer approach to be the tops of a whole family of trees. Closely grouped around the parent tree, children and children's children have come to maturity in its shadow. They afford mutual protection and shelter and have become to such an extent one single tree-family that when the progenitor in their midst begins to decay, its descendants close the gap until the ancestral tree has recovered itself as the rejuvenated and immortal tree of the species. Only the fir-trees—and of these, only the mountain firs—behave in this way. Larches and pines have no family ties. The lightning which fells one of them, the storm which uproots it, affects that one tree alone.

Anyone who imagines that he is leaving the abundance of the valley for the poverty of the mountain will be surprised when he finds luxuriant virgin forest. But he will lose his astonishment when he discovers that he is treading under foot black, peaty earth more fertile than can be found in any garden. Only where the inimical wind and snow ravage the mountain passes does the realm of the last giants end. Only whatever can live through the winter beneath the snows, and nothing else, can survive here to flourish luxuriantly during the brief summer. Here is the lovely world of alpine flora. One's foot sinks deep into rich carpets. The crocus

Baroque House in Innsbruck.

202

Innsbruck, Maria Theresienstraße

forms white or lilac islands and streams in the moist ground. The bloom of the gentian reflects a deeper and softer blue than that of the southern seas. Beneath the blue sky rises the curve of the mountain slope, dotted with yellow auriculas and besprinkled with the lighter blossoms of the anemone.

Clumps of saxifrage scent the air; creeping flax covers the stones; dusky red primulas edge the dark clefts in the rocks. Where the snows melt, leaving the ground bare of other vegetation, nod the delicately fringed bells of the soldanellas. Here on this hill the pastel shades of the bluish globularia mingle with those of the white primula and pale yellow auricula. In the depression where the little stream tinkles and twists, heavy yellow buttercups and marsh-mallows raise their shining heads out of the vivid blue of forget-me-nots. On the Sonnberg grow nigritellas, scented and chocolate-coloured. Many other herbs and flowers are to be found here whose names amidst this riot of colour slip the memory of the wanderer, though he recognizes and constantly re-discovers them.

Well may one be bewildered by the magic of contrast—the burning sun alternating with the cool shadows cast by the clouds by the tonic air, or by the snow caps in the background against which a cow shed, a tree, a cluster of alpine roses or a carpet of flowers stands out clearly.

Even in March, when the remaining snow still sparkles with great crystals like glowing diamonds, the sun rises victorious, while from the roofs of the cattle sheds the melting snow and ice drip to the ground and the stored-up hay gives forth a summer fragrance as it awaits transport by sledge to the valley, these regions remain a realm of brilliant colouring, of soft footpaths where movement calls for no effort.

Everything above the level of these alpine pastures is exposed to the fury of the elements. Only a few sheltered spots remain islands of life. Sheep graze as far up as these. These heights mark the limit of all forms of life. Yet is there not life in the rock which stretches itself and in the glacier which cuts and scours it, crushing and moulding it afresh? Here summer and winter have not yet been divorced. Is that the roaring of a torrent, or of a distant wind? The rain turns to snow and

Street in Innsbruck.

hail. Whether it is the waters of a lake, or ice which fills a hollow in the rocks, whether it is water or an avalanche which crashes downwards in a mist of spray, it is fundamentally the same thing; the transient-permanent and the permanent-transient, the fixed, the fluid and the fleeting are merged together in struggle and in play.

A WORD TO THE VISITOR. The height of summer or the depth of winter are not necessarily to be recommended as the best seasons to visit Tyrol, although—or rather because—these are the most popular tourists' seasons, when all the world travels. If you make a comparison between the seasons of the year and the hours of the day, you will appreciate this. In March, the year's morning, the countryside reveals itself full of promise, and new life is stirring on every hand. June is the noon of the year, heavy with blossoms. In the twilight of September the ripe fruit falls with the fading leaves as the new buds are forming. Peace descends with the last evening hour when the countryside, replete, goes to rest through the Christmas midnight of the year. Let then the connoisseur of delights choose from these four seasons marked out by the clock of the year the one best suited to his personal tastes and needs.

The tourist can be confidently recommended to establish his first centre in the Innsbruck area. This must not necessarily be in the town itself. Igls to the south of it and the Hungerburg to the north, the unspoiled mediaeval town of Hall with its saline springs and deposits, and Seefeld, on the plateau of the watershed between the Inn and the Isar, all belong in this sense to Innsbruck, combining the charms of a town with those of the country. After all, why should one not spend a rainy day of the holidays in museum or café, enjoy a theatre or concert in the greater freedom which goes with a holiday abroad than one can feel at the end of a humdrum working day?

All around Innsbruck lie quiet, shady forests which offer such a wide variety of walks for a whole day, half-a-day or even for an hour as could not be exhausted in a year. Here the Upper and Lower Inn Valleys run together, the valleys of the Wipp and the Stubai joining them from the South. The Sellrain also flows from the West into the Innsbruck basin. In all these valleys terraces have formed from 600 to 900 feet up called the "Mittelgebirge" which are most massive at Innsbruck where they are broader than the valley itself.

They are well populated and well developed. They lie in the fertile middle belt. The views they afford looking downwards into the valley, or of more distant prospects, are just as attractive as the views you will see on gazing upwards into the mountains or at your immediate surroundings.

Within half-an-hour the cabin of the cable-railway swings one up from a height of over 1700 feet to well over 7000 feet, to the Hafelekar, whence one gets a fine view of the mountains of the wild Karwendel range. But one cannot see as far as the heart of the Karwendel, to the mysterious and death-haunted Ahornboden. In one hour the cable railway lands the visitor amid the extensive pine-woods on the Patscherkofel, opposite the Stubaier Ferner (glacier). In half a day one can reach the Stubai Alps and the glaciers of the Ötztal and Zillertal. Three hours by road or rail take one over the Brenner, in the south, to Bozen and Meran. It is from this neighbouring other-world that the Föhn, the heady south wind, streams into the Province of Tyrol. Its burning breath does the maizecobs to a turn even in autumn. The maize stocks are left standing in the harvested fields of the Innsbruck valley until late in the year, while the reddish gold and brown cobs lend the splendours of their colouring to the gable walls beneath the protecting eaves of the peasants' homes.

The immediate surroundings of Innsbruck exhausted, a short train journey of one to three hours will present the traveller with new and attractive beauty-centres: the dark Achen Lake, set amidst steep and gloomily-romantic cliffs, the little fortress of Kufstein with its giant organ whose thunderous pipes are audible from afar and its imposing background of the many-peaked Kaisergebirge, the smiling and sunny surroundings of Kitzbühel with its mountain pastures and ski-ing areas. Or one may go further up the Inn Valley to the glacier world of the Urgebirge Valleys as far as the Paznauntal which ends so impressively below the Trisanna Bridge and Wiesberg Castle, to the sun-bathed townships of Imst and Landeck. Still further on lies the world-famous Arlberg and the Fernpass with its lakes. There is distant Ausserfern with the Plansee and the bizarre chalk mountains of the Lechtal and the Zugspitz mountain with its rack-and-pinion railway.

HOSPIT-ABLE LAND

SALZBURG

OF FESTIV-AL

WORD-PALETTE
SALZBURG

A landscape gay at the birth of the world·
Towering mountains· tree-shaded shores and
wild-foaming Ache·
Golden the sun-dust 'neath steep-arching rainbow·
A lovely world·breathing happiness'
Monks in monastic cloisters· hand carved altars·
Veiled in drifting mists· wayside Madonnas·
Princely gestures· rich vestments and ritual· archipiscopal palace·
The music of redemption· organ concerts· many-voiced choirs·
Mozart's "Krönungsmesse" in festive Abbey·
Attentive horses frozen to stone· melodious mystery·
Foreign visitors· devout or non-believers·
"Everyman"· The summons from turret and tower·
Faust's city on the heights·
Seduction of the proud spirit from earthly seraglio·
Andantino-Rondo allegro-Mirabell
Johannes Wolfgangus Theophilus
Amadeus Mozart

In former times a legendary lake is said to have covered the northern part of the Salzburg Province which is also called Flachgau. It took its origin in the neighbourhood of the Lueg Pass, following the bed of the Salzach, still narrow, until it broadened out in the high ground between Hallein and Anif. As it increased in size and strength it covered the whole district; Waller- and Mattsee were swallowed by it and even the course of the Salzach was no longer recognisable.

But this whole picture has been developed from what exists today. The actual process was the reverse. Neither river nor lake were swallowed up by that ancient sea at a time when neither Anif nor Hallein existed. It is nearer the truth to say that all this slowly emerged out of the vast expanse of water as the flood slowly receded. It was only then that the lakes of today emerged as evidence of the former vastness of these still unusually deep and restless lakes; only then did the Salzach carve out its bed, towns and villages springing up along its banks. But in that forgotten Chalk Age, when this almost boundless lake covered the land, the waters were even then broken by a few islands—the Salzburg Stadtberge. They are older than the surrounding plain, more established and calmer. They heard the sound of the receding waters, the farewell croaking of frogs and the splash of gigantic prehistoric monsters wading the fords. On their slopes many of these beasts must have sat humped together in hopeless melancholy. Month for month the darkening moon

Salzburg, 15th Century, Woodcut.

sank behind them, the all-knowing vultures encircled them. On their slopes the first birds laughed, and in their impenetrable forests the little songsters built their nests.

The charming legend of Franz Solanos tells how this holy man was accorded a rare favour on his deathbed: clouds of birds gathered at his window, flew about his weary head, sat confidingly on the edge of the bed and perched by thousands on the branches around his cell to lend beauty to his last hours with their gladsome song; blackbirds were there, chaffinches, robins, larks, thrushes and yellow-hammers. There was even, the legend tells, a canary to blend its song of triumph with the contrasting notes of an albino blackbird which warbled ecstatically from so far away that it was invisible. The soul of the holy man was raised ever higher amid the heavenly concert until it was finally wafted into eternity.

The end of the prehistoric ages before man appeared on the earth is supposed to have been similarly accompanied by the song of birds. Well may they have chorused, not their pity or grief, but their anticipation as the earth emerged from the receding waters with its promise of nesting places and abundant food.

Salzburg must have been born to the accompaniment of some sweet and impressive melody, a melody that the Province embodies today.

Not all the Province of Salzburg arose out of the waters. Going south one meets more

212

Irrsdorf, Gothic Doors.

View from the Mirabell Garden

and more prehistoric volcanic rocks and lava formations, slate flattened by pressure during millions of years, granite formed of sandstone ground up and re-formed by intense heat, porphyry and mica. The Province is not only old in so far as its history is concerned. Long before history began, what is now Salzburg was steeped in ancient lore—a lore which indefinably conveys its message to man, slowing down the steps of those who tread its soil and enriching their minds.

Seen as a whole, the contours of Salzburg Province may be compared to one of those mid-summer cloud edifices, the cumuli, which, bathed in the rosy light of evening, pile curve upon curve in baroque extravagance, rising to a slender spire. At this narrow extremity, close to Bavaria, lies the formerly famous but nowadays little known Benedictine monastery of Michlbeuern with its romanesque church and the statue of the venerable Meinrad Guggenbichler, whose carved church doors with the moving figures of Mary and Elisabeth in Irrsdorf, to the south-east, are all too little prized.

This northern part of Salzburg, characterised by pleasant hills, the lakes of Mattsee and Wallersee lying amidst green meadows and sub-alpine vegetation which often merges into moors with their reeds and heather, is crowned by the chief city of the Province.

When first approaching the city from the station, the visitor has no inkling of Salzburg's venerable beauty. The broad street is flanked on the left by the embankment of the main line to Bavaria, a pebbled walk beneath chestnut trees, placards, a kiosk. Later come grocery stores, inns, paper shops, hotels and souvenir shops, as in many another provincial town. The unusual, the characteristic note of Salzburg is struck quite suddenly by the Mirabell Palace, in the Rainerstrasse. Now rises curtain after curtain to disclose the Salzburg of legend and romance. The Dreifaltigkeitsgasse leads past the Seminary to the first church of Fischer von Erlach. Thence beneath the Sautter Archway one reaches the Linzerstrasse which from time immemorial has borne the traffic through Salzburg. The Romans themselves passed along this delightful highway, coming from the direction of Radstadt to cross the Tauern Mountains.

Tower after tower crowned by the glittering symbol of Christianity pierces the blue morning sky above the ancient heart of the city on the left bank, the church spires seeming almost to reach

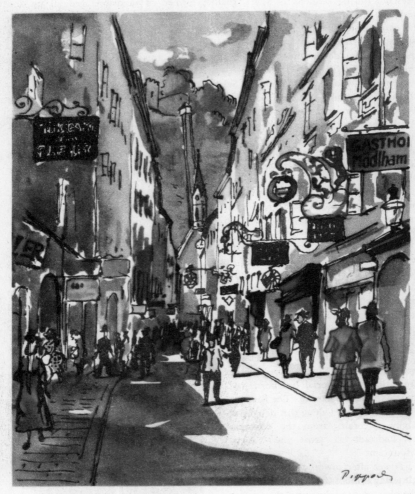

Salzburg; Getreidegasse

About the year 700 A.D., St. Rupertus built a church in honour of the Apostle Paul and a monastery for the monks of the Benedictine order on the sunken and overgrown foundations of Juventum.

Even under Charlemagne the bishops of Salzburg, Virgil and Arno, showed particular devotion to Christian church music. The surroundings of St. Peter soon rang with the real Gregorian choral chants.

Neidhart von Reuenthal and Tannhäuser are the predecessors of the "Monk of Salzburg", who wrote a great many religious as well as secular compositions

in the second half of the fourteenth century at the court of a quarrelsome archbishop. Within the Bishopric, Leonhard von Keutschach was the first of that line of sharp-profiled, religious princes, concerning whom there has been much conflict of opinion who during the changing periods of gothic, renaissance and baroque styles, placed on the face of Salzburg the stamp and sign of their own self-willed and often secular personalities. Castles are the stone evidence of their activities and their might, above all the unconquered fortress of Hohensalzburg. The turnip in the coat of arms of the bishops calls to mind the architect of Keutschach, as does the "Hornwerk", a musical

up as far as the fortress which rises sheer and stately high above all buildings of the city and the green of its own woods.

The extensive fortifications above house no dusty romances. There are apparently no ghosts in clanking armour with fluttering pennons or mist-enshrouded châtelaines to haunt them. Sober and impressive magnificence is the keynote of this unconquered bulwark of the Bishops of Salzburg.

No prince ever ruled here as heir of an inherited kingdom, no heroic knight subdued the surrounding lands by his strong arm. The law and the customs of a court muffled the blast of trumpets. No single family, but a long series of unrelated regents of a spiritual treasure peopled these finely-proportioned rooms. On the throne sat the lord of the Province who was at the same time guardian of his subjects' souls—a strange picture of duality.

The roofs of ancient Hohensalzburg were overshadowed by the call for solemn decisions, by the complexities, the temptations and the responsibilities of rule.

A traveller, one who loved the countryside, thus describes his first glimpse of the City of the Bishops in their stronghold; "Arrived at the terminal station of the lift which takes one from the city to the fortress,

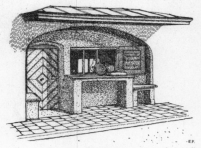

Old Bakery.

217

Elli Rolf

curiosity which still exists. This instrument is a curious musical apparatus consisting of 200 organ pipes—the so-called "Bull of Salzburg".

At the beginning of the sixteenth century the aged musician Paulus Hofhaimer after 29 years spent in the service of the Emperor Maximilian, was appointed Cathedral Organist in Salzburg. Theophilus Paracelsus named him in the same breath as Albrecht Dürer, and one of his contemporaries said of his organ-playing ;—"Master Paulus is so vastly versatile that one can listen to him for years. One does not so much wonder from what source the ocean feeds all the rivers as from where this man derives all his themes".

The great organist tradition of Salzburg was carried on in 1520 through the appointment of the master of

Rudolf von Alt : Residenzplatz.

song, Heinrich Finck, as Composer to the Cathedral, while Petschin and Glanner, talented pupils of Hofhaimer, developed the art of part singing and classical melodies as well as that of organplaying.

Wolf Dietrich von Raitenau, Prince and Archbishop of Salzburg, can only be understood in the light of the renaissance period. The words of Hamlet concerning his father may well apply to him : "He was a man, take him for all in all, I shall not look upon his like again", and for the Salzburg which was created by him there is the speech of Grillparzer : "See, how she sumptuous lies, adorned with towers and noble lines, by art made fair what God so richly decked".

A glance at those times and at Europe helps to give the picture of the

we left the car and climbed up into the fortress by means of a long flight of steps on the outer wall. The ticket-girl in the moss-covered courtyard assured us, with a patient glance at those who were waiting, that the next tour of inspection would soon begin. Inevitably the vague first remarks which our cicerone drawled out mechanically were concerned with a torture chamber, with terrible racks on which the sinners were stretched until they were so elongated and thin that the sun seemed to shine redly clear through them. I asked myself whether the tiresome imagination of later generations has not been responsible for many an instrument of torture which is shown to us as an authentic reason for our flesh to creep. The room which was shown us here as a torture chamber was anyway not used for the ignoble purpose of tormenting human beings. We were shown "sitting-prisons" which might equally well have been window nooks, and the sightseers were then led past a wonderful stove for which a million dollars is said to have been refused. Via many stairways we reached the beat of the

219

Salzburg, Horse Trough.

castle guards, which seemed to have no end, and finally the great organ which once bellowed out over the city like a bull if an enemy was sighted in the distance. At last we climbed the famous observation tower.

"Outside the confined space of the fortification, we suddenly felt free as the birds as we came out upon the topmost pinnacle, which is higher even than the bastion itself. Our guide described the surrounding beauties in homely terms. 'Over there', he said, 'you may see the Gaisberg, that green hump there, and beside it the rocky Tennengebirge, the Göll and behind them the Übergossene Alm'.

"I quickly turned away in order, solitary as one can be in a crowd, to have the entrancing panorama to myself.

"Clearly outlined, as in a vision, I saw how the Alps extend almost up to the city boundaries, but not further to the north. The magnificent eagle-like ridges of the Untersberg and the Stauffen are the last efforts of the world of rocks to extend its domains. The mountains shut the lovely city into a spacious acute angle, but so respectfully that they do not actually touch it.

"The south-east is marked out by the luscious green of conifers and grass-lands which spread over the guardian Gaisberg. To the South, a little apart from the latter, arise the bare cliffs of the Tennengebirge; further to the West lies the marble mountain of the Untersberg. In the far West, almost on a level with the city, are outlined the sharp ridges of the Stauffen. The acute angle formed by the mountains is occupied by a vividly green and very level plain which seems to have thrust itself through the gap to the South, the Lueg Pass, where the waters of the Salzach have forced their way through the rocky wall.

"From this narrow gorge of the Lueg Pass debouches not only the wide Salzburg plain, but also the silvery Salzach, which winds its way swiftly through man of Raitenau something of its right place in history. By land and by sea the Turks were seeking to plant the green banner of the Prophet in the West. Spain, the Pope and the Doges' Republic of Venice had fitted out a great fleet of galleys which were assembled in the harbour of Messina for the fight against the overwhelming traditional enemy. Austria was making an attempt to shield the open frontiers of the Continent from the forward-thrusting East during years of fighting, while in Europe itself the religious wars had broken out. In France the Huguenot War was raging, while Scotland watched its queen, Mary Stuart, die under the headsman's axe. Don Carlos died mysteriously in Spain and in Germany the subjects were expected to accept the religion of their ruler together with his bread. Philip II of Spain and Queen Elizabeth had started new epochs in their kingdoms, while Italy had found its way to baroque style and culture after the glorious period of the Renaissance.

In the Roman-German Empire the brilliant period of Karl V, whose arrival was welcomed by Albrecht Dürer and whom Titian painted before his death, was past. Emperor Rudolf II had retreated to his gloomy castle at Prague in order to forget the cares of the Empire in astrological meditations. Groups of persons exiled on account of their faith wandered from country to country, while the conflicts which were to lead to the murderous Thirty Years' War were coming to a head.

In these troublous times, in 1587, the twenty-eight-year-old Wolf Dietrich was placed on the Archbishop's Throne of Salzburg, chosen by the prelates of the Cathedral. His ambitious dreams given practical shape by travelling as a cavalier through Italy, France and Spain, there came as a flash the idea of attaining sovereign power with a

Fauststadt.

bushes to the cluster of Salzburg islands. The hill which is crowned by Hohensalzburg forms a slight hollow in the protective shelter of which the old city, guarded from above, to the rear and on its flanks by the mountain, and in front by the river, opens its eyes to the morning sun. The rejoicing peals of the bells of two dozen churches sound like the wakening cry of a happy and beloved child.

"To the North and the North-West the long plain so expands that everything approaching the city in olden times was visible days ahead. At midday the sun shoots burning arrows into this open countryside. There lies Bavaria with —far away—Passau, city of bishops. From here the northern, Germanic world reaches out to meet these territories so closely linked with the South. Here the skies above Salzburg arch dominatingly over the surrounding heights.

Leopoldskron Castle.

"The picture would be incomplete if one failed to mention the many spots where the green of the meadows, moors and hills is pierced by rocky, barren stone. Constantly the soft blanket of earth is broken by a chalky dolomite hump, a rocky ridge of the same ancient grey as the massive Hohensalzburg, which rises sharply or in milder contours from the soil. The Gaisberg also displays this almost yellowed grey tone, particularly in places where the new motor highway cuts into it, carrying a suggestion of the skin of a snake, or of the sun-bleached baroque façades which are such a feature of Salzburg. But one would seek in vain for a comparison for the proud, starkly outlined peaks of bare rock, which here and there jut out from the crest of the Untersberg.

"Turning towards the south-east, one cannot fail to be reminded of the sandstone of the Vienna Basin, the so-called Mediterranean Terraces of tertiary rock on which, as Stifter says, "the fiery stream of wine lies slumbering". The Plainer Hills are of a similar rock-formation, rising above the later morraines and the moors of the Salzburg plain. According to dependable reports, there was once a vineyard here which became the basis of the cellars of the good monks of St. Peter's in the valley below."

Our traveller, aroused at last from solitary contemplation, found himself alone on the tower of Hohensalzburg. His cheeks changed colour, for the air had undergone as great a change as the walls of the fortress, and the sun suddenly lost its power. To the West lay a leaden pall which within seconds dissolved in rain, sweeping in sheets over the blotted-out plain. The long grass visibly and gratefully revived beneath it, and from the moors rose clouds of mist. But before the ground was really damp, the sun was victorious, building its own triumphal arch across the heavens. Not enough with one, two

*miraculous chance of its realisation :
Salzburg should become the Rome of
the North.*

*During his 24 years of government
this religiously worldly Archbishop
changed the Salzburg of the Middle
Ages, the narrow and picturesquely
winding streets of which offered
dangerous hiding places for disease
and plague, into a proud city of
magnificent open squares. The Princely
Residence, the Chapter-House, the
Royal Stables, the Cloister Walk and*

*the renais-
sance Chapel
of St. Seba-
stian, the
pleasure pa-
lace of Al-
tenau-Mira-
bell, and the
re-planning of
the Cathedral
Square are
all stages of
his great building activities.*

*Music played its own part in the
splendid court ceremonies, the Salzburger Hofkapelle being founded in 1591.
The composing of religious music for
the Cathedral and the compositions for
festive concerts attracted German as
well as Italian composers.*

*That which Wolf Dietrich was unable
to complete was continued by Marcus
Sitticus. The foundations of the new
Cathedral were laid according to the plans
of Solari. The pleasure castle of Hellbrunn was built and the stone theatre*

*in the ex-
tensive game
preserves. At
the same time
that the
" Defenestra-
tion" of the
Imperial
Envoy from
a window in
Prague, 1618,*

Hellbrunn.

great vivid rainbows were painted against the
paling violet of the skies, perfect in form
and of impressive grandeur. The spot where
they rose out of the soil was clearly visible.
On the square before the Cathedral a seraphic
ray of multicoloured fire shot up, curving
joyously into the heavens, to descend to earth
at the extreme edge of the plain where it joins
the mountains. Below this rainbow again,
starting from the roof of the Bürger hospital,
the second arch bent in proud submission.

These two open gateways to the West rose
sharply defined over the landscape. Little birds
formed a living garland about the multicoloured
double doors, fluttering, wind-swept, over the
nectar-soaked plain, wheeling, returning, and
vanishing noiselessly in the skies.

A description of the sights of the city alone
would fill a book, many volumes or a whole
library. The story could start in the cloisters
of the first Salzburg Christians in Petersfried-
hof, going on through the period of the rule of

223

Werfen Castle.

the bishops, the peasant revolts and days of baroque glory to the rapid change in history after the last of the archbishops, Prince Colloredo, had fled "abroad" (meaning Vienna), to abdicate there. The Duke of Toscana succeeded to the Province, but he soon exchanged it for the rulership of Würzburg, Salzburg thereby becoming Austrian territory until, soon afterwards, it was given to Bavaria by Napoleon. Four years afterwards it was "repatriated" at the cost of money, or rather of land, namely the left bank of the Salzach, remaining from this time onwards a Crown land of the Monarchy and finally becoming the modern Austrian province.

All this and much more the swift green Salzach saw, this river which rises in the western corner of the Province, high above on the Salzachgeier and traverses the land like the veins of a transparent leaf. Following the course of the Salzach upwards from Salzburg, one soon reaches the Lueg Pass, and on emerging on the other side of the tunnel one usually finds entirely different weather. The cloudy sky which one has left behind is here clear. Glorious mountain air comes down from the Hochkönig which, with its glacier, the "Übergossene Alm" (the "Drowned Field") is some nine thousand feet high. To make the ski descent from Hochkönig to Werfen, a run of over 2400 yards, is a rare experience for sportsmen. On the opposite side the Tennen-

proved the starting point of the Thirty Years' War, the open-air stage of the Hellbrunn Steintheater, one of the oldest of the German out-of-door theatres, was producing an opera called "Andromeda". "Il Orfeo" and other plays followed, bearing witness to the Archbishop's love of art. The latter soon afterwards erected a baroque stage in the Italian style in his official residence.

In 1628 the Cathedral was completed by Paris Lodron. The sumptuous interior, with its 12 balconies and several organs concealed under the great dome, made it possible for Orazio Benevoli, composer of the Cathedral Dedication Mass, to make use of the many-choired, many-voiced style of the Venetian-Roman school with unimaginable effect. That unforgettable "Dedication Mass" has gone down in the history of great music, employing as it did 16 vocal and 34 instrumental voices with the assistance of 3 organs, the singing voices being divided up into no less than 8 different choirs which were posted on 12 different balconies. It was at this period that the Salzburg cathedral and church concerts, which were to grow into an honourable tradition, made their promising start.

So was born and developed that unique atmosphere of Salzburg musical and theatrical culture which was built up by Benevoli, Bernardi, Megerle and Hofer, Muffat and Biber, Eberlin and Caldara up to the pre-Mozart period of Leopold Mozart, father of Wolfgang Amadeus, Cajetan Adlgasser and Michael Haydn, brother of Josef Haydn.

On January 27th, 1756, a son was born to the Archbishop's Concert Director, Leopold Mozart, who was baptised under the name of Johannes Chrysostomus Wolfgangus Theophilus Amadeus. This child was destined to become Salzburg's greatest son.

"Perchtenlauf" in St. Johann im Pongau.

gebirge rises starkly with its gigantic caves of ice; the gloom, the echoes and the changing light of the latter have the fascination of the underworld. The castle high above Werfen, one of the few in these chivalric-clerical surroundings, has never been taken by storm and is therefore well preserved, although it was once almost gutted by fire.

The course of the Salzach now takes a sharp turn to the left, bringing it close to the vast bulk of the Hohen Tauern. Within this curve lies the entrance to a charming freak of nature, the Liechtensteinklamm. The Arlbach here cuts its way violently through the Radstadt chalk. The gorge resulting, the Liechtensteinklamm, is extremely narrow. Still today the inexorable water cuts into the proud and deeply wounded rock, sawing it in twain. One follows the vigorous water-saw on a slippery plank-walk, along the cleft in the path, deafened and often drenched in fine spray. From time to time one is startled

The Wolfgangsee.

by a mysterious roaring from the depths of the mountain. Soon one finds oneself within this mountain, remote from the sun even though it be at its zenith, trapped in a damp gorge, surrounded by high walls but sure of one's way on the narrow path which has been carved out of the stone. The water foams angrily through narrow passes, tearing at the rocks, wearing away the stones, swirling and growling through the hollows it has worn in the walls, leaping, tossing, screaming, as though a terrible rebellion had broken out in the usually placid element.

The next lateral valley is watered by the Gastein Ache, the healing and magical waters of which are well-known. The two Gasteins, Hof- and Badgastein, are world famous. The reputation of these health resorts has been connected for centuries with the names of illustrious visitors. These two spas which formerly slept in winter now attract crowds of visitors through their ski-lifts. They seek health in the neighbouring mountains, which vary from giants which climb to glacial heights to more gentle hills. Nearby lies the Sonnblick with a meteorogical station lying at a height of 10,000 feet above sea level. A further lateral valley serpentines in the bold curves of a car road up the gigantic bulk of the Grossglockner, providing enchanting glimpses of rushing mountain streams glittering far below and of white, foaming waterfalls which sway in the wind like the beards of ancients. Over all this, a vast sea of cloud.

This giant world of the alps rules the emotions of man with almost painful majesty, commanding his ear, absorbing his glances, and forcing him to speak almost in whispers. One can imagine this vast mass of rock with its thin covering of arid grasses groaning under the indignity which the splendid road has imposed upon it. One can almost feel the mountain rising and falling as it breathes deeply, seeking to hurl the crawling, twisting car into the depths which make one giddy as one looks down.

In the far distance light and shade change as in a Rembrandt picture. Amidst this stupendous landscape, one experiences a feeling of liberation and lives through a whole gamut of emotions, passing from sheer amazement to a sense of com-

226

prehension of all things in which time no longer plays a part. The motor road climbs to a height of almost 7800 feet, ending at the foot of the ascent to the highest peak (12,000 feet).

The Glocknerstrasse takes its start in the pretty little valley town of Bruck-Fusch, near the Zeller Lake, on which the railways and motor roads leading to the Saalach Valley also converge. Zell-am-See, in winter a happy training area

The Glocknerstrasse. View of the Edelweiss Peak.

for skiers, becomes in summer a gaily-coloured and picturesque holiday resort.

Valley after valley winds through the giants of the Tauern world until the Grossvenediger is reached, and finally one of Salzburg's two frontiers, that with Italy, which is dominated by the Dreiherrenspitze.

Let us return gradually to the eastern end of the Province where the Niedern Tauern sink by degrees to lay themselves at the foot of man, so to speak, in the Tauern Pass. It must not be imagined that they make it any too easy for him; even this pass, swept by snowstorm and avalanches, is 5400 feet high. On this high plateau lies a blue-white alpine paradise, which makes way for the road to the Lungau, a region consisting mainly of high plains characterised by their clear, sparkling air filled with the faint scent and whispering music of the otherwise rarely-seen larches. Mauterndorf, Maria Pfarr, Moosham (a casket of treasures

from a mediaeval museum) and finally Tamsweg, well-known as the coldest place in Austria, and also for its beauty. Spread out in generous profusion are a number of strong, well-built settlements, solid in construction, with beautiful old churches and a horizon of mountain silhouettes. Further away, beyond the confines of the province of Salzburg, towers the mighty Dachstein:

Behind the nobly formed Bischofsmütze and the remote stretches of the Gamsfeld the Schafberg lifts its beaky nose over the dark waters of the Wolfgangsee, the bizarrely picturesque mountains grouped about it like stage scenery.

Salzburg, Franziskanerkirche

From the heights of the "Landauer", a shady resting place opposite, one looks down into sheltered St. Wolfgang. From here a cheerfully puffing engine takes us up the rack-and-pinion railway to the Schafberg. The view from the summit discloses a picture of such divine beauty that the name given to one of the stations, "Himmelspforte" ("Heaven's Gate"), seems quite justified. Beneath the precipice which falls abruptly away stretches the pale blue of the dancing Attersee, the whitely shimmering Mondsee (Moon Lake), while the deep blue of the Wolfgangsee completes a unique Trinity which even if it should not be compared to holy things, must yet be admitted to be divine in its gaiety, and has a beauty which almost hurts the eye as it gazes upon it insatiably.

Belfry.

Travelling westwards from the Wolfgangsee one arrives once more at the city of Salzburg. The road offers variety enough as it leads past the small, jade-coloured Fuschlsee, following the bends and curves of the Gaisberg as it winds around it, passing the bare Nockstein before it reaches the city on the Salzach.

But let a visitor speak again, that same admirer of Salzburg whom we last met on the "High Fortress", who finds himself attracted again and again towards the capital:

"Even after a few days away I felt drawn again to Salzburg. It seemed to me that there was sanctuary there, and security; a feeling of being in a chosen home, such as one gets in a castle. Thus in the evening we turned towards the city. The fields became darker and darker, a deep black-green, with inky spots of pine-wood above which this or that summit was still daubed in flaming colours by the setting sun. Yellow-white houses lay scattered about like crustaceans on the sea shore. The bushes beside the pale grey roadway were rounded off, macabre as evergreens against a white wall.

"In the sky and on the earth glittered golden stars. A penetrant smell of shave-grass arose from the earth. A myriad grasshoppers filled the air with their shrill, uncanny harping. We seemed to smell the very perfume of the shadows. The moon broke suddenly, violently, through a bank of clouds. The cool of the evening softly touched forehead and cheek.

Le nozze di Figaro · Ouverture

Rondo

Tempo di Menuetto

Menuetto I   Menuetto II

Elli Rolf

"Dreamily we approached the beloved city with its nervously winking lights and faint sounds, deadened by distance. These faded until it was still and silent, amidst a sea of misty meadows, where the quiet eyes of the white water-lilies looked up joyfully into the dark blue heavens. The lights of the city held the warmth of this promised land, its noble outlines its charm. Out of the darkness rose a jagged rock, crowned for all time by the great fortress of Hohensalzburg.

"I closed my eyes to fix forever this picture which rose so movingly out of the steaming fields; this moving mingling of sage-green and cream-white, crowned by the centuries-old silhouette which had been made to fit it; a song carolled by the awakened senses, an indestructible fount of happiness."

SUNNY FRONT-

CARINTHIA

IER PROV-INCE

CARINTHIA

Eugenie Pippal-Kottnig

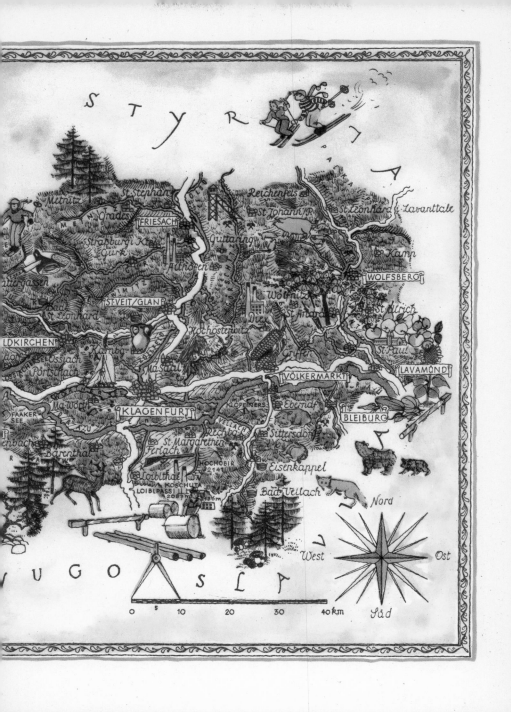

WORD-PALETTE
CARINTHIA

A land in the South·glittering frontiers·
Drifting clouds from the sea·
Alps challenging the heavens·great lakes·attractive lesser waters·
All around the frowning beetling crags·
Down from the glaciers the little streams·the cascading
veils of foaming white waters·
In far-flung forests·grazing game and sunlit foliage·
Roman remains·round-arched vaulting·frescoes on ceiling and wall·
"Lichtsäulen"·shrines·charnel houses·fortress-churches·
Abbeys·holy St·Hemma·
And holy ferryman St·Christopher·
Gleaming white roadways·turnings·sharp curves·mountain
passes·tunnels on the heights·
Alongside·vast depths·behind·the far distance·above·the circling
Of eagles in the heavens—and cloud-cast shadows on driven snow·
In courtyards and villages·games and song·"Reiftanz"of miners·
Spirited horses·Smiling and bowing·pacing and turning·
In hollows and valleys the warm lakes·
Little wavelets caressing island mountains·creeks and shore·
The reeds in the wind·
The wind in the sails·the buoys wind-blown·
Regattas and diving tower·Youth and sunshine—
The Dragon defeated·

Evening on the Ossiachersee.

Over Carinthia hovers the atmosphere peculiar to a frontier province, the perfume of·far-distant lands which, coming as it does here from the Slavonic East and the Latin South, makes one's heart beat faster even in settled times. The irresistible stream of life constantly carries a trace of foreign customs through the filter where contact is made with other territories, influencing both nature and the works of man. The force of nature is so strong that it is able to combine even opposing elements into a united whole, forming from them something individual, compact, harmonious, truly Austrian and specifically Carinthian.

SYMPHONY OF THE COUNTRYSIDE. In its physical features the province resembles a mussel-shell, with level ground and deep rills which extend far up into the surrounding framework of mountains. At first falling steeply, then more gradually, the mountains sink into the plain from the west, north and east. To the south stands a disconnected Alpine wall.

Nature has left but few passes in this girdle of mountains, and even these are barely usable in winter. All the valleys lead to the lowest level where the waters collect, to be released eastwards by a single outlet, that which the Drau has made by its own force.

But what a variety of contours, what play of colours this mussel-shaped Province offers. It would be hard to find such a many-toned melody of colour and form within another area as small as this, with its bare 10,000 square kilometres.

The types of rock and strata, of erosion and accumulation, vary within very limited areas. The work accomplished by long-vanished glaciers of the Ice Age is etched in intriguing lines. Below in the valleys lie lakes with shallow and sandy creeks of an almost southern warmth, above them terraces and debris of moraines now thickly wooded. In the hollow lie the isolated hills and the bogs. Up in the mountains you can find romantic lakes and waterfalls, harsh clefts and bare ridges and the wild confusion of the crust of a forgotten world, petrified while still in eruption, then scoured and pounded by wild storms. Add to this the colourful variety of the vegetation, enriched by the flora of the adjacent Mediterranean, Illyrian and Baltic territories, the deciduous forests and woods of mingled firs and larches, and the flowering carpet of the mountain pastures. Who can explain the presence amidst all this profusion of the Wulfenia, a plant native to the Himalayas and unknown in any other part of Europe?

ANDANTE MAESTOSO. Where the province joins Tyrol and Salzburg, it is dominated by the Hohe Tauern, which culminate in the majestic pyramid of the Grossglockner (approximately 12,000 feet) above the Pasterzen Glacier. The colours of the meadows and woods stand out sharply contrasted against rocks and snow. Through it runs the magnificently constructed alpine highway to Salzburg. On the Carinthian side the Möll foams past the well-known mountain village of Heiligenblut, to be joined by the waters of the Malta from Ankogel and Hochalmspitze. Through the glistening spray of a hundred waterfalls it flows into the Lieser, which absorbs it near the ancient town of Gmünd (traversed by a road in use since Roman times which leads over the Katschberg to Salzburg), and bears it onwards to the Drau at Spittal, the starting point of the Tauern railway. Shortly before this the river is joined by the overflow waters of the Millstättersee. This area

FROM HISTORY

In the year 976, when the Emperor Otto conferred the Eastern Marches on the Babenbergs, he also separated Bavaria from Carinthia. From this time dates the independent existence of the Province, at first as a subject duchy. In 1077 the house of Eppenstein established its independent rule, to be followed by that of Spanheim and— after the brief interlude of Ottokar of Bohemia—by the line of Meinhard, an offshoot of the family of the Counts of Tyrol. In 1355 the province became a permanent possession of the Hapsburgs. Carinthia, the frontier province, fell like other districts a victim to the disorders and famines of that period. The constant bloody invasions of the Turks, Hungarians and Venetians gave its patriotic inhabitants opportunity to prove their loyalty and courage in the face of the enemy. The Emperor Friedrich III sent word to the Carinthians that "they had earned for all time thanks, honour and praise from the Holy Empire."

Then Carinthia developed during almost three centuries of peace and achieved great prosperity. The riches found in the mountains played a big role—iron, first mined by the Romans, came from Hüttenberg, lead from the Bleibergergraben and the Karawanken, gold and silver from the Tauern. Feudal overlords were still powerful in the land : the Archbishop of Salzburg in Friesach and the Bishop of Bamberg in Villach were the mightiest. They created these towns, whose commanding positions on the great traffic routes gave them an importance which even exceeded that of the old ducal town of St. Veit. The Duke and the Court officials of the Princes of the Church gave the countryside the imprint of the rule of a mediaeval aristocracy through their numerous castles and country residences. This imprint lingers on

formerly prospered from the water-power of the mountains, as old stamping-mills and finely escutcheoned mansions in quiet valleys and on deserted heights still bear witness. Today it belongs to the devotees of mountain climbing, ski enthusiasts, and worshippers of the world of the great mountains who find happiness among the edelweiss, gentian, rhododendron and scented nigritella, to the marksman who pursues the noble chamois up the mountain clefts and to motorists who find pleasure in following the curves and twists of the excellent mountain roads.

`ALLEGRO CON MOTO. From here up to the Styrian Alps, and running parallel to them, stretch the Noric Alps. Here there are a few summits over 6000 feet, but as the world of eternal snow and ice is left behind, the majestic note gives peace to the sighing of vast forests. Within the wide crescent which they form together with the lower groups of the Gurktaler Alps, the Nockberge and the Metnitztaler Alps as far as the deep valley of the Olsa, life is peaceful,

Glocknerstrasse.

239

Klagenfurt Etching, 1547.

with a tempered gaiety. The softly rounded hills and grass-covered slopes with their carpets of flowers strike a bucolic note. This is a domain of shepherds and of modest travellers who come here in summer in search of peace and placid beauty. In winter it is a ski-terrain which not even the novice need fear to tackle. The cable railway to the Kanzel, above the Ossiachersee, which is extended by a ski-lift to the heights of the Gerlitzen, saves a long climb. Broad valleys which are all traversible lead from the Glan, the Gurk and the Lavant through a fertile and cultivated area back to the Drau. The Brennsee and the Afritzersee maintain Carinthia's reputation as a country for warm lake bathing.

High up on the Turrach Pass which leads over into the Valley of the Upper Mur one sees the dark, shining surface of a small lake. Towards the East, where gaps leading from north to south mark out the line of the mountain ranges and the flowing water, the melody of the landscape becomes softer as one crosses the saddles of the Kor and Sau Alps with their abundant fauna until it blends into the farewell song of the Drau. Along a railway line and the dreamy road which Rudolf Hans Bartsch calls "the road of the Styrian wine carrier", Carinthia's chief river passes over into the rich vineyards of what was formerly Austrian South Styria. Not far from Wolfsberg, chief town of the fruit-producing Lavant Valley, the "Paradise of Carinthia", a modern car road leads over the

Lavant Valley Costume.

Villach, 17th Century.

in the ring of castles surrounding St. Veit, of which the famous Hoch-osterwitz may be called a "Carinthian Grail", in the castles crowning Friesach and in the fortified mansions near the Italian frontier. A later creation of these proud overlords was Klagenfurt, now the chief town of the Province. Sheltered by the castles and towns splendid buildings arose—in Klagen-furt the Provincial Diet Hall, in Spittal-on-the-Drau a dream of early Renaissance in the shape of the Palazzo Porcia. Here and elsewhere grew up many a comfortable burgher's house which spoke of prosperity resulting from shrewd trading, and some fine churches.

The Napoleonic times did not spare peaceful Carinthia. General Bonaparte marched through the Province in 1797. The Imperial grenadiers occupied it in 1805 and 1809. Open rebellion against the foreign conqueror was organised by Johann Baptist Türk, the Carinthian Andreas Hofer. He moved too early in the day to be successful and it was not until 1814, under Metternich, that the great hour of liberation from foreign rule struck.

During the stormy year of 1848 the inner unity of Carinthia was again demonstrated. It was the same during the first World War, the mountain

saddle of the Pack into the Graz basin, thus affording a quicker and more comfortable connection with Styria than is provided by the railway which runs by way of Friesach and the Neumarkt Saddle. On the southern slopes the peasants' houses lie at very high altitudes. The Benedictine monastery of St. Paul, a well-known educational centre, is situated here. In the mountains are iron ore and coal. The wind sweeps through the extensive forests, and across flower covered fields in which the blue squill, a child of the South, is still to be found.

FURIOSO. South of the west-east line which the Gail-Drau Valley cuts through Carinthia, at the foot of the frontier wall formed by the Carnic-Julian Alps and the Karawanken, the melody of the landscape is different again. After the *Andante* of the Hohen Tauern and *Allegro* of the Noric Alps which is transformed into the softer airs of the Lavant Valley, comes the wild *Furioso* of the storm-swept Kalk-gebirge.

Between the Gail and the Drau, the Gailtaler Alps sometimes rise to a height of 6000 feet. To the south they fall away in impressive walls of rock. On the more gentle northern slopes

16

On the Millstättersee.

frontiers of the Province proving an insurmountable barrier. In 1918 South Serbia laid claim to Carinthian territory and foreign troops soon invaded a country which had collapsed after four years of war. But the Carinthians stood firm in loyalty to the Motherland, and the Province emerged intact from the defensive battles of the year 1919 and the plebiscite of 1920. The inflexible patriotism of its people had triumphed. History repeated itself after the second World War in which Austria was involved. The old saying "Carinthia free and undivided" will be bequeathed by the present sorely-tried generation to its sons, as an inheritance which is part of the very existence of the Province.

WHAT THE PEOPLE ARE LIKE

Anthropologically there are two main races clearly traceable in Carinthia: a blond, tall, long-skulled type and a dark, tall, long-faced but short-skulled type. Both types are about equally prevalent. The eastern type of man, smaller, with a broader skull and darker skin, is less frequently met with. Here and there in many places there are isolated traces of a Mongol race, revealed by the characteristically wrinkled eyelid and the position of the eye. It is typical of Carinthia that none of these traits indicates a national division. They result from centuries of constant racial intermingling, being found quite as frequently among the German-speaking as among the Slovene inhabitants of the Province. It seems that the original Celtic peasant inhabitants gradually mixed with Germanic, Slavonic and other elements which penetrated the Province as the result of colonisation, wars and the expeditions of merchant caravans.

Living in this area marked out by its natural boundaries, these peoples, aided by the effects of common conditions of life and progressive intermarriage, gradually developed into that Austrian-

lies the picturesque Weissensee, the only alpine lake which can boast of a bridge. The Gailberg offers a way over this mountain range connecting the towns of Kötschach and Oberdrauburg. A second road leads over the Kreuzberg between Hermagor in the Gail Valley and Greifenburg in the Drau Valley. Where the two broad river valleys meet lies Villach, on the extensive mountain plateau of the Dobratsch which has been given the name of "Carinthian Rigi" on account of the wonderful view from it. The acrothermal baths and the valuable metals won from the Bleiberger Erzberge are some compensation for the devastation caused by landslides in the dawn of history on the south side of the Dobratsch. The wierd scenery must be in part the reason why a famous colony of painters has settled in these parts, in the village of Nötsch. Among them are such well-known artists as Franz Wiegele, Arnold Clemenschitsch, Kolig senior and Herbert Boeckl, as well as Anton Mahringer and Raimund Kalcher.

Only south of the Gail Valley and of the lower reaches of the Drau is the wild character of the frontier mountains fully apparent. The wall of the Carinthian-Julian Alps stretches from Tyrol to the Gailitz Gorge through which passes the railway-line to Italy. In the Monte Coglians it attains a height of 9000 feet. It has a single negotiable pass—a military road even in Roman times—at Plöcken. The crests of the ranges tower upwards in pyramids or sheer walls of rock in a bewildering variety of forms, differing according to their height and the type of stone. Dense beech woods alternate with open fields, the meadows of the Gartnerkofel reflect the majestic violet blossoms of the Wulfenia. The Wolayersee reflects an impressive view of the surrounding country.

The Landhaus, Klagenfurt.

Lower down in the Gail Valley lies the reed-girdled Presseggersee.

Next comes the unbroken wall of the Karawanken Alps, their highest point, the Hochstuhl, lying well above 6000 feet. This range is a continuous chain of peaks, ridges, rocky clefts and awe-inspiring precipices as far as the Obir, the slopes of which in places suggest a monstrous stairway. The rose-tinted "Alpine glow" of these mountains in the setting sun is an unforgettable picture. The great pyramid of the Mittagskogel is reflected in the Faaker-see, which many consider the most beautiful lake of Carinthia. Nature has allowed few streams to flow from this mountain, but the river named after Bad Vellach is an exception. Here, in the neighbourhood of Eisenkappel, ancient volcanic formations give a picture of a prehistoric mountain world. Its wildness is modified by the beauty of the Drau Valley, a considerable part of which is known as the "Rosental"—"Rose-Valley". This picturesque name has nothing to do with roses, but may be connected with the rectangular fields of ripening buckwheat which, with their rosy shimmer, are a pleasure to the eye when one looks down from the terrace of the Hollenburg on to the old armoury of the "Gun-Maker of Ferlach". The name really derives from the lords of Raseneck-Rosegg, who owned a fortified castle at the same place. Apart from this, the rudeness of nature is tempered only by the pine forests, and, in spring, by the sea of narcissi which bloom in the mountain pastures. Josef Friedrich Perkonig, the great writer on Carinthian scenery, called these parts "the quiet kingdoms". The Karawanken can be traversed by the Wurzen Pass, the Loibl Pass and a road crossing the Seeberg; at Rosenbach they are pierced by a railway tunnel.

PASSACAGLIA. All these different groups of mountains which vary so greatly from one another combine to form a delightful enclave in the heart of Carinthia, where the varied motifs of the scenic melody are repeated in a comprehensive recitatif. From the prehistoric mountains, mighty glacial streams which dug for the lakes of today their deep beds descended to the valleys. There are more than 200 of these in Carinthia. The rivers brought gravel and clay and continued

Millstatt, Cloister Walk.

244

alpine type which is nowadays implied by the use of the word "Carinthian", creating a feeling of natural common weal, without entirely destroying specific indications of individual differences. An extravagant capacity for enthusiasm, a light-hearted joi de vivre and love of good food, an impulse towards what is great and profound, are ascribed to the Germanic element. Rough and primitive strength, loyalty, a coarse sense of humour and self-confidence are believed to originate in the Celtic admixture. From this last the people are considered to derive a certain uncomprehending tendency to reject all that is new or unusual, the much criticised tendency to leave everything as it has always been. Whether this be true or not, all these qualities do, in fact, mark out the Carinthian generally, with little distinction as to his mother tongue. They equalise out in the souls of the people, stormy contradictions blending in the calm of a purposeful attitude towards life. Light usually triumphs over the darkness of the depths.

NATIONAL CUSTOMS.

The colourful customs of the inhabitants derive from age-old sources. In Central and Lower Carinthia, they date from the Celtic part of the prehistoric migrating hordes and the days before the birth of Christ. Heathen processions around the mountains in spring which led to the heights of former Celtic places of worship, became in Christian times Easter pilgrimages, such as the strange "Vierbergelaufen" in the Zollfeld area. The customs and legends of Upper Carinthia date back to the times of Teutonic invasion. Prayers for good harvest weather and for fertility embodied in the old custom of blessing the fields, the solstice fires and the marriage customs as well as those of the "Rauhnächte" have undergone many a change since they were first

Gail Valley Costumes.

building on the inheritance of the moraines of the ice age. The mountain winds carried seeds from afar. Thus there came into being a mixed landscape of thickly covered, isolated summits, ranges of hills, meadows, ploughed fields and stretches of water.

In this enclave lies the largest lake, the Wörthersee, the centre of summer holiday life, a reservoir of warmth covering an area of some 20 square kilometres. On its shores are many country houses, colonies of bathing huts and popular holiday resorts, among which the most important are the spas of Velden and Pörtschach. The Wörthersee is also a first class centre for sport of all kinds. On its beaches are crowds of bathers, swimming and playing games of water-ball; beyond them rowing boats explore the bays and inlets, while further out again, white sails swell in the wind and speed boats flash by, many towing a surf-riding board on which a bronzed figure is precariously balanced. In late winter, the wide surface may become a skating rink of vast dimensions. On the shores of the other lakes, large and small, life is less intense, but more idyllic. The Ossiachersee dreams pensively in the shadow of

Shrine.

the Gerlitzen, with the secularised monastery of Ossiach on its shores. The broad and open Millstättersee, named after the health resort of Millstatt in the centre of which are a monastery and church of venerable age, looks serenely out at the world. Of the "Thousand Statues" which classical scholars claim to have been the origin of the name there is today no trace, unless one is prepared to find a modern version of them in the muscular figures which crowd the great diving-tower of the swimming pool, a true campanile of water sport. The Faakersee lies amidst fascinatingly beautiful scenery. Far away in the south of the Province smiles the little Kloppeinersee, which can boast of being even a few degrees warmer than the Wörthersee.

This lake owes its agreeable temperature to its sheltered position. Although the southern sun reaches it across the wall of mountains, the latter wards off cold winds. During the greater part of the year, this lake forms a calm island of fine weather amidst the surrounding storms. If one looks across the countryside from the Ulrichsberg, Carinthia's most typical mountain, one gets a good picture of how all the varied elements which make up the landscape blend harmoniously together—the central part of the great mussel of Carinthia and the surrounding mountains, with the valley of the Drau which traverses the entire Province from the Porta Tyroliae at Oberdrauburg to Unterdrauburg at the other end and beyond, receiving all the tributary streams and the ribbons of the highways which, a true network of roads, lead from all directions to the heart of the Province.

RESTING PLACE BETWEEN NORTH AND SOUTH. Whoever wishes to enter or leave Carinthia must traverse a high pass or a narrow gorge, no matter from where he comes. So nature has ordained.

For this reason the roads have stood from time immemorial, however much they may have been improved by science. Their wearisome length, their task of linking the Adriatic arm of the Mediterranean with the Danube Valley area, have influenced the way of life of human beings and their choice of settlements. Carinthia is and always has been a resting-place for recuperation after climbing up from the sea level and overcoming the barrier of the southern Alps, before preparing to cross those to the North.

The pattern of the Roman roads has been indelibly recorded. There is the Noric Road, which

Glan Valley Costume.

instituted. Hüttenberg has its "Reif-tanz", a miners' festival which expresses the longing for light of those who hew coal in darkness below ground. The "Kufenstechen" in the Gail Valley where horse-breeding is important to the people, derives from old tournaments. A ring which is held out on to the course by a girl has to be speared at full gallop. The "Kranzelstechen" in Weitensfeld in the Gurk Valley is a similar custom.

On such festive occasions, or at the ceremony of the dedication of the local church, one sees the old national costumes which are heirlooms in the valleys. At other times simple garments of home-woven linen and "Loden" (coarse woollen cloth) are usually worn.

VILLAGE AND FARM

Variety lends a special charm to farm and village. Scattered in small groups, the buildings stand in colourful and attractive gardens filled with flowers and enclosed by hedges. Built here of wood and there of stone, flat alternate with sloping roofs, and pergolas crossing the garden from one side to the other with those running the length of it. The wooden pillars supporting the veranda roofs are always carved; doors and windows are framed in colour and decorated by flowers. The "Kachelofenstube" ("Tiled Stove Room") contains hand-carved furniture and gaily painted chests. In the remoter valleys the "Rauchstube" ("Smoky Room") is still to be found. Originally it was a living room with an open fireplace and hand-made copper vessels. Shrines and wayside crosses differ greatly one from the other. Grain chests display the pleasure taken in artistic hand carving and colouring.

The food of the country people is simple and wholesome. Milk and sweet dishes made from flour form the basis of nourishment. Of the latter the most popular in town and country are the large "Nudel", a sort of cake, made of

Gmünd.

begins at Aquileia and forks north of Osoppo, the western branch crossing the Plöckenpass and the eastern the watershed of Pontebba. Where it emerges from the high mountains arose the modern Mauthen on the site of Loncium, and where it crosses the Gailberg into the Drau Valley grew up Oberdrauburg. Here one branch leads past Aguntum-Lienz through the Puster Valley to the Brenner and another past Teurnia (now called St.-Peter-im-Holz), Spittal-on-the-Drau and Gmünd to the Katschberg and on to Salzburg. The eastern fork runs from Pontebba-Tarvis to the place where the trading centre of Villach developed, and past the Ossiachersee and the Wörthersee to Virunum at Zollfeld, near the point where Klagenfurt was established, and further on to St. Veit, where the former dukes of the Province held court. Further along its course

Spittal, Castle Porcia.

to the Neumarkter Sattel and Styria arose the proud town of Friesach. From Virunum a road led eastwards. On this route lie the larger towns of Southern Carinthia, such as Völkermarkt and Bleiburg.

This natural network of roads is as much used as ever today. This has maintained the prosperity of the settlements along its path. The fulcrum may have varied its position slightly as the area developed, but it has always lain within the triangle Villach—Klagenfurt—St. Veit. The advent of the locomotive, of the automobile, even of the airplane have brought little change in this respect. These routes follow the historic, natural highways. At most, where in olden times an obstacle was circumvented, it is today surmounted by an artificial construction, or bored through by a mountain tunnel as the Tauern railway does at Mallnitz and the Karawanken railway at Rosenbach. Even the airplane flying high above follows the old Pontebba route in order to avoid dangerous storms.

THE TOWNS OF CARINTHIA. The Carinthian settlements have earned their right to be called towns more through their historic past than for any other reason. They are small in size and their economic importance varies greatly. Nowhere do they crush nature like a stone fist, forcefully suppressing it. It is nature which encircles and penetrates them, surrounding them with a framework of lovely scenery, predestinated and naturally developed as centres of a district. This may be the reason why for a long time none of them was given the absolute dominance of a capital. An additional reason may be that the three most important places all lie in the centre part of the Province close together, having originated in different feudal territories of which they formed the centre.

The old ducal town of St.-Veit-on-the-Glan, where Walther von der Vogelweide sang, as well as his less talented colleague, the Carinthian Zachäus von Himmelberg, was pre-eminently a fashionable court centre, which later came into competition with the picturesque little mountain town of Althofen, an iron trading centre. Today it is a typical provincial town,

Klagenfurt, the Dragon.

248

a soft flour paste with the edges folded over, and filled with "Topfen" (curds), herbs, poppy seeds or dried pears. For festive occasions there are the "Leinöl-krapfen" (a sort of doughnut) and the "Reindling", a cake filled with cinnamon, sultanas or currants. The chief dish is "Sterz", made of buckwheat or maize. Normally meat is only eaten smoked except on feast days. Peasants engaged on exhausting work may eat bacon at tea time or it may be eaten with potatoes, cabbage or pickled turnips at the mid-day meal. For drinks there are cider and Schnaps, home-made spirits from the fruit growing on the farm.

Although the mountainous nature of Carinthia does not afford its inhabitants a very luxurious existence—in comparison to that of the peasants in the plains it may almost be called poverty-stricken—it provides in its variety rich food for the spirit. The special temperament and mentality of the people find joyous expression in the magnificent songs of Carinthia, which have been spread, through Koschat, far beyond the native frontiers. Sung in jolly company by three, four or five voices, women's and men's blend harmoniously with that of the "over-singer" who remains an octave higher. It makes no difference whether the language of the song is German or whether, as in places near the southern frontier, it is sung in the Carinthian-Slovenian dialect. Sometimes, in fact, the two are mingled, with amusing effect. In the field of religious melodies there are many shepherd's songs which express in direct countryman's fashion the story of the finding of the infant Jesus in language which is sometimes moving, sometimes amusing. The most revered song, however, is and always will be, for Carinthians, the "Kärntner Heimatlied", written by J. Ritter von Gallenstein in 1817. Its verses describe the beauty of the Motherland Province in moving terms of deep affection.

Maria Wörth.

a shopping place for the needs of the surrounding countryside. Numerous castles and fortress-ruins are all that remain to remind of its proud past.

Villach has always been an excellent centre of communications. Belonging to Bamberg until the middle of the 18th century, it early received valuable privileges which together with a highly developed trade and the rich mineral yield of the mountains made it a very prosperous centre of culture. It likes to be called the "Town of Paracelsus", who lived there with his father for fourteen years. Its particular attraction is provided by the mountain which looks down into the streets and highroads from all sides. People say jokingly that this is the only town in the world where it is possible to hunt the chamois in the streets. This is, of course, not strictly accurate, for the forests of the Dobratsch mountain merely touch its outskirts. As a health resort it would be hard to beat, for mountains and lakes present the most varied attractions, while the warm springs of the medicinal baths offer a cure for many painful illnesses. A faint flavour of life in Italy, whose frontiers are not far

off, lends a certain
piquanterie to
Villach. It has
developed indu-
strially along lines
which have done
nothing to dimi-
nish its attrac-
tions.

Klagenfurt, the
administrative
centre of Carin-
thia, is the only
town which is
a municipal city

according to accepted ideas. Even Klagenfurt is a natural picture framed by the
most delightful scenery, and so near to the Wörthersee that it can be considered
as belonging to the latter. The life of the town benefits by the crowds of holiday
makers who visit it every year and by their demands save it from provincial stagnation. One should not be put off by the name, for it has nothing to do with
"Klagen" (moaning) as the legend of the
Dragon claims, but is simply a distorted
version of "Glanfurt". The Dragon is to
be found in the municipal coat-of-arms,
and, in stone, guarding the fountain in
the main square of the town, which bears
evidence of its distinguished past in its old
patrician houses. Emperor Maximilian I
presented them to the provincial noblemen
who had converted the small village of
those times into a strong fort protected
by stout walls against Turkish and
Hungarian invasions, and probably against
unruly neighbours as well. The prosperity
of Klagenfurt really dates from the time
when the development of Triest caused
the road over the Loibl Pass to be built up
as the shortest means of communication.
Old farms with shady walks, dreamy inns
where southern wine sparkles in the glasses,

Lesach Valley Costume.

250

St. Veit-on-the-Glan.

well-kept gardens on the remains of the city wall, and wide avenues produce an atmosphere of peace and ease. The Government buildings, museums filled with treasures of prehistoric times, the proud Diet Hall with its "Wappensaal" of the Carinthian noble families, grammar schools and theatres, bear witness to the cultural level of life in Klagenfurt. On market day it is transformed into a little provincial town, where natural produce is exchanged for manufactured articles and the industrial products of many local factories, thereby maintaining a satisfactory balance between town and country.

And Carinthia's many other small towns? It would be tiresome to name them all and recount their merits. They are all witnesses to the industry of citizens, tradesmen and labourers, the forebears of some of whom have been settled in the district for generations. All of them are in close touch with the peasantry and fit well in with the wonderful natural surroundings of Carinthia, which invite the traveller everywhere to linger awhile. Some towns, such as Friesach, are almost overloaded with the beautiful and valuable monuments of a proud past. Churches and chapels richly decorated with reliefs and paintings, strangely formed charnel houses and beautiful wayside shrines ("Lichtsäulen") bear witness to pious gratitude. That this sentiment did nothing to weaken the powers of resistance and the realisation of the value of freedom is proved by the existence of fortified churches and the remains of the *Fliehburgen*. These fortified places of refuge owe their construction

251

to the peasants' determination to resist attacks from the Styrian-Carinthian frontier districts which had often been invaded from the East.

AN ARTISTIC PEOPLE. The plastic arts have been widely influenced by the melody of the landscape and by the individual note which characterises Carinthia. This influence can be seen at work through the centuries. Even the works of foreign artists produced in Carinthia bear the Carinthian stamp.

The *Herzogsstuhl* ("Duke's Chair") at Zollfeld and the little church of Krainburg, one of the oldest churches existing in Austria, bridge the gap between the Roman remains which have been unearthed, and the romanesque period. On high points which were carefully selected you will find country churches in which services are still held and massively built charnel-houses. In the decorations of the romanesque monastery churches it is possible to trace the course of history; to see how, for example, the provincial romanesque reliefs yield to the Nordic passion for representations of the Stations of the Cross (for instance those of Millstatt), or how the style of great German buildings spreads into Carinthian territory, influencing the building of the monumental abbey at Gurk. Secret beliefs of the people in the supernatural as well as symbolic representations are revealed in the carvings on the doors and in the many-arched porch of the Abbey.

The religious severity of the choir construction is the first sign of Gothic, which blossomed in the 15th century into many pure gothic churches. Wooden statues of the Virgin Mary vie for recognition with richly carved triptych altars.

The renaissance and baroque styles are afforded little scope in secular monuments. But in the churches we find massive early baroque altars, which were succeeded by daintily carved rococo pulpits and by the famous Pieta of Rafael Donner in Gurk Abbey.

Carinthia's architectural and sculptural treasures have to yield place both in respect of quality and numbers to her paintings. There are a great number of romanesque wall paintings, noteworthy for their magnificence of conception and delicate colouring. The painting of Bishop Romanus in the Keep of Friesach is supposed to be the oldest fresco in Austria, dating from 1130, while that of the Apostles in the "Winter Church" of Maria Wörth is nearly as old. Again and again the removal of plastering

Gurk, Romanesque Fresco : Adam and Eve.

Strassen, Gothic Fresco : The Interment.

brings to light new marvels of colouring from long past ages. The smallest and most humble of churches sometimes becomes famous overnight. Even the frescoes revealed show a rough peasant uncouthness; this is always matched with a brilliant talent for painting. The pastel-coloured frescoes of the "Master Heinrich" in the western nave of Gurk Abbey are perfect in form and conception, and have a European reputation.

A well-qualified Carinthian expert in the fine arts has written of the development of Carinthian painting in the 13th century: "At the beginning of the romanesque period every scene was allotted a definite place on the wall, the colours being given merely symbolical value and the whole conception governed by severely inkonographical laws which attached little importance to the portrayal of persons, and disregarded entirely the surrounding scenery or superficially indicated it by symbols. But at the end of this period we find scenes where active beings replace the unreal puppet figures of the earlier epoch. Parallel to this change is the addition to lifeless drapery in the painting of figures of broken, serrated lines hinting at movement. Then came a flowing softness of outline which still refused to suggest the reality of the body beneath the drapery. Finally we see the artist overcoming the shapeless softness of outline, the suggestion of a living body beneath the garment and the soft lines slowly merging into lovely Gothic."

The strong urge towards painting in Carinthia has influenced the local Gothic. Elsewhere you will find that it is an aim of Gothic to curtail wall space in favour of windows. But in Carinthia, Gothic is moderated, the buildings more solidly constructed, in order not to lose any possible space for wall paintings. In small buildings with little wall space, you will find that the mural decorations have been frequently over-painted. The many churches of the Province, especially the wonderful Gurk Abbey, the abbeys of Millstatt and St. Paul, the church of Maria Saal and a host of others, some of which are in remote spots, offer striking examples of this trend in art. In order to provide still more space for special occasions there are the so-called "Fastentücher" ("Lenten Cloths")—stretched canvases something like the "Armenbibel" ("Poor Men's Bible") with painted scenes of the Passion, with which the altar is covered during Lent. One of the largest belongs to the Abbey of Gurk, a pious gift of the Countess Hemma who, canonised, has been made the patron saint of the Province.

Metnitz, Charnel House.

ROUNDING OFF THE PICTURE. The broad belt of mountains whose waters flow into the Carinthian basin, towards which their valleys also run, and the uniform transport network which has consequently developed and has its centre here, have helped to give Carinthia remarkable political and economic unity.

Within its confines there are no dividing barriers. No one area of Carinthia could exist independently of the others. They supply one another's needs. Without serious loss no one of them could be separated from the others and attached to some neighbouring economic territory dependent on a too distant centre. Their life is indissolubly united with the whole Carinthian plain and its towns which are the essential nerve-centres—Klagenfurt, with its government-offices and most of the higher schools, a scientific centre of the Geschichtsverein (Historical Research Society) for Carinthia and the museum collections provides for administration and cultural life, Villach as a railway junction of great importance looks after the technical requirements of the communications system. These two towns with St.-Veit-on-the-Glan and the rest of the smaller towns give the area its necessary economic backing.

Thus this compact organisation is permeated by all those elements of which the living body of Carinthia is constituted. It is surrounded by the eternal symphony of colourful scenery, interesting through its peculiar mingling of culture and national dress, exciting by virtue of the far-away magic beyond its frontiers.

GREEN FOR- ESTS

STYRIA

BROWN ORE

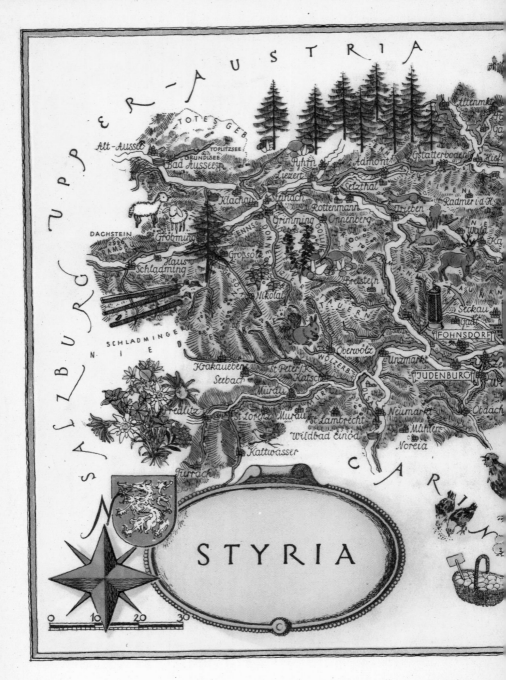

EUGENIE PIPPAL-KOTTNIG

WORD-PALETTE
STYRIA

Clearing·digging·prospecting·cutting·
Ores and woods·
Weather-beaten refuge from the foe· arsenal· armoury·
Open Turkish frontier·
Iron in the hills· hammer-masters· miners·
proud workshops·
Council Hall· Clock tower· shaded wells· bourgeois comfort·
Mill amidst fruit orchards· waggon wheel· storks·
Scarecrow in the vineyard·
Library of the abbots· abbey and priory·
Mountain famed in song·
"Schuhplattler"· yodler· benevolent master·
Procession· pilgrims· holy shrine·
Heritage of ancestors·
Wooded homeland·

Graz, Mausoleum.

This Province, on the northern fringe of which the Kalkalpen stand as shimmering walls, and into which, between the Radlpass and the Wechsel, the sources of its streams and rivers flow from the primeval formations of the Lower Tauern and the Styrian border mountains, this Styrian land, which ends with its broad valleys of ploughland and gently sloping vineyard hills to the east and the south, has never lacked admirers to sing its praises.

Styria takes its name from the Count of Steyr, who in the 12th century was entrusted with this territory as a frontier outpost in the south-eastern corner of the Empire. Frequently overrun, defeated and rebuilt in the course of the changing centuries, its history has indeed been that of an outer march. Its name brings with it the memory of stubborn struggles, and the silver panther on a green field stands to honour its spirit in its coat of arms, kept immaculate by manly courage.

How shall one try here to describe the Province in a few words? At what boundary should one begin, at what places pause to use that district and its inhabitants to illustrate the whole? Obviously from Graz, the capital, we must try to get a glimpse and general picture of past and present. A fishing village and a market-place near the Mur Bridge in the shadow of the fortifications of the Castle Rock—this was Graz more than 900 years ago. Civic industry, the good and ill fortune brought by the centuries, have filled its history. Emperors have reigned there, and there also servants of art and science have come together from all quarters of the globe. Today Graz is a town with a quarter of a million inhabitants, surrounded by busy industrial

261

districts, but the old Cathedral with the Mausoleum, the Armoury and the Joanneum are carefully preserved and living witnesses to its colourful past.

The other towns of the Province are no less worthy of consideration; Bruck, formerly so wealthy, with the famous Market Fountain in front of the Kornmesserhaus, the iron-producing town of Leoben, the trading centres of Judenburg and Murau, the last of which has grown up so charmingly around its Schlossberg.

Space calls for brevity. We must limit our wanderings to three districts; from them, we can learn to know the whole of Styria.

WEST STYRIA. It is part of the secret of Western Styria that the colourful and clamorous life of our times which is to be met within a number of mining and industrial settlements from Steyeregg to Piberstein is constantly influenced by the underlying muted tones of the ancient soul of the Province, which lives on in its quiet woodland solitudes. The southernmost point is the mountainous country beyond Eibiswald, crowned by the distant heights of the Koralm Range. The Freiland forms part of the Province and above it the tiny church of Maria-Osterwitz, which grows up into the clouds. There is that little corner behind Modriach and Pack which seems lost to the world, where they adhere more closely to ancient custom and habits of work than elsewhere. There is the Gössnitz, with its steeply sloping fields rising above the rushing mill-streams below. Still valleys sweep in attractive crescent form around and below the peaks of the Stubalpe. Everywhere in these barren farmlands from Radlpass to Lower Gleinalmspeik, the fields and meadows have been conquered from the wilderness of vast forests by means of fire and plough. Everywhere on these islands created by persistent, back-breaking peasant labour, the brown wooden farmhouses beneath their silver-grey roofs of slate defy the gales which come raging from the storm-centres of the mountain fields, and in age-old "Rauchstuben" the life-blood of ancient legends thaws again before the warmth of the open fire.

Beyond the savagery of the mountains, a world of vine-covered hills unrolls like a gay-coloured scarf before the dark girdle of the forest peasants land. On the sun-side of the mountains below the heights, the vineyards on the slopes are staked out with serried rows of vines on supporting poles. This is the picture which begins in a small way at the "Gasselberg", where with care it is possible to produce a Schilcher which has the proper tang alongside many an unassuming vintage. In the Styrian Schilchertal, between Ligist and Eibiswald, the view broadens and opens out. The vineyards there on the Hochstrassen and on the clear-cut, towering mountain ridge of Greisdorf are famous from olden times. The Engelweingarten above Stainz should be saluted with joyful respect, as should all the carefully tended vineyards where the Wildbach grapes ripen.

At the foot of this double garland of forest and vineyards is fruitful soil in which Turkish wheat prospers under a burning sun, yet despite all the riches which lie in the soil or come from the bright skies above, bad weather, misfortune and hard times have made the population adopt a grave and sometimes resigned attitude towards life.

A friend of the Styrian motherland wandering throughout the strip of country which we call West Styria and observing it with affection, would soon notice that beneath the noise and bustle of the fleeting present there lies hidden the treasure of a rich past. Roman inscriptions on stones and the tombstones of Italian officials and native Norics which are

Women of Leoben.

Graz, Diet Hall.

turned up in the fields by the ploughs of the peasants, now decorate the walls of many a building. On the towers and churches, especially of Mooskirchen, Stallhofen, Piber and Köflach they have been preserved as an indelible greeting from distant centuries when the world-wide power of the Roman Empire allowed our Homeland to share in its civilisation and culture.

Long after grass and the wilderness had erased the traces of Roman Noric civilisation, and a new way of life, Christianity and order had come to the Province of Salzburg, the castle of Deutschlandsberg became a centre of Salzburg planning and working. Later on, but of no less importance for development and trade, the nowadays so quiet town of Piber grew to be a far-reaching centre of culture when the house of Eppenstein gave their property to the Benedictines of St. Lamprecht. Their priory, in the parish of Piber, was a coveted living which once even boasted

Graz, Clock Tower.

of a bishop. The Bailiff of Piber, however, taxed the lands of the Kainachtal down to the last peasant farm in the mountains. A circle of fortified castles guarded the roads and byways leading to Upper Styria—Haunstein, Klingenstein, the Primaresburg near Lankowitz, over the ruins of which the forest of Franziskanerkogel grows, Leonrod in the Gössnitz Valley, nowadays popularly known as Höllerrock Castle, Krems, where the keep still towers steeply above the Schlossberg, and the proudest of them all, Ober-Voitsberg, in whose shadow the inhabitants have enjoyed the privileges of citizens of a princely city ever since the time of Duke Friedrich the Handsome (1367). For many centuries life was mainly a peaceful exchange

of peasant labour and civic industry, the wine carriers from Hungary and the lowlands bringing greetings from far-off lands. Occasionally great nobles who broke their journeys had brought the exciting atmosphere of the big world. Like shafts of lightning historical moments lit up this forest-hidden land when the Turks came to trouble even the lonely vicarage on the Pack, or later, when the French marched in via Eibiswald and Preding. After the modest deposits of iron ore had been exhausted, the valuable timber caught the eye of the iron-masters. The streams drove the wheels of the hammers in the scythe workshops. The manor house to which one of the largest, the Tunner-hammer, belonged, still stands today amidst the smoke and noise of the colliery. Ever since Archduke Johann drew up with his own hands the plans for the construction of the railway line from Graz to Köflach in the fifties of the last century, and had them put into effect despite obstinate opposition, West Styria has become more aware of the vigorous life of modern times.

EAST STYRIA. Four main roads give access from the chief town to the rich fruit-bearing country of East Styria. Around this territory winds the River Mur, sweeping south-wards from the sharp angle it makes at Bruck, and then eastwards to leave Austria at Radkers-burg, forming a living barrier along the boundaries of East Styria.

The white ribbon of the first road runs past Maria Trost, climbing the hill within view of the massive Schöckel, descending to Weiz where it forks, one branch leading to the northern hill country, while the main road runs dead north, right into the heart of Peter Rosegger's "Waldheimat" ("Wooded Home-land"). The second highway is that famous

one which from its earliest days has been known by its name of the Ries. Its asphalt surface climbs steeply to the high road, affording sweeping views from the inn-benches which date from the days of coach-travel. Bordered by forest and meadow, it descends gently into the Raab Valley. From Gleisdorf, where a branch leads off through Feldbach and Fehring to Hungary and another to the far-distant territory of Hartberg, its main branch continues as the Ungarnstrasse (road to Hungary) through Fürstenfeld to the Province of Burgenland.

The third road wanders towards the East Styrian hills, running past St. Marein-on-the-Pickelbach down into the Raab Valley. The fourth road over the Hühnerberg is the last in the network of roads which serves the quiet peasant life in the valleys between the Raab and the Mur.

These roads all vary, passing over hills and through valleys, past wooded mountains and vineyards linked together by fertile fields. The further east one travels along the valleys, the more they widen out as the space between the ranges of hills broadens until, in the distance, they remind one of the nearby Hungarian Plain. In the same measure that the countryside loses the shelter of the mountains do the human habitations grow together, isolated farms gradually giving place to hamlets, villages and market towns. The farms which in the middle districts consist of rambling house, cattle stalls and outbuildings, loosely grouped around one another as the terrain dictates, now move their components nearer and nearer together until on the other side of the bend in the Raab they become compact rectangles within which man, beast and the fruits of the soil are collected into one homestead.

It is not hard to discover evidence of the changing fortunes of the Province. Tombstones have been found in remote parts of the forests with inscriptions in Roman letters erected to the memory of Celtic aborigines. By the roadside are overgrown tumuli which the peasants awefully refer to as "heathen graves". If one is to believe local legends, great princes are buried in some of them—perhaps even Attila himself, the King of the Huns. Later the Avars overran the country, destroying the deserted homesteads of the Romans and their culture, and driving their slaves, the Slavs, before them with their whips. After the year 800 A.D. when Charlemagne had broken the tyranny of the Avars, there came monks from Salzburg to preach Christian doctrines and with them Bavarian peasants. But soon the Magyar invaders swept in to interrupt the peaceful work of these settlers among the natives. Only after the Battle of Lechfeld was it resumed. Then, with the vigour of the adolescent Western world as a spur, a civilisation based on the hard work of a simple peasantry grew throughout the centuries into that unobtrusive, modest culture which has survived all the hard tests of the past. In those early days the villages grew up on river banks and in sheltered corners between hills, overshadowed and protected by the castles of the ruling knights; the Riegersburg, which crowns the steep slopes of the Felsberg, is a fine example of the latter. Protection from the danger which always threatened from the East was afforded by the frontier towns of Friedberg, Hartberg, Fürstenfeld and Radkersburg. The burghers who lived in them and in the market-towns, proud of their social position, yet in close contact with the country-folk, kept the latter in touch with the develop-. ments of the age and brought to them profitable trade.

The Raab, the chief river of East Styria, flows broad, sluggish and dark from the districts where the villages melt into fertile fields and the storks nest on roof-tops and chimneys. As it hurries through Passail the river is still an immature mountain stream. From this remote and pleasant market-town Peter Engelbrecht once found his way to the Imperial Court in order to teach Latin grammar to Maximilian, later the first emperor of this name. Further on, below the old Stuben-berg castle of Stubegg lies Arzberg, where, as the name suggests, lead ore (with a silver content) was mined.

Bruck-on-the-Mur, Kornmesserhaus.

Erzberg.

Then the walls of the Goller and the Gösser close in on the river at Raab-klamm. Through this gorge a series of stone steps, foot-paths and bridges lead above the roaring, turbulent waters.

At the other end of this gorge rises Gutenberg, a fine castle which owes its impressive lines to the Stubenberg family to whom it has belonged since the 13th century.

St. Ruprecht-on-the-Raab owes its name to the Archbishopric of Salzburg which owned properties here since the year 860. Once a large parish and the judicial centre of an important district, it is today a notable market town which is sought out by holiday makers who appreciate its mild and health-giving summer climate.

Here the Weizbach joins the main stream; on its upper reaches lies the township of Weiz, a centre of industrial activity whose foundries even in far-off ages disturbed the placidity of the countryside, into which it is constantly spreading out its tentacles. Its landmark is the partly romanesque Taborkirche, records of which date from 1188. The church on the Weizberg is built high above the town. Its exuberant-baroque twin towers afford a commanding view of the countryside in all directions. The cherished "Himmelsbergerin" as pilgrims call the shrine, is the work of Veit Königer, the Styrian baroque sculptor, and the painter Ritter von Mölk. The famous Renaissance Hall of the Joanneum at Graz was removed thence from Radmannsdorf Castle, today the seat of the Prefecture. Gleisdorf, once an old trading centre, was built on the ruins of Celtic civilisation. Many a well-preserved burgher's house bears witness to the prosperity of former times.

Just before Feldbach, the old market-town of the old Duchy which was raised to the status of a municipality in 1884, the road turns off which leads past Castle Kornberg with its many towers to the Riegersburg. The little town of the same name lies snugly ensconced on the lower slopes of the steep basalt rocks which are crowned by one of the most famous castles of the Province. Through seven gateways the approach winds into the inner courtyard, where a deep well is covered by a fine superstructure in wrought iron. Although Rutgerespurc Castle dates from the

ON THE ERZBERG.

Styria is called "The Iron Province", and if one recalls the Armoury in Graz, that unique storehouse of the militant frontiersmen, one realises how applicable is this name which chroniclers and poets are so fond of giving to the Province. It applies firstly to the mountain which forms the heart and centre of the countryside, the Erzberg. Since the times of the Romans the work of the miners on its slopes has been developed from early primitive methods to those of modern technique; the tall mountains around, and the old houses below the castle of the Oswaldikirche maintain the warmth and romance of Styria amid more mundane surroundings. The buried treasures of the mountains were welded into useful implements by the mills in Vordernberg and the iron works in the forest-glades until, in the middle of the 19th century, the works were able to make use of the newly-discovered brown coal mines. On this combination were founded the great iron works of Donawitz and Kapfenberg, which have made the name of Styria known throughout the world.

The Erzberg alone is enough to make Styria a rich Province. According to the legend it was in bygone times a mountain just like any other. One day a merman was caught in the Leopoldsteinersee. In return for his freedom he offered mountain treasure as ransom—gold to last one year, silver for ten, or iron to last for ever. The natives chose the last named.

The rust-brown iron mountain rises to a height of 2,400 feet by a series of gigantic steps, at the foot of which lies the market-town of Eisenerz, crowned by the "Schichtturm" and an old fortified church. Here beats the heart of the "Iron Marches" in its metallic depths. Thousands of miners can be seen on the iron-ore terraces, many of them working on the mountain as

12th century, it owes its present form and the insolent splendour of the interior mostly to the "Gallerin", born a Baroness von Wechsler, whose adventurous career is even today the source of many much appreciated stories.

The Raab, along the banks of whose quiet, swiftly-flowing waters stand the great mills of the district, passes on into Hungary. Its basin has been made prosperous by peasant industry and toil.

The Feistritz starts its romantic course through Styria on the western slopes of the Wechsel, born of springs which arise amidst the wild mountain scenery of the Stuhleck and the Pretul Alps. For a considerable distance it is confined in a narrow valley, past Rettenegg and Ratten where the mining of brown coal has brought strange people and customs to the old forest peasant village, and is followed by the road and railway which serve the farms scattered on the mountain slopes or congregated into villages.

Birkfeld, the old market-town of the Duchy lies well above the river. Anger, on the other hand, lies in the depths of the valley, surrounded by fruit trees, its dreams of the peaceful comfort of older times nowadays disturbed by the asbestos mills and the trucks from the soapstone quarries at Rabenwald. Through the cleft between Rabenwald and the Kulm, which affords a widespread view of the countryside, the Feistritz changes its direction to flow

Hartberg.

east, and later southwards. Before it comes out into the open valley it passes below the forest-clad ruins of the ancient fortress of Stubenberg, the family seat of an old Styrian ruling family. Once again the Feistritz is swallowed up by a dark forest gorge, the Herbersteinklamm, at the end of which arises an imposing castle of the same name. Many periods have made their contribution to it— romanesque, gothic, renaissance, baroque. Peasants' straw-thatched farmhouses join the villages on the outskirts of the broad valley. Orchards follow the line of the low forest hills and on either side of the wide river lie fertile fields. Through an avenue of poplars the road leads to the picturesque and harmonious Castle Feistritz, well-hidden by the surrounding forests.

Out of the broad plain which was once owned by the Dukes of Styria rises Fürstenfeld, built up by the industry of its inhabitants, which has yet suffered the hardships of a frontier town up to the present day. The knights of Malta, evidence of an unbroken tradition, retain today their claim to a share in the property of the parish church which dates from 1232. A tobacco factory which has been established with its many branch buildings near the old castle soon recalls to lead us to the present.

The strip of land between the Feistritz and the Province of Burgenland is cut by the parallel rivers, the Safen and the Lafnitz. The hills which divide the two valleys rise up from the vineyards and forests until at Rabenwald and Massenberg they tower far above the stately Waldberge. Northwards these hills are overshadowed by the forest-clad mountains of the Jogelland which shut in the earlier course of the River Lafnitz.

At the foot of the mountains, between the serried rows of village houses which have often had to be rebuilt in the course of their tragic history, stand the residences

Riegersburg.

270

*did their grandfathers before them. On
holidays they wear the sober Maximilian
miner's formal dress as has been the
custom for centuries. Work above ground
has made the old shafts obsolete, a
giant electric crane replaced the old
trucks.*

*Three roads once led to Vordernberg,
on the other side of the Erzberg. The
brown one brought iron ore, the black
one coal and the white, flour. Up to
the time of Emperor Joseph II this
once-wealthy mining and industrial town
had the trading monopoly for all iron
ore smelted there. Since Donawitz has
been able to draw coal from Seegraben,
the blast furnaces of Vordernberg have
fallen on evil days.*

*Styria is also called "The Green
March", because of the woods which
cover the spurs of the alps, as vast
forests in the heights and as cool coverts
between the vineyards of the lowlands.
They are peopled by mountain dwellers
of ancient and hardy stock such as the
Archduke Johann knew and loved. That
princely friend of the people rescued
the Province from economic and mental
decay, making of it a pleasant garden
where the concerns founded and encouraged by him exist today. Johann gave
proof of his love for Styria by taking
one of its daughters for his wife. The
people and the forests have grown
together to make up what is implied
by the term "forest motherland."*

IN THE CAPITAL.

*The pleasantest way to reach Graz
is to cross the Ries. The road descends
in ever-sharper curves until after one
steep drop one finds oneself facing the
five terraces of the town. At once the
eye is caught by the Schlossberg with its
corpulent Clock Tower.*

*A sky of southern blue sets off the
grey stones of the main square. Outside
the Rathaus the flower and vegetable
market is a riot of colour. The character*

of provincial nobility, originally built for defence
and as a refuge for the villagers, which today
illustrate modern farming methods or have
become seats of responsible national education.
Castle Neudau, the old Wasserburg may be
named as one example of many.

Close to the edge of the mountains, at the
foot of the Ringkogel, over which the Romans
built the Säumerstrasse, lies the town of Hartberg amidst country which has been cultivated
since the earliest times. Today it is the seat
of various administrative authorities, an outpost
of northern East Styria. The fine lines of the
baroque tower of the local parish church puts it
ahead of many other pleasing pieces of architecture in Hartberg.

Pöllau, the market-town between Rabenwald
and Massenberg has become famous on account
of its old monastery church, a spacious building
distinguished by its fine workmanship. The
most important interior decoration is the painting
by the Master who created the Pöllau frescoes,
Matthias von Görz.

The ancient Monastery of the Prebendaries
at Vorau stands in solitary grandeur. Founded
in the 12th century, razed to the ground
by fire and rebuilt, ravaged by wars and consequently fortified like a castle, showing signs of
decay yet refurbished in the styles of successive
periods with added beauties, it has always been
a centre of monastic discipline and learning,
and of the religious and educational work
carried on by the priests in the mountains
and valleys of the district. The church has
two German towers. On the walls of its
brightly-lit interior the Masters of the early
18th century have put all the joyful triumph
of the baroque age into their paintings, colouring and stucco work. The sacristy is known for
its "Judgement Day", and "Last Supper",

by J. C. Hackhofer, and the library for its treasures of old manuscripts.

Space must be found for a word about the hill country between the Raab and the Mur, the Land of the Seven Valleys which, separated from one another by forested heights, all guide their dark streams past quiet rural villages and mills hidden behind alder groves, flowing in the same direction towards the Mur. The latter, sweeping eastwards, forms a natural boundary for Styria. In the forests the edible chestnut is common, here and there casting its shade over a tumulus, which bears witness to long-forgotten settlements. Summer warms the air with southern strength, autumn bringing clear skies and the finest views from the footpaths which wind through vineyards and woods to white chapels.

The Gleichenberge and the Stradner Kogel are of volcanic origin. The curative properties of their springs are widely known. Bad Gleichenberg enables numerous visitors to combine the healing qualities of forest solitude, with up-to-date medical equipment.

The vine, which is cultivated in East Styria with varying results north of Hartberg, steadily improves in quality towards the south, reaching its zenith in the Klöcher Gebirge and around Halbenrain where the fine vintages are stored in the wine-cellars.

Mureck is a town of ancient Styrian civic culture, but its crown, the castle of Obermureck, lies on the other side of the Mur in what is today foreign territory, as does Oberradkersburg, the ducal castle which since 1918 has been separated from the most southern town in Austria, the ever-loyal Radkersburg. None of the sufferings of a frontier town has been spared it. The tombstones in the churchyard of the gothic parish church are witness to the origins of its inhabitants. The venerable relics of Styrian civic life of olden times which are preserved in the tower of the Rathaus below the solemn frescoes of Fritz Silberbauer will encourage future generations to emulate the loyalty and watchfulness of their ancestors.

THE STYRIAN ENNSTAL. Where the train leaves the narrow valley of the Palten to enter the broader valley of the Enns, it is greeted by a noisy network of sidings, signals and rails in the big station of Selzthal. The time-table describes it as a junction where many passengers change trains at an important crossing of north-south and west-east routes. Its name is better known in and outside the Province than many another which formerly meant fame and surviving tradition in the Enns Valley. A hundred years ago Selzthal was not much more than the name of a district, of a forest valley in which the charcoal-burners worked for the *and appearance of the old town is determined by a mingling of Late Gothic, Lombardian Renaissance and Italian Early Baroque. The well-known double-spiral stairway is a specimen of the extravagances in form of the 15th century. Half a century later the Diet Hall was built, a renaissance building of mature beauty. Within the severe exterior, dominated by massive cornice mouldings, one is surprised by the southern spaciousness of the three-storied arcaded courtyard. A harmoniously blended stairway leads to the banqueting hall. The bronze well in the courtyard is the work of native bronze casting. The adjoining Provincial Armoury, established in 1640, contains the greatest collection of historical armour and weapons in Europe.*

The best work of the early baroque period is the tomb of the Emperor Ferdinand II. It was designed as a reminder of the triumph of the Counter-Reformation. The 16th and 17th centuries are responsible for the many arcaded courtyards. It was in the 18th century that the palais and residence of prosperous citizens were built.

SOUTH STYRIA, LAND OF VINEYARDS.

On the mountain tops shine small, white churches and summer bungalows gleam palely among groves and thickets. The shaded side of the mountain slopes are covered with forests, the southern sides bear sunny vineyards. The vines are often trained up poles which are usually the tops of fir trees, planted in the soil so that each vine looks like a well-grown tree. In the leafy vineyards are dozens of rattles, operated by the wind, which chatter at every gust. They are like wooden stars, little ones and big ones, which reflect the sunbeams, lending an unusual charm to the countryside. They give tongue at the least breath of air, their varied and often

Pöllau.

iron hammers of Admont Monastery, the iron-bearing rocks affording a meagre existence. Its few houses were not enough to form a village, and it belonged to the parish of Versbühel in the district of Rottenmann. But where the railway lines came to meet and cross, there the noise and bustle of the new life brought new inhabitants, new houses. Workshops and homes grew up amid the ever increasing noise and drifting smoke. In itself no beauty-spot, it is the gateway to a world of high mountains and age-old valley culture, the Ennstal.

To the right following the course of the river runs the Pyhrn railway, which then crosses the valley and disappears into the Bosruck Tunnel behind Ardning, emerging into the open to carry traffic to Linz in Upper Austria.

The track of the other line which leads to Amstetten follows the course of the Enns. From it one sees one picture after another of the ever-changing beauties of nature. The moss which spreads over the valley has in places been torn

Admont Monastery, Library.

musical notes enlivening the warm nights and sun-drenched, dreamy days. The more abundantly the vines have blossomed, the sweeter the ripening grapes, the more wind rattles are set up to protect the cherished fruit. In their thousands they are supposed to scare away the bold thrushes and starlings. Although when they sound loudly a cloud of scared birds rises into the sky, they soon settle again among the sweet grapes. The wind-rattles really contribute more to the atmosphere of this part of the country than to the effective protection of the wine. Visitors as well as natives adore them; you quickly learn to distinguish the notes of one from another. On stormy nights of hail and thunder, it is as if they were calling in alarm to the ruler of the clouds.

Styrian attributes:
Dour but galant the Ennstaler,
Charming the Ausseer girl,
Thoughtful and grave the Murbodner.
Solemn, good trencherman the East Styrian,
Easily roused the Grazer,
Soft of heart the Lower Styrian.
And all tough and courageous in the cause of the Motherland.

up or dug out to form ditches and pits; between them stand the narrow sheds containing slabs of dried peat. The valley extends as a wilderness filled with the humming of a myriad busy insects above the red carpet of wild mustard out of which rise blackberry brambles and the white trunks of young birches. The Kulm, a tree-clad hill on the pale summit of which stands the pilgrimage church of Frauenberg, rises steeply from the banks of the Enns. With two towers and light coloured walls the old shrine reflects the light of the surrounding mountain peaks, which look like a festive garland supporting the blue of the heavens. For half a century the abbots of Admont have cherished this church of Our Gracious Lady with artistic and more than loving generosity. In the "Turkish Year" (1683) the church was invested with its baroque pomp as a worthy framework for the old shrine, to which Johann Thaddäus Stammel later added a glorious wreath in the shape of a delightful choir of angels.

A narrow avenue of chestnut trees leads to a Calvary Mount on the fringe of the mountains. The group around the Cross rises above a weather-beaten wall. It is the work of peasant hands and has an impressive solemnity seen against the background of the distant mountains. In the valley below the Enns emerges, a green and glittering torrent, to flow through meadows and alder bushes to Admont.

The two slender towers of the Abbey which are seen by the tourist from a long way off, were only built after the great fire of 1865, but the surrounding settlement and the foundation of the monastery date back to the earliest history of the Province. Latest research claims to have established that the name Admont is of Illyrian origin, and that the "region of plentiful water" which this name suggests in Illyrian had therefore long been inhabited by human beings—by fishermen, woodsmen and hunters—when monks from St. Peter in Salzburg came, in 1047, to the monastery. It had been built by Archbishop Eberhard with money given by St. Hemma of Gurk, there to found what became one of the most prosperous and best known cultural centres of the Province. Worship and science, art, agriculture

Bad Aussee.

and forestry all found a home here. Progress and civilisation were spread through the surrounding virgin forests and through the properties which had been given to the monastery in Sausal and Untersteier. Often threatened by fire, the monastery has succeeded in preserving undamaged its famous treasury, the library with the frescoes of Altomonte and the masterpieces of J. T. Stammel up to the present day. During the heyday of the monastery, the flower of Austria's youth took their vows here, a long line of artists, men of learning and priests being noted in the chronicles of the monks during the course of a whole century. The great world, however, has forgotten most of their names, although historians still speak of Abbot Heinrich II, whose gifts of statesmanship resulted in the dignity of a Governor of Styria being added to his title of Abbot before he was treacherously murdered in 1297.

Better remembered in our own times are the names of the scholars Richard Peinlich and Albert von Muchar, after whom streets have been named by the provincial capital.

After a short, enforced pause, the rule of St. Benedict was re-established in the almost 900 year old cloister, a monastic revival in modern times of a venerable past.

Towards the north, beyond the little village of Hall, where salt was crystallized out of the waters in the 12th century, and the hidden, solitary mills, the Haller Mauern majestically enclose the Admont Valley. How grand are the names of the Steinberge—Pyhrgas, Hochturm, Hexenturm and Natternriegel! And how grandly their cliffs and peaks glow beneath the summer sky. For nearly half the year through clear and frosty wintry days they are covered with a glittering mantle of snow.

To the South the jagged Hahnstein rears its head, blocking the view to the higher peaks of Sparafeld and the Reichenstein. On the slopes of the Klosterkogel lies Röthelstein Castle. Lime trees stand in the outer courtyard, which is surrounded by a turreted and loopholed wall. A massive archway leads to the Residence which is known as a fine example of 17th and 18th century architecture.

On the left bank of the Enns, running eastwards, the road leads past the Grabner-hof, a modern agricultural college, and through the little village of Weng, climbing steeply to Buchau.

Through meadows and woods the little road leads out of a realm of solitude past traces of the bygone days of the "Ironmasters" to come gradually into more populated and livelier surroundings. In 1150 this place was called St. Gallus-in-Silva, i. e. St. Gallen-in-the-Wood—and the descriptive name is still applicable.

The main road from Admont to the East runs towards the Hohen Buchstein, at the foot of which road, railway and river enter that unique natural phenomenon which the Enns through countless aeons has carved out of the chalk cliffs, the Gesäuse. A sunny, cheerful forest valley, the river tearing its way through the rocks below, and on both sides high forests filled with the rushing wind and the songs of birds in the tree-tops. Now and again a stone avalanche falls from distant heights with the re-echoing crash of falling debris. Where small lateral valleys join the Ennstal they afford above dark forests glimpses of the gorges and heights of the Gesäuse-berge. It is an exciting excursion, no matter whether the traveller looks out from the window of a train or the back of a car, or, disregarding the fatigue of going on foot in the old way, enjoys the beauty of the Upper Styrian mountain world in a four-hour walk.

Into the Gesäuse runs the Johnsbach Valley, once filled with noisy life by blacksmiths and their apprentices, but now a popular point of entry for mountaineers who whish to climb the heights of the Reichenstein, Ödstein, Planspitze and Hochtor. In Gstatterboden, on the calmer reaches of the river, the mountain giants are again visible in all their majesty.

Where the Erzbach joins the Enns lies Hieflau, long famous for its output of Styrian iron. The nearby Erzberg and the waterway of the Enns enabled Hieflau to establish and develop its furnaces, to turn out iron ingots and to build workers' houses. There are still some remains of the great Enns Dam, a picturesque construct-ion of the hydraulic engineer Hans Gasteiger, who was buried in Kirchlandl in 1577.

The Enns, now flowing northwards, buries itself deeply between high plateaus on which farmers have long been settled amidst meadows and woods. Hastening past Gross-Reifling with its castle-like houses dating from the times of the iron carriers

and raftsmen, leaving Altenmarkt behind it, the Enns, today the favourite torrent for adventurous souls in collapsible boats, flows across the frontier into Upper. Austria.

From Selzthal the railway runs upstream along the left bank of the Enns to Radstadt and Bischofshofen in the province of Salzburg. All along-its course north-wards stands a chain of the characteristic peaks of the Kalkalpen in exciting diver-gency—Hochmölbing, Totes Gebirge, Hochtausing, Grimming, Stoderzinken and the lower flanks of the massive Dachstein. Different again, less wild, but as unique in their own way, are the forested subalpine hills which run off here to the left. Behind them lies the wilderness of the Niedere Tauern with their many lakes.

Liezen at the northern edge of the valley, mention of which occurs in documents of 900 years ago, was the most important transport junction before the railway came into being. Trade and barter brought prosperity from the salt carriers and the traders who arrived by way of the Pyhrnstrasse. The growth of the neigh-bouring town of Selzthal has brought losses to the former roadside settlement, but the persevering inhabitants have found other means of livelihood and today its flourishing industries have raised Liezen to the status of a town.

Wörschach, a pleasant and peaceful spot at the entrance to a gorge, attracts from afar holiday visitors and health seekers year after year to the healing springs of its radio-active sulphur baths. Mountaineers and ski-ers climb from here into the mountain world of Hochmölbing, Warschenegg and Hochtausing, the climber often finding summer conditions on the verdant heights of the Schneehitzalm and the Bärenfeuchten between the numerous herdsmen's huts. The mere pedestrian crosses the Taschnermoos within view of the towering Grimming and goes on to the Putterersee by way of Aigen.

From Wörschach the road leads westwards to Niederhofen, whose little gothic church deserves the attention of all lovers of art—and of Styria. This building contains curious tempera paintings from about the year 1500 and three carved altars from the 17th century. According to Ferdinand Tremel, the Styrian historian, we have in it one of the oldest churches of the Enns Valley. In Stainach, to which the junction of the Salzkammergut electric railway and the Bischofshofen—Selzthal line have brought new life and trade, we catch sight of the rocky nest of "in der Pürgg" above. The great gothic church there, noteworthy for its antiquity as well as for its unusually artistic architecture, well earns its local name of "Steyrisches Kripperl" (Styrian Crib). Inns and farmhouses surround it, completely filling the gap in the rocky cliffs.

On the other side of the valley lies Irdning, an impressive market-town whose busy life confers many advantages on the wide mountainous hinterland.

From Liezen onwards one is impressed again and again by a mountain which rises above lower wooded heights like a vast, glittering castle of rock—the Grimming.

Mariazell

It is not surprising that in the Middle Ages it was described as the highest mountain in Styria and that the people paid tribute to its majesty in awe-inspired legends.

The market-town of Gröbming is worth a visit. Holidaymakers are attracted to it because of its fine situation and wonderful scenery. People from a wide area come to deal with officials who long ago established themselves here because of the central position. Art lovers come again and again on pilgrimages to the beautiful gothic church whose great carved triptych altar of the year 1510 stands out among other art treasures.

Going upstream, we find the Enns flowing through increasingly cultivated and civilised country the nearer it gets to the old mountain town of Schladming. This place has been well planned and beautifully proportioned about a great square. Overshadowed by the towers of the Catholic parish church of the 16th century and the Evangelical church (1862), it presents a picture of dignified calm. In the past it has seen much want, warfare and tumult. It was the scene of peasant and religious wars. Fires and economic collapse ruined many an old family. The civic rights which were lost by Schladming in the year 1525 were restored to it again in 1925 in recognition of the courageous temperament and vigour of its population. The Schladming countryside gets its individual note from two plateaus, the Rohrmoos and the Ramsau. The latter, lying at a height of over 3000 feet at the foot of the Dachstein, has been populated and cultivated for ages. The picturesquely-scattered farm-houses bear many evidences of their occupants' unquenchable love of the homeland. Thanks to its healthy situation in the heights and the approach it offers to the Dachstein via the Austriahütte, Ramsau is one of the most popular holiday centres of the Alps.

From Rohrmoos, a little further off, the view of the Dachstein range is if anything grander and more impressive. Here, as on the Ramsau, the farmhouses have in many cases retained the local peculiarity of the flatly inclined purlin roofs (as they are to be found westwards in the adjoining province of Salzburg). Together with the wooden shingle roofs weighted down by stones, they give the countryside its distinguishing note. These comfortable and homely dwellings are fast disappearing. Modern ideas and times call for economy with wooden shingles, pointing to the greater space and other advantages afforded by the steep roof.

HOCHSCHWAB AND MARIAZELL. On the borders of Lower Austria rises the broad and mighty complex of the Hochschwab. The range covers a surface of 400 square kilometres and includes over a hundred separate peaks. When the townsman sees these mountains, he has the feeling that Faust's magic cloak has transported him into another world. The magnificent though distant views across the Danube to the high-lying plateau of the Waldviertel, to the West towards the Dachstein and beyond it to the Glockner, to the South as far as the barrier of the Karawanken are not easily forgotten.

No less impressive is the wilderness of surrounding peaks and snowfields. The

Dachstein, Southern Slopes.

Hochschwab, that mighty giant, is approached through defiles and valleys where stand old foundries and deserted smithies. One's eyes are continually drawn to the towering walls of this gigantic range.

That is how the monk had seen it who is mentioned in the legend of the founding of Mariazell. In the middle of the 12th century, Otto VII, Abbot of Lambach, sent one of his monks eastwards to spread the teachings of Christ in the wilds of the mountains. He carried with him on his arduous journey an ikon of the Virgin, carved out of the wood of the lime-tree. But before long he found that he could no longer find his way out of the mountains, range upon range rising before him to bar his path. At last he sank down exhausted before a wall of rock, calling on the Virgin for help and rescue. In answer to his prayers the unscaleable barrier of rock parted asunder, granting him a miraculous passage to the valley behind it. There the holy man stayed and decided to build himself a cell in honour of the Virgin.

Now a town, Mariazell is delightful in summer as in winter because of its position and the surrounding scenery. Its central point is the great pilgrimage church, the largest in Styria. Gothic forms and baroque roof are impressively united. To the rear of the middle part of the nave is the chapel of Our Lady and the revered picture of the Virgin Mary and Child which is the object of worship.

The simple "Marien-Zelle" has developed into a place of pilgrimage, its religious influence reaching far beyond Austria into other lands. Processions of pilgrims seek comfort and strength here. Women and girls who wear a picture of the Virgin Mary of Mariazell on a slender chain about their necks, are supposed to be protected by it from sin and distress, and to retain for life a share in that charm and gaiety which enshrines this little jewel of a town in the mountains and spreads over the whole Styrian countryside.

PROVINCE ABOVE THE ENNS

UPPER AUSTRIA

UPPER AUSTRIA

EUGENIE PIPPAL-KOTTNIG

WORD-PALETTE
UPPER AUSTRIA

Church spires in a broad countryside.
Hills · hillocks · and furrows.
Farmer's calendar · sundials · hailstorms · summer lightning.
Yellow hemp · white unbleached linen ·
the soft murmur of spinning-wheels.
Mountain forests · emerald-topped · high as thought can reach.
Rock crystal and many-hued stones.
Danube barges · boat builders · stacks of salt · stacks of iron.
Fields of rye and maize · wheat tall as man ·
wind-swept seas of grain.
Wars of the peasantry · open markets · towns of proud burghers.
Prosperity · joie de vivre · devout and thankful hearts.
Village churches · cloister · abbey and monastery.
Chalices · panel paintings · fish ponds · choirs.
Organ and jubilation.
Poplar avenues · fruitful countryside · picturesque
mountains on the horizon.
Salt in the lakes.
Water lilies · lovely play of light and shade.
Wind-driven wavelets.
Gay abandon of nature and man.
Blissful lives.

ƒ

our quarters make one whole: this expression was coined for Upper Austria. Security and tranquillity are the key-note of this province which stretches from the Alps to the forests of Bohemia, embracing a considerable stretch of the Danube.

The Upper Austrian peasant is not in the habit of making much fuss about his work and the city dweller is equally modest. But such modesty cannot be allowed to detract from the solid achievements of the peasants and townsmen which are Upper Austria's two first claims to fame. After these come her monasteries and convents.

But let the Province speak for itself and its inhabitants.

DOWN THE ENNS. Where the Enns leaving its narrow valley flows swiftly northwards to join the Danube, the "Green Province" joins Upper Austria at Steyr. Softly, gradually, the mountain ranges decline to smoothly rolling hills, until they subside restfully in the old iron town at the juncture of the Enns and the Steyr. For hundreds of years the hammers of armourers and cutlers have been pounding away on the banks of the river, for it is here that the iron of the Erzberg is welded into implements of peace and war. Together with the names of such well-known products as Werndl Rifles and Steyr motor cars, one comes across the name of Michael Blümelhuber. His part it was to produce delicate ornamental objects from the iron by his skill in steel-cutting.

287

Schwertberg.

Downstream the raftsmen see from afar the massive blocks of the city tower of Enns. Known already to the Romans, Enns has been since olden times an important depot for salt, wood and iron. Goods not discharged there for road transport, stayed on the barges until the Danube Maut (customs house) was reached. The market-town there is still known as Mauthausen, and commands the waterway to Vienna and Hungary.

IN THE MÜHLVIERTEL. In the great quarries carved out of the steep Danube cliffs one glimpses the primitive Mühlviertel scenery, based literally on granite. How many blocks of it have been cut and shipped upstream and downstream from Mauthausen, and used to build railways, roads and bridges, making the name of this picturesque market-town known throughout Europe! On the same bank further downstream before the Danube enters the narrows of the Strudengau is a fertile stretch of land known as the Machland. The chief town is Perg, once famous for its sandstone quarries from which millstones were cut. Close by is Baumgartenberg, which rises abruptly with the massive tower of its entrance gates and its high-roofed church out of the spreading orchards.

A secular building of equal interest is the massive Greinburg with its granite arcades built on a cliff jutting out towards the Danube, dominating the town of Grein, framed by the forests and reflected in the waters of the Danube. Ships navigating this part of the Danube have to be on the lookout for rapids and whirlpools. Warnings are exhibited on the banks near danger spots and where necessary, hoisted on flag poles. The tugs toil upstream laboriously hauling heavily-laden barges past the picturesque riverside villages of Sarmingstein and St. Nikola.

Northwards from Perg and Mauthausen the Mühlviertel countryside broadens

Steyr; the old Dominican Church.

Steyr; Market Square.

SALT FROM HALLSTATT.

Thousands of years before the birth of Christ, the salt deposits in Hallstatt brought settlers to this remote spot and soon gave them comparative prosperity. Mining was also carried on, bronze cast, coarse wool woven and many a beautiful vessel of clay skilfully formed, although without the help of a potter's wheel. In baskets and sacks the salt was brought along byways to the trading roads and there exchanged against Roman goods. When the overlordship of Rome came to an end, Hallstatt fell into oblivion, the barbarian invasions temporarily obliterating its very name.

In 1292 Duke Albrecht I of Austria ordered the salt works of Gosau to be opened. This led to friction with Archbishop Conrad of Salzburg, as salt was also produced in his territories at Hallein. Possibly this prince saw danger to his revenues in the competition. Possibly the new works at Gosau really lay on Salzburg soil. In any case when the news of Albrecht's death became known in 1295, the soldiers of Conrad of Salzburg, accompanied by a mob from Hallein, overran the Kuchental, destroying the salt-pans and the new trading-centre.

Salt mines in Hallstatt were first mentioned in 1311, as a concern run by the State. A new method of producing the salt had been developed; instead of it being simply hacked off in blocks, it was dissolved in water, and the solution pumped above ground into pans. For a time the salt thus recovered was transported just as it had been 1500 years previously ; that is, it was brought in sacks to Lambach and there shipped down the Traun.

Hallstatt's production in 1311 was considerable, amounting to about 4800 tons a year. By 1534 it was already 10,000 tons, rising to 25,000 tons in 1571.

The discovery of the Ischl salt mountain in 1562 caused Hallstatt's

out. Circumventing the deep cut valleys, the high roads lead to the hilly uplands. Before long one glimpses the wooded rolling summits with the Alps on their southern horizon. The surrounding hills are covered with dark green forests, against which ploughland, pastures and farms stand out beneath the sunlit clouds. The slender-spired, white-walled churches on the heights might be pilgrims' ships about to set sail towards shores in the heavens. From the depths rises the sound of the rushing waters of the Feldaist, which after flowing placidly through meadow land at Wartberg, has been trapped in a wide and narrow rocky gorge through which it has to storm its way into the open. There its dark sister, the Waldaist, which has its source among deep forests where in remote villages the inhabitants paint religious pictures on glass, flows placidly to join it.

Amid such surroundings lies Kefermarkt, whose gothic church contains a well-known carved altar, a fine example of late mediaeval art. It breathes the spirit of an artist who was at one with the people. St. Wolfgang occupies the central shrine, with St. Peter and St. Christopher on either side. The delicate tracery of the lime-wood carving branches upwards like the tops of trees. Something of the old-world peace that permeates the hill region which the traveller has just left seems to be embodied in the gentle inspired features of the central figure. In the face of the "Holy Ferryman" St. Christopher, one finds traces of the severity of the northern landscape. Any day you can run across people with such impassive faces, with such dour expressions on those inclement uplands of the Upper Mühlviertel, where spring arrives a month later than elsewhere in Austria, and where even in summer the solitary farmhouses are endangered

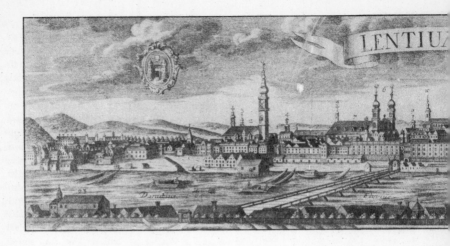

by raging storms. Here an early winter may often come to destroy the harvest, the fruit of bitter toil, and sweep away bridges and footpaths, so that neighbour is isolated from neighbour.

At such times life is easier in the Upper Austrian towns—for instance, in Freistadt, the former frontier fortification north of Kefermarkt. Round the mediaeval town with its wide, turreted square lies a broad moat. On the wall which once defended the citadel whisper ancient lime-trees, casting their shadows over the children who play beneath them.

Not far from here runs the line between Linz and Budweis, the first "railway" line constructed on the continent of Europe, which unites the former Crown Lands of Bohemia to Upper Austria. In biedermeier times the citizens of Linz used to make excursions on this railway, travelling far into the country in horse-drawn railway carriages resembling post-coaches. These were in use for 40 years before the horse-drawn was replaced by the steam railway.

Up hill, down dale, sometimes in deep valleys, sometimes climbing up to the heights, the Mühlviertel, which has been called, not without reason, the "hunchback"-land, stretches further and further out towards the dim vastness of the Böhmerwald. At the foot of the Dreisesselberg, where Bavaria, Bohemia and Upper Austria meet, rises the broad Mühl from which the district takes its name, its golden-brown waters flowing on to the Prämenstratensian monastery of Schlögl. For many hours one can trace its meanderings through solitary mountain forests, following the sound of the woodsman's axe or the smoke of the charcoal-burners, where the grey wisps float above the lofty crests of the pines. From courtyards and houses come the muffled rhythm of hand-operated spinning wheels. Here flax is grown, spun and

importance to decline, but on the other hand production on a large scale was planned for the whole district. A conduit for dissolved salt in solution was constructed from Hallstatt to Ischl and later extended to Ebensee, thus laying the foundations for an industrial development, the principles of which are still valid today.

A difficulty inseparable from the recovering of salt was the considerable amount of wood required. The two salt-pans at Hallstatt in which the solution was evaporated needed 380 cubic metres of wood per week. Gradually but surely the forests disappeared, for apart from the need of fuel for the pans, building and mining timber was also necessary. In the middle of the 16th century Hallstatt had a consumption of 88,000 tons of wood per year. These proved the maximum figures for salt production. The discovery of the salt mountain at Ischl and the subsequent laying of the salt-solution conduit saved the forests of the Hallstättersee.

In 1750 the transport of salt underwent a great change through the regulating of the Traun. From now on the

bleached. At Rohrbach and Neufelden the country opens out. Hops flourish on long poles and the Mühl is dammed to form a lake, the falls of which produce much needed water-power.

The wide ribbon of the Danube borders the Mühlviertel on the southern side, but the wild Urgebirge impedes the river's course, forcing it into creeks and side-arms. So were created the confined, deeply forested Danube narrows from Bavaria to beyond Lower Austria. A journey through those romantic reaches of the great river is not easily forgotten.

THE CAPITAL. Linz is a retiring town, a coy beauty. Anyone arriving from the railway station will not appreciate it. Nor will the motorist, if he follows the main road passing the iron foundry. The proper way to arrive at Linz is to land from the Danube. Then you will take it to your heart, for Linz is born of the Danube. St. Martin-über-dem-Felsen is its most ancient church.

The castle is an outpost. It has seen many changes, from monastery to castle, later to a

princely residence and then to barracks. Since the time of Rudolf II it has stood, a massive block-house, above the town. The old town lies at the foot of the mountain, where the little houses start to rise towards larger ones. The growth of Linz dates from the establishment of its market; originally it was just a broad street adorned with lime-trees and wells, an example of the interpenetration of town and country. The middle-class houses of the square speak of old-fashioned comfort. Narrow house fronts conceal long courtyards with ornately arched entrances. The Rathaus with its baroque façade and octagonal tower is hardly more noticeable than other buildings.

Linz has always been a bourgeois town. Each stone proclaims that this is no creation of monarchs, that this is a town of self-satisfied middle-class folk. Its history is a record of industrious citizens.

The northern porch of the fine Diet Hall reminds one of the great days of the 16th century. During the Reformation Johannes Kepler taught here and wrote his first work, the "Harmony of the World". The severely monastic renaissance buildings contrast with the elaborate baroque outlines of the Jesuit Church. Ignoring the busy bustle of nearby factories, the charm of this town of free burghers lies in its quiet and dreamy atmosphere, the baroque note of the buildings on the main road and the hour when the far-famed women and girls of Linz stroll of an evening on the main square and along the Danube banks.

UP THE DANUBE. Linz and (on the opposite bank) Urfahr are suitable points of embarkation for Danube steamer trips. The adjacent slopes of Frein- and Pöstlingberg, to which the little suburban houses on the river banks cling like birds'-nests, confine the bed of the stream at the start. The steamer passes between the impressive Kalvarienbergkirche and the slender tower of Puchenau, following the curve of the legend-haunted Kürnberg, in the forests of which are the walls of an ancient, weather-beaten refuge from invaders. Above the far-flung wall of mountains lies the Cistercian monastery of Wilhering. Built during the Crusades on an isolated strip of river bank, it was rebuilt after a disastrous fire with all the splendour of Austrian rococo.

salt from Hallstatt—still 10,000 to 15,000 tons a year—was rowed over the lake and taken down the Traun in small boats. From this time on a separate industry developed—that of ship-building, for there was a considerable fleet to keep in order. There were six-oared and nine-oared boats; upstream they were drawn by horses. The knowledge of ship-building acquired by the inhabitants of the Salzkammergut proved of good service during the wars against the Turks, for many hundreds of war vessels were built by them, to be used on the lower reaches of the Danube.

At the beginning of the 17th century, as a result of the Plague and the Turkish Wars, the Salzkammergut was involved in grave economic difficulties. In 1714 the Salt Office in Gmunden refused all responsibility for steady salt production "while the salt workers are literally dying of starvation". In 1715, people in Hallstatt were reduced to eating soup made of salt water and bran bread.

In 1717, scurvy broke out in Aussee. In 1770, the want was so great that the miners saved the tallow issued to them for lighting purposes in the mines in order to be able to take it home on Fridays as extra fat.

The time was ripe for social upheavals, and in France the flag of revolution was unfurled. In Austria radical reforms were proclaimed by a progressive monarch, the Emperor Joseph II.

ANCIENT CUSTOMS.

The traditional customs of the Province follow the seasons of the year. Just before Christmas families work with devotion and skill to build up a Manger scene, often several yards long. From moss and roots a Salzkammergut scene is built up in which the Crib is placed with its carved wooden figures, which generally date from the 18th century. Midnight mass is solemnly

Wilhering Monastery.

As one passes through a romantic countryside, villages crop up here and there, crowding their red roofs around lofty church spires. Elsewhere the mighty keep of a mountain castle challenges the skies. The steamer threads its way among sandbanks where herons stand motionless as dream figures until suddenly one of them flaps his wings and writes the cryptic signs of his flight in the morning sky. In the far distance one can see where, to the south, the wall of the Alps blocks out the horizon; at times it seems to draw nearer and at times it seems to be swallowed up in the misty distance.

The boat steams cautiously past the rocks of the Aschacher Kachlet, giving the passenger time to look at the tower of Eferding Parish Church, in which a certain Johannes Kepler once married the daughter of a simple citizen, Reutlinger. Beyond the ruins of Schaumburg we approach the hills of Aschach. The grapes embodied in the coat-of-arms of this market-town are a reminder of bygone days of Upper

Aschach-on-the-Danube.

Austrian wine-growing. The green grapes on the sunny walls of many a farm-house seem to be dreaming of these bygone glories. To-day, the mugs in the "Bauernstuben" ("Peasant Parlours") and the glasses on the inn tables are no longer filled with wine, but with the cider and perry from apples and pears which in late summer lie in great heaps before the old home presses, richly carved and decorated with mottos. The Upper Austrian is a great drinker of cider in pauses between his warm work in the fields, and at "Jause" (tea time), in cool, paved rooms or in the shade of an inn lime-tree in summer.

The wooded charm of the mountains lining the Danube Valley strikes an ever more solitary note. The hills and cliffs twist the ribbon of the river into loops until at Schlögen it makes a great bend around the foot of the mountain on which stand the ruins of Haichenbach. Next come the villages of boat-builders; further upstream we see on high ground the market church of Engelhartszell on the right bank, near the Bavarian frontier.

IN THE INNVIERTEL.
Rich harvests are usual in this part of the country. The four-square farms nestle comfortably and with an air of independence in the rich fields. In the stables, side by side with the long row of sturdy cart-horses are fast trotters, which draw the farmer and his wife on cross-country trips, or when they enjoy the hospitality of a wedding feast in some neighbouring village. Baroque church

296

announced by trumpets from the tower, and hundreds of candles burn in the cemetery.

In the "Rauhnacht", before the Feast of Epiphany, you can watch the "Glöcklerlaufen" in many parts of the country around Ischl. Young men in groups of up to 30 and more carry transparent head-dresses on their heads in the form of chapels, fish, crosses, ships, etc., which are lighted up from within by candles. They are dressed in white, with dangling bells and run from house to house at a definite steady pace.

In the spring, at Candlemas, the time for changing servants, there is "Aperschnalzen". This is a rhythmic cracking of whips which welcomes the first patch to be clear of snow. Later comes the "Almauftrieb" (the driving of cattle up to the mountain pastures) to be followed in autumn by their being driven back to the valleys. The procession up to the green pastures is a great event. The cattle are decorated with coloured ribbons and garlands of flowers, the leading bull carrying a bell. The calves often bear crowns of real flowers between their tiny horns.

On Palm Sunday the palm bush is constructed. Branches of pine, willow and spring flowers are twined together in bunches to which ribbons and apples are attached, and are then fastened to long poles and carried to the church. Afterwards they are placed in the middle of the fields to make them fruitful, and left until the new grain or high grass has grown up all around.

Corpus Christi Day is a religious holiday throughout the Catholic countryside. Everywhere there are processions. At Hallstatt and in Traunkirchen, where there is too little space between lake and mountains, the Corpus Christi "Procession" is held upon the lake. On the water, verses are read from the four gospels, while guns thunder from the shores or in the mountains.

Braunau-on-the-Inn.

towers and the steep span-roofs of the houses look out over golden fields of wheat and barley, over level plains and gently sloping hills of arable land, over orchards heavy with fruit and extensive forests. Like a constantly recurring *leit-motif*, the chain of the Alps thrusts the many-shaped zigzag of its peaks into the sky wherever one glances southwards. Whether it be in the prosperous market-towns on the Inn, in Schärding or Braunau or the land up-country, in Ried or Haag, in old riverside-shipping towns like Obernberg or in the distant villages, everywhere you sense the Innviertler's *joie de vivre*, his passion for dancing and song, his simple enjoyment of marriage and church festivals. Trace this to its source and you will find that it is love of the soil, of the Province, of home—as you will find it interpreted in the dialect verses of Stelzhamer.

If you are looking at altars and similar church decorations in this area, you will surely come across the name of Schwanthaler. An artist whose imaginative sketches have been exhibited all over Europe lives here in a romantic castle at Wernstein-on-the-Inn—Alfred Kubin.

IN THE HAUSRUCK. Across the Province of Upper Austria runs a forest-covered range of alps, the Hausruck. Its massive height may well have seemed to popular imagination like the body of a giant resting embedded in the surrounding hills, lost in mysterious dreams.

297

Schärding-on-the-Inn.

When this sleeping giant stirs—landslides of the underlying gravel beds, say the geologists—the giant Hausruck often shifts houses from their anchorage. Yet the people love him as a well-meaning giant, especially since he presented them with a treasure which adds to their prosperity. In the time of Emperor Joseph II, fields of brown coal were uncovered here. Since then a mining population has grown up. Wolfsegg, a market-town over which stern battles raged during the Peasant Wars, has given its name to the second greatest coal area in Austria. The fertile slopes of the Hausruck stretch out to the Danube Valley. At its lowest point lies Lambach, the old Benedictine settlement on the Traun. Its splendid baroque porch is worth attention. On leaving the neighbourhood of this monastery, one enters an area of almost irresistible beauty.

THE SALZKAMMERGUT. It is impossible to paint in words a convincing picture of the glories of the Salzkammergut. One can mention its name, together with those of various favorite spots there, to stir up feeling or memories. There is that feeling of elation which is inseparable from this area; everyone is susceptible to it, whether he comes from Upper Austria, Salzburg or Styria. A sense of expectancy masters eye and mind. Impatiently one's gaze wanders from the lovely immediate surroundings to the exciting view ahead, both impossibly lovely. An involuntary cry, a sudden embrace, may afford vent to the emotions—the Austrian will suddenly cry out: "God must have made this world in seven holidays!"

298

These are a few among many such customs. There is the cavalcade of the peasants on St. George's Day, and other peasant processions. There is much competition among the young men. It is real work dragging logs to the summits for the "Sonnwendfeuer" (Solstice Fire) or the tallest fir tree down to the valley for the maypole. If the youths of one village manage to cut down the carefully-guarded maypole of a neighbouring village, it is a notable achievement.

Inseparable from the customs of the people are their songs. Hence the many folksongs to be found everywhere— the "Almruf", the "Jodler", poacher's songs and Christmas lays. The themes underlying the traditional folk dances are love and play. The "Ländler" and complicated figure dances alternate with the difficult "Schuhplattler". Thus do old customs give a clue to the people and their character.

What names of districts, lakes and mountains shall one cite? There is the towering triangle of the Traunstein, Schafberg and Dachstein, the latter a part of Styria, emblems of the three provinces they dominate, the beauty of each reflected in surrounding lakes. Then the lakes themselves—the Traunsee, with its two aspects, the one gay and southern, and the other romantic, gloomy—behind it the rocky silhouette of the "Schlafende Griechin". The Attersee, a vast stretch of water, home of softly-gliding yachts, with rows of summer villas on its banks. The sunny Mondsee calmly rocks its waterlilies in face of the steep and menacing Drachenwand. On the other side of the Scharfling is the Wolfgangsee, framed like no other by towering mountains. Theatrically they stand encircling the lake, the Zwölfer-, the Retten- and the Mittagskogel, the haughty Sparber and the long Bleckwand. The sharply-silhouetted Schafberg dominates them all. In the midst lies the lake—dark, dreaming—princess or child of this encircling range. On its shores lie unreal townlets like illustrations to a fairy tale, St. Wolfgang the loveliest. Morning, noon and night one can watch the fascinating interplay of fresh breezes, light and shadow. Clouds drift across the mountains like playful cherubs, to be joined by pudgier cherubs, born of the mists over the little river in their mocking contemplation of the earth beneath.

Further down the valley stands Ischl, the summer residence of the old Emperor Francis Joseph. In the fields you may find planted tall poles bearing bunches of flowers left over from the Easter celebrations, or twigs of palm-willow, which the superstitiously devout plant in the soil, believing that it is a protection against hailstorms.

Orth Castle.

Corpus Christi Procession on the Traunsee.

Further up the Traun lies the Hallstättersee, a tight-lipped storehouse of ancient secrets. The houses of the little market-town are piled one above the other on the narrow rocky terraces leading from the shores of the lake to the slopes of the Salzberg, on whose heights lies a famous ancient burial ground. Lines of Hamlet come back involuntarily as one inspects the charnel-house with its many rows of skulls with religious inscriptions painted across the bony foreheads.

Indifferent to man's changing fortunes, the Dachstein, its royal peak towering above the mountain forests, watches eternally in its glacier armour. Below, the Gosau Lakes look up at it with unrevealing eyes of green in whose depths one can read only the reflection of primitive natural forces.

In the Salzkammergut, beauties of nature and of handicraft are never far apart, and on turning from the one you meet the other. There are carved statues and pulpits, sacred images and churches with famous altars—Hallstatt, Mondsee and, at St. Wolfgang, Michael Pacher's wonderful altar triptych.

There is the old monastery settlement of Traunkirchen; on a steep hill jutting out into a creek of the lake which the Romans called "The Happy", the monastery lies adjacent to the church and the dreamy courtyard of the now solitary garden, cut off by an arched gateway from the outside world. Next again comes the cemetery, protected by a low wall of rock which runs down to the lake. The graves are huddled together, the mounds and crosses covered by rambler and ivy. Those whose minds incline that way may reflect in this lovely spot on life's reconciliation with death.

Turning back to pulsating, exuberant life, the picturesque streets tempt one to travel further, mountain railways wait to carry one up to the summits which afford such unique views of the lake district of the Salzkammergut.

Just as in Rome one drops a coin into the Fontana di Trevi if one wishes one day to return there, so one should linger for a parting glance at the promenade in Gmunden. Built in a series of rising curves, the epithet it seems to call for is "graceful". Country mansions, castles and middle-class homes rub shoulders with one another. Boats rock softly on the water, swans glide elegantly towards the shore and the silver-grey outlines of the lakeside castle are reflected in the waves.

FROM KREMSMÜNSTER TO ST. FLORIAN. Swiftly and smoothly the pastel-green waters of the Traun run through forest and field out into the fertile moorland near Wels, a town which has a colourful and distinguished past. The course of the Traun is followed closely by the smaller Krems. This river has given its name to a splendid abbey. Anyone seeing Kremsmünster for the

Hallstatt

301

St. Wolfgang.

first time is immediately struck by its mighty, castellated walls with their great cupola-crowned roof. From the high belfry of the monastery towers with their helmet-like domes come notes of praise to the Creator. Standing before the interesting arcades of the fish-tanks, one is filled with admiration for the architect of the abbey. When (for the arcades of this unique building go far beyond the utilitarian purpose for which it was intended) one looks at the skies reflected in the crystal-clear surface of the fish-pond, listening to the fall of the water pouring from the moss-covered carved figures round the spring above it, one has a feeling of having caught a glimpse of a forgotten and enchanted world in which the strange story that the fish here were once called to feed by the notes of a bell sounds quite reasonable. Looking out from the top of the "Mathematical Tower", from the Observatory, one can see far into the valley of the Krems which spreads before one like a beautiful garden following the slopes of the foothills. To the south one sees the multitudinous peaks of the Tote Gebirge. With its rugged ridges and snowy, glittering peaks, it is majestically overshadowed by the wall of the Hohe Priel. There are many all-day excursions to be made in this area across rising plateaus and a landscape of primitive beauty. As one approaches it through the Almtal or by way of Hinterstoder one enters the realms of great heights and brooding silence.

St. Wolfgang, Pacher's Altar.

Mondsee; Stiftskirche.

The world which is
revealed at St. Florian
is vast and majestic in a
different sense. Below the
heights of the Ennstal the
towers of this magnificent
building of the venerable
Augustine Prebendaries
rise into the sky, a brilliant masterpiece of the
Austrian Baroque.

Bad Ischl, Pump Room.

One cannot help being deeply impressed by the beauty of this complex of monastic
buildings, especially if the approach is made from the highroad up the steep hill
and one passes through the main archway on to the outer courtyard. The effect of
the delicate lines of the façade is irresistible. In the middle stands the massive
gateway, inviting one to pass through and on to the point where stairways appear on
either side and, straight ahead, the spacious inner courtyard.

The names of Carlo Antonio Carlone and Jakob Prandtauer appear here once
again. Illustrious visitors have stayed here through all the centuries—emperors,
popes, artists and great masters, the last
of these being Anton Bruckner. The
Monastery is indebted to Albrecht Altdorfer for a number of valuable panel
paintings which, in their passion of
portrayal, in the splendour of their
glowing colours, represent all that is best
in the Danube School.

Bridging the centuries, the rainbow
of art reaches Bruckner's symphonies in
which the spirit of the baroque period
and of rustic scenery are expressed by the
blending of ardent themes with clear
and simple melodies. Grand stairway,
"Emperor's Room", Library, gay ceiling
frescoes, the carving on the dark choir
seats and jubilant, trumpeting angels—all
are born of that spirit which pervades the
Province of Upper Austria, rooted in the
primitive strength of the soil and religious
belief.

St. Florian Monastery.

PROVINCE

LOWER AUSTRIA

BELOW THE ENNS

EUGENIE PIPPAL-KOTTNIG

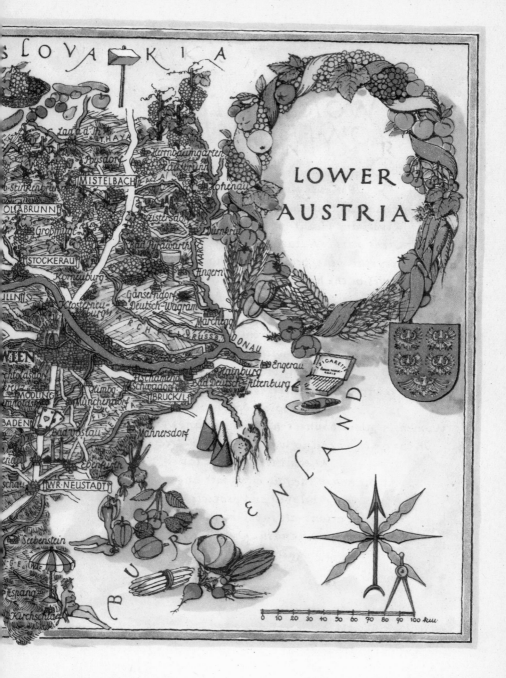

SLOVAKIA

LOWER
AUSTRIA

Poysdorf
Herrnbaumgarten
MISTELBACH
Hohenau
OLLABRUNN
Großmugl
Leiersdorf
Dürnkrut
STOCKERAU
Bad Pirawarth
Korneuburg
Ungern
Gänserndorf
Klosterneu-
Deutsch-Wagram
burg
Marchegg
DONAU
WIEN
Engerau
Lichten-
Hainburg
MÖDLING
Schwadorf
Bad Deutsch-Altenburg
Münchendorf
BRUCK/LA
BADEN
Bad Vöslau
Mannersdorf
Ebenfurth
WR·NEUSTADT

Seebenstein

BURGENLAND

Aspang
Kirchschlag

0 10 20 30 40 50 60 70 80 90 100 km

WORD-PALETTE
LOWER AUSTRIA

Primaeval migration·battlefield·frontier·
Soil of many races·cradle of Vienna·
Four quarters to a whole·Charm of variety·alps·hills·
Rivers and plains·great expectations of mothers·
Great gifts of Nature: Corn·poppy-seed·apples·
The crystal wine·brown bread·honest sons of the soil·
Monasteries in the heights·cloisters in valleys·city gates with
heraldic bearings·
Sunny courtyards·four-square·Lofty threshing-floors·well-filled stables·
The cellars deep and cool—a hospitable folk·
Northwards·wild forests with abundant game·In the midst
the great river
Baroque towers·ruined castles·bow windows and angle-nooks·
cooing doves·
Women in gilded bonnets·harvest garlands·vintage festival·
In the south—healing waters·black fir-trees·red beeches·
Ancient track to the sea·
At the heart the fair city·safe and surrounded·
beloved and protected·
All generations·all races·mingled and scattered·
Seal and handshake·Eternal hills·
Austria's Escorial·

ƒ

Variety of scenery, of work and of people, multiplicity of colouring and tone, differences of speech, song, verse and custom, in village and in town—all this goes to make up, all this is given by our bountiful, inexhaustible, motherly homeland of Lower Austria.

Let thy sons tell of thee to friends:

IN THE SEMINARY AT ST. PÖLTEN. It was a long and exciting journey as your mother travelled with you from the northern vineyards across Vienna and the Wienerwald to St. Pölten. As the great cupola of the mighty Abbey tower rose above the horizon you could not suppress a slight quiver of excitement, and as the other towers joined it, spires and then again cupolas, you felt, without being able to express it, that there was something spiritual about this picture. Then it gripped you, the riot of colour and the flowing lines of Baroque. Overcome, you stood in the great abbey square, and then passed through the gates in mute expectancy. Marble columns, gilded capitals, ornate ceilings and the glittering gilt and colouring of the altar pictures impressed you deeply.

Rathaus and Trinity Column, Franciscan Church and Carmelite Monastery, bold tracery of gables, blossoming clouds of stone, haloes spreading rays of gold, they all plunged you in a single day deep into the rich treasures of a vanished world. Since that day your acquaintance with the great names of Jakob Prandtauer, Daniel Gran, Altomonte, Mungenast and Kremser Schmidt have meant much to you.

In those times the board of the seminary was a frugal one and outside, overhanging the road to the town, there was a solitary pear, forgotten in the glossy green of the mighty tree-tops, tempting, round and invitingly yellow. For half an hour or more you tried to knock it down. The one who finally hit it was envied, but when he bit into it he made a face. For weeks it had to be kept in a cupboard, and only then did it become chocolate brown on the outside, the inside silver-hued and delightfully sweet. You soon found out that St. Pölten lay near the perry country.

311

The teachers took good care of you. They let your surroundings speak for themselves. You will never be able to forget the arcaded courtyard of the Schallaburg with its wonderful terra cotta work from the hand of an Italian master. Seitenstetten was rather far off, but you managed to visit it. Quiet and beautiful, yet busy in its own way, it is set in a fertile countryside.

Once two of you decided to go off together. Above your heads you bore a flag which was supposed to express the longing of its bearers for the open spaces and all things beautiful. They found their way to Mank, to Amstetten and further afield, discovering that this province possesses as many real farmers as it does great, rounded hills. Like castles on the latter stand the two-storied farms of the landed farmers. Theirs is the world in all its essence—ploughland, meadows, forests. Black-trunked, heavily grown pear trees stand before the farms, in gardens, in hedges. The peasant dialect is soft, easy going, manly and kindly.

Later you once stood with a girl up in the mountain-pass village of Annaberg, in the porch of the church. The curious high tower with its covering of metal plates showed clearly against the blue winter sky and in the far distance before you was the snow-topped ridge of the Ötscher. Then you set forth into the boundless glistening world through the dark-green snow-covered forest. There a wonder arose out of the earth, a wonder for you, child of the hills. Through the crystalline crust of the ice broke the faultless bloom of the first christmas rose, born of the silent force of winter. Carefully you picked the blossom, and carefully you gave it to the girl. Pure and white as the rose was this hour, pure as the eternally sparkling snows, young as the potent breath of the woods and as free of dust as the beckoning blue heavens.

You have not forgotten the sparkling summer waters of the Erlauf and Lunzer lakes. Surrounded by flowers and forests, tranquil, glitteringly blue, they call to you, offering rest to the weary visitor from the cities, and tempting the peasant pilgrims of Lower Austria away from their pious, easy walk of penance to the Virgin Mary at Zell.

STUDENTS IN THE WACHAU DISTRICT. Your St. Pölten teachers wanted you to see many and varied things, and so you found yourselves in the wine-gardens of Göttweig Monastery. Oh unforgettable hour! Blue as the night, golden as the moon, milk-white as the surrounding chestnut blossoms. St. Benedict is fond of building on mountains. Before us were the valley and the low country and there beyond, half hidden by fields, the Danube. Above were many hundreds of lights, gables, roofs, towers and mountains. On the morrow you passed through Krems, singing, because you were students, "A wandering apprentice I, knowing no cares ..."

How it echoed in the narrow streets! The past took you warmly by the hand. If you had found a blue-uniformed sentry standing guard at the Steiner Tor with

312

Göttweig Monastery; view from Stein-on-the-Danube.

red top-boots and white leather accoutrements, you would not have been surprised.

When the happy crowd went on to Dürnstein, was it still an excursion? Was not it rather a dipping into the romance of the past? "At the Sign of the Singer Blondel" or "At the Sign of King Richard the Lion Hearted" are names of inns there. And when you lay up above on the remains of a castle wall, the dark water streaming past below and the dark forests gleaming on the slopes of the mountains, you had for the first time the feeling of getting to know the spirit of a countryside and of being close to all the fateful events it had seen.

Melk is throned in majesty. From a massive parapet of stone rise Prandtauer's glorious towers. The Monastery is vast and overpowering. It was the birthplace of law and order in the Danube district, as of Austrian culture and literature. The treasures which the magnificent library offers to the mind can hardly be grasped by the eye.

Everyone should at least once have seen the colourful silk dresses and shimmering gold bonnets of the women from the Wachau district. How lovely when the evening light falls on them as it did that time in Göttweig, and you hear the moving rhythm of the song: "So home we go in the full moon's light."

THE WALDVIERTEL. Eggenburg lies almost on the dividing-line between vineyards and forests, gently warmed by virtue of the declining and widening slopes. But high above, around the Nebelstein, the wind blows chill and raw. There the oats have to be mown by mitten-covered hands. As the Ottenschlag saying has it:—"Three-quarters of the year winter, one quarter cold." In places there are enormous blocks of stone which have carefully to be avoided by the plough. Vast forests of pine give the countryside a dark and rugged hue, relieved only by

Weissenkirchen.

the austere yet lighter shades of oats and rye. Colour is lent by blue flax, red and white poppies and verdant green fields.

The view is dominated by range upon sweeping range of eternal mountains. White highways curve gracefully up and again down the steep slopes. Everywhere at the highest point stands a dark-green forest of pines. At times the ground stops abruptly, and you can see whence the gigantic stone masses fell—and are falling still today—which formerly towered above field and forest as ancient mountains. A precipice drops steeply away, the debris of fallen stone-masses lying at its foot

Apricot Gathering in the Wachau District.

among the many trees. Past great piles of stones large and small flow the Thaya and the Kamp, sweeping stones with them. They swirl in endless bends around the foot of cliff after cliff. About their sheer walls stand defiant castles and dreamy ruins.

Once you were invited to visit the forest district. For a whole day you journeyed through the woods and then you were forced to stop. Before you arose a great baroque tower, below it a forest of gothic pillars reaching towards the heavens, cloisters and a shaded well, the whole complicated gothic blossoming and romanesque fading—the monastery of Zwettl in its lovely situation on the banks of the swift-flowing Kamp amidst mighty forests. Continuing, you came to the frontier, high above. A piece of secular and chivalric history confronted you like a rock—Heidenreichstein, the most beautiful river-castle of the Province.

Usage and custom are rooted in the soil of the woodlands. On the house gables appear May blossoms in many colours. Young men plant green fir-trees, decorated with waving ribbons, for their girls. Mischievous "May paths" are devised with sawdust or water mixed with lime which are suddenly found leading over streets and byways from a certain door to another, thus making public what the parties concerned had kept a closely-guarded secret.

In many places the winter evenings still see the traditional "Rockreise". Women and girls "visit" friends in order to spin thread. Softly the delicate wheels turn, young men come and sing, and the women and girls tell stories of the robber chief Grasl, of the wicked Waldschrat and of God's vengeance on the inquisitive girl. Here and there an old loom is still standing.

Melk abbey.

*All the Provinces of Austria have
frontiers with foreign countries, with
the exception of Vienna. All the
Provinces of Austria have capitals
of their own, with the exception of
Lower Austria. Vienna is surrounded
by Lower Austria, providing it at
the same time with a capital. Thus
the Province of Lower Austria occupies
a unique position in relation to the
capital of the entire country, being
closest to it in times of sorrow as
well as in times of joy.*

*This Province is fourfold, the
Danube dividing it from West to
East. To the south of the river one
part lies below and the other above
the Wienerwald and in the North
the third lies before the Manhartsberg
and the fourth behind it.*

*The four quarters may also be
regarded from another aspect. On
the map, above and to the left is
the Waldviertel, sombre and of manly
strength. Adjoining it, consisting of
broad, low and sunny hills is the
fertile Marchfeld. Below to the
left one finds charming sub-alpine
country and finally the Wienerwald
with falling slopes and plains in the
east.*

*A many-rayed star of roadways
spreads outwards from Vienna over
the countryside. Parallel to the
Danube, the Linzer Bundesstrasse
follows an old Roman road over the
Strengberge to Amstetten and
St. Pölten. To the north of it the
highways run towards Bohemia, the
one heading for Budweis, the second
straight for Prague and the third
for Brünn. Pressburg (Bratislava),
on the other side of the frontier, is
passed on the journey to the Carpathians.
On the way to Budapest or down
to the Balkans one may pause awhile
at Bruck-on-the-Leitha. Eisenstadt
is on one of the roads to the vast
Hungarian plains, while the serpentines
of the Semmering continue to where*

THE WINE DISTRICT. Your home lies
below the Manhartsberg, its people and landscape familiar to you as a picture book which
you have looked through countless times.

There above stands the hill you love the
most, the Hutberg, just 890 feet high. From
it, on clear autumn days, you can see the
Schneeberg, Rax, Ötscher and Hochschwab;
you can see over the boundaries of Lower
Austria into Styria.

SPRING IS LOVELY. Approaching the
vineyards, you find a young peach tree. Its
delicate branches are full of pale, ethereal flames,
daintily burning garlands of roses without origin
or connection. You can see no leaves, only
blossoms below which grows not the slenderest
blade of grass. The vines are still cracked,
brown and withered, their shy green shoots
still pale and tiny. Innumerable grey sticks
seem weather-worn and dead, the yellow earth
still lies naked. Thus it is that the wonderful
pale pink garlands of peach blossoms seem to
have grown straight out of the dry wood and
wintery earth. You could walk for hours and
find nothing except beckoning bushes of flame
above brown vines and endless rows of grey
spikes.

This picture before you is full of a delicate
grace, of a strange beauty of shading. From the
lowest vineyards which rise gently before your
feet, you meet three delightful colours, old
acquaintances and yet uncannily strange. A
vineyard hut, washed grey by the rain, without
walls and straw-thatched. A cherry tree, heavy
with shining white blossom, arising from deep-
yellow earth! It is hard to believe that this
picture lies on the banks of the Pulkau, not on
those of the Yang-tze-kiang. Grey, white and
yellow, that is the quiet, dainty widespread
tricolour of all the flowering clay mountains

Raab-on-the-Thaya.

of the Pulkau, in the Danube area—and in China.

BEAUTIFUL IS OUR SUMMER! Millions of vines reaching out towards the setting sun, a low, thick-set endless forest of pale green. Before you the fertile valley in its lovely frame. Ahead, hundreds and thousands of fields, ribands of flame through which one can walk for two hours, golden seas of shimmering grain. And in between, green clover and vegetables, caught in the rays of the setting sun.

In the middle of the valley, along the Pulkau, lie the villages. Large and solid roofs, a strong, bulky tower, and round about a circle of trees characterise the isolated vineyard market-towns and villages. They are large and straggling settlements, virile in character. You should pay them a visit and enter one of the houses. A strong and penetrant smell of home-made bread, bubbling pots, flour-bins, eiderdowns bursting with feathers, the breath of man and beast, warmth of straw and stables will greet you with familiar welcome.

Where the valley sweeps broadly round are again pale green hills, vineyard upon vineyard. Next comes a wooded mountain, its crest gracefully sloping down and leading the eye on to the great beech and oak forests of Ernstbrunn. Hard is the life of the peasants here—never-ending round of toil. On winter nights when the vines are endangered, they tend the fires whose smoke fights the frosts. When at last they have completed the protection of the vineyards against damp, against drought, against insect pests, they turn, weary and worn, to the fields awaiting the reaper. As black clouds gather they fear for both. Through sleepless nights they aid the beasts in the struggle to bear their young. When they go to haul the trunks of great oaks from the forests, it is midnight before the horses are fed. The population has preserved its ancient manner of speech, as lively and as deeply rich as the ocean. The forces of long past centuries and an ancient home-land linger on in word and custom. Marriage splendours, the dance of the vintage, "Weizauslösen" (de-husking the grain) and "Federnschleissen" (stripping the feathers of their down) lend colour to days and nights.

In summer everyone should see a "Kirtag" (church festival). This is more than an annual fair, it is the great festival of the year, two days and two nights of feasting *they fork out into Yugoslavia and Italy.*

The roads are on the whole the same which the Roman legions used 2,000 years ago when they traversed the Province, to· be followed by the great barbarian hordes, by Attila the Hun, the "Scourge of God", the Avars going in one direction and the Franks and Bavarians taking the other. Swedes, Hussites, Turks and Janissaries, Poles, Pandurans, Napoleon's Guards, the song-loving regiments of the Austro-Hungarian Monarchy—and now the German and the Allied Armies—have succeeded one· another.

On the same roads dukes, counts, princes and emperors, kings of Bohemia and Hungary went their ways. Here also passed itinerant monks and flagellants, merchants and preachers, travelling students, scholars, minstrels, troubadours, abbots, cathedral builders, painters, copper-workers, organ builders, the Brothers of the Rose, Father Abraham a Sancta Clara, hurrying couriers and ladies in swaying litters. In later years came Casanova, Augustine of the ballad singers and Mozart on his journey to Prague.

What multitudes have passed along these highways during the last thousand years and in the thousand preceding them. The land is a book of stone— a living book of the people who have walked it. In these parts life has marked faces with the signs of joy and care, of knowledge gained through endurance and wisdom through suffering, until they have become such as we see them today, formed as an old master paints a face on canvas.

Like the unchanging Danube, the vines and the gentle doves, the sons of this province cling to the· customs of their forefathers and to their beloved soil.

Let us supplement the quartering of the Province by the mentioning of

at a generously decked table, after the walls have been freshly whitewashed, the doors newly varnished and the windows cleaned and polished.

HOW BEAUTIFUL IS THE VINEYARD COUNTRYSIDE IN AUTUMN! In the vineyards bells are ringing, not as a summons to festivities or to express joy, as the poets like to tell us. The narrow tracks sink into the soft yellow clay to a depth of three or four waggons and in the vineyards stand so many great tubs laden with grapes that the night is often far advanced before the last has been removed. Then it is that the tinkle of bells and the crack of the whip can be heard

Lilienfeld.

from afar, so that approaching farm waggons can draw aside wherever the track widens to let the neighbour's laden cart go past.

The wine cellars are spacious. Not every wine-grower has a house for himself and his family, but all have storage room for barrels and utensils. A real wine district numbers more wine-presses than private dwellings. They are to be found in dry and narrow valleys, looking from a distance like compact villages.

The wine-presses are built against the mountain, steps leading up to them through meadows and bushes. Above them sway acacias, lime and chestnut trees and elderberry bushes. Beneath their shade the children find a pleasant spot for play and games.

To the song of the wine-mills the dull gold juice runs off the pressing-board, guided downwards by pipes and wooden conduits. The youngest apprentice drives up the cart with its tubs of grapes and goes back for more. The landlord and his men press them until nearly midnight. It is difficult work, toying with giant forces and needs to be understood. The great, dark press groans in all its joints when the massive stone rises, swaying, and the slender bars, taking the enormous pressure, crack and snap ominously with the noise of rifle shots. Below in the cellar drifts a ghostly mist, whitish or almost invisible. Above in the vineyard stands a curious, squat sort of mill above a manhole. It is the hand-worked pump which draws up the powerful fumes. Despite it, every year one or two men have *places and towns. Dark are the woods around Weitra, Harmannschlag and Karlstift on the Bohemian-Austrian frontier; the countryside lies high with its heavy, dark earth. Zwettl, the town and the venerable monastery, are surrounded by vast forests. Above Ottenschlag and Martinsberg the Waldviertel closes in on the Danube, broken delightfully by the descending valleys of the Isper and the Weitenbach. Those wishing to proceed from Gmünd, the frontier station, or from Allentsteig or Waidhofen to the Danube, prefer the road through Gföhl, passing Senftenberg on the way down to Krems. Above on the Bohemian frontier, and also in the Thaya Valley, stand fortresses and castles: Heidenreichstein, Karlstein, Raabs and Riegersburg.*

The ploughed fields gain more and more on the forests, the vines creeping up the sunny slopes. Near Horn the countryside opens out attractively. Here there is a plentiful choice of routes—uphill to Drosendorf and Retz, downhill through the Kamptal to Langenlois and the spacious Tullnerfeld, or straight across country to Eggenburg and Hollabrunn, or by a sharp turn through the Maissauer forest and mountain towards Stockerau and Korneuburg.

So with a wide detour one arrives at the quarter lying below the Manhartsberg. Corn and wheat gradually replace forest and vineyards, increasingly so towards the March. Laa-on-the-Thaya, Poysdorf and Mistelbach lie on the way to the oil district of Zistersdorf. To the south the fertile corn-growing lands link up—Gänserndorf, Wolkersdorf, Deutsch-Wagram, Gross-Enzersdorf, Marchegg and Orth.

Around the hub of the Danube, the Alpine forelands penetrate deeply into Lower Austrian territory in the

Lilienfeld, Porch of the Monastery.

to be dragged unconscious from the cellar, overcome by the fumes of the wine.

In the vineyards you see men's jackets and hats amidst the vines, appearing and disappearing, for their job calls for bent backs most of the time. The day may be fine and sunny, here and there a grape picker full of fun and the harvest a bumper one—still, there is no romance about their task. All day long they shuffle with bowed shoulders from vine to vine, of which there may be easily a thousand in one vineyard, one vine alone often bearing a dozen bunches of grapes. Even the wine-grower's wife, despite the watchful eye she keeps on yield and profit, may straighten her shoulders with a groan among the tangled masses of heavily-laden vines to look out over the vineyard and exclaim: "God Almighty, will it never end?"

BEAUTIFUL IS WINTER AMONG THE VINEYARDS. One sees a blending of golden earth, immaculate snow and the red thorns of blue-grey acacia trunks.

Along the roadside, steep steps below protecting arches amidst trees and overgrown with brambles and bushes lead down into the wine cellars. On a holiday, many old hands return gladly to the place they were once so eager to leave. One hears familiar salutations—"Grüss Gott, Herr Professor"—"Servus, Franz"—"Servus, Schani".

Such greetings empress the brotherhood of those who work amidst the vines, a comradship which seldom dies. However distinguished the position some of them may have attained in the great world beyond, they are glad to return to the comfortable corner seat which was theirs of old—perhaps the more so because it is now unfamiliar. You could do worse than find such a corner yourself one day.

The white candle sputters and drips, held in a black iron spiral, as its gold-tipped flame lightens the surrounding shadows. Glasses hanging from the rough hooks of the black-wood glass-rack, reflect delicate or brilliant hues. The landlord, coming from the barrel with a brimming wine-siphon, takes them down one after the other and lets the thin stream of wine run into them, fragrant with summer, foaming and bubbling. As the traditional toast—"Gesundheit!"—"Good Health!"— goes around, one might think it the password of some secret society.

Day fades unnoticed into night as tongues are loosened and secrets shared. The wine and the earth which nourished it establish their rule over the hearts of men. *In vino veritas*—the inner soul of men, be it good or bad, reveals itself in words while the world beyond is wrapped in silence. Whatever the sounds of the street outside, they fail to penetrate into this roadside cave. Emperors and kings, battles and epochs cease to count. The world is that which lies within the orbit of the flickering candles. Here village school-teachers, priests, professors, doctors, their fathers and their brothers are one!

For many, Retz is the fairest town of the wine country. Here, during the dark days of the Thirty Years' War, the first Austrian hymnal was put together; it enshrines the soft and moving lyrics of Mediaeval German. That which Stifter's "Nachsommer" (Indian Summer) expresses in words, is told in stone in the beautiful municipal square of Retz. Below the square and under the houses lies cellar after cellar. In some of them you could drive with a carriage and pair. Above towers and crenellated walls, on the way to the forests higher up, stand two stately windmills, solitary and lovely, with no fellows in all Lower Austria.

IN THE MARCHFELD. You once stood day after day as the tireless lark filled the blue heavens with his song, while the great world stirred like a strong man awakening from a sound and refreshing sleep. This world seemed to be one vast wide-stretched field of green and brown, bounded only by the blue-forested Bisamberg and the Carpathians. Between these two were fields of pale, shimmering corn or misty plough-land. Above all arched the mighty dome of the skies.

Village Street in the Tullnerfeld

Klosterneuburg.

The tree-girdled villages with the red church spires were unpretentious and companionable. Around Easter the straight roads bordered with cherry trees became long avenues of fantastically beautiful blossom.

Gross-Enzersdorf marks the limits of the extensive island known as the Lobau, an unspoiled wilderness of water, trees and bushes. The river broadens out as the current flows more rapidly.

A son of Essling grew up to become a great master: Rafael Donner. Through Dürnkrut and Kroissenbrunn which appear in "King Ottokar, His Rise and Fall", Marchfeld has a link with Grillparzer.

IN THE DISTRICT BELOW THE WIENERWALD. Anton Wildgans called one of his books "Fate of Mödling". He lived near St. Othmar in a house above which grew dark umbrella pines between cliffs and sky. Any of you who want to appreciate the beauty of your country should read these books, the original manuscripts of which are preserved in the Wildgans House.

*quarter above the Wienerwald. Waid-
hofen-on-the-Ybbs, Lunz, Scheibbs and
the stretch from Mariazell to St. Pölten
are far-famed for their rustic beauty.
Further to the north of the Styrian
boundary lie Türnitz and Lilienfeld,
Hainfeld and Gutenstein near the
contrasting shapes of the Mittelgebirge.*

*Along the road to Greifenstein,
on the Danube, through Neulengbach
and Altenmarkt, descending to the
Hohe Wand, Schneeberg and the Rax,
runs the boundary of the "quarter
below the Wienerwald". Encircling
Vienna in a mighty arch from Klosterneuburg to Heiligenkreuz and Baden,
it descends to the plains along a line
of thermal springs. On one side of
the Südbahn grows a heavy wine;
on the other is a chain of industrial
centres—Traiskirchen, Sollenau, Leo-
bersdorf, Berndorf, Wiener Neustadt, Neunkirchen, Ternitz and
Wimpassing. The factory chimneys
do not end until the Semmering
district is reached at Gloggnitz and
Payerbach. The Pittental leads to
the "Bucklige Welt" of Edlitz, Kirchschlag and Aspang, while to the
east of Vienna the approaches to
Hungary lie in the flat triangle formed
by Schwechat, Ebenfurth and Bruck-
on-the-Leitha.*

ON THE BANKS OF THE RIVER.

*Restless flows the Danube through
Lower Austrian territory, until it
is reluctantly compelled to submit
to control and regulation. At Strudengau it still gives birth to leaping rapids
and circling eddies, twists itself at
Ybbs to a dangerous bend, narrows
to the legend-haunted valley of the
Wachau and constantly forces the
current to move now towards this
bank, now towards the other, until
it at last subsides into a broad and
placid stream below Tulln. With*

Baden, where the healing waters flow close
to the roadside, proved a great attraction for
you. To drink them you only needed to go
down a few steps. On all the bridges over the
Schwechat, you could smell the sulphur from
the springs which were discovered by the
Romans. The modern medicinal baths were in
their time the temple of a goddess. In the piping
times of peace you found there many people
who had come from far off countries. The rich
glow of the tulip beds in the Kurpark is a sight
which you should not miss.

Kornhäusel, an architect of late classicistic
style, built for Baden a town hall with Greek
temple columns and a flat roof adorned by
stone statues. His work, specimens of which
can be found throughout the town, is of modest
but genuine beauty. You keep finding pillars
and rows of columns, Doric and Ionic capitals
and caryatids, which, although of unequal value,
lend a distinctive air to the town through their
variety of form and the attempt to reproduce the
beauties of antiquity.

Mozart's "Ave verum" and Beethoven's
"Missa solemnis" are particularly treasured
by Baden. Grillparzer, Schubert and further
southwards, Raimund have all enriched this
countryside with the breath of their art.

At the foot of the forests are extensive vineyards. Light, stony soil and a favourable situation give the grape a
choice quality which has
been further improved
by careful tending.
Gumpoldskirchner wine
was taken around the
world on one occasion
on a Zeppelin flight. It
kept its high quality
throughout.

Hainburg, Wienertor.

You once stood in May in Wiener Neustadt on the Ungarfeld. There was the rocky wall of the Hohe Wand in the south. The Rosalien range appeared as a light coloured, enticing forest. Eastwards the green pasture-land opened out like a gateway. The two gothic towers of the Theresian Military Academy were an unchanging landmark of the "ever-loyal town".

You first drove over the Semmering in time of peace. Then you were able to enjoy yourself quietly and at leisure. Giants must once have played in this area, using as dice the mountains which begin here, wild and majestic. A man of the determination of Karl Ghega was needed to tame this wilderness. He bent the mountains and the deep gorges to his will. His tunnels and viaducts alternate in carrying the railroad to its highest point. The Semmering railway was the first mountain railway of the world which all others used as a model. All the railways of the Andes in South America learned from it.

The Semmering district, in a pocket of warm air above cold and misty valleys, is Lower Austria's show-piece. People from all the world over come here in search of health and peace. The Viennese regard the Semmering, Rax and Schneeberg as their own estates in the Alps. Towards the east the landscape slopes gradually down to the forested knolls of the hill country. In Mönichkirchen the work of Anton Wildgans reached epic status.

IN THE WACHAU DISTRICT. In the first days of creation there may have been some question as to which was the stronger, land or water. In the Wachau, the river triumphed over the mountains, although it has still to follow a course prescribed by the former, as to where it should narrow, should turn, should form bays and inlets; rocks jut out to spur its flanks, hidden granite builds hurdles over which it is forced to leap. Between Melk and Krems nestle a dozen charming villages whose picture lingers long with the wanderers along the banks and the passengers on the Danube steamers. Weissenkirchen lies in the heart of the Wachau district in a sunny position to the south. Old courtyards, arcades, rounded archways and vinecovered houses call for attention. In the small village of Schwallenbach they will show you the old parish church and the "Devil's Wall". The boatmen of the Danube tell the story of its origin. The Devil's grandmother is said to have scoffed regularly at the columns of pilgrims and the ships of the Crusaders, moving the Archfiend one night to try to block the flow of the Danube by building this stout wall. At Willendorf was found the sandstone figure of a "Venus" which archaeologists admire as a relic of matriarchal, pre-historic times. Spitz, a sleepy little Danube town at the foot of the Jauerling should not be overlooked. Backed by the four-square tower of the Hinterhaus ruins, it is in blossom time a fairy garden of pink and white. Standing out against the mountains behind are multi-coloured forests—pale green larches, rust-brown fir trees and dark pines.

Baden near Vienna.

it, it carries rubble and sand from the mountains, laying down its burden wearily in autumn when its level is low, only to drag it vigorously forward again on the swelling spring waters. In winter, ice-floes form into a barrage starting from the direction of Hungary, slowly advancing against the current and constantly fed by drifting ice. The ice-floes mount with loud reports one upon the other until, in some years, people are able to cross the river on them as on a bridge.

Flood warnings may be given at any time of the year. People are still caught unawares by the rising

To pay special attention to any one place of the Wachau would be to wrong all the others. There are St. Michael, Vösendorf, Rossatz, Arnsdorf, St. Johann, Aggsbach, Emmersdorf, Groisbach and Loiben. Every where are dreamy corners, arches and arcades, steep stairways and cliffs, ivy-covered walls overlooking the river.

Built on a rock high above the Danube, the monastery of Melk holds undisputed sway over the wide countryside. For 300 years the massed roofs of the village below have marched with the columned façade of the front elevation. It took a whole generation to build this

Seebenstein.

mighty Benedictine monastery according to Prandtauer's grandiose design, the Prelate's Courtyard with its quiet fountains, the Imperial Wing, the great half-moon of the terrace between the two monumental and at the same time delicately contrasted towers, the high dome of the cupola, the library, the fine reliefs of the archways and the artistic ceiling frescoes. Stand beneath this baroque canopy and look upwards: Virtues, Wisdom and the Arts are seen attempting to lead the human soul to higher things.

Here one is confronted with a part of the spirit of Austria. Side by side with the inescapable reality of everyday life and the material world, thought and emotion have built an unattainable but equally real world of the imagination in baroque style. It is in conformity that the Wachau district does not possess any broad, straight motor roads. Here everyone is forced to linger, to regard quietly his surroundings, perhaps also to ponder a little over himself and the world.

Melk stands at the beginning of the Wachau, which now passes Schönbühel to become the most famous part of the Danube Valley. Church and castle stand here on rocky ground near the river, showing a marked individuality of design. You would be well advised to stop at Aggsbach to climb to the ruins of Aggstein. The countryside here opens up like a burst and overripe fruit. Along the horizon roll the green waves of the mountains, hill upon hill. Far below the remaining walls of the once mighty castle gleams the "Rosengärtlein". Scattered around are farms, churches and fertile fields. Down in the valley vineyard follows vineyard. The sharp tang of woodruff rises on the air, and may later be met again floating in a refreshing wine-cup.

A culminating point in this feast for the eyes is Dürnstein. It rises up abruptly in complicated lines and its harmonious blending of ochre and white. Sheltering beneath the dominating ruins of the old castle and a baroque monastery tower is the clean little market town where the moving story of Richard the Lion-Hearted and his minstrel Blondel is still honoured today.

waters. Maliciously the latter lift the well-stacked piles of firewood, which they carry off with the same ease or difficulty as they do the rough-hewn logs which have been rolled to the river brink to serve as rafts. Using these as battering rams, the river attacks houses and barns, tears skiff and boat from hook and chain and drives terrified animals into the fatal current.

Then once again the Danube flows peacefully past the watchful water-gauges, to trickle cunningly above the dams on to the fields and meadows. Grassland and forests follow the river's course for long distances. The vegetation grows luxuriantly in the damply-warm climate of the Danube Valley, producing a primaeval, awe-inspiring picture. On the sand-banks of the river lives a polyglot world of birds. Cormorants and grey herons stand watchfully in the

In Krems the Middle Ages live on into modern times—the old city gates, the patrician residence with its bow window jutting out above the street, the Parish Church with paintings by the Krems baroque artist Schmidt, the inns with their dark, carved furniture and pewter vessels on the walls. Behind the town the vineyards follow the river, the steep clay slopes threaded by horizontal lines of stone supporting walls.

The Wachau ends with a monastery on the right bank of the river, as it began with Melk above. Göttweig, in an open situation on the mountain side, may be seen from afar. Set back from the Danube harbour and the shipping routes, it stands calm and solitary, remote from the noise of the workaday world. It can boast of Dutch tapestries and delicate chairs in the Imperial Suite, these and the

The Legend of Habergoas.

Wiener Neustadt.

ornate copper washbasins bearing testimony to the illustrious guests who have stayed here. Placid and secure behind its walls lies the first courtyard; from the walls one has a clear view of the surrounding countryside in all directions.

THE CHIEF CITY OF LOWER AUSTRIA—not under the law of today, but historically, is Vienna. The Province supplies this great mill of life with thousands of sons and daughters every year. There they become workmen, tradesmen, professors and priests. Many of their children and children's children fulfil noble tasks, becoming famous doctors, explorers, artists, technicians and statesmen. Their creative genius reflects honour back to their native valleys and farmlands, to humble homes, workshops, schools and churches.

Semmering.

Harvest Workers from the Cities.

bright sunlight, paying no attention to the peaceful raftsmen. Storks nest in the tall trunks of the silver poplars, quacking ducks and pheasants live amidst the labyrinth of bushes and reeds. Around solitary pools moves a world of beetles and dragonflies. Duckweed, river weeds, bracken and moss play their ageless game with the sunbeams. There the majestic step of the deer breaks through the undergrowth. Far from the dog's quick ear the rutting-call of deer rings out. Thrushes and reed-warblers trill their happy melodies.

The mother of Vienna is Lower Austria. Beethoven's fury-ridden journey to Wiener Neustadt, Schubert's gay excursions to Atzenbrugg, Raimund's forest refuge of Gutenstein, all arose from their dreams of the homeland, their life stories.

Great as a mother are you also, Lower Austria, in suffering and overcoming trials. A Province disturbed by the clash of arms throughout the centuries, a Province of battlefields, the tournament field of Europe, often laid waste, violated and ruined, you are always raised up again through the primitive forces of the soil, through a loving Providence and the work of ever-confident hands.

You, Lower Austria are truly an empire in your manifold life, your flowing distances and your directing centre.

331

PROV-
INCE
ON THE
BURGENLAND
LAKE OF
THE
STEPPES

WORD-PALETTE
BURGENLAND

Foothills of the Alps, fanning out into the plains.
Soft carpet of moss, rich and luxuriantly fertile.
A breath of the South in colour and distant space.
Unshackled play of the winds over vast open steppes.
Golden sheaves of sunbeams over land where once the ocean rolled.
Majestic stillness of eternal noon.
Wide heaths, herons in the reeds.
Feathered grasses by ponds of gleaming copper.
Far-off shimmering twilight – darkened lake.
Freestone arches of torture-chamber in an ancient keep.
Martial terra-cotta statuettes above the soft yellow facade
of a castle
Dead-straight highway fringed by wild acacias.
Soldierly ranks of gleaming whitewashed houses.
Village drummer, Martini Day, flock of waddling ganders.
All-day hunting through great estates and ancestral forests.
Slow-plodding oxen-team drawing the creaking farm-waggon.
Green-in-green mosaic of vines, up-hill, down-dale.
Be-shadowed soil, sunlight falling on vines and grapes.
Round-dancing to tamburizza.
Scarlet poppies, purple sage, reed-song and rhapsodies
Creative hymn, anthem of Austria, Haydn.

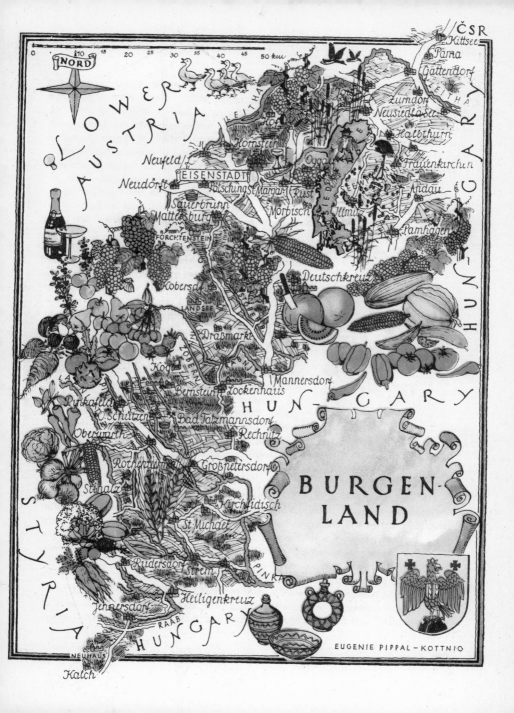

The Burgenland has some strange features. It is the youngest province of Austria, yet it claims to be one of the oldest. For a time it belonged to Hungary, and just during this period it held a brilliant position in Austrian intellectual life, boasting of such mighty names as Haydn and Liszt, Hyrtl and Semmelweis. Its name is taken from three castles which no longer lie within its frontiers, but is justified by other castles as well. It is of considerable length— 160 kilometres from North to South, corseted somewhere in the middle to a waspwaist only four kilometres in diameter. Its plains are sparsely inhabited, while its mountain land is densely populated. It has a raw climate in the south, while in parts of its northern areas, the climate resembles that of Helwan in Egypt. Its frontiers with foreign countries are longer than its inland boundaries, yet it is Austrian to the core.

The inquiring stranger who has set out on a voyage of discovery should first

drive by car along the Bundesstrasse to Bruck-on-the-Leitha and here turn off to the right into the Leitha mountains which in the centre separate the Burgenland from Lower Austria. From the summits of the mountains one looks down on to the Neusiedler Lake. Over 900 feet above the shining surface of the lake one finds oneself beneath sighing trees growing on what was once the bottom of a great sea. The sea itself, it is true, disappeared thousands of years ago, but the work of its maritime life remains in the form of rich deposits of mussel chalk. Walking along any forest path in the Leithagebirge one can easily trace in the stones the fossil forms of long vanished animals and plants.

When the tourist is weary of scientific research he can clear his brain in the sparkling Neusiedler Lake or with the no less inviting wine which ripens on its shores.

The plain to the north of the Neusiedler Lake was always one of vast estates. Between the scattered villages lie the dairy farms of the great landowners, who have their castles and manors in the villages. In Kittsee, Gattendorf and Halbturn there are many examples of baroque art. Lukas von Hildebrandt, Maulpertsch and others were commissioned to work there for the Magyar feudal landowners, Esterházy, Batthyány and so on.

Adjoining this countryside, the moor-land district, is tucked away on the eastern shores of the Neusiedler Lake a cloud-overcast and wind-harassed group of lakes. There are a number of warm and brackish little lakes, scattered over steppes of pronouncedly eastern character. Sea-sparwort, feathered grasses and copper-

gleaming pools lie generally beneath heavy masses of clouds whose great shadows move constantly over the inhabitants, houses and flowers. St. Andrä near Frauenkirchen is the place which has a climate in summer similar to that of the Egyptian Helwan. Here, as on the eastern shores of the Neusiedler Lake, flourish almond trees and other plants usually only to be found

Up in the Leithagebirge, near the village of Winden is the Ludlloch, a place where, according to the evidence of human remains discovered there, cave men and cave bears lived in the time of the later Stone Age, i. e. 6,000 or 7,000 years ago. Unfortunately there is no menu of the times extant, and it is therefore uncertain whether the cave men eat the bears or the cave bears the men. But as there are considerably fewer bears than men in the Burgenland today, it may be safely assumed that the bears headed the list of table delicacies.

The Burgenland is not unfamiliar with the question of land reform. Should the great estates be preserved as grain producing property or should homes be found for thousands of people in new villages? There are arguments on both sides.

A farm is a book of wisdom. The Burgenland owes its fertility to the hard working hands of its farmers who never neglect their soil, and who meet all their trials with placid good humour.

Although nine-tenths of the Burgenland is devoted to agriculture and forestry, it has over 200 industrial undertakings. There are saw-mills, wood-carving centres, parquet-flooring

in the South. Between the lake corner and the heath district lies a strip of specially favoured countryside, one of the chief Burgenland wine districts, with its centre at Gols and Weiden.

The tourist may now find it hard to make a decision: what should come first? Here beckons wine. Ochre yellow is the earth which produces it. Blue shadows toy with every shade of green, that of the firmly tied vines and that of the serrated, dull-surfaced leaves. Soon the glasses sparkle with Ruländer and Furmint, Welschriesling and Blaufränkisch and other famous vintages.

Above the water a silver heron sails majestically through the air, reminding us that the shores of the Neusiedler Lake are unusually well-stocked by nature with wildfowl. In the reed belt surrounding the lake live the grandest varieties of herons; here you also find nests of the bustard, willow-wren and bearded titmouse—a colony of birds such as can be seen nowhere else in Austria. When a flight

of wild ducks settles down here with rustling wings you may be meeting with old acquaintances again from the Wiener Stadtpark. The only difference is that there they allow themselves to be tamely fed by children, strutting like actors in the pay of the Municipality of Vienna, while here they lead a free marauder's life in the nightly-stirring reeds of the Neusiedler Lake.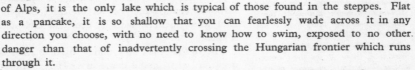

And the centre of all this, the lake. As you will expect, it too possesses strange features. In Austria, country of Alps, it is the only lake which is typical of those found in the steppes. Flat as a pancake, it is so shallow that you can fearlessly wade across it in any direction you choose, with no need to know how to swim, exposed to no other danger than that of inadvertently crossing the Hungarian frontier which runs through it.

On what one might call Western Austria's corresponding lake, Lake Constance, you find proud steamers sailing over the bottomless depths famed in ballads, but on the lake in the Burgenland the reckless sailor must only beware that the wind does not blow away all the water from under his keel. This must not be taken too literally, yet it is a fact that when the wind blows for days in a certain direction the whole water is actually driven together in the extreme corner of the lake. This phenomenon of the bewildering "Windstaue" is only one of the many peculiarities of the lake.

Another strange thing is that nobody knows whence its waters come, for the only tributary is the Wulka, an insignificant little trickle. Four times as much water as the brook contributes is regularly lost from its wide surface by evaporation. Logically, the lake should have vanished long ago. In defiance of all the laws of hydrography, it continues to exist, leaving scientists to puzzle out from what hidden sources it manages to keep going.

Occasionally the lake falls on hard times, and about once in a century it disappears altogether. This provides an occasion for the peasants on its shores to measure its bed painstakingly, and to resume the bickerings about the ownership thereof which had been dropped during the preceding century or even the one before it. About the time that the legal costs of these quarrels have so accumulated that the lawyers begin to be afraid that they will not be able to collect them, the lake quietly rises again, taking possession of its old bed as if it had never chosen to *factories, brick kilns, lignite works. There are factories which turn out linen, hemp and jute, blankets and felt, pencils, artists' chalks, asbestos, jade, sugar and methylated spirit. There are canneries for fruit and vegetables, and workshops producing stucco supports from the reeds of the Neusiedler Lake.*

BURGENLAND—THE GARDEN OF VIENNA.

Fruit, vegetables, grapes, the first early cherries, fresh lettuce, cauliflower, asparagus, strawberries, apricots, tender french beans—the first, long awaited harvest, doubly welcome after the winter, rolls in the spring towards the Vienna markets in a chain of high-piled lorries.

OGGAUER WINE.

In Oggau there is a Roman cemetery which dates back to the third or fourth century A.D., in the graves of which clay vessels have been found. Archaeologists say that these vessels contained the wine given to the dead to take with them on their journey to the other world. This calls for reflection. In those days every mortal expected that he would be served with nectar and ambrosia at the table of the gods. But the inhabitants of Oggau preferred to take with them their choicest wines rather than have to be dependent on the drinks of the gods.

Gustinus Ambrosi, the deaf sculptor, says of his Burgenland:
"How fortunate that I have travelled through the whole of Europe and have been able to drink in the splendour and magnificence of its many countries, with their thousand types of scenery, peculiarities and variations. Certainly it is nice to stay at home, but I felt the urge to get away and would have gone to the ends of the earth,

disappear. In former times it seems to have behaved even worse, for old documents mention it sometimes as a lake, once as a swamp, once as a river, then as a stream, while others appear not to have known of its existence.

The country lying between Eisenstadt and Ödenburg, Mattersburg and Rust, is the real heart of the Province. The lake parishes of Oggau and Mörbisch and the small "free town" of Rust are far-famed for their wine. On the gabled roofs and the chimney-pots stand pensive storks, in the vaulted cellars lie the massive wine barrels. As far back as the year 1364 the inhabitants received royal permission to mark them with the coat-of-arms of Rust—a trade-mark protected by law nearly 600 years ago!

Leaving the delights of Oggauer and Ruster wines, let us turn to Eisenstadt, the city of Josef Haydn.

One does not need to be especially sensitive to atmosphere to feel the genius of the great master in this little town which is so closely united with the surrounding countryside. The tiny house where he lived is still standing. How

Esterházy Castle, Eisenstadt.

Mountain Church in Eisenstadt.

even to exotic climes, in order to learn.

If I add up, I find I have spent nearly half my life so far in eight European countries. And yet of all the impressions, of all the wonderful scenery which I shall never forget, which was the most wonderful? I found it in my little home province of Burgenland, which hardly knows of the existence of the great world outside . . ."

Softly rolling slopes, hedges, distant hills are blended in a mystic harmony. A wonderful green, almost olive grey tint reflects in still majesty the glowing rays of the sun. The landscape is a series of undulating waves in which the farmers tend their fields. In the distance lie the white rows of village houses. In some of the fields the red poppy grows so thickly in spring that the deep red patches spread over the countryside as if God had underlined in this red ink, the poppies waving in the wind, that this is a happy countryside.

At Güttenbaeh, in the district of Güssing, a buried relic of the Celts was found—a hoard of silver coins which aroused the enthusiasm of numismatists until one day some cold-blooded investigator established that they were only copper coins with a thin silver-plating. Lest we should think too badly of this Celtic official counterfeiting, let us remember that at the same epoch, in distant Asia, the forging of banknotes had long been a flourishing industry.

BURGENLAND—STORK LAND.

If a girl is born, violets are put into the oven so that the child may not get freckles. The first actions of every newborn babe are of the utmost importance. If he stretches out his hand towards money, he will become a thief, if he tries to grasp a whip, he will make a good farmer.

small a space its walls enclose, and how far has the spirit of the human being who lived within them shone out across land and sea and across the changes of time. In Haydn's day the mail-coach still rumbled heavily over bumpy streets, but the simple Burgenländer Haydn, who made his first journey abroad only in old age, could say with quiet pride: "My language is understood everywhere!"

Haydn's home has been turned into a museum. Yellowed leaves with jottings from his hand are precious reminders of the creator of unfading beauty. Haydn is not alone in this tiny room. He shares it with Liszt, Burgenland's other great son, and with the daughter of his music copyist, the dancer Fanny Elssler—a glittering three-pointed star in the heavens of music.

Near by stands the palace of the Esterházys, strange, arrogant, yet impressive, built on the foundations of a mediaeval castle and renewed in baroque style by Italian architects at the end of the 17th century. The plain façade has inharmonious ornaments in the shape of terra cotta busts which are clumsy representations of former Esterházys and of Hungarian monarchs. But the garden front, in classic style with a view across a fine natural park on the slopes of the Leithagebirge, is impressive. From the terrace in front there is a no less wonderful view of the almost Tuscan landscape, framed by the Rosaliengebirge and the Ödenburger Mountains.

Although Eisenstadt is still so small a place, its new dignity as capital of the Province (since 1924) has meant a considerable increase in the number of modern

Eisenstadt, Synagogue
Death-Glass.

buildings—the Council Hall, attractive official buildings, the homes of civil servants and villas. Side by side stands the history of old Eisenstadt written in stone—the old royal free town, the Esterházy residence, the Jewish Ghetto in Unterberg and the more recent settlement of Oberberg. The Wolff Collection in the Provincial Museum has some unique monuments of Jewish culture. The Calvary Mount in the Bergkirche gives a glimpse of another world, with its painted, strikingly realistic wooden figures in curious grottos. A first inspection of Eisenstadt may well be rounded off by a visit to the wonder-working picture of the Virgin and to the tomb of Haydn in the Bergkirche.

Other attractions await us. Above Mattersburg appear the slopes of the Rosaliengebirge, covered with the luscious purple of flowering sage. One could wish that here spring might last for ever for us to admire the sea of blossom, cherry tree after cherry tree intermingled with peach and apricot, and the yellow-white blossoms of the plum, with their tangle of intertwined black twigs; great beds of strawberries flourish in the rich and fertile soil.

Far above the little village of Forchtenstein stands a well-preserved castle of the same name. It was once the seat of the Counts of Mattersdorf, whose forebears, Simon and Bertram, came from Spain in the year 1200 with their sister Tota, of whose beauty it was said that it had no equal throughout the world. A poet might well harbour the fancy that her beauty lives on in the spring splendour of the flowering hedges on the Rosaliengebirge. The student of history may remember that in the year 1374 the Counts of Mattersdorf and Forchtenstein placed this part of the Province under the jurisdiction of the Duke of Austria. Their escutcheon, combined with that of the Güssingers, forms today the coat-of-arms of Burgenland.

The early Stone Age has left evidence of human progress in the Wulka Plain. The Bronze Age which succeeded it was marked by a consi-

Forchtenstein.

342

When Croatian girls are singing
To the tamburizza's sound,
You hear ancient lays a-ringing,
Every eye casts smiles around.

For they're singing of Junaken,
Their love's rapture and distress.
Of the king's descendant, Marko,
And his wife, the proud princess.

― ― ― ― ― ― ― ― ― ―

derable development of traffic and trade. The Bernsteinstrasse, that famous trading highway of prehistoric times along which, about 1000 years before Christ, the honey-coloured amber, tears of the sea, was brought from the coasts of Samland to Italy, passes through the Burgenland. It crossed the Danube at Hainburg, a predecessor of the Roman road which later lead to Italy by way of Carnuntum, Ödenburg, Steinamanger and Laibach. Today Ödenburg (Sopron) belongs to Hungary. What the "Ödenburg Sack", connected to Hungary by a narrow tongue of land only five kilometres wide between the frontier and the Neusiedler Lake is to Hungary, is to Austria the "Ödenburg Spur" which limits the Burgenland to a width of four kilometres and almost cuts the northern and southern parts of the Province off from one another. Seven roads and three railways are thus cut off. The only road which connects the two regions had to be built by the Austrian Government.

"The bloody Hall", Lockenhaus Castle.

Southwards this road leads to the Oberpullendorf district, a hilly country with varied scenery and attractions of its own. Anyone interested in tracing historical developments must hasten through the Province to the spot where a range of mountains forms a barrier dividing Burgenland into two parts. The eastern corner which at the same time marks the Hungarian frontier, is the Geschriebenstein, the tallest mountain of the Province, some 2,700 feet high. Its summit affords a wide view across the plain of Raabau. On its slopes, just on the other side of the frontier at Wöllembach, on the St. Veitsberg, stood one of the best-known foundries in the Bronze Age, a prehistoric industrial centre.

Here the Burgenland reveals itself to the traveller. At the foot of the Geschriebenstein lies the forest-surrounded castle of Lockenhaus, which, with its Gothic Knights' Hall and a keep five stories high, dates back to the year 1200. Almost as old are the ruins of Landsee Castle on the borders of Lower Austria, one of the biggest castles in the country.

But to bore a tourist by dragging him from castle to castle as far as Kobersdorf would be risky, since it would—finally land him on volcanic soil.

343

Güssing.

Burgenland's volcano—Pauliberg is its name—is of course no longer active. But it provides the Province with indispensable basalt for road building.

The Burgenland volcanoes—there are more than one of them—although non-eruptive, have the hot springs which still flow along the thermal line. That line of healing springs which begins in Vienna and continues through Baden and Vöslau, unites in Burgenland with the sulphur baths of Leithaprodersdorf, northwest of Eisenstadt. It carries on to the unpretencious health centre of Sauerbrunn at the foot of the Rosaliengebirge and feeds the mineral springs of Kobersdorf at the foot of the Pauliberg. Parallel to it runs a second line from the radioactive baths in Edelstal to the mineral springs of Deutschkreutz.

Far off in the south of the Burgenland the basalt cone of Güssing is still recognisable as a part of the volcanic chain. The narrow strip of land where three countries meet and where the castle ruins of Neuhaus look down from the mountain, is in its isolation one of the most lovely spots of Austria. Here the Raab traverses the Province. Its name has survived from the days of the Romans, who may have adopted it from the

Kobersdorf.

Celts or the Illyrians. The town of the same name situated where the river joins the Danube is called Györ in Hungarian, preserving the memory of the Avars who, when the barbarian flood had subsided, remained as rulers of Pannonia, and thus in the Burgenland. "Györ" means "ring", the Avars designating as "rings" the earthworks behind which they defied a superior force, while their mounted hordes ravaged the countryside.

Bernstein.

In Southern Burgenland there are no surviving traces of the Avars, although the names of many places bear witness to their not always willing followers, Slavonic tribes who, as farmers, were forced to contribute to the support of the Avar nomads. Welten,

344

Gritsch, Doiber and Oberdrosen are examples, while Windisch-Minihof has preserved its eloquent name unchanged.

Minihof—does it not sound as if this village had been named after one of its favourite inhabitants? On Sunday, when the women and girls of the Burgenland go to church, many of them in the traditional and proudly preserved national costumes which differ from village to village, more than one pretty girl, whether Mini, Kathi or Liesl, attracts attention.

In the Province there are about half a dozen Minihofs. But the name means nothing other than Münichhof, Monks' Dwelling. The monks, whose memory has thus been recorded did much to further the development of the Province.

About 800 A.D., Charlemagne defeated the Avars, and established the Pannonian Mark, which included the best part of the Burgenland territory on both sides of the Raab and the adjoining strips of Lower Austria as far as the slopes of the Wienerwald. This became the nucleus of Austria. The monasteries of Salzburg, Kremsmünster and Mattsee, together with those of Passau and Freising, were given vast estates in the Burgenland by the Carolingian rulers and attracted settlers. The ruins of Scarabantia and Sabaria, which had the appearance of an "öden Burg" ("desolate castle"), lying about like "Steine am Anger" ("stones on the slope") then awoke to new life. Purbach and Donnerskirchen between the Leithagebirge and the Neusiedler Lake, Lutzmannsburg in the district of Oberpullendorf, close to the Hungarian frontier, and Pernau, further to the South just the other side of the frontier, all date from this time. So does Minihof, the "Hof", or residence, of the monks.

Let us here recall St. Martin, the most venerable of all the famous sons of the Burgenland. Born in 316 A.D. in the little town of Sabaria, he became through his efforts as Bishop of Tours the patron saint of the Franks. Reverence for his name was brought back to the Burgenland and to Pannonia through people who settled

Mörbisch.

there in the days of Charlemagne. In 1926 St. Martin was made the patron saint of the Burgenland. But the fact that every self-respecting Burgenländer insists on eating roast goose on St. Martin's day is not necessarily due to his piety. Since the days of the Carolingians, a number of places in the Burgenland have been connected with St. Martin either by their names or by the dedication of a church. The most southerly is St.-Martin-on-the-Raab.

Schlaining.

From St. Martin it is not far to St. Gotthard. This monastery, just across the frontier, was founded by French Cistercians in 1184. It is a curious coincidence that in the Battle of St. Gotthard in 1664, where the Turks were defeated in open conflict for the first time, French troops played a decisive part. The battlefield lies within the Burgenland parish of Mogersdorf. The name of the neighbouring village, Maria-Bild-bei-Weichselbaum, recalls the legend that a wonder-working picture of the Virgin was brought from a forest shrine to the village church, but transferred itself back to its original site, where a church was then built.

Kittsee.

Even in the days of the Carolingians the rivers of Lafnitz and Pinka contributed to the establishment of settlers in the Burgenland. The Lafnitz today forms a natural boundary with Styria. If you follow the line of the Pinka northwards you will find that it crosses the frontier of Austria seven times. The same typically Burgenland villages are to be found on either side, inhabited by a mixed Croat and German population. The river fortress of Eberau in this district is perhaps the least known castle in Austria.

In its upper reaches the Pinka like the other Burgenland rivers—the Raab, Lafnitz, Güns, Rabnitz, Eicha and Leitha—unites the Burgenland with the Styrian-Lower-

Landsee.

346

Village Street in Mörbisch.

Austrian alpine foothills, to which it by its character belongs. Sandwiched in between, on the upper Pinka, one finds a living witness to Burgenland history in the Magyar enclave of Oberwart.

The Magyars came to Pannonia about 896 A.D. In 907 A.D. they destroyed the Bavarian armies near Pressburg, thus putting an end to the Frankish-Bavarian Pannonian Mark. For half a century hordes of Hungarian horsemen overran Europe, spreading out even to France and Italy. The Battle of Lechfeld in 955 A.D. put an end to this, and the Magyars then tried to secure themselves a permanent home in the Danube Basin. Their "Westwall" was the impenetrable forests of southern Burgenland, and, further northwards, the swamps of Rabnitz. The valleys in the forest belt were defended by barricades and troops.

Oberwart.

In one of these "Warte" or outposts, which is today the Hungarian-speaking village of Oberwart, the Magyar garrison maintained itself for 1000 years. Here the Magyar origin of the population is still evident in their speech and picturesque dress.

There are traces of almost every period of Burgenland history in the district of Oberwart. The most valuable heritage is that left by the extinct volcanoes at Tatzmannsdorf, a healing centre for heart complaints and feminine ailments—an Austrian version of Franzensbad.

Geologists will find much to interest them in these parts. The brown-coal mines of Tauchen, the antimony and sulphur-stone deposits at Schlaining, the iron ore which was mined even in Celtic-Illyrian times at Eisenzicken and on the Eisenberg and the pyrite rocks at Redlschlag are instances of the varying types of soil.

Unique in Central Europe, however, is the asbestos of Rechnitz and the Styrian jade from Bernstein. The green, veined stone is really beautiful. It comes to the

workers who have inherited their trade from father to son as uninteresting stone splinters. The final products can be seen at the Vienna fair—unbelievably delicate vessels and translucent vases. The finest examples have gone to all parts of the world. The late King Alfonso of Spain even took some of them with him into exile.

The Burgenland is a country of ancient traditions, legends and memories. The story of the good prince Giletus and his wicked wife is supposed to explain the origin of the Neusiedler Lake. Then there is the legend of the "Wasserstoffel", a creature like a human being which lived in the Neusiedler Lake like a fish and, caught and tamed, emptied a whole sack of frogs, snails and water-snakes on to the banqueting table of his adored young mistress at her marriage, because this seemed to him to be a most delicate dish. The wedding gift was anything but well received, and the poor Wasserstoffel, who had meant it well, fled in despair and was never seen again. The Templar knights, who lost the castle of Lockenhaus through treachery, are said still to haunt it. In one of the most beautiful castles there occasionally appears a "White Lady", gentle and gracious.

The son of Wolfers von Güssing and his grandsons were called Henz, and from these proud lords whose family was one of the most powerful in the Burgenland the inhabitants are supposed to have received the name of Heinzen.

Between Güns and the Carolingian Lutzmannsburg lies the monastery of Marienberg. It was founded in 1194 as a branch of the Austrian Cistercians of Heiligenkreuz, who about this time were granted estates on the shores at the Neusiedler Lake, where the name of Mönchhof still recalls their memory.

Frankenau and a number of neighbouring parishes are inhabited by Croats. This race is to be found in many other villages scattered throughout the whole Province. How they got there, we shall see later. First let us visit the basket weavers

Basket-Weaver.

of the beautiful Rabnitz Valley and the potters of Stoob where the ancient craft of pottery is still carried on by hand. Then let us cross to Raiding. Here the small house is still standing where a great man in the world of music first saw the light of day—Franz Liszt. He was triumphant the world over, from Russia to France and England. Everywhere the smiles of lovely women welcomed him but more and more he was affected by that melancholy which is reflected in the verses of Lenau. The latter had connections with the Burgenland through his mother; his lyrics won as many friends for the land of the *Puszta* as did the Hungarian rhapsodies of Liszt.

Past Ritzing, where the surface belongs to the Burgenland but the coal below it to Hungary, because the tunnels of Brennberg, near Ödenburg, burrow below the frontier, our way leads us to Sieggraben. This is the home of the Semmelweis family, whose most famous son brought salvation from the scourge of puerperal fever to the child-bearing mothers of all times. From here the road climbs to the summit of the Rosaliengebirge, where a view opens towards the east across the Wulka Plain, taking in Ödenburg and the Neusiedler Lake and westwards, the Bucklige Welt, Wiener Neustadt and the Leitha.

Village Drummer.

On the Leitha also lies the battlefield of 1246. Friedrich the Quarrelsome, last of the Babenbergs, made the territory which had formerly belonged to the Mark of the Carolingians the subject of his first demands.

The Burgenland was long contested. Not for nothing do the many churches in its pleasant villages stand on commanding heights, surrounded by walls which give them the appearance of fortresses, and not for nothing were the many castles and fortified towers set up.

The days of the Turkish invasions brought poverty and desolation to the land, but at the same time a new population which was fleeing from the Turks and found a new home in the Burgenland—the Croats. From Kroboteck in the district of Jennersdorf through Stinatz, Punkitz, Podgoria and Kroatisch-Minihof there

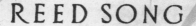

REED SONG

To the pond, where it reposes
drop the moonbeams softly down
twining their ethereal roses
in the reeds' encircling crown.

Deer move in yon hilltop, seeming
watchful of the velvet sky.
Now and then the geese stir, dreaming
where in tangled depths they lie.

Tear-filled sinks my glance revealing,
through my inmost spirit bare
a sweet thought of you is stealing
like a silent evening prayer.

NIKOLAUS
LENAU

Village Street.

are many village names of Croat origin. These Croats not only repopulated the devastated areas but also cleared the forests to build new settlements. The "Displaced Persons" of the Turkish Wars have become an indispensable part of the Burgenland population.

They are called "Wasserkroaten". It is uncertain as whether this refers to their having come from the coasts of Dalmatia, or whether "Wosser Kroaten" points to their having come from the province of Wossen, i. e. Bosnia.

The soil of the Burgenland is not capable of feeding all its children, so that thousands of its inhabitants become bricklayers who work for the whole week in other parts of Austria during the season, to return on Saturdays to their native villages. Their busy hands have helped to create the splendid buildings on the Ringstrasse. In the plaster and stucco decorations of these are concealed the reeds of the Neusiedler Lake. The Votivkirche, in Vienna, is built of stone from the quarries of St. Margarethen, between Eisenstadt and the lake. The Italians who were summoned to the Leithagebirge in 1550 as stone masons had barely become Burgenlanders when they were commissioned to work on the imperial "Neugebäude" in Ebersdorf. Thus there is a close connection between Kaiser-Ebersdorf in Vienna and the Burgenland parish of Kaiser-steinbruch in the Leithagebirge.

Without designing it, we are back at our starting-point. Kittsee has still to be mentioned, lying in the extreme north opposite Pressburg, where Josef Joachim, the famous violinist, was born, and Zurndorf, the native town of the Vienna Capucine preacher, writer of Hungarian history and Protestant bishop of Saratow in Russia, Ignaz Aurel Fessler. Nickelsdorf looks over the frontier towards the Nibelungen town of Wieselburg, where Josef Kainz (famous actor of the Vienna Burgtheater) first saw the light of day.

There are castles and churches where the art of the Burgenland is represented by the paintings of Dorfmeister, Maulpertsch, Altomonte-Hohenberg, Köpp von Felsenthal and Storno, an art which lives on today in the work of the famous modern sculptor Gustinus Ambrosi.

Let us glance again over the wide and sunlit countryside to Eisenstadt, where the festivals in the historic Haydn Hall have revived the music traditions of the Burgenland, to the villages where one hears the tamburizza orchestra, and the airs of old folk songs from which Haydn took the undying melody of his hymn. Once again let us glance at the people, the farm labourers at Friedrichshof or Edmundshof, the workers in the chalk and jute factories, the reed-cutters by the lake and the vine-dressers with their aprons stained green by copper sulphate, the farmers and the labourers, as far as the smallholders in the extreme south who industriously till their four *joch* of ground, keeping records of the weather as their fathers did before them. Don't be surprised if one of them appears round a bend in the forest path, nods approvingly at the fleecy evening clouds and pats you on the shoulder to say—"That's the weather we need here. But you—come back again soon to our Burgenland."

METROPOLIS ON THE DANUBE

VIENNA

VIENNA
SECTION

LEGEND

1 ST·STEPHEN'S
   CATHEDRAL
2 OPERA HOUSE
3 HOFBURG PALACE
4 RATHAUS
5 NATIONAL THEATRE
6 KARLSKIRCHE
7 FINE ARTS MUSEUM
8 NATURAL HISTORY
   MUSEUM
9 BELVEDERE PALACE
10 SCHÖNBRUNN
   PALACE
11 VIENNA FAIR BUILD-
   INGS—COURT
   STABLES
— TRAMWAYS
— METROPOLITAN
   RAILWAY

THE CONTOURS OF A CITY.

Vienna is not merely the name of a city.
Vienna is not merely a symbol of European history.
Vienna is not merely the world's musical centre.

Vienna is all this and much more. Vienna is the sum of the knowledge of life of generations and peoples, it is the effort of many states to draw together. Vienna is the conversation between men, the arts and nature, the link between present, yesterday and tomorrow. Vienna is a suggestion to the world to adopt its way of life and being. Between that which constitutes home—the register of births, the wedding ring, a trade inherited from one's father—and that which calls one abroad—opportunity, a far-off future, parting and settling down in new surroundings,

Vienna is a third alternative. It is the adoptive home of musicians and men of intellect. It is a hospitable centre of pleasure and luxury where difficult and pointless journeys come to an end and sojourning in this world becomes wonderful everyday life.

Vienna is the expression of life itself. Life with all its terrors and its great moments. Not only the expression of the will to live and not merely the imperative of Kant or a "You may, You shall, You must". No, everything and everyone lives in Vienna and is loved—the hunchback, the deaf, Falstaff and Don Quixote. Everyone in Vienna is equally important, the great as well as the little stars drift at night on the same road towards eternity.

Vienna is a place of recuperation from all ills, even if it is not listed as such. In its air and its atmosphere one finds the right standard by which to judge the problems of life, which exist before the eye of the new-born child has focussed on the surrounding world, and are still there when that eye closes for ever. To inherit this earth and yet not fall a prey to Mammon, to possess it and yet to remain penniless, to conjure up a vision of Heaven without becoming a Utopian, to blend these things properly together and to fill the hours of one's life with them—in short, to possess the art of living humanely as a human being—all this is essential Vienna.

Why otherwise should there be such contradicting opinions about Vienna and the Viennese? Every such opinion is similar to the picture reflected in a badly-made mirror—it is hopelessly distorted.

Come, therefore, and see for yourselves what Vienna is—even now and despite everything. Vienna, born of the surrounding countryside, is, as you will soon recognise, still a part of it. The rolling lines of the forested mountains in the West, from which in summer a cool breeze blows even in to the narrowest streets, reach far out towards the city. One constantly catches glimpses of nature in the distance, of the sunny plain of the Marchfeld, or of the broadening valley of Vienna's river known in song as the Blue Danube.

This city whose suburbs stretch from the vineyard-covered heights of the Kahlenberg and the Bisamberg to the richly-wooded Danube meadows is truly at one with the smiling landscape and benevolent Mother Nature. Its streets and squares were not laid out according to geometrical plans, but grew up naturally, as men felt the need to build them; the very routes of the tramcars which take one so quickly from the heart of the city to the verdant world of forest and meadows follow the course of various streams and brooks which have long disappeared under the cobblestones and asphalt.

The landscape around Vienna retains its historic outlines. Roman hands planted the sunny slopes with the precious vines. Later on, Christian monasteries spread the blessings of education. Crusaders rode through the Danube Valley, watering their horses in the Nibelung river. The plain of Marchfeld became the scene of bloody conflicts between powerful lords who sought to dominate the capital. At

The Hofburg before 1848.

the end of the Turkish Wars the relieving forces came down from the heights of the Wienerwald to fight a decisive battle, at Aspern and Eßlingen Napoleon lost for the first time the halo of invincibility.

Time after time the countryside has won back its inhabitants from political storms to the enjoyment of its own eternal melodies. All those with a talent for painting, building, music or poetry, have drawn strength and inspiration from their native soil. The countryside is linked with the soul of the creative work which has been completed in its midst. In the songs of Schubert, in his "Unfinished Symphony", the Wienerwald lives again. Beethoven expresses it thus: "Here, surrounded by this scenery, I often sit for hours, my senses delighting in the contemplation of the conceiving and life-bearing children of nature. Nobody can love this landscape so much as I."

Poets have sought to immortalise the rhythm of Vienna and its surroundings in verse. A happy band of painters has found in it an inexhaustible source of inspiration.

Few cities are so rich in history and drama, in glory and in suffering, as Vienna. Nothing is ever lost in this world, not even the tremulous heart-beat of a child, nor the words of lovers beneath flowering jasmine, the melodies which so strangely linger on in the city. That is why Vienna can unfold that fascinating drama of life which exists for its own ends, for you, for me, and for everyone.

ON FOOT THROUGH THE INNER CITY.

Come now straight to the heart of the city, but forget for a time your occupation and the time of day. There are towns which may be hurried through hastily. Others—and Vienna is one of these—need to be enjoyed in leisurely fashion.

The difficulty of understanding Vienna lies in the contrasts and parallels with which one is everywhere confronted, the baroque fusion of concrete objects and abstract ideas. The pulsing heart of the city, its centre in every sense of the word, is the Stephansdom. Six modern streets, busy and bustling, converge there to pour their teeming crowds and traffic into the Cathedral Square. There is nothing visible to recall the fact that this square was a cemetery until the time of the Emperor Joseph.

Viennese Girl, 1898.

Let us approach it from the Graben. The kaleidoscope of moving traffic keeps the picture of street life constantly changing. Above a tall house stands a globe as an advertisement for sewing-machines. A few steps further and we face the Cathedral, standing aloof from the workaday world which surrounds it. Before this grey, noble pile, everything round about seems to dissolve into unreality. Never can this picture be forgotten, the tower, at once massive and delicate, its slender height leading up to the window of the fire-watchers, up and up to the blossoming of the spire and to its topmost pinnacle above which there is only the majestic peace of the Vienna skies.

This cathedral in the midst of a bustling world of shops radiates a solemn calm, a hallowed spot amidst competing vanities and material interests. Like some worldspirit rising clear of the life

Viennese Girl, 1899.

of the senses, its tower reaches up to the heights of immortality.

This church is no sermon in stone, but a building which appeals to every sense and thereby multiplies its eloquence. Its speech can only be heard by those who listen with their inmost souls—there are many thousands who hardly catch the faintest whisper as they hasten past. Yet to everyone, surely, the moment comes when he hears and understands this speech.

Do not confuse yourself with details. Listen only with one ear to the explanations offered you, for the general impression is more important than the parts which go to produce it. But one cannot overlook the old romanesque west front. It stands solemn and massive in comparison with the supporting columns which rise upwards to lose themselves in the delicate tracery of arching windows. There in front, near the small porter's lodge begin the seemingly endless steps leading up to the tower. Behind the water-spewing gargoyles hangs the "Pummerin", a mighty bell which was cast from the metal of Turkish cannons.

Before we enter the Cathedral let us take a quick glance at the exterior. There are niches sheltering figures which look down on us—Jesus on the Cross, the Virgin Mary, and, towards the front, an open air rostrum from which Johannes Capistranus preached a crusade against the Turks. The small door at the side leads to the catacombs. It was at this spot that the body of Mozart was consecrated in 1791. The subterranean chambers are extensive and many-storied. In the crowded city of the Middle Ages it was often necessary to bury the dead

below the streets of the city itself. From 1735 to 1783, 12,000 bodies were buried here.

The North Tower of the Stephansdom has never been completed. Need we regret it? Could one nowadays picture this landmark of Vienna with a second companion tower? Over the Adlerturm

Vienna. Kärntnerstrasse.

Dominikanerkirche.

(Eagle Tower) spreads the twilight of expiring Gothic, but a few paces further on we can admire the luxurious, vigorous Gothic of the porch before the Bishop's Door (leading into the transept). The plain façade across the street is that of the Archbishop's Palace.

Let us now enter through the reverent half-light of the Cathedral. What a vast hall confronts us. The light of the candles which pious hands are for ever placing before the picture of the Madonna give an idea how high is the centre part of the nave. Gradually shapes take form in the gloom—statues, columns, canopies, tombs, memorial tablets, the wonderful stalls of the women's choir, the pulpit, a portrait of the Master Pilgram, the Tirnakapelle where Prince Eugene sleeps, the baroque altars against the pillars and the tomb of Friedrich III.

BURGOMASTER DR. KARL LUEGER.

When the Ringstrasse was nearing completion and Vienna had not yet finished filling in the wide gaps between the districts on the near and on the far side of the Gürtel, when there was a never-ending stream of people moving towards the capital seeking work, happiness and well-being there, when the city's outer suburbs were reaching out further and further towards the horizon—at this moment a man arose from amidst the people who was to complete Vienna's transition to a large city with vision, courage and energy during his few years of office. This was the memorable burgomaster, Dr. Karl Lueger.

He was a true child of the people, his father being curator in a museum and his mother the owner of a tobac-

The Dorotheerkirche before 1787.

conist's shop. He himself started as an insignificant and unkown lawyer, but soon became the advocate of the small man. He had an unequalled knowledge of Viennese dialect, which he spoke himself.

This was the beginning of a new era. The industrial development of Austria had reached a peak during the seventies of the bygone century. Finance and industrial capital completely dominated the economic system of the Monarchy, backed politically by the Liberal Party. At the Freudenau races the offspring of great aristocratic families rubbed shoulders with those of the new-rich „gulden millionaires". They raised their grey top hats in salutation to each other, the one with casual good breeding, the other with demonstrative self-assertiveness, exchanged bows and greetings from their rubber-tyred carriages in the Hauptallee and soon found themselves in full accord over mutual business

How evil were those men who set fire to this wonderful cathedral as they retreated from Vienna in 1945. This is the most painful wound in the martyred body of the city.

Let us forget such sad memories in the sunny, pleasant streets where we can join the bustle of the Old Town. We may cut through the narrow side streets quickly, seeking the hidden heart of the city. Converging on the noise of the Kärntnerstrasse are deserted corners and the backs of houses where washing is hung out on the balconies and a cat calmly licks its paws in the sunshine. Round-arched double doors stand half open to the inquisitive gaze. Old ladies live there who hobble daily to Mass with enormous prayer books, funny, proud old things with the hearts of children. Pretty, fair-haired children smile confidingly from the windows or laugh as they play in the courtyards. There is

State Opera.

such a small-town atmosphere here that it seems as though the biedermeier period lingers on.

These pictures are all to be found here within a comparatively small space. The same number of steps which we had to take from the Cathedral to reach this quiet corner will suffice to take us on to other great gothic churches. The solemn and massive Augustinerkirche stands in a street which is filled with the noise of motor traffic. Its Early Gothic form is still cool and severe, far removed from the decorative exuberance of Late Gothic. The famous Christina Monument created by Canova at the beginning of the 19th century is a remarkable example of the symbolic portrayal of sorrow and mourning.

interests or at times in the conclusion of strange marital alliances.

The great town mansions near the Ring were in sharp contrast to the houses in other parts of the city, in the outlying districts. In the latter a single pump had to suffice for four, eight or ten families and what was called a "light-shaft" was not worthy of the name. It was a gloomy, narrow tunnel down which the sunlight only penetrated as far as the upper stories in the hottest summer.

To be a Liberal meant to leave things as they were, not to interfere, to leave the peace of the upper classes undisturbed and to remain deaf to the plaints of those below.

Lueger, however, had an ear for the low mutterings of the crowd, for he lived next to the small man, to artisans and shopkeepers, simple citizens and factory workers. To replace isolated and ineffective outbursts of discontent, he formulated a radical programme of demands, using language which could be understood by all, shaking the Imperial City until it awoke from the slumbers of Liberalism with his fiery speeches.

While society—baronesses, bankers and officers—continued to waste idle lives in flirtations, while the Prater meadows echoed in the early morning to the sound of shots exchanged by duellists, Lueger was considering how the pressing municipal problems which had arisen through the crowding together of enormous masses of people could be solved in progressive fashion, to the advantage of the community and in the teeth of corruption and vested interests.

The population of Vienna had risen from 680,000 in the year 1875 to 1,727,000 in the year 1900, but the horse-drawn tramway, the steam tramway and the few electric trams were not linked together. They were inadequate to meet the demand for transport, and charged very high fares.

Apart from these concerns a few small gas and electricity works had come into being, all of them privately owned and most of them the property of foreigners, who had built up for themselves a circle of paying customers and now proceeded to make enormous profits.

Lueger recognised with infallible instinct that the supplying of the Vienna population with gas, electric light and modern means of transport must not be made the subject of greedy exploitation by private capital, but that it was the duty of the municipality to retain the monopoly of this branch of the administration in its own hands, thus making these facilities available to the general public on the most favourable terms.

The quiet peaceful Minoriten Church has a solemn, other-wordly air. The fine main entrance in French Gothic is the work of Jakobus of Paris. The façades of baroque palaces, which now house Ministries and the Diet are neighbours in the intimate square.

Hidden away in a corner of the Old Town lies the attractive church of St. Maria-am-Gestade, at the foot of which formerly flowed the Danube, a place of worship venerated by salt-shippers.

Residence of the Archbishop.

The sevensided tower, the open tracery of the decorative stone cupola, the delightfully hideous gargoyles, the charming covered porch and the richly ornamental network of the arches are a series of glorious surprises.

Emerging from this church, it is as if its noble proportions had not yet quite released the visitor from their spell. The narrow surrounding streets through which we approached the church seem to have acquired something of its air of quiet and repose. Vienna is often criticised as being backward. All it amounts to is that the city is too wise rashly to discard what time has tested and found worthy. To do otherwise would be to murder its own soul. Vienna wants to remain always Vienna. In the development of the city, this wish has never been forgotten. You will never be able to understand Vienna until you have grasped one secret. The soul of this

With these basic demands Lueger became the founder of Communal Socialism, gaining with this programme the support of the small man. After nearly 20 years of political struggle, he entered the Vienna Rathaus at the head of the Christian Social Party which he had founded. Austria generally remained under the domination of the Liberal Party, which had four times been successful in securing that the Emperor four times refused to sanction the choice of Lueger as burgomaster. The fifth election in the year 1897 was finally approved by Francis Joseph I.

Capital sought methodically to find a way to block the socialistic tendencies of Lueger in the city council, and he continually met with great difficulties in financing important projects. Finally he founded the Zentralsparkasse der Gemeinde Wien in order to have a bank at his own disposal. He also created

Plate IX

Rudolf von Alt; Stephansplatz (section). Vienna, Municipal Collection.

Plate X

Albrecht Dürer; Mary with many Animals. Vienna, the Albertina.

the Städtische Versicherungsanstalt in order to make cheap and reliable insurance available for the masses.

Vienna's rapid development into a great city which culminated during Lueger's term of office as Burgomaster, forced the municipality to undertake new responsibilities. Lueger recognised the needs of the situation and proved himself competent to satisfy them along modern lines.

If one reviews the extent of his activities as Burgomaster, one has to admire Lueger's administrative genius even more than the oratorical gifts of this man of the people. Within a few years he created the extensive organizations of the Municipal Gas and Electricity Works and established a network of tramways. Gradually schools arose. He met the needs of the city for drinking water by building a second pipe-line system to the springs in the mountains. For the living he built the Krankenhaus der Stadt Wien (the Vienna City Hospital) in Lainz, the Städtische Altersheim (Municipal House for the Aged) and the Heil- und Pflege-anstalt Am Steinhof (Lunatic Asylum). For the dead he established the great garden area of the Zentralfriedhof (Central Cemetery).

The building of the municipal warehouses, the taking over of a brewery as city property and the establishment of the central cattle market in St. Marx enabled the Burgomaster to influence trading developments and to institute a measure of price control.

Lueger's greatest gift to Vienna was the creation and dedication to the city of the belt of forests and meadows, which brought it health together with the beauties of nature.

The progress which marked the year 1900 and subsequent years bears the stamps of Lueger's own personality. The necessary measures were born of his own initiative, and had often to be carried through by his personal

Jesuit Church at Am Hof.

bewildering city lies in the past, rooted in the baroque period, yet holds fast with lively enjoyment to all the beauties of this warm earth.

The centre of Vienna as the "Kaiserstadt" is the Burg. There is an Old and a New Burg, the older part dating from the Babenberg days of the 13th century. Behind a short and deep ditch, once a moat, stands the gateway to the Schweizerhof. Its massive rustic blocks call to mind the magnificent porches of Lombardy. The strong pulleys over which ran the chains of the drawbridge are still plainly recognisable.

The courtyards and wings are extensive. Towards the Michaelerplatz the complex of buildings ends in the "White Tower". In the

Vienna; Heldenplatz.

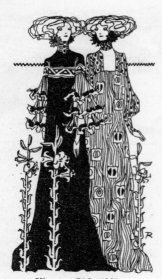

Viennese Girl, 1902.

insistence in the face of general opposition. Thus the great Burgomaster
prepared the way for the idea of collective provision for general economic
through the municipality. He may be
said to have built the bridge which led
to the fulfilment of the demand of the
mass of citizens for collectivism in a
communal-political sense. Ten years
after his death this work was continued
by new methods in other directions, and
once again became an example to the
whole world.

WITH BAEDEKER IN HAND.

No matter how easily Vienna reveals
itself to you and throws itself open to
you, you will not get to know it without
an effort. On the contrary, you must
take your Baedeker and scan it con-
scientiously as though you were back

semicircle of the front façade are two monu-
mental groups of statuary symbolising the
"Sea Power" and "Land Power" of the former
Austria.

The sombre façades of various centuries unite
in calm dignity to form the impressive square
of the Inner Burgplatz. Here the ceremonious
changing of the Castle Guard took place. Here
the privileged Dampierre Dragoons were allowed
to parade before their Highest War-Lord with
martial music, and to set up their recruiting table.

In the Schweizerhof steps lead up to the
Castle Chapel where the Wiener Sängerknaben
sing Mass, Sunday for Sunday. Adjoining it
is the entrance to the Religious and the Secular
Treasuries. Once inside the enormous building
of the Hofburg one can walk through wing after
wing. There are the rooms where Emperor Francis
Joseph once lived and laboured; next to these
are the apartments of the beautiful Empress
Elisabeth, followed by sumptuous gala halls
which lead to the vast wing of the New Burg.
How lucky that the plans of many an edifice
in Vienna have been only half executed. The
view of the Heldenplatz detracts attention from
the explanations of the most experienced guide.
Original in its unfinished symmetry, it is a
square, panorama and a landscape scene at the
same time. It forms a square with the two
museums, the Royal Stables and the three
monuments which decorate it. It becomes a
panorama as we see how it connects with the
Ballhausplatz, the Burgtheater, Parliament and
the Ringstrasse. It is landscape by virtue of the
park and adjacent buildings which carry the view
on to the Rathaus, the Votivkirche and the hills
of the Wienerwald which seem so close. The
medley of people strolling backwards and
forwards on the paths of the Volksgarten suggests
a painting by Brueghel. But in the month of

Viennese Girl, 1912.

May the colour-loving eyes of Waldmüller seem to have been at work when the circular clumps of heliotrope and purple lilac close in the walks and open spaces in scented profusion.

One should traverse the Heldenplatz in all directions as if looking for a lost drachma. It is everywhere varied, and everywhere a part of Vienna. One may go there on a March morning when young mothers are pushing their prams backwards and forwards in the sunshine, sheltered from the wind, beneath the windows of the study of the President of the Republic. Its vast extent is brought home when the Viennese stream in through the Heldentor and surround the statues of Prince Eugene and Archduke Karl in their hundreds of thousands on some festive occasion. Or you may visit at five o'clock in the afternoon when the path alongside the Volksgarten suddenly springs into life as some hurry home from work while others crowd in the opposite direction into the Inner City for recreation or a rendez-vous. In "Fasching" (Carnival) you may see how the lights of the many-candled chandeliers shine forth from the tall windows of the gaily-illumined state apartments. In the great Redoutensaal across the way the lights

at school. Here are a few things you can mark in advance for special attention.

The STAATSOPER (State Opera House), although it became a ruin in 1945, should be visited for the sake of its memories. Read how this building, which many people described as the most beautiful opera house in the world, looked in the days of its glory. Spare a thought for those two luckless builders of the '60s, van der Nüll and Siccardsburg. The loggia with its attractive façade and statuary, the gilded vestibule and the main staircase have remained intact, but nothing is left of the magnificent interior, of the rows of seats and the boxes, of the ceiling paintings of Rahl and the imposing wall decorations of the gala room.

The spirit and tradition of the house, however, have remained alive. Burnacini's gala operas in the 17th century, the performances at Laxenburg Castle, in the Old and in the New Favorita, in the grounds of Schönbrunn and later in the Kärntnertortheater—all this formed an unbroken chain to the opera bouffe, the "magical opera" and to Mozart. For Fanny Elssler's triumphant rise to popularity the old opera building was too small, and the new opera house on the Ring had its gala opening with "Don Juan". It ushered in a glorious epoch. Verdi came to Vienna, Wagner was discussed and fought over. A generation of singers, the House itself, the Philharmonic Orchestra and the conductors grew together in one concept which throughout the world is more honoured than the diplomatic corps—the Vienna Opera.

The fine building, beloved of the Viennese as the setting for so many memorable and wonderful hours, now lies in ruins, but the Vienna opera, the talent, the love of music, the enthusiasm, the orchestra and the players have remained. In the Theater-an-der-Wien stands Rodin's splendid bust of Gustav Mahler. New names win fresh fame, joining those of Schalk, Richard Strauss and Bruno Walter. Way up in the "Fourth Gallery", youth criticise with acid impartiality the values, the talents, the performance of the artists.

Like the Opera, the BURG-THEATER retained little more than its façade after 1945. This theatre was held to be the finest in which the German language was spoken and occupied a unique position in Vienna's cultural life. At its foundation, in 1776, Emperor Joseph impressed one duty upon it—that of becoming a national theatre.

From these beginnings—the first theatre on the Michaelerplatz is charmingly portrayed in old etchings—the theatrical dreams of the Viennese progressed towards fulfilment—the establishment of a repertory theatre of world literature, based on the collective talent of a first-class cast.

A crisis in the management of the Burgtheater even today is more important to the Viennese than a change of government. To become director of the Burgtheater is the dream of many which only few, of course, have ever realised.

In the NATIONAL LIBRARY students find one of the greatest book

Griechengasse.

suggest gilded clouds which hang motionless in space. On mild June evenings you may cross the Heldenplatz when the city fathers decree the festive illumination of the Rathaus, making of it a flaming piece of Brussels lace. After the theatre you may walk over the great, quiet square with echoing footsteps to the Ring, or go there the next morning, when the sun bathes it in a golden flood and lifts up your heart in gladness.

Viennese Girls, 1914.

Opposite, on the façade facing the Inner City, still within the extensive grounds of the Burg, lies the solemn and dignified Josefsplatz. No successor to Max Reinhardt has arisen who could transplant this impressive scenery on to a stage—the classic façades of the National Library, the Royal Riding School and the enchanting proscenium of the Pallavicini Palace. Behind high windows is the famous domed hall of Fischer von Erlach, a dream in marble, gold and sunlight, which is considered the most magnificent library of the world. The streets leading from it narrow suddenly, as if unwilling to let one leave the square.

And now let us wander through the Inner City without any special goal, to the hidden beauties which are so easily discovered. There stand mysterious courtyards with covered stairways, cage-like balconies, noble weather-beaten porches dreaming of baroque fantasies beneath spider's webs, little old houses and shops of the dealers in antiques—a garland of beauty hidden in the heart of an active, bustling and teeming metropolis, a fascinating juxtaposition of yesterday and today.

The Plague Column on the Graben was erected by the Emperor Leopold to commemorate the end of the epidemic in 1679. This stone allegory, this bold mixture of realistic and religious ideas, the work of Fischer von Erlach as well as other sculptors, has been compared to a splendid opera. Only a few steps behind it, cut off from the lively Graben by a modest little square, is the venerable Peterskirche, full of colour and rich decorations. Rottmayr's frescoes in the interior radiate a golden brilliance which makes an almost carnal appeal to the senses. A little further, on the Tuchlauben, the clothmakers used to offer their wares in old Vienna, and one-and-a-half centuries earlier the Roman military lines stood here. Every walk through Vienna can be made a game of question and answer with time and history.

Viennese Girl, 1913.

Vienna, Stadtpark.

Josefsplatz ; The National Library.

The Hohe Markt leads into the Wipplinger-strasse, at the beginning of which the former Bohemian Court Chancellery faces the old Rathaus. In the courtyard of the latter is an artistic creation, the Andromeda Well of Rafael Donner. Donner came to the monastery of Heiligenkreuz as a poor choir-boy and gave shape to his dream pictures by moulding secretly at night the grease which had dripped from the church candles. Another late masterpiece of his art, the Donner Fountain on the Neue Markt, is known and loved by all Viennese. It was created at the end of the baroque period to the order of the burghers of Vienna, who wished to rival the aristocratic and religious patrons of art. It shows two male and two female figures grouped around the principal female figure, "Providentia", with her mirror.

collections in the world. Established in the year 1526, it was moved in 1726 to the baroque building designed by Fischer von Erlach Senior. The central oval of the unique Gala Room contains the private library of Prince Eugene of Savoy. In all, the Institute possesses about one and a half million printed works and over 8000 incunabula. Treasures of untold value are included in the various departments of manuscript, music, maps, theatre, portrait and papyrus collections and in the picture archives.

In the HAUS-, HOF- UND STAATSARCHIV (Archives of the Imperial House, the Court and the State) are documents and treaties of all kinds going back for twelve centuries, valuable manuscripts with the seal of Pope or Emperor attached, state treaties, declarations of state councils,

The Graben.

proclamations of the Estates and treaties of peace. Anyone wishing to write the history of Europe is bound to have resort to these unique documents.

The number of collections and galleries, museums and archives seems inexhaustible. The Austrian's love and understanding for art and science have created for themselves a permanent monument in these.

At the head of the list of great MUSEUMS stand those of FINE ARTS and of NATURAL HISTORY. Both date back to the old Hapsburg collections, such as the Treasuries with contents which date from the 13th century. Picture Gallery, Tapestry Collection, "Wagenburg", Medal and Coin Museum, Pre-Historic Section— the problem is where to begin.

The ALBERTINA Collection of Graphic Art, with about a million

Further on, past the Crypt of the Capuchins is the Albertina situated on a high bastion—a treasure store for art-lovers. Here is an almost complete collection of the drawings of Albrecht Dürer which once belonged to Prince Eugene.

Almost in the shadow of this Albrechtsrampe and backed by the green spaces of the former Kaisergarten is the white statue of that witty divine, Abraham a Sancta Clara. His entertaining and moving pulpit discourses helped his enormous congregation to forget their hunger, thirst and weariness. He was preacher, narrator and satirist in one. His influence, which did not stop short at the Imperial Court was to a great extent due to his perfect command of Viennese dialect.

Viennese dialect! This is a faithful mirror of the spirit of Vienna, wonderfully soft and

expressive, full of slurred and muted vowels, of musical cadences which come from the contact with Italy, of expletives of Bajuvarian origin and noble survivals from the treasure of mediaeval German which have elsewhere long since been discarded. Wit and humour, drastic comparisons, diminutives and tender expressions and traces of all European languages —Italian, Spanish, French and Slavonic—are to be found in it. In the course of centuries, Vienna has come under the influence of many tongues, and each has left its mark on the dialect. The city's power of assimilation has moulded them all into "Wienerisch" and we in Vienna still draw on this rich heritage. To take one instance out of many—there is a Spanish

drawings, contains work from every school of art and every country. It is the most important collection of its kind in existence.

The State KUNSTGEWERBE MUSEUM is a unique display of textiles, pottery, glass, furniture, goldsmiths work, pewter, oriental carpets, East Asiatic stone carvings, table implements and china.

The MUNICIPAL COLLECTIONS and the ARCHIEPISCOPAL MUSEUM OF CATHEDRAL AND DIOCESAN COLLECTIONS add to knowledge of city and ecclesiastic life.

The rest must be left to your own initiative, or—you will soon know more than the Viennese themselves.

Bohemian Court Chancellery.

word "prado", meaning "meadow". A foreign word, the Viennese seized on it, made it their own, the stranger soon became a real Viennese, the "Prater". So it has been with many another expression which may have been Greek—or Spanish—to the Viennese at the outset.

The elegant Kärntnerstrasse leads straight from the Ring to the Stephansplatz. We can stroll through it and enjoy its fascinating shop windows another time. Now let us cross it to enter the Himmelpfortgasse where the Winter Palace of Prince Eugene of Savoy is situated. Because the narrow street does not afford a clear view, the statues which usually decorate the entrances to such palais are missing, the three gateways being ornamented only with reliefs. The impression made by the grand staircase in the interior is all the greater, Fischer von Erlach and Lukas von Hildebrand united to create a magnificent palace for the great military leader, although the Belvedere Palace on the other side of the Ringstrasse is a monument to Prince Eugene which is even more imposing.

Let us wander on through the complex of narrow streets in the old city, through the venerable, twisting Schönlaterngasse with its dormer windows and porticos, its legend-haunted houses, through the Sonnenfelsgasse in which there is not a single modern house and follow the Bäckerstrasse up to the Alte Universitätsplatz, with its view of the early baroque Jesuitenkirche and the venerable Aula.

The Jesuits have still another place of worship in the Inner City. It stands near by in Am Hof, the church called "Zu den neun Chören der Engel" ("The Nine Choirs of Angels"). Am Hof is picturesque, and its name is ancient. As far back as the 12th century there stood here a country seat of the Babenbergs, which later became their palace. Old records describe the square as a tournament field. Nowadays, at Christmas time, the "Christkindlmarkt" (Christmas Market) is held there, with glittering Christmas trees full of lights, brightly coloured toys on the stalls, rocking-horses and trumpets, bringing a merry sparkle to children's eyes.

Dreamy houses of long-dead burghers frame the great square, in the centre of the whole is a delicate column to the Virgin.

Much of Vienna's history has been written here. From the terrace of the church, in 1782, the Pope gave his benediction to thousands of Viennese. He had arrived unexpectedly to try to persuade the Emperor Joseph II to abandon his plans to reform the Church.

From the same terrace the Emperor Franz II announced the birth of the new Austrian Empire in 1806, after he had laid down the German Imperial Crown under the threats of Napoleon. The revolutionary year, 1848, saw Latour, the Minister of War, hanged here on a lamp-post.

Beyond the hollow of the Tiefer Graben the Freyung leads to the Schottenstift, where the oldest pictures of Vienna are preserved.

Now let us come out on to the Ring, following it down towards the quays of the Danube Canal. Leaving the Canal on our left we may glance on our right at the venerable Ruprechtskirche above a steep flight of steeps.

Following the broad sweep of the Ringstrasse we may catch a glimpse above the roofs of the grey Cathedral and continue past the long façade of the Ministry of War opposite which stands the modern Post Office Savings Bank designed by Otto Wagner.

We glance at the extensive Stadtpark, resist the temptation to linger at the Schwarzenbergplatz and finally come to a halt before the Opera, realising with sorrowful amazement the full beauty of its construction, now alas open to the sky.

Viennese Girl, 1903.

Am Hof : Armoury.

VIENNA VISITING CARDS.

On the other side of the Ringstrasse we must abandon all attempt to proceed systematically. Vienna consists of 26 Districts, and although the First is far more important than any other, there is still so much to be seen that even quartering the ground would lead us nowhere. All that remains is to select a few places at random.

Where the Kärntnerstrasse joins the Ringstrasse, or moving along the Ring from the Wollzeile, the eye is caught by a majestic, green patina dome rising harmoniously against the sky.

THE KARLSKIRCHE. This is Fischer von Erlach's masterpiece, a marvel of conception and construction whose charm and gaiety of spirit enshrines the soul of Vienna. A startling blend of fundamental baroque with recollections of antiquity and rich ornamentations combine in a magnificent monument. It is a happy task for that reflective visitor to try to interpret for himself its manifold symbolism.

The two gigantic pillars, copied from the Trajan Column in Rome, were intended to represent the Pillars of Hercules in Spain, for the possession of which Karl VI, who commissioned the construction of the church, fought without success in the Wars of the Spanish Succession. The reliefs portraying scenes from the

The Freyung, with the Schottenkirche and Harrach Palais.

life of St. Charles Borromäus symbolise the triumph of the Counter-Reformation. The junction of the cupola and a Corinthian portico points to the temples of antiquity and the quality of Karl VI as ruler of the Holy Roman Empire. The great architect consciously rejected all colour and heavily decorative scrollwork in planning the magnificent proportions of the lofty interior in order to increase the monumental effect.

Not far from the Karlskirche is the broad and sunny Schwarzenbergplatz. Let the visitor decide for himself whether there is any other square in Vienna which can compare with the generous expanse and distinguished reserve of this one.

Adjoining the Schwarzenbergplatz is an architectural district with a character of its own.

THE BELVEDERE. From whatever direction you approach the grounds of the Belvedere you feel that you are about to be the guest of a Prince, a true cavalier. If it belongs to the soul of Viennese culture to combine the significant or rather the truly great in art with an element of irresistible charm, then the two Belvederes, Upper and Lower, can be accepted as the most typical examples of Vienna art. The world has to thank Lukas von Hildebrandt for these peerless baroque masterpieces.

The Lower Palace used to be the summer residence of Prince Eugene, although he was only able to visit it at short intervals between military campaigns. After his death, much was changed inside and outside, but the ceiling frescoes of Altomonte

Michaelerplatz

and Fanti still glow in their pristine colours, the two-storied Marble Hall still displays magnificent mouldings. Allegorical reliefs depict Eugene, not merely as a tactical genius, but also as a peace-maker and apostle of culture.

The two palaces are harmoniously connected by a terraced park in which it is easy to imagine proud cavaliers with powdered wigs and swords strolling with smiling ladies in elaborate gowns of rustling silk.

At the top of the park is the Upper Belvedere, with its corner pavilions and mansard roofs. In the time of Prince Eugene it was a proud residence which made a fitting background for great feasts and receptions. How clear-cut are the finely ornamented roofs of the two wing towers at the corners against the blue of the sky. We pass into the ceremonial Sala Terrena, the entrance hall with its mighty figures of Atlas supporting the ceiling arches. The splendour of the broad well-lighted staircase which leads to the Marble Hall, and goes on up to the third story, takes one's breath away. Here the full glory of Hildebrandt's interior decoration is revealed in slender pillars, mouldings and cleverly-painted imitations of architectural features. Naturally the brilliance and luxury which filled these halls in baroque days will never return to them.

Plate XI

Albrecht Dürer; The Adoration of the Holy Trinity.
Vienna, Museum of Fine Arts.

Plate XII

Rembrandt; The Small Self-Portrait. Vienna, Museum of Fine Arts.

Plate XIII

Velasquez, The Infanta Margareta Theresia. Vienna, Museum of Fine Arts.

Plate XIV

Peter Brueghel the Elder; The Peasant Wedding (section).
Vienna, Museum of Fine Arts.

From the balcony there is a magnificent view over Vienna, embracing the lower garden palace, the green domes of the Karlskirche and the Salesianerkirche and the silhouette of the great city as it loses itself in the clear-cut, rolling lines of the Wienerwald hills.

In front of the south façade of the Upper Belvedere Palace, near the main entrance, is a quiet pond. Its clear surface reflects all the lovely outlines of this loveliest of all the Vienna palaces. In the festive halls the great mirrors along the walls gather the light and prolong their length into infinity. Dream and reality mingle where, as in baroque churches, the ceiling frescoes show the heavens opening with their saints and cherubs, and we can hardly distinguish the architectural features painted on the walls from the plastic actuality of marble. That is the spirit of the Baroque—an illusion which delights is better than a depressing truth—the spirit of an age in which western people found a form of cultural expression which has survived to this day.

People often speak of the wild extravagance and redundance of the baroque style of building. Princes, noblemen and monasteries did indeed squander great sums in those times in order that art should prosper—the art which went to enrich palaces and cathedrals, parks and marble statues as a triumph of the spiritual over the material. But if we pause to reflect how Vienna has been enriched by the glory and beauty of this art, we shall value and praise this extravagance.

With the name of the Belvedere in Vienna is linked—

SCHÖNBRUNN. The Palace and the Park form one harmonious whole. The first design for the grounds of Schönbrunn came from Fischer von Erlach. The great architect had planned to place here a splendid building right in the midst of the then unspoiled beauties of meadows and forests of the Wienerwald. It was to be a glittering fairy palace, with flower-covered terraces, porticos and fountains, commanding the whole countryside. This plan was over-ambitious and for that reason was never carried out. The Emperor died, the available funds were exhausted and the architects of his daughter Maria Theresia, Pacassi and Hohenberg, were only able to lay out a part of the grounds.

There is a trace of Italian palace architecture about this palace; the conception of the great central tract and of the statues along the coping was taken directly from the south. The two galeries on the lines of those in Versailles and the combining of palace and grounds in one harmonious whole exemplify the quieter French style of architecture.

The whole building glows with the warmth of that attractive shade of colour which is described as "Maria-Theresia yellow". Its lines emphasize the horizontal and everywhere seek to strike a note of gaiety and happiness in being alive. The main block is made up of three sections which blend together with the two wings into a wonderfully harmonious piece of architecture. The two outer flights of steps with their great ornamental lanterns and the richly decorated wrought iron gates suggest two arms widespread in welcome, inviting to an inspection of the Palace. This is the façade which faces the front entrance courtyard. On the other, that on the garden side, green balcony doors reach down almost to the ground, suggesting a link between the palace and the extensive grounds behind it, giving the building from this side the appearance of a hospitable country manor.

From a spacious, sunny courtyard one finds oneself on the first floor at once in the heart of the palace, with the gala rooms which are a triumph of the gifted interior decorator Pacassi who designed and completed them. Everywhere one feels the charm of French rococo—in the decorations, in the apportioning of space and in the abundance of graceful ornamentation. But the laughing grace of the flower motifs, the harmony of the colours—red, white and gold—in furniture and tapestry strike a definitely Austrian note. Stucco, always a typically Viennese medium, has here and there grown almost into mouldings in full plastic, framing ceilings and wall paintings with curlicues, rosettes and gilt scroll work which have a naive exuberance of form. Great mirrors, so placed along the walls to secure the maximum effect, create the illusion of unending space.

The crowning glory of the interior is the Great Gallery, a long hall with eleven enormous windows, glorified by the magnificence of the chandeliers of gilded wood. One cannot see enough of the glittering mouldings, the wall candelabras and the bronze chandeliers. The eye wanders to the ceiling and the blue frescoed heaven of the Italian painter Guglielmi; Maria Theresia reigns there above with crown and sceptre; with her, obviously to encourage recruiting, are portrayed officers and soldiers of the Seven Years' War.

During the time of the Vienna Congress, representatives of power, riches and renown used to assemble here in this Great Gallery of Schönbrunn Palace—the emperors, kings, army commanders and diplomats of Europe.

Vienna; Ringstrasse.

Mariahilferstrasse about 1780.

The intoxicating magnificence of the "Million Room", so called because its construction and decoration is supposed to have cost a million gulden, stands out even among the other richly decorated apartments. There is the Napoleon Room with its priceless tapestries in which the Corsican lived in 1805 and again in 1809. Here, too, died his son, the young Duke of Reichstadt. The great Ceremonial Hall with the representative picture of Maria Theresia painted by Meytens, the two Chinese Circular Rooms which again are decorated with extravagant luxury, the Mirror Room, the "Karussel-Room", thus called after a great wall painting of the Meytens School of Art, the living rooms and reception rooms of Emperor Francis Joseph—all these great rooms impress one as a dream vision of some highly coloured and lovely historical panorama. In sober contrast are the simple sleeping quarters of the Emperor Francis Joseph with the iron camp bed on which he died in the year 1916 amidst the horrors of a world war which he had tried in vain to prevent.

The little Schönbrunn Palace Theatre strikes a note of intimacy and charm with its red, white and gold colour-scheme. Here young Marie Antoinette, the daughter of Maria Theresia, danced the shepherd-and-shepherdess pastorals of the Poet Laureate, Metastasio; here Mozart conducted his opera "Der Schauspieldirektor"

Vienna; Mariahilferstrasse.

THE STRAUSS DYNASTY

Pizzicato-Polka

SEF STRAUSS 1827 – 1870

Soldiers' Greeting

EDUARD STRAUSS 1835 – 1916

and here his "Don Juan" was produced. Nowadays this historic stage is at the disposal of young actors of the Reinhardt School.

Something quite unique for sightseers is the Wagenburg, or carriage park. Its show-piece is the eight-horsed Coronation Coach of the Emperor Karl VI, fashioned in the shape of an enormous gold crown and supposed to be the most beautiful coach in the world. Its interior is decorated with valuable paintings of the Rubens School. This coach was used at seven Hapsburg coronations, the last of them being that of Emperor Karl, crowned in Budapest during the First World War in the year 1916.

Wide gravel parks and avenues conduct one to the lovely grounds of the Palace, a compromise between two art trends—born of the enthusiasm for nature of Rococo and the joy in antiquity which characterised Baroque. Figures taken from legend and ancient history, the rich statuary of the park, reflect the living spirit of those times, commemorating many historic events. Tall, formal hedges clipped in the French manner flank the wide flowerbeds, running diagonally towards fountains with their surrounding statues.

In the far distance are the Neptune Fountain, the "Roman Ruins" and the Kaiserbrünnl with the "Beautiful Fountain" from which Schönbrunn takes its name. On the other side are the Palm House and the extensive Zoo. Half way to them a zig-zag path winds up to the heights of the Gloriette, a light and decorative structure with slender columns and stone roof through the round arches of which the skies look down.

From here we get a fine view of the wide-spread city, an attractive

island in a sea of green. Vis-à-vis lies the lovely belt of the Wienerwald. Directly to the rear the low-built biedermeier houses mark out a picturesque pathway to the castle and grounds of Hetzendorf. This again is in the neighbourhood of Laxenburg Castle, with its lake and its game park.

The people of Vienna who visit Schönbrunn realise that reforms come not only from below, but sometimes from above, for Joseph II threw open these exclusive grounds to the public of his own accord—Schönbrunn, the Augarten and the Prater.

IN THE PRATER. The Prater was formerly a game preserve for noblemen of high rank, who were furious with the Emperor for deciding that the public in future should have free run of the place: this meant, the aristocrats grumbled, that they could no longer be among their equals. Joseph answered with biting irony:

Schönbrunn; gloriette

"If I always wished to be among my equals, I should be forced to take my walks in the Kapuzinergruft, among the deceased Hapsburgs."

The Prater is a vast stretch of untouched open country which lies on the right bank of the Danube. Just as the mountains behind the city reach right up to its suburbs, so does the wooded plain of the Prater with its open fields and pools. One can wander for hours in this natural park, the most extensive recreational area for the Viennese. However many tens of thousands come here, the Prater has room for them all as they spread over the broad expanses of meadows and woods which offer shade, rest and repose after the din of the city.

Right through the middle runs the Hauptallee, with the romantic Lusthaus at one end, beyond which the road leads on to the Freudenau, Vienna's racecourse. At all seasons of the year it attracts visitors. But in May this avenue forms an unbroken ribbon of flowering chestnut trees. When the petals fall from the blossoming candelabra, the grass, the footpaths and the roadway are all covered with white and red snow.. Later on, in autumn, children eagerly collect the shiny brown chestnuts lying among the dead leaves.

On one side of the Hauptallee lies the little lake near the Konstantinhügel and further on the Heustadel Water, on both of which are rowing boats for hire. On the other side are the Trab-rennplatz (Trotting Race Course), the great Sport Stadium, three historically famous coffee houses and the "Wurstel-prater" (Fun City). Here at the foot of the Big Wheel, holiday crowds find a centre of light-hearted happiness, where the cares and sorrows of a harsh everyday world may for a space be forgotten. The "Wurstel" (Punch) still delights children as he did in the days of Adalbert Stifter. Fascinated, they sit before the small stage where their imaginations are ever again successfully led astray into a world of illusion and fantasy with very primitive aids—chiefly adroitness of the fingers and a native gift of wit. Ancient wisdom finds its expression here, a wisdom which recognises failings with a smile. Born of

Viennese Girl, 1948.

395

Avenue in Schönbrunner Park.

Vienna; Prater.

Praterstern.

the spirit of **Baroque**, tempered by Biedermeier and handed on by Raimund and Nestroy, popular fancy and humour have here been translated into verse and music. In the "Plane Song" and the "Ashes Song"—and before the "Wurstel" in the Prater—the Viennese recognises his spirit of resignation and is resigned to his recognition of it. Thoughtfully he mingles dream with reality, relieved of something which can be neither assessed nor grasped, and turns back, smiling, to the warm pulsating life, to the fascinating turmoil of the Wurstelprater.

THE BELT OF WOODS AND MEADOWS. The Wienerwald is, to the Viennese, an inviolable and hallowed spot—almost sacrosanct. For this reason it is an unwritten law of city planning that Vienna must never lose its appearance of being part of the countryside. The written law of the great Burgomaster Lueger speaks of the belt of woods and meadows, of its protection and its inviolability.

The belt of woods and meadows, as this deep and extensive green garland of sighing forest and luxuriant meadows is called, encircles a great part of the city, planting outposts deep into its territory, looking over its own shoulder in all directions at it,

Danube Wharf (Kai).

enlivening and refreshing it day by day with fresh forest winds and cool breezes from the Danube.

From the vineyards of Nussdorf rises up the forest-crowned head of the Kahlenberg, favourite mountain of the Viennese and a last outpost of the Wienerwald, the extensive hill country to the north-west of the City. Its fields and deciduous forests form a vast recreational garden of recreation for tired city folk in search of fresh air. Few other cities can boast of such a large and unspoilt natural preserve in the immediate neighbourhood of the granite sea of tenement buildings.

A short walk brings us to the adjacent Leopoldsberg. Here you can sit in the little tavern gardens drinking the excellent wine which is grown a little lower down, near Grinzing and Nussdorf, and gaze at the green domes of Klosterneuburg monastery, the steamers on the Danube with their trailing banners of smoke, the fields along the banks and the Stefansturm which rises like a fountain of stone. One thinks of the days when the merry Babenbergers still held sway here above and pious Margrave Leopold founded the monastery of Klosterneuburg on the spot where he found the wind-tossed veil of his lady.

Downwards from the Leopoldsberg leads a beautiful, shady, wooded path. A visit to the monastery is well worth while, for all our Austrian monasteries have been very important centres of art and learning by virtue of their architecture, their art collections and their libraries; Klosterneuburg enjoys apart from this the best of reputations as a college for church music. The famous school of the town of Klosterneuburg for vine and fruit-growing dates from the times when our monasteries were strictly organised working communities which spread considerable material culture.

The Trautsohn Palais.

The buildings of the monastery lie on a rocky plateau, the western part of which appears as a picturesquely gothic tangle of dark stairways and steeply towering supporting walls, while the east of the plateau, crowned by the two mighty cupolas beneath the German Imperial Crown and the Austrian Ducal Coronet, reveals the entire splendour of the mid-baroque period. The best view of the two domes is to be had from the monastery park. To the South the slender, new-gothic church spires are etched against the blue of the sky.

Climbing a long, steep flight of steps, the Pfisterstiege, one reaches the Leopoldihof with its splendid gothic bay window and its fountain with the renaissance figure of the Babenberger Leopold III. The outward sign of the power with which it was invested at the time of its foundation and which it succeeded in asserting for centuries, is the great monastery church.

The most valuable work of art of the monastery is the Verduner Altar which stands in the Leopoldskapelle—a world-famous work dating from the end of the 12th century.

In the building of the monastery we enter the realm of dreams and magic of true Austrian baroque. Its creator was the Milan architect, Donato Felice d'Allio.

The greatest curiosity of the rich monastery museum is a collection of romanic ivory objects, small boxes, portable altars and Italian bronzes. In its very

Plate XV

Canaletto; Schönbrunn Palace (section). Vienna, Museum of Fine Arts.

Plate XVI

Waldmüller; Prater Trees (section).
Austrian Gallery of the 19th Century.

The Praterstrasse with the Carltheater.

extensive library the art-lover is fascinated by the beautiful illuminated manuscripts and the family tree of the Babenberg rulers. The treasury contains the Austrian Ducal Coronet and rare goldbeaters' work of the Middle Ages.

The city itself climbs up to the heights of the Hermannskogel and the Kahlenberg, extending as far as Klosterneuburg, Mödling, Schwechat and even beyond the Lobau district. But it is hoped that this virgin zone of woods and fields will prevent the disappearance of many cherished villages, prevent the picturesque biedermeier gardens being swallowed up by tenement houses and ensure that the wonderful boating and bathing centre which Vienna possesses on the Old Danube does not lose even a foot of ground to industry and factories.

The historic little country parishes of Nussdorf and Heiligenstadt, Sievering, Grinzing and Liebhartstal, of Hietzing, Mauer and Perchtoldsdorf have grown together in a semi-rural region where nature, modern villas and ancient structures blend pleasingly. The "Heurige" wine-gardens of Kahlenberg, Neustift-am-Wald, Rodaun and Maria Enzersdorf hold within their little flowered courtyards that true Viennese "Gemütlichkeit" (easy-going cordiality) which loves life and the fleeting moment for its own sake. You clink glasses with your neighbour, drinking, in the joy of your heart, to the health of the stranger beside you, who himself feels the same about you. Many an

Vienna; The Old Bed of The Danube.

On the Kahlenberg.

old vineyard tavern which is listed for protection under the Ancient Monuments Act evokes lively pictures of biedermeier days, when the suburbs were holiday resorts and Schubert, the eternally young, wandered the countryside with his friends. Bauernfeld, Beethoven and Grillparzer sought rest and relaxation here among the green fields. Here Waldmüller proved the power of his brush and Ferdinand von Saar, the poet of solitude, wrote his rapturous elegies on Vienna, the city of his dreams.

From the higher parts of the suburb of Döbling one can recognise the peaks of the Lower Carpathians, the Schneeberg and the Ötscher. To realise the whole charm of the surroundings of Vienna, you must see it from the heights of the Kahlenberg. There you will understand how the city has really grown into its natural framework and how its Cathedral and many towers, the river, the mountains, the plain and broad horizons have come to form parts of a single whole. This is a picture which never fades from the memories of those who have once seen it.

If one then approaches Vienna from the north, from the direction of Prague or Brünn, the whole city seems to have been swallowed up by the mountains. Then the Wienerwald looks like a great, green and shady creek past which the silver Danube flows, broad and lazy, downstream. Mountains rise up one behind the other, followed closely by the alps in ever-higher ranges.

As the journey to Vienna usually ends in the afternoon or early evening when the sun is over the alps in the south or west, one feels in the magic of these sub-alpine woods, an irresistible temptation to hasten on to the valleys of the Wienerwald, to rest and linger there in a spot so favoured by nature.

Coming from Budapest or Pressburg (Bratislava), the picture is again different. There the wide river, the broad plain fill eye, ear and senses with their unchanging rhythm. Something of the Puszta melancholy still lingers; when such feelings translate themselves into music they find their expression in Schubert's "Der Tod und das Mädchen", or Beethoven's "Moonlight Sonata".

From the south one enters by the gates of gaiety. To pass by the swimming pools off the high road, to cross the vineyards or walk alongside them, Pfaffstätten and Gumpoldskirchen not far off, to recognise the lime-tree before the doors of the Höldrichs Mill, to catch sight of the cheerful black pines behind the Türkenturm of Petersdorf on the Parapluiberg, to see the bold profile of the Kahlenberg ahead and finally to look for the silver-grey needle of the tower of St. Stephen's—all this induces a mood of light-hearted gaiety. It is a part of the "G'schichten aus dem Wienerwald" ("Tales of the Vienna Forest"), or a bar of the Blue Danube Waltz.

Beethoven's House.

PART III

FROM THE FIRST TO THE SECOND REPUBLIC

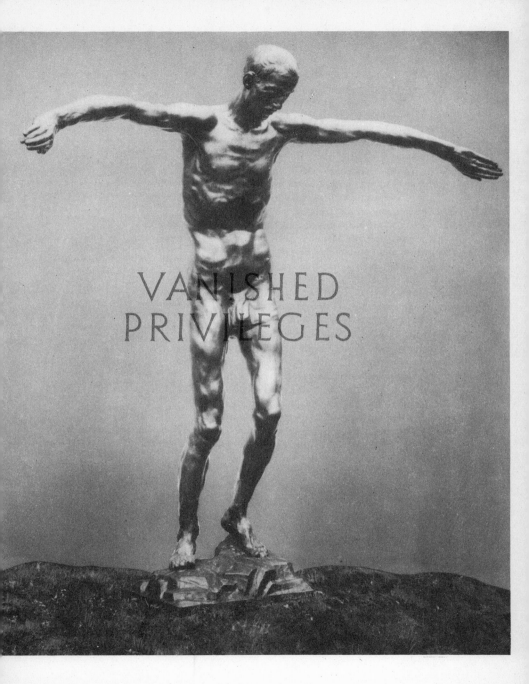

VANISHED
PRIVILEGES

When the Austro-Hungarian Monarchy broke up at the end of the first World War, this collapse meant more than the tragic end of a state or empire. In the heat of nationalistic fervour and in the enthusiasm generated by successful *Revanche* on the Rhine it was not at first realised what damage had been done to the whole European concept, and thus to every country of the Continent without exception through the destruction of the Austrian economic unit. The effect was felt far beyond the limits of the little country on the Danube.

Austria, an important keystone in the building of the European balance of power, had dropped out. The intoxication of victory hindered the conclusion of a constructive peace. The stabilising balance of two major states was lacking. President Wilson, it is true, had laid down his 14 points, but America soon returned to her old policy of isolation. Through the October Revolution Russia was for the time being deprived of all voice in foreign affairs and thus peace was in fact dictated solely by Clemenceau, the "Tiger", the Succession States formerly parts of the Hapsburg Monarchy frantically applauding his extreme chauvinism at the very one-sided peace congress. An attempt at extreme severity in the case of Germany resulted in half measures. Aiming at the exaction of a maximum of reparations, the dictated peace in this very way enabled a gigantic industrial development to take place on the Ruhr, thus involuntarily re-establishing its potential for the manufacture of armaments.

The German delegate left the gloves which he had worn in signing the peace treaty lying ostentatiously on the conference table—the challenge to a second world war!

October 27th, 1918. Appointment of the last Imperial Government under Lammasch.

October 28th, 1918. Proclamation of the Czechoslovak State.

October 30th, 1918. State Council set up under Chancellor Renner. All-Party Coalition.

November 3rd, 1918. Proclamation of the Polish Republic.

November 11th, 1918. Emperor Karl renounces all claim to exercise ruling powers in Austria.

November 12th, 1918. Proclamation of the Republic in Austria.

November 16th, 1918. Proclamation of the Republic in Hungary.

December 1st, 1918. Proclamation of the Kingdom of the Serbs, Croats and Slovenes.

February 16th, 1919. Election of a Constituent National Assembly.

April 2nd, 1919. The Hapsburgs banished and Titles of Nobility abolished.

September 10th, 1919. Treaty of Saint-Germain signed.

October 1st, 1920. The National Assembly ratifies the new Constitution.

October 10th, 1920. Plebiscite in Carinthian frontier districts goes in favour of Austria.

October 17th, 1920. Election of the First Austrian Parliament.

October 22nd, 1920. The Social-Democrats leave the Coalition Government.

December 4th, 1921. The Burgenland is restored to Austria.

April 1st, 1922. The Death of Emperor Karl I.

August 20th to 27th, 1922. Chancellor Seipel visits Prague, Berlin and Verona.

September 27th, 1922. The League of Nations approves the plan for Austrian financial reconstruction.

March 2nd, 1925. The Krone is replaced by the Austrian Schilling.

June 30th, 1926. End of financial control by the League of Nations.

410

October 20th, 1926. Seipel's fourth term of office as Chancellor.

November 3rd, 1926. The "Linz Programme" of the Social-Democratic Party.

July 14th, 1927. Verdict of "Not Guilty" in the Schattendorf Trial.

July 15th to 17th, 1927. Serious disorders in Vienna. Burning of the Palace of Justice.

March 11th, 1928. First demonstration of the Heimwehr in an industrial area.

October 8th, 1928. Simultaneous demonstrations of the Heimwehr and the Republican Schutzbund in Wiener Neustadt, separated by a cordon of the Austrian Army.

September 16th, 1929. Failure of the Bodencreditanstalt.

October 27th, 1929. First demonstration of the Heimwehr in Vienna.

December 7th to 10th, 1929. Austrian Constitution changed.

May 18th, 1930. "Korneuburg Oath" of the Heimwehr.

November 9th, 1930. Last parliamentary elections before the Second World War.

May 12th, 1931. Government action to save the Creditanstalt.

September 12th to 13th, 1931. Attempted Putsch by the Styrian Heimatschutz.

May 20th, 1932. First Dollfuss Government.

September 5th to 20th, 1932. Conference in Stresa.

March 4th, 1933. Resignation of the three Presidents of Parliament. Crisis for democracy.

March 7th, 1933. Prohibition of all public meetings. The freedom of the press curtailed.

March 18th, 1933. The German Cabinet Minister Frank threatens Austria on behalf of the Nazis.

March 30th, 1933. Republican Schutzbund disbanded.

May 1st, 1933. The Socialist May-Day celebrations forbidden.

In the meantime history had taken its inevitable course. The black and yellow flag had been hauled down in Austria and a disinherited generation hoisted the red-white-red tricolour over the ruins of the Hapsburg Empire. While in Vienna the Republic was proclaimed on the 12th of November, 1918, and the principle established that in future all power would emanate from the people, the Succession States—Czechoslovakia, Hungary, Poland and Yougoslavia—had hastened to invoke the principle of self-determination in order to declare their independence, and thus to burden the remaining rump of Austria with all debts and obligations.

To this country of barely seven million inhabitants, whose frontiers had been torn up by violence, the remnants of the army now came streaming back—officers from garrisons in Hungary and Croatia, administrative clerks from Cracow and Laibach, ship-builders from the docks of Pola and Trieste, merchants from Belgrade and the harbours of the Adriatic, teachers and doctors from the Ukraine and the Carpathians, professors from the German University in Prague, mining engineers from the Upper Silesian collieries, governors' staffs and employees from the vast forest districts, judges, diplomats, ambassadors, builders, foremen, railwaymen—all streamed back into the mutilated torso of what only four years previously had been a prosperous empire.

The fate which now overtook Austria was without precedent. The worst horror of those days was not the stormy happenings all around and the starvation, but the utterly catastrophic reversal of every aspect of life, and the disappearance of Austria's proud position. An Austrian nocturno had begun, the privileges of centuries had been extinguished.

Egon Schiele ; The Sister-in-Law of the Artist.

If there were any need to emphasize or to prove the indestructibility of the conception of Austria, events subsequent to 1918 might be called as witnesses before the bar of history. With quiet determination, the Austrians pulled themselves together and prepared to tread the stony path towards the formation of a new state. Now the call came to the simple citizens, the peasants, the city workers. The privileges of a class who for the last ten years had meant no more to the various peoples of Austria than a loose bond forged by tradition and official position were swept away in the general collapse of 1918. The blackballing of socially ineligible candidates for membership of exclusive clubs and the privilege of having green shutters to the house windows—documented evidence of membership of a privileged class—together with the old uniforms and the titles of nobility became just a part of historic memories.

The Austrian people know by instinct how to determine what is part of a precious heritage from the past and what is merely outworn convention. This instinct has constantly enabled them to adjust themselves to new modes of life during the ups and downs of the centuries. The Austrian has the gift of human comprehension, a readiness to respect opinions diametrically opposed to his own. Averse from the use of force and revolted by unnecessary violence, he cherishes freedom and hates tyranny. The Austrian has no respect for an empty skull, even if it is covered by a top hat or the brass hat of a general. But he is capable of deep reverence for every person and every thing really worthy of it.

Austria's path which led from the First to the Second Republic was a painful and difficult one. She was no more free from errors and mistakes in home policy than from reverses

413

coming from abroad, for Europe as a whole had not yet found peace. The shadows of great crises fell athwart the land in the middle twenties at a time when it enjoyed only a makeshift financial stability and consolidation. Now came the stagnation of world trade, and the birth of the dictatorships. The internal political events can only be partly understood if considered in conjunction with events in the outside world.

Austria is the barometer of Europe. Lying on the Rome—Berlin axis, partly surrounded by the semi-circle of the lands of the Little Entente, with eyes hopefully turned towards the peace policy of the League of Nations, this country found itself amidst ideological material forces which only too soon began to extend their activities beyond their own frontiers, until opposing policies in this small and tortured country put an end to civil peace. A factor to be remembered is that men without employment were marching in all the various armed formations—Schutzbund, Heimwehr and Storm Troopers. Despite lack of unity, Austria still found the strength to resist the aggression of the Third Reich until the invading troops of Hitler trampled—for the time being—Austria's freedom into the dust.

During the years of 1938 to 1945 there arose and spread through Austria a valuable quality, the will to tolerance and cooperation when the Motherland should at last be liberated.

April 11th, 1936. Schuschnigg orders disarmament of the Catholic militant formations.

May 4th, 1936. Compulsory military service in Austria.

June 11th, 1936. Germany recognises by treaty the full sovereignty of Austria.

July 23rd, 1936. Political armistice for the Nazis.

October 10th, 1936. Disbanding of all private armies. End of the Heimwehr.

June 18th, 1937. National-Political Section set up in the Vaterländische Front. Infiltration of the Vaterländische Front by Nazis.

September 25th to 29th, 1937. Mussolini visits Hitler in Germany.

February 4th, 1938. Hitler purges the German General Staff.

February 12th, 1938. Schuschnigg visits Hitler at Berchtesgaden.

February 24th, 1938. Campaign speech of Schuschnigg to the Federal Council at Vienna. Final struggle for Austria.

March 9th, 1938. Schuschnigg announces National Referendum.

March 11th, 1938. Ultimatum of the German Government. Fall of Schuschnigg.

March 12th, 1938. German troops invade Austria.

March 13th, 1938. Proclamation of the annexation of Austria by Germany.

NEW ORIENTATION
OF INDUSTRY

THE AUSTRIAN ECONOMY AFTER 1918.

The disintegration of the Dual Monarchy was immediately followed by severe economic disturbances. These were by no means small, even in comparison with the position after 1945. The heart of Austria, with its highly developed trade, was suddenly completely cut off from its former inland sources of raw products and markets. The oilfields of Galicia, like the important coal deposits in the lands of Bohemia, Moravia and Silesia, were lost, having fallen to the Succession States, and the loss of the agricultural surplus areas produced a threat of famine.

The Succession States—Czechoslovakia, Yugoslavia and Hungary—each attempted to build up a national economy, to balance its economic structure and to make itself as far as possible independent of raw and semi-manufactured materials and finished goods. A division of labour which had grown during decades into one complete organism was thus broken up, to the detriment of all peoples living within this territory. For Austria this meant that an intensive system of internal trading suddenly turned into one of foreign trade, where great difficulties had to be overcome. At first even inter-state transport communications were further complicated by barriers created by the Succession States.

The nadir of those days was reached with the signing of the Treaty of Saint-Germain, which revealed the full extent of the catastrophe. Austria's tragic path at that time was blocked by a series of apparently insurmountable obstacles to the procuring of essential foodstuffs, coal and raw materials. Inflation to an extent never before seen set in and led to a selling-out of national assets. The unfavourable basis of the rump economic structure as well as the instability of Austria's relations with foreign countries seemed to doom all her efforts to failure.

After difficult but very skilfully conducted inter-state negotiations, the governments of Czechoslovakia, France and Italy were persuaded to advance credits to the Austrian Republic. The Allied Powers convinced themselves that Austria, if help came from the League of Nations, would exert her own energies to the utmost in order to put her finances and trade on a sound footing. The will of the Austrian Government to stabilise the budget, demonstrated by the previous abolition of food subsidies (in December 1921), did much to assist these efforts. The Financial Recovery Plan which was signed at Geneva on October 4th, 1922, proved the turning

416

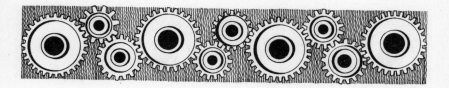

point. The banknote printing presses were stopped and national administration put on a firm footing through drastic measures of economy.

However praiseworthy the efforts which led to a balancing of the budget, the difficulties which still confronted Austrian trade remained considerable. Austria's productive capacity was far greater than its markets (which had shrunk to an eighth of their former size) could possibly absorb. As a great part of Austrian industry was devoted to manufacture, the country was dependent on the import of foreign raw materials (textile, metal and chemical raw materials, hides, furs etc.) and auxiliary materials (above all coal). On the other hand, the social services (unemployment pay, emergency aid, health insurance etc.) which were more extensive than in all the other Danube States made the costs of Austrian production comparatively high.

All Austria's efforts were directed towards export. In 1931, 25 per cent of all inland output was exported, 45 per cent of this being industrial production. If one works out the value of goods exported per head of population and compares it with the exports from other countries it will be seen that in 1937 Austria was ahead of Germany, France and the U. S. A., the comparative figures being 39 : 36 : 34 : 28.

As an industrial country, Austria was forced through the ceding of her agricultural surplus territories to rely on the import of foreign foodstuffs. These imports had to be paid for by the export of industrial goods, as had also the raw and auxiliary materials.

According to the balance of payment figures for the year 1934, the exchange of commodities, which amounted to 63 per cent of all listed inter-state payments was the most important item of Austria's inter-state economic transactions. Second in importance were payments under the heading of invisible imports and exports (balance of services), which amounted to 23 per cent of the total payments. Austria made a profit on these transactions of about 200 million schillings. That proportion of the goods imported which could not be covered by exports alone was therefore paid for by services in the strictest sense of the word. Of these services, the tourist trade and transit trade were the most important.

Through the loss of former markets, Austria was forced to form new export connections in the north, south, west and overseas. As the goods which had formerly been exported to the east and south-east were not automatically marketable in these

territories, Austrian producers were forced to adapt their output to these new conditions. This was of course only possible through the painful process of making certain changes in the economic structure.

The main bases of Austrian trade, as vital then as now, were:

a) the abundance of forests which ensure timber for export as well as for the furniture-making and paper industries.

b) The deposits of iron ore which form the basis of iron and steel production and the iron-working industry.

c) The wealth of water in the alpine districts, constituting an extensive source of power which is being increasingly exported in addition to supplying Austrian industry with current.

d) The recently-discovered inland oil fields (at Zistersdorf).

e) The fashion and luxury-article industry, an export factor of increasing importance.

f) The credit balance of services (tourist trade and transit trade).

It is one of the characteristics of industrial-commercial production that Austria, as a result of her comparative lack of capital, should be at a disadvantage whenever it is a question of mass production. But wherever there is a chance for painstaking finishing, special skill or workmanship, as well as good taste and original ideas on the part of the producer to play a rôle, the prospects of success are excellent. It is not only, as is often mistakenly imagined, the fashion and luxury industries to which this applies, but all the many branches of manufacturing where it is the quality of the work which counts. These factors are strengthened by the prevalence of small concerns in Austria. Factories with up to 100 employees amount to 75 per cent of the total, those with 100 to 1000 employees to a little over 20 per cent, and the factories employing over 1000 persons to only 4·4 per cent.

After the stabilisation of the currency, production and export trade showed a favourable increase between the years 1923 and 1929. Production rose during this time by nearly one third. Then followed the general slump, especially serious for Austria on account of her great dependence on export. The development which had begun so hopefully was now brought to a standstill through the external crisis.

418

ROADS AND RAILWAYS.

The roads of Austria are as ancient as her history, dating back to the Roman military and posting roads which followed the line of frontier fortifications right through the country. In their Provinces the Romans usually built flint or gravel roads with a uniform width from three to three and a half metres which were kept in good order by soldiers.

The Roman roads, based on surprisingly exact knowledge of the territory—in the alps they were all boldly conceived crossings via alpine passes—survived the flood of the barbarian invasions, forming Austria's principal highroads until well on into the Middle Ages.

Although very fine ecclesiastical and secular buildings were erected during this period, and the nobility and burghers created flourishing towns, the roads were sadly neglected and their condition became desperate. The apparent contradiction in progress can be explained by the political situation and general conditions. Most people lived within the fortified areas—the castles, markets and towns in which even countryfolk were forced to take refuge in the constantly recurring periods of war. When danger from the Turks became a constant threat for Austria during two centuries, the roads were still more neglected, partly, perhaps, with the intention of making it more difficult to march from village to village and to penetrate into the interior of the country.

Thus until late into the 17th century the roads were allowed to degenerate into dirt tracks, without any attempt to surface them. Following the lie of the land, they ran uphill and down dale, unplanned and unregulated. The few existing fords were at the mercy of the slightest floods and there were almost no ditches at the side of the roads. Such roads were naturally only negotiable for vehicles in fine and dry weather and it was a work of art to bring a load intact to its destination. A special class of freight carriers grew up who created a monopoly for themselves. Travellers as well as merchants were very much at the mercy of the skill as well as the moods of the carriers.

The great change in politics created by the victory over the Turks and the new urge to build which reached its apex in the blooming of the baroque period, soon brought about a complete alteration of these conditions. Under the Emperor Karl VI, Vienna became a great European traffic and trading centre. Step by step extensive road planning was carried through. In the forefront stood the need of a link with the Mediterranean harbour of Trieste, so the "Kommerzialstrasse" was built. The road over the Semmering Pass took only 48 days to complete. At the same time the

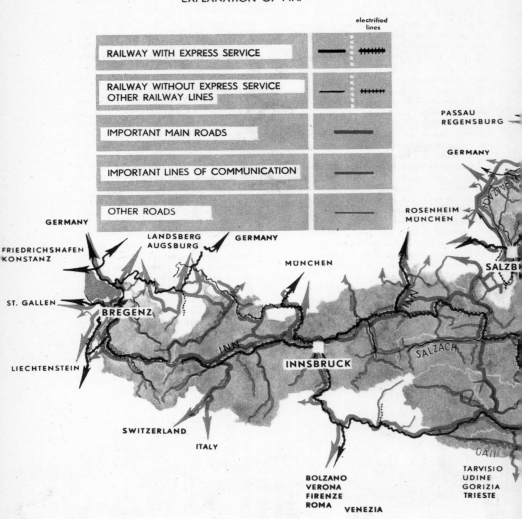

EXPLANATION OF MAP

electrified lines

RAILWAY WITH EXPRESS SERVICE

RAILWAY WITHOUT EXPRESS SERVICE
OTHER RAILWAY LINES

IMPORTANT MAIN ROADS

IMPORTANT LINES OF COMMUNICATION

OTHER ROADS

PASSAU
REGENSBURG

GERMANY

ROSENHEIM
MÜNCHEN

SALZB

GERMANY

LANDSBERG
AUGSBURG   GERMANY

FRIEDRICHSHAFEN
KONSTANZ

MÜNCHEN

ST. GALLEN

BREGENZ

INN

INN

SALZACH

LIECHTENSTEIN

INNSBRUCK

SWITZERLAND

ITALY

GAIL

TARVISIO
UDINE
GORIZIA
TRIESTE

BOLZANO
VERONA
FIRENZE
ROMA   VENEZIA

Road an

420

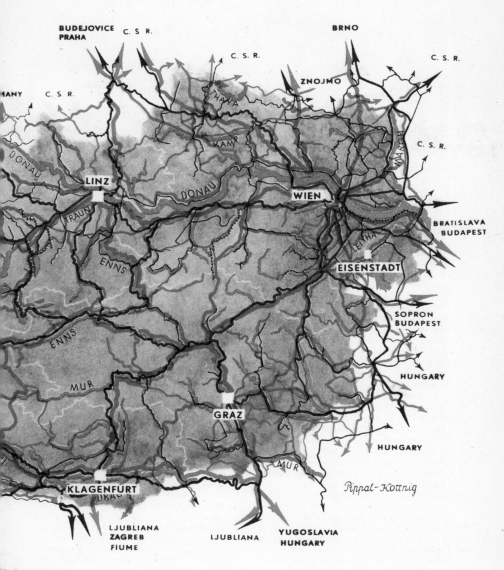

BUDEJOVICE
PRAHA
C. S. R.
C. S. R.
BRNO
C. S. R.
ZNOJMO
C. S. R.
MANY
C. S. R.
THAYA
KAMP
MARCH
C. S. R.
DONAU
LINZ
DONAU
WIEN
TRAUN
BRATISLAVA
BUDAPEST
ENNS
LEITHA
EISENSTADT
ENNS
SOPRON
BUDAPEST
MUR
HUNGARY
GRAZ
HUNGARY
MUR
Pippal-Kottnig
KLAGENFURT
DRAU
LJUBLIANA
ZAGREB
FIUME
LJUBLIANA
YUGOSLAVIA
HUNGARY

Railway Map.

Salzkammergut Local Railway.

building of main roads from Vienna to Brünn, Olmütz, Iglau and Prague was started.

Hand in hand with the construction of a modern network of roads went the development of the mail service. When Napoleon made preparations for the conquest of Europe, the way had quite literally been prepared for him.

When steam instead of horse power began to make the wheels go round in the 19th century and the first engines crawled puffing through the country—in short, when technical development revolutionised all previous ideas, covering the countryside with a dense network of railway lines, Austria took the lead among continental countries in railroad construction.

In 1837 the first train left Vienna in the direction of Wagram. By 1841 there were already 350 kilometres of railway line in use. The year 1848 saw work started on the daringly planned Semmering Railway, with its succession of tunnels and viaducts, the world's first exciting attempt to build a mountain railway. The Westbahn was built in 1858 and the Ostbahn completed in 1868. Since that time Austria's key position in the transport system of Central Europe has been undisputed. Soon goods trains from Germany, Bohemia and Poland, heavily laden with coal and industrial products of all kinds were rolling between the Brenner and the Semmering on their way over the Alps to the Mediterranean, bringing back in return southern

fruits, rice, fish and silk. Southern France and Switzerland sent costly finished products in exchange for grain, cattle fodder and pigs from Galicia, Hungary, Serbia and the Ukraine.

The Arlberg Express has long been the backbone of the European transport system, collecting passengers from the West, from the Channel ports, from Brussels and Paris, from Zurich and Geneva and carrying them down through the gateway of Austria to the Balkans— to Budapest, Bukarest, Belgrade, Sofia, Athens and Constantinople.

For the lover of the beauties of this world a journey through Austria is itself an unforgettable experience. It is difficult to select for mention any of the countless scenic beauties to be seen from the Austrian railways without slighting the rest. There is the Mittenwald line near Innsbruck, the line by which one passes from Salzburg to Carinthia through the Valley of Gastein, the ascent of the Arlberg and the Brenner, the narrow-gauge Salzkammergut local railway, the cross-country connection from Attnang-Puchheim by way of Gmunden, Ischl and Bad Aussee to Selzthal, the Ennstal stretch, the Pyhrn railway, the line through the Styrian mountains, the views from the line which cuts through the mountains to Mariazell and the innumerable mountain and cable railways. Here we must stop, otherwise it will become just

The Trisanna Bridge.

a matter of transcribing from the time-table, for in Austria every rail journey is enchanting.

The scenic beauties which the state railway has missed are covered by a carefully planned network of motor roads, totalling over 70,000 kilometres in length. One name may stand for all the roads over the alps or through mountain passes, along the shores of lakes and by the Danube and through long poplar avenues—the Glocknerstrasse, which climbs up to and penetrates a monstrous world of mighty mountains and glaciers. A motor journey over it brings home Austria's wish to offer of her best to guests from abroad, and with them to see and enjoy her wonderful countryside.

Trade stagnation lasted until the middle of the 1930s, when the armament programme of the Axis Powers, Germany and Italy, was launched, to be followed gradually by an armaments race between all the world's most important trading countries. Austria was excluded from the development which led to the catastrophe of the Second World War, firstly through her political differences with the Third Reich (which answered by a cruel economic boycott in order to force Austria to her knees) and secondly on account of her economic structure, which was suited to the production of peace-time goods but not to that of armaments.

Austria had to make a tireless and purposeful search for new markets before she succeeded in forming and consolidating foreign trade connections with distant territories—the United States of America, British India, Japan, China and the Argentine. If this development had not been interrupted by the occupation of Austria in 1938, the results of Austria's successful attempts to revive her foreign trade would doubtless have soon been apparent in the growth of typically Austrian exports.

Even though the visible results of this change of direction may seem modest, it must not be overlooked that parallel with the deleterious results for Austria of the protectionist policies pursued abroad, there were serious internal problems of economic reconstruction to be solved. One of these was and still is the structure and the development of agriculture.

For many reasons unconnected with economics, but also in order to increase home supplies of the chief articles of food, agricultural development was encouraged. The most important changes in agricultural production were brought about, particularly in the years 1930 and 1931, by radical economic-political measures. The customs tariffs for these years showed a considerable increase of duties on grain, flour, sugar, cattle and meat, the protective tariffs being even further increased in the following years. The resulting rise in prices meant an increase of cultivated areas and the production of the most important kinds of grain.

A further far-reaching measure affecting cattle raising was the regulation of imports of cattle and meat through the setting up of tariff barriers against the most important of the neighbouring States. Apart from this, in April 1932 the import of the most widely sold types of cattle and cattle products was forbidden.

The increase in production resulting from all these measures was bound to increase the difficulties of marketing during the slump. In pig-raising it at last became necessary to resort to curtailment of output (prohibition of pig-raising for the market). An attempt was also made to increase the costs of cattle-rearing and thus limit the supply by raising the so-calledli cence fee for the import of fodder.

As a stimulant of milk production, a milk-equalisation fund was created to content with sales difficulties, through which the means for the export of dairy products at prices below production costs were raised by the imposition of a tax on fresh milk.

Thus it came about that in the 1930s Austrian products such as standard butter, high grades of cheese and cream could compete successfully on the markets with the dairy products of such leading countries as Denmark, Switzerland and Holland. The western alpine provinces especially profited by this arrangement, but at the same time a great demand was created for home milk products throughout the whole country. Gradually, in the Danube City which has been known from Roman times for its enjoyment of sweet wines, depôts were established where milk could be drunk in the busy streets and on public squares, giving the City a new attraction.

The doubtless necessary encouragement of dairy farming, just at this time, how-ever, brought with it new problems which were aggravated by the effect of the world economic depression. The situation was made worse by the fact that the prices for agricultural and dairy products had sunk far lower than the prices for technical aids to agriculture. The discrepancy between these two sets of prices became still greater from 1933 to 1937. The comparative fixity of wages and the increase in public debts accompanied by sinking prices were not inconsiderable factors in bring-ing about general deterioration.

Problems of agrarian policy were bound to have a reaction on industrial-commer-cial economics. Austrian products had to compete with those of countries which had the advantage of considerably lower agricultural prices and thus of a lower cost of living. For a land such as Austria, which in the main can only secure the goods she needs through the export of her own products, it is essential that wages, an important factor in costs, should not be affected too unfavourably by the high price of grain.

Apart from the necessity for the existence of agriculture, the chief problem is to find a reasonable compromise between the legitimate aims of agriculture and the need of Austrian trade and industry to export at competive prices. This end can only be attained by the pursuit of a suitable economic policy and by an increase of agricultural productive capacity through measures of rationalisation, the discouragement of the drift to the towns and the setting up of a suitable system of administration.

The period between the two World Wars was too short to allow of full success on these lines, especially in view of the long duration of the world slump.

For the same reasons the efforts to develop the industrial-commercial system along new lines could not be brought to full fruition; attempts to maintain the status quo frequently held up progress. In times of international trade shrinkage any change of policy is not only exceptionally difficult but sometimes also a considerable risk.

In spite of this Austria made repeated attempts in the course of the years to develop plans for economic rapprochement with neighbouring States. These efforts, however, were doomed to failure through the existence of most-favoured nation clauses and political obstacles. Already in May 1931, conferences were being held in Rome concerning the possibility of increasing trade connections between Italy, Austria and Hungary. From this time onward the preference

THE BANKING SYSTEM IN AUSTRIA.

The structure and economic activities of the Austrian banks since their foundation round about the middle of the last century have followed a different course to that of the credit institutes of the West. For while industrial progress in the latter was based on the active participation of a large circle of interested persons and a well-organised capital market, the development of the far-flung territories of the old Austro-Hungarian Monarchy was left almost entirely to the initiative of the Vienna banks, at first in connection with mechanised transport, and later in connection with industry. Thus, in contrast to the Western type of pure deposit banks, they became universal banks with much more comprehensive functions. Apart from receiving deposits, they gave credit of all kinds ranging from discount credit to long term mortgage credit, dealt in shares and put through stock exchange deals as well as carrying on note emission and syndicate business.

The end of the Monarchy in the year 1918 made it necessary to adapt the Austrian banking system to new conditions. How close the connections of the Vienna banking institutions were with the territories of the old Empire which have since separated from Austria is shown by the fact that of the 127 branches of the Vienna banks which existed under the old Monarchy, not even 10 per cent fell to the new Austria and that, for instance, the Creditanstalt had 16, the Anglo-

bank 34 and the Wiener Bankverein 29 branches outside the territory of present-day Austria.

Adapting the Austrian credit system to the conditions and needs of the Austrian Republic actually took more than one and a half decades. It was not until the year 1934 that this process could be considered as completed with the fusion of the Creditanstalt and the Bankverein. The enormous difficulties involved were still further complicated by the fact that the change coincided in point of time with far-reaching international crises of trade and finance, so that certain grave reactions on the Austrian economy were unavoidable. Notwithstanding this, the latter and its credit system proved themselves strong and vital enough to survive those troubled times and to prepare the ground for the favourable development of Austrian trade in general and the Austrian banking system in particular.

This development was broken off in abrupt and catastrophic fashion through the establishment of the National Socialist regime and the outbreak of the war which soon followed. Although the end of the war restored Austrian independence—in theory, at least—it left behind chaotic conditions—both figuratively and literally a heap of ruins.

In the realm of finance, the first attempts at reconstruction had to be directed towards the re-establishment of the means of payment, a solid national currency being of course a primary condition for the normal

system in foreign trade became the guiding principle, the narrowing down of inter-state trade relations being shortly afterwards still more strongly emphasized through currency restrictions and the clearing agreements connected herewith. The currency devaluations of the gold-standard countries towards the end of the year 1936 created new difficulties for Austrian foreign trade. As devaluation was out of the question and an export subsidy was not considered to be a suitable political-economic instrument, the only remaining alternative was to lower the costs of production. The difficulties of such a course have been proved by practical experience in all countries, as the questions of fixed prices and wages combine to form an insurmountable obstacle to such a development.

Nevertheless Austria still succeeded in linking up with the world boom which began in 1935—1936. In the year 1937 her figures of production were 6 per cent higher than those of the last characteristic boom year of 1929. The tourist trade developed exceptionally favourably, despite the "1000 mark limit" imposed by Germany, and the volume of foreign trade was constantly on the increase.

In view of the heavy burden of debt which the country had to assume after 1918, of the increasingly protectionist tendencies throughout the whole of Europe, especially among Austria's immediate neighbours and considering the severe and long-continued world trade depression, as well as the crises of international currency,

the budget of Austrian administration at the end of the First Republic must be considered to have been thoroughly satisfactory. The often apparently insurmountable difficulties which confronted economic policy in those days were dealt with in such a manner that the state of Austrian trade in 1937, judged by production, income and consumption, could in every way bear comparison with that of other countries. During the whole of this period the national budget was balanced and the currency was considered to be one of the most stable in Europe. The Austrian Schilling was known in general as the "Alpendollar" on account of its stability.

The administration of the Federal Government as well as that of the various provincial governments was developed on the basis of a balanced economy as a framework of a general working programme. In the first place road-building was started, improvements carried out and private building activity encouraged to make investments. The number of unemployed ceased to increase and even showed a slight tendency to fall from season to season through large-scale recruiting of workers for the land. The actual unemployed were able to draw on unemployment insurance funds. Weekly payments of about 28 Schillings per person meant that even during those difficult years nobody had to suffer hunger. These social measures, passed during the first ten years of the Republic, still remain in force for the

functioning of the Austrian credit system. This aim was principally served by the Bank Reopening Law and the Banknote Transition Law of July 1945. These were followed at the end of 1945 by the Schilling Law which restored the Austrian Schilling in place of the Reichsmark currency and attempted to combat symptoms of inflation (which in part had appeared before the fall of the Nazi Government) by the blocking of accounts. Two years later the Schilling Law was reinforced by the Currency Reform Law which declared forfeit the greater part of the frozen assets which had been created by the Schilling Law and changed the remaining accounts (then only partly free) into liabilities of the National Treasury. The stabilisation of the currency at which the Currency Reform Law aimed has been successful, and the Schilling has once again become a real standard of value as a result of this measure.

Apart from the prominent part they played in carrying through the currency measures, the credit institutions were naturally chiefly concerned with providing a basis for their primary economic function, that of collecting superfluous money and directing it to the most useful channels of general trade.

Progress made in both these directions, and future prospects are by no means inconsiderable. There is an obvious return of confidence in the banks. This is shown by the slow but steady increase in deposits, encouraged by re-adoption of the principle of the secrecy of bank transactions and by

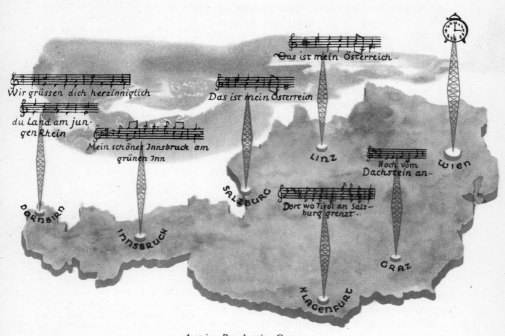

Austrian Broadcasting Centres.

protection of individuals who have lost their work and, of course, contribute the social security of the State.

The annexation of 1938 and the Second World War robbed the Austrian People of its freedom and the fruits of twenty years of painstaking reconstruction.

THE ECONOMIC POSITION AFTER 1945.

Austria's liberation had to be paid for by severe economic sacrifices. Compulsory incorporation into German armament production had been followed by far-reaching changes designed to increase Germany's output of war materials. The necessary investments for renewals and replacements could not be made, while machinery deteriorated more rapidly. Apart from this, Austria had been exposed from 1943 onwards to the effects of bombing, which increased towards the end of the war until in the final stage the whole country became a battlefield. Thus apart from the considerable consumption of stocks and capital goods owing to war production, there was a great deal of material damage.

In addition to the losses directly caused by the war, new restrictions arose for Austrian trade at the conclusion of the fighting. The internal trade links of the country had to a great extent been disrupted through the setting up of four zones of occupation. At a time when in view of the tremendous losses it would have been advisable to ensure the full development of all the means of production, the necessary connections between the various parts of the country could often only be established or maintained under the most difficult circumstances. It is perhaps typical of this period that the various provinces entered into barter agreements with foreign countries independently of one another, often in order to get goods which would have been available within the country itself had unhindered trade been possible.

During the first days after the liberation a goods vacuum arose. Transport had almost completely broken down owing to the extensive destruction of roads and bridges and the lack of the necessary vehicles. Clearance and repair work was first necessary before trade activity could develop at all, and if the Allied Forces of Occupation and UNRRA (as well as other help granted by Congress, private charity organisations and credits) had not aided in bridging the gap,

the payment of interest on deposits since the beginning of 1949. On the other hand, credit demands on the banks resulting from the economic revival are so numerous that they are hard to meet, however severely they are scrutinised. This is all the more the case since Austrian industry, owing to the extensive damage and losses suffered by it during the last stages of the war and after its end, has a great need of capital and long-term credit for investments, as well as of business credit. In such cases, where genuinely justified demands for credit are concerned, the Marshall Plan will be of assistance. The main idea of this is to permit the technical modernisation of Austria's system of production, thus increasing her ability to compete in the international field, to encourage full exploitation of her natural assets, and to provide the country with a sufficient amount of raw materials essential to production during a certain initial period. It is to be hoped that this measure will assist Austria to attain economic independence and help towards the re-establishment of her position in international commerce.

The Austrian banks have a further duty indispensable to the security of smoothly running finance in the re-establishment of the Vienna Stock Exchange as the proper market for dealing in shares, not only to serve legitimate private interests but also to prove itself a suitable medium for the State issues which must be expected.

Banking in Austria is carried on chiefly by joint stock banks, some of which have an extensive branch business. A few of the smaller concerns are situated in the provinces. Apart from these there are a number of highly respected banking houses and nine provincial mortgage banks. Two special characteristics of the first named are their ability to give individual attention to clients and their valuable foreign connections. The provincial mortgage banks are public bodies which have the principal duty, apart from other banking transactions, of attending to mortgage and municipal credits, financing the loans they grant through the issuing of deeds of mortgage.

Despite the difficulties still to be encountered in the reconstruction of Austria and its economy, the Austrian banks will continue to place their services at the disposal of the nation's commerce in accordance with their traditions, and to assist in securing for the Motherland a brighter future after long years of impoverishment and peril.

THE AUSTRIAN INSURANCE SYSTEM.

Insurance, with its estimation of risk and liability, of success or collapse, forms a mirror of Austria's development from the First to the Second Republic.

Within the space of not quite thirty years—1918 to 1945—the Austrian insurance concerns were faced with

a food catastrophe would have been inevitable and the work of reconstruction have been indefinitely postponed.

From the outset, everything possible was done to help build up foreign trade again. At first, in view of transport difficulties, only trade with neighbouring countries came into consideration. The initial results were not great, since all these countries were busy with their own reconstruction and usually themselves needed the goods which Austria wanted. It was only gradually that by means of compensation agreements and later of clearing agreements, the trade relations which in 1938 had been broken off with Austria's most important suppliers and customers could be resumed.

In this way raw materials and auxiliary products as well as the means of production for industry were brought into the country, thus forming a basis for the recovery of industrial-commercial production. With the improvement of food conditions, the power situation and the increasing exploitation of available resources, output again began to rise.

In 1947 it was possible to reach 61 per cent of the industrial production of the year 1937; for the first time in 1948 output rose above 85 per cent of the former figure. Industrial employment figures for 1947 were 19 per cent and those of the year 1948 were about 30 per cent higher than those of 1937.

The most rapid strides in industrial production were first made in the branches more remote from

the consumer—mining, the iron industry, metal works and the chemical and silicate industries, while progress in consumer goods was comparatively slow.

This was due to the prime necessity of reconstructing the country's own trade and of a similar need in those European countries which buy goods from Austria. In proportion as world trade again becomes normal, however, the structure of Austrian commerce will take another shape and the share of specific export goods in the total sent abroad will increase. It is thus necessary to avoid excessive development of the industries manufacturing capital goods, or there will be a danger that the problem of supporting undesirable investments which arose just before 1938 may once again rear its head to hinder the progress of Austrian trade.

In any case the threatening economic vacuum of the year 1945 has been overcome and the development of the productive powers of the Austrian economy is growing. But there is still a great deal to be done in the way of reconstruction. This does not mean only the replacement of objects and material destroyed by the war. Still more important is it to work out the new shape of Austrian trade and the forms best suited to it. Conditions are in so far more favourable than those in the period after 1918 in that the work of reconstruction itself offers an opportunity of adapting the new framework to actual economic conditions and thus of gradually completing the

the double task of coping with the results of two wars and of adapting themselves three times to altered territorial conditions.

Despite the political liquidation of Austria-Hungary in the year 1918, Austrian insurance companies were generally able to keep, in one form or another, the position which they had built up during decades of pioneer work in the territories of the newly created states. One may say that with the setting up of the insurance system in Austria-Hungary, an economic and civilising mission had been carried out. Until quite recently the management of important businesses in the territories of the former Monarchy meant— either through the systematic grouping of affiliated concerns, through reinsurance connections or through the establishment of branches of the main concern—a useful fusion of trade interests in the Danube region with a consequent favourable effect on the prospects of peace in this area.

Even though it has been possible to avoid inflation since the Second World War, the year 1945 placed Austrian insurance in a much more difficult situation than that in which it had found itself in 1918. The period of German occupation had left behind it an unenviable inheritance. There was first the direct effect of

432

war on the country, then the occupation of Austria and its division into zones, with ensuing damage to trade, the devaluation of the compulsorily accepted German state bonds, with the complicated problem of "German property", and finally the disappearance of the basis for Austrian insurance in a number of neighbouring states.

Just as before, the Austrian insurance organisations attach the utmost importance to international connections. These have always been of the best and it was luckily possible to resume them quickly after the end of the war and the restoration of national independance. This explains why in Austria—in contrast to other European countries—there has never been any difficulty over coverage even during the first post-war hardships, rearrangement of reciprocal insurance necessary after separation from Germany being carried out smoothly and without friction. Austrian insurance firms are untiring in their efforts to consolidate their position as far as possible in the international re-insurance market. The Austrian National Bank appreciates the desirability of this and has facilitated dealings in foreign exchange within the framework of its limited powers.

Further development of life insurance business, however, will depend on problems connected with the devaluation

readjustment of Austrian commerce which had been forcibly interrupted in the year 1938. The former successes of Austrian commercial policy justify the assumption that this goal will be reached in the not too distant future. It may also be assumed that the experience which the whole world had of the results of exaggerated protection just before 1938 will have created a more favourable attitude towards free trade, thus ensuring that Austria's efforts to increase her foreign trade will fall on more fruitful soil than before. The possibilities of internal trade in Austria are not sufficient to give a nationalist economic policy a chance of success. Foreign trade will always remain a decisive factor for the Austrian economy and thus all other commercial measures can only be considered in the light of its demands and of its development.

The progress made since 1945 has shown that Austrian economic policy is not treading outworn paths, but is adequately adapting itself to the needs of the moment. Government intervention in questions of price control, rationing, foreign trade etc., which proved necessary in the year 1945 owing to the situation at that time was gradually been dropped as soon as this became possible. Financial conditions, which were in a state of complete disorder, have been so far straightened out that money is once again able to fulfil its function in commerce as a means of exchange and as a standard of values. The path which has been followed from the "Schalter-

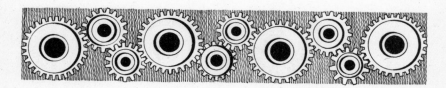

gesetz" (Bank Re-opening Law) to the Schilling Law, the Wage-Price Agreement and the Currency Reform Law is a perfect example of wise and experienced currency regulation worthy to be recorded in history alongside earlier Austrian success in this field, the best-known of which is the credit and currency policy of the old Austrian-Hungarian Bank.

A comparison of the present state of Austrian trade with the position in 1945 must tend, in view of the many obstacles with which reconstruction had to contend even though there was generous foreign aid, to arouse confidence in the commercial future of Austria and finally banish the legend of her non-liability to the realm of fable.

of the capital of existing businesses and other questions of the money and capital markets. At the moment interest is centred chiefly on the coverage of life insurance risks. The improvement in living conditions for the Austrian people is already beginning to have a favourable effect on new business in life insurance, although the social insurance system which is very highly developed in Austria leaves less margin for private insurance than in other countries.

Economy, perseverance and optimism characterise the Austrian insurance system, which is in itself a barometer of Austrian trade.

Kaprun Power House.

AUSTRIA'S RICHES—THE "WHITE COAL".

The power system of the Austro-Hungarian Monarchy was based entirely on rich coal deposits mostly located in Upper Silesia, and later re-inforced by the discovery of great oilfields in Galicia. At the end of the war in 1918, the young Republic saw itself faced with the task of replacing as far as possible the loss of almost all its coal by the available water power. The exploitation of native water power, however, was badly neglected during the First Republic because of shortage of capital; for this neglect a heavy price was to be paid after 1945.

In Western Austria, an important power producing plant—the "Ill Works" in Vorarlberg—was set up, the midway stage being reached between 1925 and 1935. It was used, however, solely to export current to Germany, and the electrification of the Austrian railways which had been begun long before was stopped half-way.

Between 1938 and 1944, the extension of the Austrian water power system was not carried out in the interests of home industry. The works built during this period were designed to supply current from the highest Austrian Alpine regions to Germany, while our own country was supposed to be supplied in winter

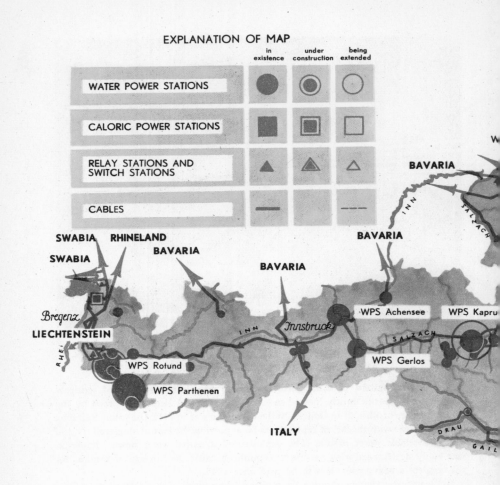

EXPLANATION OF MAP

	in existence	under construction	being extended
WATER POWER STATIONS	●	◉	○
CALORIC POWER STATIONS	■	▣	□
RELAY STATIONS AND SWITCH STATIONS	▲	◬	△
CABLES	──	- - -	

BAVARIA

SWABIA   RHINELAND
SWABIA   BAVARIA

BAVARIA   BAVARIA

Bregenz

LIECHTENSTEIN

WPS Achensee   WPS Kapru

INN   *Innsbruck*

WPS Rotund

WPS Gerlos

WPS Parthenen

SALZACH

ITALY

DRAU

GAIL

Power Stations and

with calorific current from the brown-coal districts of Middle- and Western Germany.

Austria was to be torn in half in an industrial sense and re-formed according to the ideas of Greater Germany. Thus Vorarlberg was given electric cable connect-

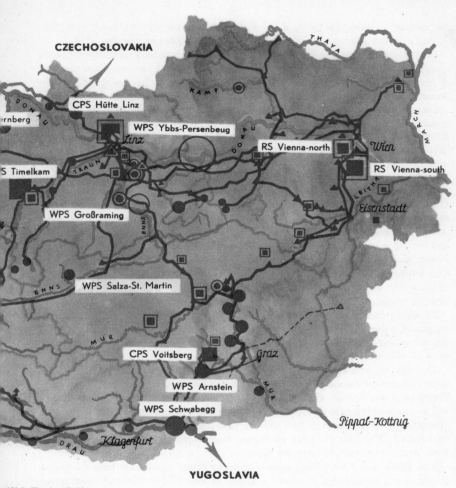

CZECHOSLOVAKIA

CPS Hütte Linz

WPS Ybbs-Persenbeug

RS Vienna-north

Wien

RS Vienna-south

rnberg

Linz

S Timelkam

Eisenstadt

WPS Großraming

WPS Salza-St. Martin

CPS Voitsberg

Graz

WPS Arnstein

WPS Schwabegg

Pippal-Kottnig

Klagenfurt

YUGOSLAVIA

High Tension Cables.

ions to Swabia, Tyrol to Bavaria and Eastern Austria to Bohemia and Silesia. There was no provision for direct connection between the Western and Eastern parts of Austria. Although building was begun on the power station of Gerlos, the Enns Power Station and the Danube power station of Ybbs-Persenbeug during the German

Occupation, construction in these years was of a thoroughly "wartime" standard. A characteristic example was furnished by the Gerlos Power Station.

In 1945 a resurrected Austria found a thoroughly disorganised power system with no system of compensating the difference between winter and summer power supplies or between river and mountain stations. There were only the beginnings of a purely Austrian cable system, for in the years 1938—1944, the existing 110,000 volt system was connected up to the power system of the German Reich. Development of the Austrian system now had to be directed to laying a main power conduit in a west-easterly direction which would run the entire length of the land. In the few years since the end of the war there has already been considerable progress in this direction. For the first time since the erection of the 110,000 volt cable over the Arlberg in 1947, the great Vorarlberg power stations are linked with the inner Austrian network. First the power stations of Tyrol were provisionally connected with the eastern provinces by a 110,000 volt line carried by wooden pylons over the Gerlos Pass. In April 1948, the first part of the future 220,000 volt main cable was put into use from the relay station of Ernsthofen to Pottenbrunn. The prolongation of the main cable to Kaprun and beyond is planned to take place at the same time as the extension of the Tauern Power Station, work having been started in the autumn of 1948. The future Austrian high tension network will not only provide a uniform and smoothly running system at home, but will also make possible a generous exchange of current with all neighbouring states.

Although man power was crippled at the end of the war and is still not properly organised, it was possible by 1948 to start construction in 60 different places. Austria, the richest land for water power in Central Europe, has so far only utilised one sixth of this treasure-store of nature.

Through the efforts of the United Nations Power Committee there is already close cooperation among the countries of Europe with a view to creating a pan-European power service. Owing to her enormous resources in water-power, Austria will be in a position to supply all the electric current still lacking in Europe, after the extensions of the present power stations have been completed and new stations constructed. Plans for exchange of current from Upper Italy to the Lower Rhine have been under consideration for years.

The Tyrolese and Vorarlberg sources of water power which have been developed or are worth developing, estimated together at about 11 milliard kilowatt hours yearly, are designed mainly for export. Water power east of the Gerlosplatte, on the other hand, will have to be used to cover inland demands. Austria most needs power in the eastern provinces, since her industries are mainly located in the Vienna and Linz districts. The principal power stations which have been designed for the supply of inland current are the Tauern Power Station of Kaprun, the Enns Power Work and the Danube Power Works of Ybbs-Persenbeug. After completion

River Power Station, Schwabegg-on-the-Drau.

of the 370 foot high Limberg dam, the building of which was begun in 1948, Kaprun will produce 180 million kilowatt hours of valuable winter peak current. A chain of river power stations is under construction on the Enns which will thoroughly exploit the falls of the river. After its completion the Danube power unit Ybbs-Persenbeug will produce a milliard kilowatt hours per year, thus becoming the biggest river power station of Central Europe.

The water power which is awaiting development in Tyrol and Vorarlberg will yield when completed about 9 milliard kilowatt hours of current yearly. In the area of the Bregenzer Ache there are several weirs which can be harnessed for power, six power stations meaning a yield of 1 milliard kilowatt hours yearly. On the Ill there are three power stations working and a fourth is nearing completion. The extension of the Ill Works for which additional accumulators and power stations are planned will make available almost 2 milliard kilowatt hours of current yearly. The exploitation of the Inn River and the water power of the Ötz District will bring in 4·4 milliard kilowatt hours a year. Apart from this there are important power projects for the Isel District of East Tyrol and in the Reisseck-Kreuzeck group on either side of the Möll Valley.

Despite her lack of coal, Austria is in the enviable position of being able to carry out her plans for producing electric power on a generous scale, thanks to her "white coal". The water-power of Austria is to a great extent capable of being dammed and allows of favourable regulation according to changing pressure. Its development has a dual aim. On the one hand it is planned to meet the increasing demand for electricity from home sources and to make the country independent of imported current, previous caloric supplies being replaced by water power as far as possible, thus reducing coal consumption to the lowest possible figure. On the other hand Austria will have at her disposal a considerable exportable surplus of electric energy after full exploitation of her water power, thus permitting this country to play a central and equalising role in the electricity production of Europe.

Austria approaches this task with the knowledge that the linking up of the various economic interests of individual states in a planned continental economy is the best guarantee for a long period of peace and for general well-being.

FAIR 'FASHIONS'
MONOPOLIES

In the history of Austrian commerce the week from the 11th to the 17th of September, 1921, is heavily underscored with red pencil. The first Vienna Fair was then held in its new form as a sample fair.

The sponsors were taking a risk, and as is often the case with new ventures the confident reassurances of those in charge were at first drowned by pessimistic voices and criticism. What was the good of an exhibition of samples in Austria three years after the defeat? Of what use was this guarantee of spurring on production and trade activity in face of the landslide of inflation?

Despite depression, resignation and desperation and in spite of all the "ifs" and "buts", the Vienna Fair entered the race as an unbacked outsider. The opening day itself forecast the coming success. Before the ticket offices stood long queues and from beyond the frontiers, Vienna's century-old reputation as a market had attracted merchants from all countries. The number of visitors and of those interested increased day by day. The exhibition started a wave of fresh confidence and optimism; the Austria which had recently collapsed was extending to an astonished world a new visiting card.

Since that autumn of 1921 the Vienna Fair—held since then without a break at the beginning of each March and September—has survived the difficult times

after the First World War. It has assisted in the transition from war to peace production, helping to satisfy the first rush for goods after the years of privation and to direct trade into its old, legitimate channels again. The Vienna Fair has gradually modified and finally brought about the end of the foreign exchange controls which shackled industry and the exchange of goods. It has found its way successfully out of the labyrinth of burdensome compensation and clearing agreements and did not even allow the most threatening tariff barriers of other states to hinder its development of free trading competition. Against the political and economic difficulties which confronted international trade Austria set the drawing power of her products. At a time when almost every little town in Europe felt itself called upon to hold an industrial fair, the reputation of the city on the Danube as a natural centre for the transit and exchange of goods was convincingly re-affirmed.

The Vienna Fair carries on a tradition which grew up naturally and has continued for centuries in Central Europe and the Balkans. When Rudolf of Hapsburg conferred the rights of a market town on Vienna in the year 1278, this was merely confirmation of a long-existing practice. From Babenberg and Crusading times, the markets of Vienna had born testimony to civic industry and manual skill, as they had to the honest labour of her artisans and her far-reaching trade connections.

These market rights were confirmed to the Viennese and extended by every ruler in turn. A visitor to one of the two fairs, held at Candlemas and on St. Jacob's

Day, who transported his goods by one of the prescribed highways enjoyed, no matter whence he came, the local governor's protection for his person, his goods and his waggons, a truly enviable privilege in the unsettled times of the closing 13th and the 14th century.

During the Middle Ages it was open to anyone from every country to bring what goods he liked to the two great Vienna markets, with the exception of wine and beer, which were available in abundance on the spot, and of excellent quality. People of every trade and every guild could sell and offer their wares freely.

After the Turkish Wars there was a fresh revival of Vienna market life in the 18th century. But then the discoveries of the weaving loom and the steam-engine began to take effect on production and trade. In the 19th century the railway rendered goods fairs superfluous and the markets began to be transformed into sample exhibitions.

The economic system of the Austro-Hungarian Monarchy was so well-balanced that it had at first no need of any special display of sample products within its frontiers. The exchange of goods between the agrarian and the industrial areas went on smoothly and although samples of all the products of the Empire were occasionally displayed at great exhibitions—Vienna owes the building of the Rotunde to the Great Exhibition of 1873—there was actually no need of special methods to advertise or boost them, for demand and supply were well adjusted, and connections between producers and their customers dated from the times of their fathers and grandfathers.

After 1918 more than a third of Austria's population was engaged in industry and commerce, nearly a further third being occupied with agriculture and forestry. In both cases the small or medium sized concerns were predominant, a fact which explains the ability of Austrian economy to weather the storms of crises. It had never taken special measures to promote war industries. Never through war, but through the years of peace had the Empire prospered. When in 1866 Austria lost the war against Prussia it was because, despite the better training of her troops, the Austrian rifle was inferior to the Prussian.

It is in concerns in which intensive labour and detail is important that the individual talent of the Austrian can find expression, not in great concerns resorting to capitalistic mass production methods. Thus at the Vienna Fair one finds a varied profusion of articles and goods. On the stalls and in the various departments in the halls and pavilions are to be found samples of all the industrial, commercial or agricultural goods produced in Austria, from the simplest tools to complicated precision and tool-making machinery, from building materials to the most modern power plant. Commerce, industry and agriculture unite here to present a complete picture of the Austrian economy.

Agriculture plays a big rôle in the Fair, which not only provides farmers with an opportunity of selecting their requirements in tools and machinery but also a choice of advertising methods to aid them in selling their own products. The latest developments in many fields are displayed with pride—stock-raising, grafting, crossing, products of the soil, qualitative and quantitative record achievements of every kind from field, stable, vineyard and forest.

The Vienna Fair, which is for the Austrian producer the most successful sales market and the most effective propaganda organisation at his disposal, is for the foreign producer not merely a place where he can find just Austrian products and customers. So many foreign firms take part that apart from Austrian goods, eastern and south-eastern European wholesale and retail trades are well represented. In Vienna producers, traders and direct consumers meet from the whole of Europe and from the Near East as well as the Balkans, offering many possibilities of transit deals. Here the agrarian East of Europe and the industrial West exchange their wares.

The Vienna Fair is international and is open for all commodities and to all firms from all countries. There are at least 19 countries to be found regularly represented

EUGENIE PIPPAL-KOTTNIG

at the Vienna Fair: Belgium, Bulgaria, Denmark, Germany, France, Greece, Great Britain, Italy, Yugoslavia, Holland, Poland, Rumania, Sweden, Switzerland, Spain, Czechoslovakia, Turkey, Russia, Hungary and the USA. To these must be added overseas colonies and dominions which often send goods. The two fair areas of the Messepalast and the Rotundengelände are so arranged that Vienna luxury and ornament goods, textiles, fashions, furs, knitted goods, articles of gold and silver, music instruments, glass and chinaware and leather goods etc. are housed in the Messepalast in the city, while all technical products and articles of common use, all accessories of agriculture, machinery and implements as well as building materials are arranged in the exhibition halls of the Rotundengelände.

Special exhibitions which serve no immediate business purpose but pursue aims of a general commercial or cultural character are always held in conjunction with the sample fairs. These special exhibitions are frequently arranged by the trade organisations. They provide useful information as to internal economic requirements, the high standards of development, methods of work and the trading capacity

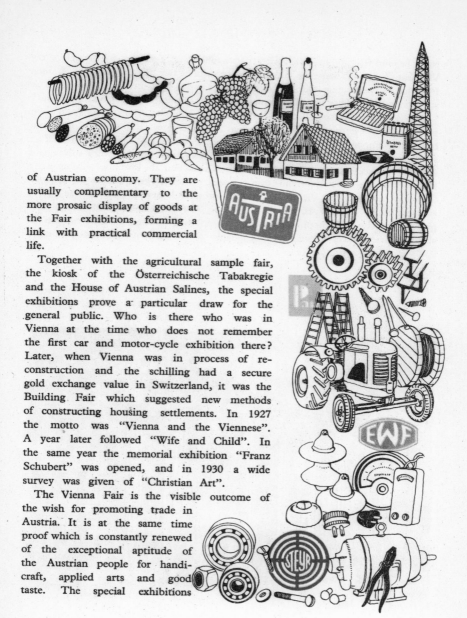

of Austrian economy. They are usually complementary to the more prosaic display of goods at the Fair exhibitions, forming a link with practical commercial life.

Together with the agricultural sample fair, the kiosk of the Österreichische Tabakregie and the House of Austrian Salines, the special exhibitions prove a particular draw for the general public. Who is there who was in Vienna at the time who does not remember the first car and motor-cycle exhibition there? Later, when Vienna was in process of reconstruction and the schilling had a secure gold exchange value in Switzerland, it was the Building Fair which suggested new methods of constructing housing settlements. In 1927 the motto was "Vienna and the Viennese". A year later followed "Wife and Child". In the same year the memorial exhibition "Franz Schubert" was opened, and in 1930 a wide survey was given of "Christian Art".

The Vienna Fair is the visible outcome of the wish for promoting trade in Austria. It is at the same time proof which is constantly renewed of the exceptional aptitude of the Austrian people for handicraft, applied arts and good taste. The special exhibitions pass beyond details to the general atmosphere of everyday life which every Viennese longs to make as pleasant as possible. For this reason the Vienna Fair has a permanent display which proves a special attraction, to men as well as women. That is the permanent exhibition entitled "Vienna Fashions".

It is a matter of especial pride to the Second Republic, that it has again been possible after 1945 to revive the Vienna Fair in its old glory. Despite the "Zones" and restrictions imposed through the war the Vienna Fair has once again proved what an attraction it is for the world of commerce at home and abroad every spring and autumn. In place of the former landmark of the Vienna Fair, the Rotunde building in the Prater, hall after hall now extends over the wide exhibition grounds. In the heart of the city, however, the Vienna Trade Fair presents a new profile in the "Hof-stallungen", a suitable blend of decorative rows of exhibits and individually planned displays. The popular amusement of strolling through the Fair exhibits in all their variety never becomes boring, thanks to the attractive methods of display and the ensuing activity.

Vienna
Fashions

Special Display

What would be the use of all the fruits of the Tree of Life, the Viennese thinks, if there were not delightful moments in which to pluck them for the women, to share them with them or, in the case of the creations of fashion, to drape them about neck or shoulders?

Vienna Fashions, Viennese women! Two words from the cup of delight which Vienna proffers to those who wish to recuperate from the toil of this weary world. The Viennese are sometimes criticised for their irrepressible love of life, for those unable themselves to smile are quick to reproach the cheerful. Thus what is condemned as frivolous is in reality a victory over the difficulties of life; what is called fickle flirtation is only a playful coquetting and light-heartedness with no evil to it.

Vienna Fashions! They take their origin in the naturalness of this city and its inhabitants. These are natural as children, discerning good from bad hours like the doves in the story of the enchanted princess. They know how to reject this and accept the other, how to enjoy, reverting to happiness, to elemental happiness. To seek for joy in everything—is not the longing for it one more bit of evidence of a lost Paradise! Finding delight in all that lives and loves, in colour and in sound, in gestures, in the step of the man rejoicing in his labour and in the care-free games of boys; the joy in melody—in written music as well as in that which is felt without being expressed—bubbling, pulsating joy in all shades of the colours of life around, from the brilliant scarlet of the Cardinal to the modest violet of Eastertide. The bodily, earthly joy in the shape of things, in successful work, in a clinging and softly draped material. The eye's delight at the sight of a circular bed of brightly coloured tulips whose flaunting heads turn towards and follow the sun on straight green stems, in order to complete the circle back again under cover of a spring night.

Vienna fashions through joy and life! Informed longings and bravely beating hearts are the things which urge on humanity to find this great happiness in living. It calls to the world that nowhere have people come so close to finding this lost secret as here in Vienna. It is like a call which echoes from every street, it is as though people were hidden behind the

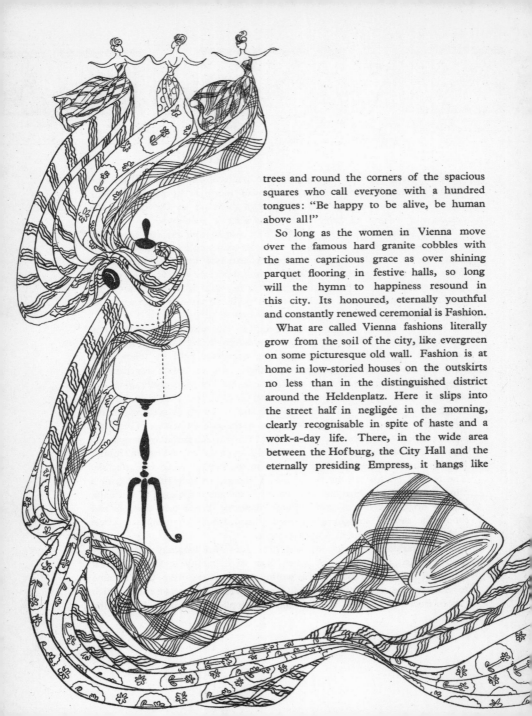

trees and round the corners of the spacious squares who call everyone with a hundred tongues: "Be happy to be alive, be human above all!"

So long as the women in Vienna move over the famous hard granite cobbles with the same capricious grace as over shining parquet flooring in festive halls, so long will the hymn to happiness resound in this city. Its honoured, eternally youthful and constantly renewed ceremonial is Fashion.

What are called Vienna fashions literally grow from the soil of the city, like evergreen on some picturesque old wall. Fashion is at home in low-storied houses on the outskirts no less than in the distinguished district around the Heldenplatz. Here it slips into the street half in negligée in the morning, clearly recognisable in spite of haste and a work-a-day life. There, in the wide area between the Hofburg, the City Hall and the eternally presiding Empress, it hangs like

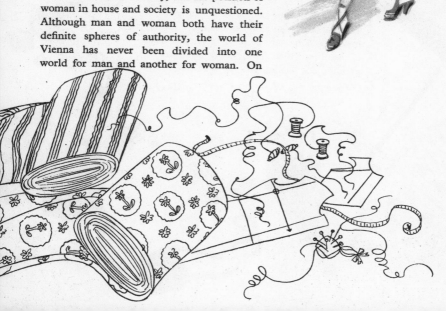

dancing sunshine over the Bruegnel-like masses in the Volksgarten and the crowds streaming along the pavements. The plump lilac bushes flower with unrestrained grace, and the chestnut trees of the avenue in front of the Leopoldian Wing look as though they were forming an escort for the petrified *levade* on its high stone column. Life is clamant here, life, women and fashion.

The chapter "Woman" is written in Vienna in a language of its own. Let us open it in the middle: Woman cooks, of course, but many men have a wonderful knowledge of the culinary arts. Man, of course, is the master—but the most famous ruler of Austria was a woman. Naturally man is the head of the family, but the position of woman in house and society is unquestioned. Although man and woman both have their definite spheres of authority, the world of Vienna has never been divided into one world for man and another for woman. On

the contrary, there is a mutual recognition, a sort of reciprocal politeness between the sexes, and the Strindberg and Ibsen problems are consequently as rarely met with as is any kind of movement for emancipation, for these can only arise where women are misunderstood or neglected by men. In short, they hold in Vienna that man and wife belong together, that one should wed for love and that a chill wind blows over marriages of convenience.

Among the qualities attributed by the world to the women of European capitals—of Paris, Rome or Madrid—those of charm and amiability are ascribed to the daughters of Vienna. The repetition of this throughout the centuries causes it not only to be absorbed into the blood but confers special qualities. One of these is a natural ease of manner, which leads many strangers to suppose the Vienna girl to be more seduc-

tive than she really is or wishes to be, so that they accuse her of promising more than she ever had any intention of allowing —or keeping.

The protective consideration which is accorded to young girls, "Backfische" ("flappers") everywhere results from another privilege, while a third is the special respect shown to old ladies. These latter form a broad class which extends from the much applauded actresses who play "mother rôles" in the Burgtheater, through all classes of the population to the country villages. All these dear old faces seeming to radiate benevolence in the soft glow of life's evening. Woe to the man who is guilty of offending one of these women!

Thus in Vienna two words are robbed of their sharpest sting: "As a woman to grow old" and "To become a grandmother". Theoretically the mothers may still,

through their appearance, be the keenest rivals of their own daughters, but between grandmother and grandchild there is a bond of womanly friendship, ripe experience giving the best advice to youth.

In Vienna it is not only the rare and striking woman of dazzling appearance who is singled out for attention. Woman as such is privileged irrespective of age or rank, and man profits from it. Fashion is not primarily a method of attracting attention, it is not so much a carefully devised system, the mere servant of woman in a jealous struggle to give pleasure. Fashion is neither a courtesan nor a procuress but is rather added to the union of man and woman as a third, joybringing partner to heighten the intensity of life.

Thus fashion in Vienna is not the exclusive prerogative of the upper ten. It is like a melody for all to sing. It is like a free improvisation in all keys of natural good taste and native coquetry. Vienna fashion translates and popularises the *dernier cri* of the moment to a refrain which every woman understands and it is therefore not possible to hold it prisoner in the leading fashion houses of the *haute couture*. It steps through the revolving doors out on to the street, moving boldly among work-a-day folk. It is not limited by anyone's occupation or station in life, but touches every daughter of Eve: it is as ubiquitous in the morning as in the evening. Personal taste and individual skill play a big part in the final result. Everyone in Vienna can catch the trend of fashion, and the women and girls look as though they all belonged to the upper ten.

Adaptation to the individual and the occasion so alters the feminine picture in Vienna that it is often not easy to recognise the fashion of the moment at first glance. The general impression is one of smart and well-dressed women, but therein lies the secret. The

VIEN-
NESE
LEATHER
GOODS

Viennese woman has never been a fashion plate but always a lady of fashion. Dress, hat and accessories are never allowed to extinguish the personal note. The last court of appeal is the general picture reflected by the mirror, not the fashion columns in the newspaper, nor the illustrated fashion periodical—not even what other women are wearing.

If the Viennese woman sees that something dictated by fashion does not suit her, this only fires her ambition. If large hats are absolutely unsuited to her type of face she will oppose them with courage and resource until the small hat which she finally chooses is preferred by everyone, in defiance of the current mode, as unique and charming. And if the fashionable colours are green and purple the Viennese girl who finds that they do not suit her hair or the colour of her skin will never capitulate or surrender with a sigh, but will search until she has found something between turquoise and terra cotta which is exactly the right shade for her.

The Italian wedge shoe with its stressing of form has found its way quite automatically to the slender-ankled foot, while it is certain that more firmly developed legs will balance their way through the streets on the narrow surface of graceful Parisian high-heeled shoes. Fashion may show a preference for flat heels; they will be boycotted in individual cases where they

460

Viennese shoe styles

do not give satisfaction. The tall woman is delighted to accept the advice from a high-class dressmaker that she should choose the long-skirted model with narrow waist; the shorter girl would never in Vienna fall to the ambition of imitating her. The latter would, it is true, have her dress as long as she can reasonably carry it, but at the same time she would cleverly distract attention from her lack of inches—perhaps with a belt, a daring lack of symmetry in the cut, or a piece of artistic embroidery, without anyone noticing that she has tried to *corriger la fortune.*

The Vienna blouse is a traditional speciality which all women love to wear. Made of billowing georgette, muslin, lace or real silk, its rich hand embroidery, frills, a Mozart ruff, a biedermeier jabot or intricate pleating makes it a delicate creation of Viennese good taste, yet at the same time the antithesis of the assertion that there is nothing new on earth.

The conception of the "smart Viennese" was born of the "Jersey" (woollen) dress, a product of the twentieth century, a costume for every hour of the day. Plain and severe for business wear, smart and chic for the Derby, quiet and unobtrusive for visits, pleasingly gracious for the five o'clock tea-dance, the Jersey dress is today a treasured and indispensable item in every woman's outfit. The summer companion of the Jersey dress on its recruiting campaign round the world is called "*Mode à la tyrolienne*". This mixture of motives from old national costumes, bright colours, summer comfort and bubbling effervescence is the most alluring dress for every holiday occasion.

One word on the skill of handicraft without which Vienna fashions would be unthinkable. That talent which is at once inborn and acquired is to be found in the smart showrooms, the art ateliers and equally at the simple milliner's or in the cutter

of a dressmaking coopera-
tive. What an astonishing
combination of eye and
dexterity, of measuring and
execution, of thoughtful
calculation and improvisa-
tion; what painstaking art is involved, for
instance, in the work of hand-stitching and
embroidering.

No material escapes the influence of fashion,
but leather seems to have a special interest
for the Viennese. Whether for ornamental
or luxury purposes or for practical use when
travelling, the number of articles which are
made from it are legion. With leather goods,
fashion—late, but at last—has thought not
only of women but also of men. Masculine
fashions, alas, are very conservative—or should
men console themselves with the fact that they
are not so dependent on external assistance as
women?

The saying that festivals should always be
celebrated as they come round is well accepted

in Vienna. Though no time of the year is an exception to this, the great season is that of winter when the old brilliance of the capital lives again in its women. These junkettings in the Hofburg, the Rathaus and Schönbrunn Palace, in the Concert House und the Musikverein—and, it is to be hoped, soon again in the incomparable Opera building—to them all Vienna society flocks as though invited to a ball by Prince Orlofsky and as though all Vienna were a scene from Johann Strauss' "Fledermaus". Fashion becomes a wild ovation to the charm and good taste of the women of Vienna.

Ball in Vienna

la Cin. Dans
la Pastorale. Dans
le choeur des voix hum...
Nul ... pareilles oeuvre,
Léonore ... concerto.
cantiques des ... urs, de leur fidèle amour.
... adre de l'action ... ou ....
l'Appas...
met sur un pied d'égal...
... ont suffi pour lui ouvrir toutes grandes le
... i six, sept

...strument
suprême.
...es de Coriolan, d'Egmont,
... ir violon; Fidelio ... cantique o
La Missa Solem... ... fait éclater
Les ... tes au clai de lun... ... reutzer, à Waldstei
...phonie en ut ...ine)
...es princes et les souver

THE AUSTRIAN TOBACCO MONOPOLY.

The Austrian State Tobacco Monopoly ("Tabakregie") was founded in the year 1784, through letters patent of the Emperor Joseph II. It extended to all the lands of the Monarchy, thus taking in Bohemia, Moravia, Silesia, Galicia and the Bukowina, Carniola, Istria, Dalmatia and South Tyrol as well as the territory of the present Republic. At the time of its maximum expansion—about the middle of the 19th century—it also embraced Hungary, Venetia and Lombardy, as well as the principality of Liechtenstein.

The vitality of the old Austrian tobacco monopoly was evident after 1918 both through the new-born monopolies of the newly created Succession States and through the Austrian Tabakregie itself. Although suddenly confined within a territory populated by only seven million inhabitants, it survived all the shocks of the previous decade and developed into a modern and efficient industrial undertaking of the State.

After the First World War there were only 9 factories left to the Austrian Tabakregie out of 30, the whole comprehensive organisation having come to an end. Its markets which had been carefully mapped out and developed were mostly destroyed or permanently closed to it.

By the end of the second World War the number of factories had been reduced to seven. More serious still was the widespread damage done to buildings, tobacconists' shops, machinery, transport vehicles and stocks. The stock losses included 162 million cigarettes, 37 million cigars and about 1,800,000 kg of raw tobacco. The internal organisation had been thrown out of gear and cramped by external forces; important

The Preparation of Tobacco in 1763.

foreign connections had been severed and both exports and imports had come to a standstill. Such was the difficult position which confronted those called upon to rebuild the monopoly.

Future prospects may be estimated from a comparison of the figures for the sale of cigarettes in former times and today.

In the year 1913, 6,349,000,000 cigarettes were sold throughout the entire Monarchy (which had then a population of 56 million), i. e. one cigarette every third day per head of population. In the year 1933, under the First Republic, 5,409,000,000 cigarettes were sold (to a population of 7,000,000), seven times as much per head as in 1913. In the year 1947, when supplies were limited and strictly rationed, 3,233,000,000 cigarettes were sold. Thus this much reduced Austria consumed a quantity of cigarettes which proportionately compares favourably with the figures for the old Empire. This will almost certainly continue to increase, as women are smoking more and more.

The Austrian Tabakregie is capable of coping with every increase of demand which may be expected. The elastic organisation of the concern as a modern joint stock company enables it to readjust itself rapidly to meet changing conditions. It is now only a question of obtaining supplies of raw materials, of restoring regular connections with foreign markets and of the provision of a reasonable amount of foreign currency for the Regie to be able to work to full capacity again as before the last war.

472

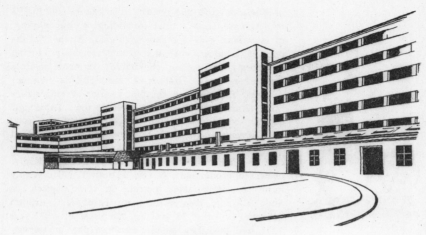

Linz, Tobacco Factory.

The traditional high quality of Austrian tobacco products is due to the use of high-grade foreign materials, chiefly certain oriental tobaccos. These can never be replaced by inland tobacco, since climate and soil do not permit the growth of similar types here. Nevertheless, the inland cultivation of tobacco is encouraged as much as possible.

The great importance of oriental tobacco to the Tabakregie is shown by the fact that in the course of modernisation of the concern, the important task of tobacco buying was delegated to a branch organisation, the "Austria Einkaufsgenossenschaft der österreichischen Tabakregie im Orient, G. m. b. H., Wien". Its main task was to restore severed connections with the most important tobacco producers in Bulgaria, Greece and Turkey. Hungary, North and South America and the Dutch colonies also formerly supplied raw tobacco to the Austrian Tabakregie, but here there are still difficulties in the way of a restoration of trade which arise from the foreign exchange situation.

The Tabakregie is a very important factor in the Austrian economy. Firstly it acts as a big employer of home labour with an inland sales organisation consisting

of 8 warehouses, 258 tobacco distributors and 13,253 tobacconists' shops, thus providing a large number of Austrians with a secure livelihood. As the Tabakregie is a valued customer in the tobacco-producing countries compensation transactions are made possible for other home industries through its foreign dealings. Even during the first months of reconstruction (April to December, 1945) the Tabakregie contributed in taxes about 10 per cent of the total state revenues. In 1946 it provided about a third of these revenues (corporation taxes about 30 per cent and customs dues over 40 per cent), despite decreased production. A rise in output will certainly mean a considerable increase in these figures. It must also be mentioned that Tabakregie exports brought in over 55 million schillings in the year 1933, and that they should therefore play an important rôle in stabilising finances as soon as foreign markets are reopened.

The staff of the Tabakregie varies according to available supplies of raw materials and depends on the preferences and satisfaction of the smoker. In the year 1937, the concern employed 5421 workers, including 3912 women, and at the end of 1947, 2930 workers, of whom 1581 were women. The dwindling of the number of workers is only in a minor degree due to the effects of the war. The main reason must be sought for in the decrease in cigar consumption which has been in progress for some time. The smoker of today is turning more and more to the cheaper type of cigarette which is quickly consumed. The cigar is one of the victims of our hustling and mechanical age. Cigar production, which depends mostly

on manual labour, is on the decline, while the cigarette, which is produced entirely by machinery, is becoming more popular. This explains the reduced number of employees. It may increase one day again, if people find time in more leisured days to blow heavy smoke rings from fat cigars.

At all events, the Austrian Tobacco Monopoly is doing its best to see that the smoker is well supplied at all times with his needs, which are those of so large a section of the community.

Hallein, Salt Freighters.

THE SALT MOUNTAINS OF AUSTRIA.

Salt-mining in Austria dates back to the prehistoric times of the Celts, was developed by the Romans and is closely connected with the growth of civilisation in the country.

The Austrian salt works in Upper Austria, Salzburg, Styria and Tyrol for a long time led an independent existence until Emperor Maximilian I put an end to it in the year 1490 by uniting all the Austrian Crown Lands under his rule.

His successor, Ferdinand I, set up a model organisation for the control of salt mining in his first edict.

In the year 1835 a salt monopoly was established in Austria as part of the introduction of other monopoly administrations. Technical discoveries made and developed in the course of the 19th century were first applied to the production of salt in the latter half of that period. Pressdrills using hydraulic pressure replaced boring machines worked by hand at Bad Ischl.

Electric power was introduced into the salt mines in the 'nineties, special power stations being set up in the mines themselves. Subsequently many hydraulic boring machines were replaced by power-driven borers.

Salt Pans in the Lambath Area.

Great advantages were secured at this time by conducting surface water under pressure to the mines to water the underground facings. A passing attempt to introduce an irrigation process in 1908 was discontinued on account of the amount of gravel washed down from the Haselgebirge.

The second half of the 19th century brought great progress in the boiling process through the use of steam heat for preliminary warming of the saline solution. The works which were started at Ebensee for this procedure were subsequently considerably improved.

At Hall-in-Tyrol, a new electric thermo-compression plant is under construction for the production of fine salt.

Austria's salt mountains have been inhabited for hundreds of years by an ancient race of miners. Happy in the beauty of the surrounding countryside and inspired by love of their lovely native Austria, they hold fast to their ancient rights, customs and traditions.

This long-rooted attachment of the miner to his beloved salt mountain proved its value after the most terrible of all wars. The Austrian saline works were among the first concerns to resume work immediately after the collapse of the German

occupation, thus allowing completely destitute Austria to procure a certain quantity of foodstuffs through compensation deals with foreign countries.

Salt, the white treasure of the mountains, serves humanity in a modified form in another manner. Wherever salt is recovered, there have grown up famous spas such as Bad Ischl, Solbad Hall and Bad Aussee, where the same substance helps to heal various disorders.

VIENNA
UNDER RECON-
STRUCTION

Clemens Holzmeister: Austrian Broadcasting House.

The end of the First World War and the fall of the Austro-Hungarian Monarchy had similar paralysing results for Vienna as did the end of the Second World War, when there was not only a collapse of the existing regime, but in addition extensive war damage to be faced. The general reorganisation of the State which took place after 1918 proved less difficult, not only because there had been no actual war damage in Vienna itself, but also because the forces released by the conclusion of the war were not hindered in their development by the pressure of an occupation. Nevertheless, it was years before the Austrian economy and the capital city had so far recovered that it was possible to go beyond efforts to satisfy the daily needs of the population and start constructive municipal schemes.

The political revolution of November 1918 secured the full triumph of democratic principles. Universal, equal and direct suffrage, with a secret ballot, was extended to women and, for the first time, applied to the election of members of a Vienna city council. As a result the influence of the masses of citizens which had until then been artifically suppressed now took full effect on the composition of the Council Chamber. Power in the municipal assembly consequently went to the Party of the workers, the Social-Democrats. By securing the majority in the City Council the latter found themselves in a position to put their principles into practice in various fields of municipal activity. During the 15 years after the First World War that the Social-Democrats were able to run the municipal affairs of Vienna, entirely new principles were applied to the administration of public welfare, housing, the conduct of public utility services, the educational system and to questions of personnel. As the basis and support of all these innovations a new financial policy was devised and put into practice. The successful achievements of this exceptionally fruitful period of Vienna municipal administration—it must be remembered that they were not carried out during a period of general prosperity and easy-living,

Vienna, the Stadium.

Amalia Baths.

but were born of the destitution of the people and more than once endangered by political and economic pressure—have been admired and emulated, not only in Austria but throughout the world as a glorious example to others, and have been adopted as a model in many countries.

Under the Burgomasters Jakob Reumann and Karl Seitz, assisted by active and vigorous city councillors, Vienna, contrary to the dismal prophecies of those who would have preferred to see Austria vanish from the map, obstinately refused to die, but blossomed out as a reborn and flourishing city. Based on the indestructible determination of the Viennese to survive which these leaders directed and inspired, gigantic housing schemes were quickly put into practice after the collapse of 1918 and caused astonishment and admiration far beyond the frontiers of Austria.

The eminent physician and advocate of social reforms, Dr. Julius Tandler, based his activities on the principle that care for social welfare was a duty incumbent on all and that those in need had a right to be helped by the community. On the basis of these principles, Tandler brought into being a social welfare organisation which not only brings aid to all those who call for it, but going beyond daily necessities, seeks appropriate means to overcome helplessness itself, and to enable the needy of today to become again active and creative members of the social system. This is applied to welfare work for the youth of the city as well as

Karl Marx-Hof

to that for adults. The Vienna Municipality has therefore set up a welfare system which makes use of welfare officials who are carefully trained for their task as well as of honorary workers who are the representations of the population and exercise the function of controlling as well as that of assisting the activities of the officials. Within the framework of this welfare organisation, and in accordance with the individual needs of certain branches of the work, there are special personnel trained in youth welfare work and others schooled in the care of tuberculosis patients. The principle of prophylaxis has been made the guiding principle of the whole public welfare service. Accordingly, welfare care begins before birth and extends to all babies and children, healthy or ailing. Every mother who applies for it receives a complete layette for her new-born child. Expectant mothers are encouraged by money grants to submit to the Wassermann test in order to combat hereditary syphilis. Medical examination of school-children at regular intervals was instituted, and women welfare workers appointed for the schools. Provision of school meals ensures that the attention of the children should not be adversely affected by hunger. School dental clinics, optical inspection at regular intervals and holiday schemes complete the programme of preventive welfare for young people of school age. A gust of

Children's Open Air Bathing Pool of the Vienna Municipality.

modernity swept through the established youth welfare centres of the Municipality. The uniformed Mr. Squeers with his rod had to make way for the teacher. The new crèches of the Municipality of Vienna may be regarded as a crowning achievement of youth welfare progress. The Municipality also struck a completely modern note by instituting and fitting out kindergartens based on the principles of the famous child psychologist, Maria Montessori.

The measures taken to carry on the war against tuberculosis were equally revolutionary. Tuberculosis welfare centres now take over the victims of this disease and either send them off for the necessary curative treatment or at least keep a regular check on their state of health. In the Krankenhaus der Stadt Wien at Lainz, a new pavilion for tubercular patients was constructed and the former sanatorium of the "Steinhof" lunatic asylum became the tuberculosis sanatorium of Baumgartner Höhe. The other municipal hospitals were brought up to date, five grammes of radium were bought, a cancer ward was established in Lainz Hospital, special wards for diet treatment and for the care of rheumatic patients were instituted and the municipal Old Age Homes were modernised and extended.

One of the few good results of the First World War was that it taught people to appreciate the value of a healthy body. Sport became a popular demand of the masses, which the municipal administration did its best to satisfy. The establishment of the Stadium and many sports grounds and youth playgrounds, of the Amalia Baths and many summer swimming pools, the extension of existing municipal peoples' baths and the construction of 23 children's free open air bathing pools all served to popularise sport among the masses of the people and improved the health of the population of Vienna.

The Tenants' Protection Law, born of war-time necessity, put a brake on private building enterprise after the First World War as it does today. As general economic conditions made it unthinkable that this law should be abolished and the old system restored whereby there was no limit put on the rents which landlords could demand, though at the same time the shocking housing conditions in Vienna called imperatively for sweeping and effective measures, the Vienna Municipality saw itself obliged firstly to raise funds to complete the housing schemes which had been dropped during the war. Secondly, it had to adopt a positive building policy of its own. On September 21st, 1923, its housing programme was adopted, the Vienna City Council deciding that it should be financed from municipal funds. Over a period of five years, 25,000 homes were to be built for the public. This programme was not only completed, but was followed by further great building projects, so that by the year 1934, about 65,000 homes had been built by the municipality, either in blocks of flats or in groups of small houses. This gigantic scheme was covered in part by the steeply and progressively scaled house-building tax.

The Vienna Municipality considered its building activities as a welfare measure to which it was compelled by existing social and economic conditions. It therefore treated the whole cost of construction as irrecoverable building investment which must be regarded as capital expenditure. Rents were fixed to cover the costs of maintenance and anticipated repairs and replacements, thus keeping them within the range of the Tenants' Protection Law rents.

House planning was developed by the Vienna Municipality in accordance with entirely new principles of hygiene and cultural progress. The building regulations in force in Vienna since the year 1883 permitted actual buildings to cover eighty-five per cent of the available surface, but the Vienna municipality only allowed 30 to

Reumann-Hof

40 per cent of the surface to be covered by bricks and mortar. This led to the construction of large housing blocks enclosing wide spaces which allow direct light to reach every flat and every room. The interiors of the first flats were very simple; with the improvement of the economic and financial position of the Municipality, those subsequently constructed had more comfort and elegance. Every flat has parquet flooring, hall, lavatory, attic and cellar, water, gas and electric light. Many flats have balconies or bay windows and in the bigger housing blocks the work of the housewives is made easier by central washing kitchens fitted with mechanical devices. Baths, douches, libraries and lecture rooms, gymnasiums, kindergartens and other communal conveniences serve the mental and physical wellbeing of all occupants. The architects of this period employed all their talents to make the blocks of flats of the Vienna Municipality as beautiful and as practical as possible, flats in which a quarter of a million people have found homes. Most of these buildings are real gems which improve the appearance of Vienna and have helped to increase the city's reputation throughout the whole world. The Municipality itself has done its share in beautifying the flats by employing artists of all kinds to work on them. So arose those imposing municipal house-blocks in various districts of Vienna— above all in Meidling, Ottakring, Favoriten, Brigittenau and on the Margaretengürtel, each of which comprises from 400 to 1600 flats. They are fitted out with every possible device to add to the comfort of tenants. In addition, more than 5000 homes have been constructed on the outskirts of the city in villa groups, partly at the sole cost of the Municipality, partly as co-operative settlements with financial assistance from the municipal authorities. Large fruit and vegetable gardens are attached, and often sheds for small live-stock.

The building activities of Vienna Municipality have opened up completely new fields, both from the standpoint of commercial policy as from that of architecture. The principles put into practice by their own building achievements the city fathers

Kahlenberg : The Höhenstrasse.

'legally embodied in the new building regulations of 1930. These put an end to the traditional construction for profit of tenement barracks with kitchens opening only on to an interior corridor, so-called "light-shafts" and back blocks. Since then, Vienna's housing principles have been adopted by many countries. They served as a model for the great building programme of the British Government, and have even influenced projects for the building of millions of flats in the United States.

A radical change has also taken place in the administration of the public utility services of the Municipality. The principle that costs only should be covered was introduced—i. e. the monopoly undertakings have to be self-supporting without trying to earn a profit for the municipal exchequer. In this way every improvement, every reduction of costs is a direct gain to the consumer—the Vienna public as a whole. At the same time extensive modernisations of all these undertakings were carried out. The Vienna gasworks were transformed into a great chemical factory which was enabled through its by-products to play an important rôle in the country's economy. The municipal electricity works were provided with new machinery and water-power plants were constructed. Gas and electric light became so cheap in this way that it was possible to introduce them to almost every Vienna household.

With these great innovations in the service of the masses (which made heavy demands on municipal finances), the position of municipal employees was put on an entirely fresh basis. Not only were working conditions improved for all categories, but wages were increased. Since then no worker or employee in municipal employment has been dependent on tips.

The basis of all the great achievements of the Vienna Municipality after the First World War was a stern financial policy which gathered in money where it was to be found—in the hands of the property-owning classes and of those who chose to live luxuriously.

Between the years 1934 and 1938 many large-scale road constructional schemes were carried out. First the Höhenstrasse was built through the belt of forests and meadows on the western outskirts of the city, then the Kobenzlstrasse and the Kahlenbergstrasse were constructed, the whole providing a wonderful motor highway. Another road important for modern traffic is the Wientalstrasse, which greets the motorist from the west far outside the city boundaries near Purkersdorf, and conducts him through Hütteldorf, past Schönbrunn Palace deep into the heart of Vienna.

Thus the activities of Vienna Municipality in the period following the First World War may be put on record as having been constructive in the best sense of the word, serving the welfare of the people at large and the progress of mankind.

THE
SPANISH RIDING
SCHOOL

AUGARTEN
PORCELAIN

THE VIENNA CHOIR
BOYS

When Austria drew up her balance sheet after the First World War to see how she could survive as a state, she found in the annals of her past three names which had a sound and well-established reputation—the Spanish Riding School, Vienna porcelain and the Wiener Sängerknaben (Vienna Choir Boys). All three institutions had splendid traditions dating back for centuries. The youthful Republic hastened enthusiastically to add new fame to that inherited from the past.

THE SPANISH RIDING SCHOOL.

In Fischer von Erlach's magnificently designed edifice in Vienna, the incomparable Lipizza horses can be seen today displaying their unique mastery of the *haute école* exactly as they did three centuries ago. It is a display of pacing and jumping which is the last word in animal grace. It is directed towards a single objective— a demonstration of perfected movement for movements' sake alone. Setting, rider and horse blend to form a single unit.

490

When the Bishop of Trieste no longer felt secure from Turkish raiders—his country house had been burnt down by robber bands—, he sold his estates near the village of Lipizza to the House of Hapsburg. In the year 1580 a stud was started there on the barren rocks of the Karst mountains in the healthy Adriatic air. There the noble strain of the Lipizzas was bred. The finest stallions were always sent to Vienna to be trained there for the *haute école*.

In 1785, the baroque passion for building gave birth to the wonderful hall of the Spanish Riding School. The Imperial Court commissioned Fischer von Erlach the Younger to design and construct it. It is so large that it gives the impression of a grandiose and vaulted city square rather than of an enclosed interior.

491

Grey wooden panelling surrounds the yellowish earth of the rings. Over the massive parterre construction rise the slender columns of the first gallery. Above the cornice of the main building a plain balustrade runs all the way round, while the entrance façade displays an antique and richly ornamented gable.

It is in this princely riding school that the *haute école* is ridden, the "school on the ground" first being gone through at the pillars, to be followed by the "school above the ground". After trotting and the "passage", the horse is untied from the posts to perform "circles" and "pirouettes". Then comes the "levade", a movement in which the horse rears its forequarters while keeping its haunches together without shifting from the spot. The horse of the Prince Eugene Monument on the Vienna Heldenplatz is rearing thus. A forward jump in the levade position without the forequarters touching the ground is called "courbetting". "Croupade", "balotade" and the "capriole" form the climax of the display.

To a fanfare of trumpets the imposing figures of the horsemen appear, slowly riding on their wonderful gold-saddled horses. They are equipped with brown or scarlet jackets with white leather breeches, high riding boots, sword and two-cornered hat which in accordance with custom they doff in greeting before the picture of the Emperor. The white horses, their manes and tails plaited with gold, contrast glowingly with the dull grey of the wooden panelling. There is a glint in their great dark eyes, and their pink-edged nostrils quiver. Beneath the gleaming hide the muscles and sinews ripple in incomparable beauty. A picture of perfect discipline, these animals go through their difficult programme. Their performance is a feast for the eye and the senses—the world-famous *haute école*, whose venerable traditions are now practised and kept up only by the accomplished horsemen of the Spanish Riding School.

VIENNA AUGARTEN PORCELAIN.

In former times, when Austria saw the triumphant progress of Baroque through town and countryside, when within fortified zones the gothic severity of the Middle Ages was forced to make way for the elaborate façades of the new style, a demand arose for suitable ornaments to decorate the new palaces, for the gala room of the town or country house. It had to be something which would go with the general scheme of interior decoration—artistic ornaments for chimney-piece, shelf and table. It was then, in 1717, that the Dutchman Du Paquier established the Vienna Porcelain Factory, of which the "Porzellangasse" is still a reminder. In the Middle Ages, when the first Chinese porcelain came to Europe, the tables of princes and knights displayed pewter, more rarely silver, but mostly vessels of wood or clay. The manufacture of china, the "White Wonder", a product of the mysterious mingling of the four elements, still remained a secret. Not until the beginning of the 18th century did Böttger of Meissen succeed in solving the great mystery. Shortly afterwards, Paquier started his factory in the Porzellangasse. A bare fifteen years later Vienna had developed a technique of its own—the delicate shading of the clay, the glazing, and the gilding. Through "flower and figure painting", old Vienna porcelain soon became world-famous. Flower-painting became so popular that the Chinese attempted to copy Vienna motifs, and wares produced to appeal to Viennese tastes were shipped to Europe through the East India Company. But just as "chinoiserie" is never more than an imitation of Chinese painting, so this Chinese attempt to reproduce Vienna patterns did not come near the originals.

Maria Theresia, who recognised the importance of applied art, took over the porcelain factory and made it a State undertaking. From this time on the manufacturers adopted the historic coat of arms of the Babenbergs as their trade-mark. The popular designation for it was "Beehive". This was the origin of the subsequently famous name for real Vienna china. The undertaking flourished, and was soon employing decorators of skill, painters in blue, rainbow-shades and gold. Orders poured in from abroad; one worthy of note was an order for 120,000 Turkish drinking vessels from Constantinople.

Motifs for decoration were taken from painting, various allegoric figures, shepherdess scenes in the French style, subjects from mythology and later designs according to rococo taste. Landscapes and the so-called mosaic patterns took the place of leaf and ribbon work. Copperplate patterns made a change in subject and technique. About the middle of the 18th century, porcelain vessels as a whole became lighter and more graceful, relief work was added and the baroque handles gradually gave way to more natural styles. Figure painting was executed with a perfection of detail, based on Watteau scenes, mounted combats, shepherds and shepherdesses, rural and hunting scenes and lovers' meetings. Then the influence of Sèvres made itself felt. This period is recalled to mind by dinner-services with rounded gold-network on a dark blue background and coloured figures on a white background.

Towards the end of the 18th century Director Sorgenthal brought new prosperity to the factory. Vienna vases were produced with pictures on the classicistic model, bowls with grotesque ornamentation and Raphaelite paintings. These designs were inspired by the antique wall paintings which at that time were being discovered in Herculanum and Pompeii, as well as the grotesque paintings by Raphael in the loggias of the Vatican, the engravings of which had made them widely known. This period was responsible for a number of charming old Vienna figurines and vessels which are among the masterpieces of ceramic art. At this time the Viennese also invented the famous "relief gold", an unequalled process for dissolving gold in oils and painting it on china.

When Napoleon's army invaded Europe and Talleyrand appeared in the Vienna factory in 1806 with his generals, Director Niedermeyer dispatched in good time the most valuable specimens to Budapest. At this epoch the now famous Napoleon Service was made for Schönbrunn Palace, a set remarkable for the wonderful forms and colours of the best Empire period. The Vienna factory survived all the losses and dangers of 1809, the ensuing Vienna Congress bringing a host of art-loving visitors who give new impulse to the factory.

The biedermeier period was devoted heart and soul to porcelain. "Middle-class intimacy" and the development of an affectionate family life created a sincere demand and sentimental longing for the products of the factory, which had meantime secured the services of a popular Vienna painter. In the year 1801 Daffinger, who later became famous as a miniature painter, entered the porcelain factory as an eleven year old apprentice. A coffee cup on which the fourteen-year-old boy painted an idyllic group of a mother with three children in perfect harmony of form and colour became a sample of the best composition of the "Old Vienna School". The plate with the Three Graces (after Rubens) is one of Daffinger's finest pieces of porcelain painting.

The tendency to the idyllic, the closeness to life of the biedermeier period made porcelain the fashion during those years. Interior furnishing took advantage of this in an over-elaborate manner, for there was no cupboard without trinket boxes, no wall without ornamental plates and the festive board as well as the everyday table was enlivened by daintily painted services. Monogrammed chocolate cups became birthday and name-day presents. Jugs, pots, pipe-bowls and box lids were wafted from their mundane atmosphere into a gay world through the designs of Daffinger in which a whole company of Greek gods descended on to a white porcelain field.

The discovery of china clay deposits near Karlsbad with coal seams adjacent and cheap labour created a powerful rival to the Vienna porcelain production. Various private circumstances brought the Vienna factory into a difficult situation and led even to its temporary closing down.

The young Austria of 1918 recalled with pride the great history of Vienna porcelain. The name and the site of the Augarten were added to the old trade mark of the firm. Historic drawings were looked up and re-designed. The Augarten Porcelain Factory soon became a centre for post-war Viennese artists, and although the first years after the re-opening of the factory fell within the inflation period, the stabilisation of Austrian currency soon enabled it to regain its former position on the Continent. Vienna Augarten china is an old and at the same time a new proof of Austrian skill. The people of the biedermeier period made no secret of their love of miniatures painted on porcelain. Many such souvenirs of a past age are still to be found in Vienna drawing-rooms, in homes where time has failed to wipe out all trace of byegone days.

Vienna, the Augarten Palace

THE WIENER SÄNGERKNABEN (THE VIENNA CHOIR BOYS).

When the Hofburg Orchestra and the "Löwenburgsche Kaiserliche Hofsänger-knabenkonvikt" in the Piarist Monastery were disbanded after the Revolution of 1918 and most of the boys were sent home, the Rector of the Burg Choir, Josef Schnitt, saved from the collapse what it was possible to rescue and re-assemble. In an obstinate fight crowned with complete success, the untiring Rector transformed the former Hofsängerknabenkonvikt into the Institut der Wiener Sängerknaben.

What a far cry it is from that difficult start after 1918, when the new epoch was started without outside assistance, without money, with only 15 boys, in a few dingy rooms of the Old Hofburg, to the all-embracing triumphal journeys of the Wiener Sängerknaben round the world. It is at the same time a pattern for future Austrian cultural progress. Although subsidies have been discontinued and patronage by the wealthy has ended through the impoverishment of the country, the traditional values of art and civilisation in Austria have the necessary vitality in themselves and in the energy of the new generation to persist and even to expand.

The Sängerknabe who stands before the footlights in his sailor suit and bows in greeting with his arms formally crossed, fresh and unembarassed, has a long

Augarten Porcelain: the Viennese Girl.

line of ancestors! They date back to gothic Vienna when song occupied an important place in the ducal Burg Orchestra under Rudolf the Endower. The Emperor Maximilian I founded in 1498 the Boys' Choir in the Hofburg Orchestra. In 1580 the Hofkapelle had 83 members. The choirmasters who in subsequent times were no longer priests but professional lay musicians were enjoined by strict Court orders to "feed and care for the Choir Boys carefully". They were to be given good food, roast meat three times a week, plentiful fruit and decent clothing.

Many great musicians are intimately connected with the history of the Wiener Sängerknaben. Gluck accompanied the choirs of the Hofkapelle. Mozart was more or less the official composer of the Sängerknaben when he was only 12 years old. His charming early composition "Bastien and Bastienne" is, like Haydn's "Apotheker", still one of the best numbers in the repertoire. Bruckner, who grew up as choir boy in St. Florian, was appointed Hofkapelle Organist in Vienna in 1867. Schubert spent five years as a choir boy in the Vienna Institute.

Now year by year posters in all the great cities of the world herald the concerts of the Wiener Sängerknaben. The programme is taken from olden and modern times, the boys beginning the evening with religious A-cappella music dating from the 16th century onwards. Then there are difficult four, six and eight-voiced movements by Palestrina, Lasso and Gallus, solemn and inspiring compositions in which the choral severity of the juvenile voices have a moving effect.

Choral plays in historic costume follow, music by Mozart, Haydn, Schubert. Fresh and natural Viennese boys are transformed into powdered and dainty ladies and gentlemen of rococo times, pirouetting with graceful charm and presenting their quartettes, arias, quarrel- and love-scenes with such ringing and silvery voices that one has the illusion of listening to an old-fashioned musical box.

The third part of the programme is made up of many-voiced folk-songs. Then come the national anthem of the country visited and at the end—Vienna waltzes.

Of the three choirs which the Institute now has at its disposal, one is always on tour, while the other two take duty on alternate Sundays in the Burgkapelle where the solemn Mass is sung. The Wiener Sängerknaben take part in the Staatsoper productions, in films, and appear on festive occasions. Work at self-perfection and progress is their slogan. Through their tireless energy they have created for themselves a home of their own, and have revived an ancient name, to cover it with honour. These boys of between seven and fifteen years of age are the melodious youth of Austria. This institution of the Vienna Choir Boys in its present shape is a striking example of how outward forms can change to correspond with the march of time, while the essential is preserved unaltered. The structure of the institution resembles that of a college. The boys are received into it, regardless of their social background, at the age of six or seven. The sole criterion is that of their talent and inclination for singing. When they have completed their preliminary training—that is to say at the age of about ten years—the young choristers receive what amounts almost to individual further training in accordance with their own wishes. It is the great endeavour of the institution to secure for the choristers when the time comes for them, to leave an extensive and uniform education. As a result, the boys cherish the memory of their chorister days. Many of them come back later as conductors or teachers, or, as part of the audience, re-live their early days as singers.

Food is not, as ascetics proclaim, just a means of prolonging a puritan existence. Far from it. Feeding—the exquisite pleasure of absorbing nourishment—is a very intimate part of the most important and the most pleasurable experiences of life. Manners and costumes associated with eating often give a faithful picture of a whole epoch, reflecting the various stages of its development whithout artificial gloss or sham. The standard of cooking and table manners reveals human—or all too human—characteristics, both of individuals and of races.

In Austria—as you will already have noticed—everything dates a long way back, the most modern things originating at the latest in the days of Maria Theresia. Very much dates back to Leopold, the saintly Babenberg, and even to the Romans. Gastronomy, the art of the epicure, goes back to prehistoric times, for in Vienna the fact has never been overlooked that taste is the first sense to awaken and the last to fade. Literature expresses its universal importance with the words: Eating is life intensified.

The words "Wiener Lebensart"—the Viennese manner of living—implies first of all a cultivated appreciation of all the pleasures of life—something which the non-Viennese may dismiss as self-gratification. The Viennese know how to interpret gratification, and find in it nothing derogatory. On the contrary, delight in pleasures of the senses, a desire to enjoy the good things of life contribute towards creative achievement. These things are the inexhaustible source of the Austrian people's artistic gifts, the primary urge to stretch out one's hand towards violin or palette and brush. From them arise the vagaries of fashion, the inspired variations of applied art and that style of living and being which the ancestors called "the life of the Phaeaces".

Would Odysseus ever have returned to his Penelope without the help of Nausikaa, the well-disposed daughter of the Phaeaces of the pleasure-loving island of Scheria? The reproach implied in the word "Phäakentum" only arouses a smile here. People are well contented that pleasure-loving Vienna should be an island in the wearisome and baffling journey of life.

But let us approach the important subject of gastronomy with a respectful obeisance to bygone days:

A HERITAGE FROM GODS AND ANCESTORS. One can hardly speak of a culinary art prior to the arrival of the Romans and the Germanic tribes in the country, for the Celts were very primitive eaters. Their food consisted of very little bread but plenty of meat, which was boiled in water or roasted on a spit.

From the Teutons two principles have been handed down unaltered—that nothing should be begun on an empty stomach, and that the famous Teutonic hospitality was a first duty. As Tacitus says in his "Germania": "No other race is so eager

Guido de Columna: "The Trojan War" (First half of the 15th Century, National Library, Vienna).

Benvenuto Cellini : Salt-Cellar
(Museum of Fine Arts, Vienna).

to offer unlimited entertainment and hospitality. For these people it is wrong to close one's doors to anyone, no matter whom."

Early Austrian guide books praise Viennese hospitality in the same way. The Viennese, according to many later accounts, were always fond of eating and drinking, especially in public places such as the Prater, Schönbrunn or the Augarten, a fact which earned them among foreigners the reputation of being heavy eaters. It was also their custom always to cook something special for the guest and to feed him lavishly.

But to return to the ancients. The Roman way of life had a greater influence on the stomachs of the Viennese than did that of the Teutons. In ancient Rome eating was a science in which delicate tastes were combined with unlimited luxury. Over the city on the Tiber hovered the spirit of culinary art. According to Plutarch, Caesar understood how to plan banquets with as much care and forethought as battles. Horace and Ovid reveal to us great interest in food and drink, refined by poetry. Ovid describes how a young man dipped his fingers in red wine during a feast in order to write a declaration of love on a small table. The feasts of Lucullus are still proverbial today and the gluttonous orgies of the parvenue Trimalchion are known to us through the tales of Petronius. Many a Viennese may have felt a spiritual bond with Cato as he repeated with a sigh his complaint: "How hard a thing it is to try to talk to one's belly, which has no ears to hear."

Cabbage, which they like to serve in Vienna as a garniture to the traditional beef, was known to the gods of the Greeks. It originated from the tears which the Thracian Prince Lycurgus shed when Bacchus bound him to a vine-pole for frivolously destroying grapes. The ancient Egyptians could consume quantities of beer and wine without getting drunk because they ate cooked cabbage before beginning their drinking bouts. Cato recommended the same practice to Roman drinkers.

Lettuce was sacred to Aphrodite because she once hid the new-born Adonis among lettuces. To the Greek gods salads came third among their favourite foods, following nectar and ambrosia. Viennese cannot have forgotten this, for in the preparation of this olympic dish they employ qualities required by other favourites of the gods, the poets—imagination, perseverance, instinct and the gift of composition.

The egg, which is supposed to have given birth to many divine, heroic and unwordly beings, was associated by the Teutons with hares, brightly coloured eggs being sacrificed at the feast of Ostara, the Goddess of Spring, whose favourite animal was the hare. Until the early Middle Ages it was the custom for godparents to bring painted eggs as present, to the christening. Searching for Easter eggs is still a pleasing custom in all parts of the Austrian provinces, and there is hardly a table at Easter which is not decorated with coloured eggs.

Among the many berries in Austria the strawberry is highly prized as a table delicacy and is known to the world as "Schöne Wienerin". The Viennese safeguard themselves against the rash which some people get after eating them by adding *Schlagobers*—whipped cream. A special attraction for eye and palate are the little yellow boats made of pastry topped by whipped cream, thickly sown with wild strawberries.

So up, supposed to have been the first food of the giants, has always been a favourite dish in Vienna. Such a variety of soups developed from the original soup which was made from bread, that in the year 1300 monks were forbidden to eat more than one kind of soup on a week-day.

The goose, honoured in Roman legend as the saviour of the Capitol, became St. Martin's bird in the Christian era. Roast "Martin's Goose" on November 11th is a special festive dish today in the Burgenland.

A glance at the history of sweetmeats is specially interesting in reviewing the Vienna cuisine, for what would this be without Vienna pastries! According to Pliny the Romans first obtained sugar cane from Arabia. Before that, honey was used for sweetening. The Crusaders rediscovered sugar-cane near Tripoli and brought it to Europe, but cane sugar had a long and expensive journey to make, and was therefore very costly and beyond the reach of most people in the 14th century, twenty pounds costing as must as a Ford car nowadays. Consequently, sugar in the Middle Ages was used almost exclusively in chemists' shops for medicinal purposes. Confectioners did not yet exist. It was the Emperor Maximilian I who brought the first sugar-blower to his Court in 1514.

Salt on the other hand, symbol of hospitality, was found in profusion in Austria.

COOKING IN THE MIDDLE AGES. The great gap which we find between the complicated cooking recipes of Apicius, the Roman epicure in the third century, and the first records of the 13th century can only be bridged by isolated references and incomplete accounts. In general, the culinary art deteriorated seriously during the Middle Ages. Stale bread, smoked fish and beef formed the staple food of the knights. The great thing was that enormous quantities should be served. It must have been exhausting work walking about encased in iron on badly paved streets, swinging the two-handed sword of battle and heroically dealing with one horrible adventure after another. The ostentation at wedding feasts contrasted strongly with the simple meals of everyday life. A detailed description of the former is given by the historian Ottocar v. Horneck in his account of the marriage of King Belas of Hungary to the niece of Ottokar of Bohemia in the year 1264. He says: "There was indeed more than enough. The Danube was scarcely able to bear the ships heavily laden with food, and many a container burst under the pressure of its contents." Elsewhere he speaks of bread to the baking of which went a thousand bushels of wheat, and of wine enough for the inhabitants of two countries.

Gülich, Inheritance Congratulation Feast, 1705. Table of the Fourth Estate (National Library, Vienna).

Before the 12th century, in accordance with the strict custom, the two sexes ate separately in different rooms. Later they were allowed to eat in a common dining hall, the knights sitting along one wall and their ladies by the other, the middle being left free for the servants to move up and down. In those days plates were made of wood and pewter, stoneware first coming into use at the end of the Middle Ages.

In minstrel times it was the duty of the host to seat each lady next to an admirer. The pair received one plate between them; people still ate with their fingers. The knight plied his beloved with affectionate words and choice morsels. This common platter was still the custom until the 19th century, after the minstrels had long vanished.

The two-pronged fork first made its appearance in Italy towards the end of the 15th century. Anna of Austria, born in 1601, still plunged her whole hand into the ragout, according to the chroniclers. It was not until the 17th century that the use of the fork became general in Europe. In the 18th century came the three-pronged, and later the four-pronged fork. Although the spoon dates back to the Stone Age, soup was still sipped from hollowed rings of bread until nearly 1500, spoons being only used to fill these. It was the same thing with the knife. As a tool it has a long history and there were cutlers even in the 10th century. But at table it was only used by the head of the house for carving. Tooth-picks, on the other hand, were found even in prehistoric graves, and were carried in costly cases in the Middle Ages.

Until the middle of the 15th century it was the custom to cover the festive board—which was placed loosely on supports and removed at the end of the meal—by enormous tablecloths, which stretched over and protected the knees during eating. Before dipping into the dishes, the hands were wiped each time on the tablecloth, so that this had to be changed several times during great feasts. The table napkin was not introduced until 1450. It is hardly recognisable as such in the luxurious squares of coloured velvet which were used for the purpose at the court of Leopold II.

There was of course no lack of etiquette and table rules. In an Italian manual of the year 1480 we read: "Do not stuff too large mouthfuls into both cheeks. Do not keep your hand too long in the platter, and put it in only when the other has withdrawn his hand from the dish."

Elegant table manners were displayed by dipping with three fingers only. The common drinking glass was in use until the year 1550. It was wiped with the tablecloth before each drink, as was the mouth. If possible the glass had to be held with three fingers only. When a lady drank, the serving-man approached and held a bowl under her chin. In serving, all food was covered with a serviette on account of the powder on wigs and faces. Before a prince partook of a dish, the food taster had to sample it before the eyes of all, even wiping the table implements with bread which he afterwards ate, such was the general mistrust and fear of poisoning. The talisman was long used at table: it was laid beneath glass or plate.

In the 15th century, Vienna cooking was considered to be among the best in Europe, and when the Viennese went to war, he took his best cooks to camp with him. The doughty Capuchin monk Abraham a Santa Clara more than once flew into a passion over Viennese gormandizing. He was not surprised, he said in one of his sermons, that house and farm were so often ruined because of the owner's overeating and that the noble soul was suppressed by the fat paunch.

DAYS OF SPLENDOUR. Splendour and luxury reached their climax in Austria in Leopoldian times, under Karl VI, under Prince Eugene and during the days of the Vienna Congress. Table decoration was a special feature of every official banquet. Fantastic shapes in sugar-icing, arabesques, ornamentation and groups of merry figures were the fashion in the days of great court banquets. The arrangement of the dishes competed with the table decorations; roasted doves and chickens, for instance, would be grouped about a pelican made of baked bread.

In this decorative period, they went so far as to produce gilded sucking-pigs. Astonishing pastry ships were filled with fruits of marzipan: the latter are still popular today. At other times table fireworks competed with disguised foods and artistic creations such as statues, fountains and castles of edible materials. Many confectioners of the period were trained sculptors.

The most luxurious days for the city were those of the Vienna Congress. Entertainment at the Imperial Court cost 50,000 gulden a day. The wealthy Austrian aristocratic families gave banquets to as many as 700 guests at a time, one day in the week being reserved for such brilliant affairs.

The so-called table d'hôte was never a success in Vienna. To these "Landlords tables" a certain number of people came at a fixed hour in order to partake of a meal which was served to everyone simultaneously at a fixed price. He who could eat quickest with the smallest regard for others was at an advantage, but as the Viennese dislike haste at mealtimes, the tables d'hôte were little patronised.

Apart from the customary eating-houses, there were also what were called the "tracteurs". Here one could eat at any time between eleven a. m. and three p. m., lunch costing up to a gulden according to what was chosen. The customers were drawn from a wide range of social classes. The manager stood in the middle of the room like a major commanding his troops and gave his orders to the waiters. The eaters sat packed together like sardines, gulped down their food and were quickly replaced by others.

In biedermeier times the middle classes lived most of their lives at home in the bosom of the family, where they also entertained guests, and took little interest in appearing in public. For this reason their history is bound up with family tradition. Their way of life and customs inspired an art style which embodied and preserved

507

them. Although the Viennese woman, superficially regarded, may have achieved the emancipation of the self-supporting woman later than those of other countries, she early became the unchallenged and particularly respected representative of a well-defined and charming type of culture in the family, the home and in her salon. The average middle-class woman in Vienna has always lavished her imagination, her good taste, her emotions and her love on the home and its cultured atmosphere. The famous Viennese "Gemütlichkeit" (comfort) is eternally to her credit. This was not difficult for her to achieve in the days of plenty, but she has the art of lending the poetic touch to the simplest meal. A snow-white tablecloth, a tasteful vase with flowers, an old china service, the dainty mat for a wine bottle and a touch of greenery as decoration can make the plainest meal attractive. Or the cobwebby teacloth of the Vienna Jause (tea table) with the hand-painted biedermeier cups, the charmingly arranged flowers, the sugary white and crisp "Guglhupf" (a sort of sponge-cake) in the centre and the aromatic coffee combine to bring a welcome break in the daily round.

This is also the reason why the restaurants in Vienna are less frequented than in other big cities. The stranger who remains more than a week in Vienna looks for private lodgings. If he is a man of name and position he soon finds acquaintances and free board. It was the custom when making a longer stay for a visitor to rent a room for the month and to eat only in restaurants.

In Vienna everything was cheaper than in most other cities. Karl Julius Weber wrote:—"Where is the great city where a philosopher may live so pleasantly for such a small sum of money and a man of the world can enjoy the fashionable world for an expenditure of 3,000 to 4,000 gulden? In any case one can live in Vienna twice as well as elsewhere with half as much money."

Glasbrenner writes with enthusiasm of Vienna:—"The Viennese is above all a human being. In Vienna there is hardly a trace of class-consciousness, for in the same tavern lackeys and cab drivers sit next to artists, rich citizens and merchants, side by side with clerks. The Viennese goes on his way untroubled and finds his own pleasures. If he feels hot he takes his coat off, if he has an itch in his legs he dances, if he likes the look of a girl, he courts her; if he feels he wants to drink, he drinks. He is always human, always without embarrassment, a quality which he has saved from the wealth of imperial days and preserved for these days of impoverishment."

VIENNA SPECIALITIES: Many foreigners have believed that Austrian cooking is the best, the most nourishing and the most piquant. The English are content with roast beef, the French with roast mutton, ragout or a few pies, the Italians with stracchino and spaghetti. Russia has her nourishing herb soups with meat balls, the Hungarian his paprikagulyas, the Dane his buckwheat and cream. But the Viennese is interested in the multiplicity of the dishes. On great occasions he expects to see every bird from blackcock to pigeon, and every fish from trout to tunny on the festive board. In Viennese cooking the condiments are not emphasized and meat is served more à la nature. The Englishman is fond of Worcester Sauce, the Hungarian of red paprika, the Frenchman favours various spices and mayonnaises, but the Viennese prefers the natural taste of the meat. The Viennese cuisine also knows how to combine the favourite dishes of all these nations in its menu, for Vienna has learnt the art of international cooking.

Among the bakers' specialities the first to be mentioned must be the Vienna roll. These have a history, for the Emperor Friedrich IV had the first rolls of the type called "Semmel" baked in 1487 with his portrait stamped on them, and gave one to each of the children who were called together in the city moat. Since then, the rolls have born the name of "Kaisersemmeln". Two hundred years later the "Kipfel" was baked in the crescent form of the Turkish sabres, being at first called "Mond" and later "Gipfel" (peak) after the spire of the Stephansturm which in those days carried a crescent at the top; the soft letter "G" was later changed to the crisp-sounding letter "K". The Vienna Bretzel also made its appearance about this time and was gradually followed by the salt "Stangerl", the "Girafferl", the "Schnecken" and the brioches.

Another Vienna speciality is the Vienna "Faschingskrapfen" (a glorified doughnut). This was invented in the year 1615 by a luxurious confectioner named Cäcilie near the Peilertor, where the Naglergasse now runs. In those days it was called "cillikugel" in her honour. Not until thirty years later was it improved through the addition of a jam filling. A Krapfen broken in half and given by a girl to the young man with whom she was in love was considered as a token of engagement. In Vienna there was many a well-known Krapfen house, and during the carnival period of 1815 alone, eight to ten million Krapfen were eaten.

Another simpler home-made sweet of which Vienna has made a speciality is the Zwetschkenknödel, or damson dumpling. Once when Prince Metternich sat deep in conversation with the Czar Alexander I and Talleyrand, the Ambassador of Saxony thought they were having a highly political discussion. Softly and quietly he approached, all ears. He was greatly disappointed, for the Austrian Chancellor was explaining to his eager listeners the recipe for the original Vienna "Zwetschkenknödel".

Apart from these damson dumplings, in which the damson is enclosed in a paste made from finally mashed potato or flour, dusted with golden-yellow roasted breadcrumbs, and afterwards served warm and covered with castor sugar, there are many other kinds of Knödel, perhaps the favourite being the juicy apricot Knödel.

A combination of pastry and fruit is a favourite type of sweet served in Vienna households. There are, for instance, the Apfelstrudel of flaky pastry and luscious filling and the Cherry Strudel. The best of all strudels, however, is Cream Strudel with a filling of sweet curds, cream and currants which must surely appeal to every palate.

We are indebted to Metternich for a further speciality, the "Sachertorte". The story goes that at a special banquet, the prince wished to give his guests something absolutely new and of exquisite delicacy for the occasion. This founder of the House of Sacher then created that cake which has since then gone triumphantly round the whole world. The guests of the Prince were as delighted with the cake as are its countless admirers still today. Shipments have been sent by 'plane to England, America, India and even to Japan. The Sachertorte has won premiums as a supreme

Vienna achievement at countless international exhibitions of cooking. It is as much at home on the royal table at Buckingham Palace as it is at a ceremonial dinner of the President of the French Republic or in the cunningly-devised menu of an Indian Maharajah. This cake is a well-planned composition and none of the attempts to imitate it have been successful. Form and colour are characteristic. Its flavour is delicate, blended, mild, not too sweet; it is not too soft, not too dry and not too spongy. It melts on the tongue and has the great advantage of

keeping well, for it stays fresh for at least two weeks without any sign of staleness.

Fried chicken and Wiener Schnitzel have become typical Viennese dishes. At home the Viennese is content with an omelette for his "Gabelfrühstück" (elevenses or second breakfast—first breakfast is only coffee and rolls) but away from home he demands a small portion of "Kaiserfleisch", an "Einspänner" (sausage) or "Krenfleisch" (meat with horse-radish). Baked ham is also a speciality of Vienna cooking.

"Beinfleisch" (boiled beef served with the bone), ribs and the "Tafelspitz" (another cut of boiled beef) have also often been designated as national dishes of the Phäaken people on the grey "blue Danube". This is true if one is thinking only of favourite weekday dishes.

It is characteristic of the Austrian to hit upon one particular place for each of his favourite dishes, where he has decided that it is prepared to perfection. Thus a true "Wiener" will willingly take the trouble of going all the way to Thallern because fried chicken can be eaten at their best there. In Breitenfurt, near Mauer, on the other hand, they make the best "Millirahmstrudel". For a lucullan banquet of crayfish you must go to Prohaska's restaurant in the Prater. The place to eat roast goose where the slice from the breast is crispest is the Schottenkeller. For variety in cooking, especially for a wide range of cold dishes, the Rathauskeller is recom-

mended first. Freshly caught trout accompanied by just the right wine provide an excuse for a Sunday excursion to Heiligenkreuz. The best Danube fish can be eaten in Fischamend behind the "Alte Tor". The women have their favourite confectioners to which they find their way to or from shopping as a matter of course.

You can be fond of Vienna cooking and still like the culinary specialities of the Provinces. In mountain farms meals have naturally to consist as far as possible of produce of the farm. In the morning and the evening the farmer usually has a soup made of sour milk and flour, with which black bread is eaten. At midday he has dumplings with cabbage or pickled swedes. Smoked meat or pickled pork is only eaten on Sundays.

The more well-to-do farmer is fond of boiled beef. He also eats many kinds of sweet or salt puddings such as dumplings, maccaroni and so on. On festive occasions there is usually a luxurious spread, dishes baked in lard being a staple food. At such times there are "Krapfen", "Schneeballen", "Polsterzipfe" and so on. At Christmas they often bake "Kletzenbrot", containing many kinds of fruits.

In the Burgenland cabbage strudel is very popular. The "Schöberl" has always been a great favourite. This is a mixture of flour, milk and eggs, poured into an earthenware bowl, which is gradually filled with hot lard in ten or twelve layers each one finger deep poured in at short intervals.

The "Baumkuchen" or "Prügelkrapfen" of Lower Austria, the "Schnür-krapfen" and the "Schmerstrudel" are indispensable at such festivals as weddings, dedication of church bells, church festivals generally and christenings.

Upper Austria has won fame in the Austrian cuisine with its "Linzertorte" as well as with its Linz pastry and the "Traunkirchnertorte". The "Reinanken", a fish netted in the Salzkammergut lakes, is well-known. The "Schwarzreiterl", a special type of lake char from the Gosau Lakes were once reserved for the Imperial family and were therefore supposed to be a particular delicacy.

Salzburg was formerly famous for its "Salzburger Zungen". Nowadays every visitor tastes the delicious soufflé called "Salzburger Nockerln" before his departure. "Mozartkugeln" are a special kind of sweet which is attractively packed in Salzburg and makes a charming present.

"Green Styria" excels in the preparation of "Sterz" (rather like the Italian polenta) and of various dishes made from maize. Foreigners prefer Styrian chicken and mutton, which are a speciality in Austria.

In addition to the Tyrolese "Gröstl", which is an everyday dish, there are a number of sweets in Tyrol which are popular delicacies—the "Hupfauf", a fine pudding, the "Schutzauf", a dish of curds, and the "versoffene Kapuziner", made of rolls, wine, almonds and currants.

The "Kärntner Reindling" replaces the "Guglhupf" in Carinthia.

If someone puts aside a rich menu and calls instead for "Kässpätzle" or "Bodenseefelchen" it is sure to be a frugal Vorarlberger.

VIENNA RESTAURANTS. During the Thirty Years' War, manners deteriorated, the inn parlour re-echoed to the jargon of the streets or the brawling of mercenaries. The end of the 17th century saw an attempt made to curb rough manners. France was the first country to establish stiff forms of etiquette, which gradually spread over the frontiers. Inns slowly developed something like comfort, although visitors still whistled for the serving boy through their fingers instead of ringing a bell.

In the era of pastoral romance, the inns became really popular. Princes used them to give informal costume feasts in the gallant manner; "Wirtschaften" were held where even emperors and empresses appeared as host and hostess, while the rest of the court either acted as servants of the inn, or played the rôle of visitors. Incidentally this obviated disputes about precedence, which made everything more comfortable. In 1698, Peter the Great stayed incognito at the Vienna Court, taking part in a "Wirtschaft" which was arranged in his honour, disguised as a

Friesland farmer. The Emperor Leopold served him wine in a costly crystal chalice, begging him to accept the latter as a gift.

In the year 1678, when Prince Johann Georg of Anhalt-Dessau appeared at such a Wirtschaft at the Vienna Imperial Court in the guise of a Dutch sailor, Emperor Leopold toasted him with the words: "Since I believe that nobody knows more about the wind than a Dutch sailor, I drink his health with the wish that the wind may be favourable to the Roman Empire, to my House and to yourself, in accordance with whatever you may desire."

All royal personages, male and female enjoyed taking part in these Wirtschaften. A lot of thought went to devising the menu, and amusing ideas were often introduced into it.

The oldest eating house of Vienna is supposed to be the Griechenbeisl on the Fleischmarkt, dating back to the year 1500. If one drank more than two glasses of beer one had to keep the reckoning by laying the appropriate number of matches on the table; some had quite a little pile to show before the evening was over. Even the "liebe Augustin", the forerunner of the public singer who was himself born at Vienna in 1643 as the son of a tavern keeper, played the bagpipes there and sang there his famous tragi-comic song:

"O, du lieber Augustin, alles ist hin . . ."

It is a far cry from him to the "Schrammelmusik" and beyond to Girardi and his immortal carriage song. The Matschakerhof, which is also mentioned in the 15th century, is about as old as the Griechenbeisl.

During the Vienna Congress the attachés of the various Powers met regularly for lunch at the hotel "Kaiserin von Österreich", which soon received the name of "Diplomatenbörse" (Diplomat's Exchange). The table reserved for them in this hotel was called the "Chronicle of Vienna". Here confidential cabinet questions were discussed during informal conversations and events of the day talked over of which the Press only learned very much later.

"Die drei Hacken", later called the "Römische Kaiser", was adjudged Vienna's most exclusive tavern in Congress times. Unfortunately it no longer exists. On its site stands the building of an insurance company in the Renngasse.

The Hotel Sacher was frequented by members of the Austrian court and aristocracy. In its garden, the old Austrian uniforms struck the dominating note. The hotel's exquisite cuisine was renowned; the owner, Frau Anna Sacher, was a well-known figure in Vienna. Like Danish women, she smoked cigars, not little cigarillos but big, fat cigars. She had the gift of making all her guests feel at home and well understood how to flatter the peculiarities of each one, to satisfy every wish and to remember a guest's favourite dishes. Sachers, because of its distinguished clientèle, became the first hotel in Vienna, and was often the scene of meetings which decided the fate of Europe. The diplomats of the whole world were numbered

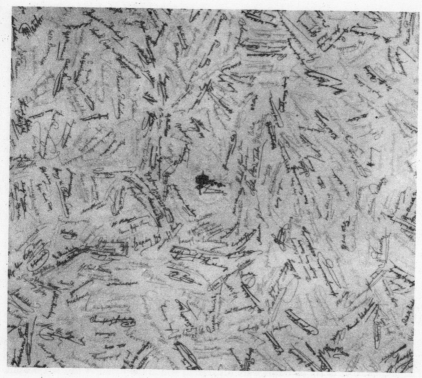

Vienna, Hotel Sacher: the "Signature Table Cloth" with the names of famous personages.

among its guests. They still show the menu there which the unhappy Crown Prince Rudolf wrote out himself for a dinner he ordered there a few days before his death: Oysters, turtle soup, lobster cotelette à l'Americain, blue trout with Venetian sauce, ragout of quails, French poulard, salad, cheese. To drink with it he ordered Chablis, Mouton-Rothschild, Röderer-Chrystall and Sherry Superieur. The famous tablecloth which served as a guest-book is a treasure of the House. More than 140 of the most distinguished guests have recorded their signatures here. These autographs on a white damask cloth were embroidered by Anna Sacher herself.

Franz Schubert used to frequent the "Ungarische Krone". A circle was formed there which was called the "Canevas Society", because Schubert's constant question

on entry of a newcomer was: "Kann er was?" ("Can he do anything?") To this circle belonged Schwind, Schnorr, Bauernfeld, Lachner and others.

The Prater restaurants are peculiar to Vienna. Some of them rank as "noble establishments" because of their higher prices. Prosperity first came to them when the "Blumenkorso" was instituted in biedermeier times. When people are happy, they generally behave well; in Vienna the contrast between grinding poverty and great luxury is not so sharply defined as in most other cities. The Vienna Prater offers happiness, recreation and comfort to all classes. An ice-cream at the Eisvogel, a cup of coffee in the Sacher Pavilion or a bite at the Lusthaus was always within the reach of many.

On the left hand side of the main avenue of the Prater, coming from the City, you see one coffee house after another. What the poet Adalbert Stifter wrote of them in 1844 is still true: "From each of them comes the strains of music. Under the trees are many thousands of seats filled with people in their best clothes. There is a laughing, a talking, a clinking of glasses, and before the eyes of the crowds the elegant carriages roll along the avenue, which stretches away with no end as far as the eye can see."

Vienna is very well off for cafés. It was from Vienna that coffee set forth on its conquest of the world. In 1683, after the city had been liberated from the Turks, large quantities of coffee beans were discovered which the invaders had left behind.

The Pole Kolschitzky, who had done valuable work during the siege, was presented with the strange beans as a reward. In a house which was placed at his disposal for the purpose he opened the first coffee house called "Zur blauen Flasche".

Vienna has always cherished the old Arabic saying to the effect that coffee must be black as night, sweet as love and hot as Hell. Coffee house life sprang quickly and definitely into being. To the question "where?" the Viennese soon had no other answer than "in the coffee house!"

"Where can I speak to you?" "From where can I pick you up by car?" "Where can I play cards—or billiards?" "Where can I dodge a curtain lecture?" "Where is the latest news to be found?" "Where can I start a club?"—The Viennese answer to each is "in the café". In course of time every class and group acquired its own coffee house. There were cafés for young men, artists, pensioners, ladies, bohemians and many others.

In the café lies illusion, and the smallest illusion is capable of making the Viennese happy. Coffee has actually become the favourite drink of the Viennese since 1683. It is a drink which they know how to prepare deliciously at home as well. The Vienna coffee house has developed in so many directions and become so unique that it has become almost an article of export—the Vienna "Stammcafé!"

You are not limited to ordering an ordinary cup of black coffee. Far from it. For the initiated there is a whole catalogue of variants. There is black coffee with or without whipped cream, the "Einspänner", the "Melange", the "Kapuziner" a "cup of gold" or a "cup of nut-brown" coffee. With these a "Kipfel" may be eaten to bring out the flavour. A glass of water is always served at the same time and the glass is refilled gratis innumerable times when the customer has ceased to order anything to be put on the bill. You sit at a small, marble-topped table, surrounded by well-dressed people. In the café as on the street outside, the picture is lively and colourful. If you wish to read there are any amount of newspapers and magazines available, as well as fashion journals and art periodicals. Just by ordering a cup of "Melange" and a "Kipfel" you acquire the right to sit there for hours if you will.

Franz Schubert, who could not do without coffee, often made it for himself at

Gasthof zur goldenen Kugel

Menu

Alpeneier
Rindsuppe mit
Leberschöberl
Gefüllter Karpfen
Lungenbraten mit
Rahmsauce
Thronfolgerinnen –
Kartoffel
Serviettenknödel
Preiselbeer
Biskotten-Igel
Mandeleiscreme
Mocca
₰

home, humorously naming his small hand coffeegrinder the home of his Holy Spirit. He swore that the best ideas and tones came to him through the monotonous noise of grinding coffee beans, instancing his D-minor-quartette. Beethoven's approved recipe for coffee was sixty beans to a cup.

After a time, chocolate was also served in the coffee houses. When Fernando Cortez landed in Mexico in 1519, he came across the drink of the native inhabitants. This was served ceremoniously in golden cups at the court of Montezuma, the last of the Aztec rulers. The doctors of Europe were of divided opinion concerning the cocoa bean, its oponents being in the minority in Vienna. In 1694 the Vienna Professor Rauch was bold enough to criticise chocolate unfavourably. As a result he lost his position and his book was destroyed. The Viennese stand no nonsense when a culinary addition is called in question.

The lemonade booths were a later development. They were most in demand of course in the summer months and were well supported by women. They were tents set up in public squares where lemonade, "almond milk" and ice-creams were sold. They sprang up on the Graben and Am Hof, on the Bastei, at the Kärntnertor and on the Neuer Markt. In good weather they were sometimes patronised—lover's whispers on summer nights and by bright moonlight—until the dawn.

For the men there were wine-cellars and "Heurige". Austrians drink more than some other races because they eat more, but they are no drunkards. At a meal good wine increases the pleasures of the palate, ensuring the thorough digestion of lunch before dinner time comes along. In the 18th century it was the custom for every host to keep a wine list for his guests to choose from. This furthered ambition so that there were houses in Vienna where eighteen to twenty varieties of wine were held in readiness for guests.

YES, THE WINE! Just as the Austrians vary in type according to whether they come from Graz, Linz, Salzburg, Tyrol etc., so does the wine vary. In this Austrian wine scores óver most foreign wines. Within the wide choice it affords, every taste can be satisfied. From the light, full-flavoured or the rather sour and thirst-quenching wines to the high-grade *premiers crus*, there is a whole gamut of excellent vintages always ready to satisfy the most exacting demands as to quality and bouquet. As the Viennese combines in himself the qualities of all Austrians, so is Viennese wine typical of the whole country. It embodies the magic of the flowers and the strength of the mountains. Few are privileged to understand and appreciate to the full the multiplicity of often very subtle differences between the various growths. Not to everyone who drinks it does the wine reveal all its soul, all its intimate secrets. It calls for wooing, for a testing; it demands of its devotees love and reverence of tongue and palate.

The vineyards of the country are older than the name of Austria itself. When the transport of wine from Italy for the use of the Roman legionaries on the Danube became difficult, the Emperor Probus lifted the ban on planting vines in the Roman provinces. Then the first vineyards came into being on the sunny hills lining the military road from Aquileja to Carnuntum and on the slopes of the Wienerwald. Subjected like all else to changing history, grape-growing flourished afresh under Charlemagne. The priories and monasteries, the monks of Passau and Salzburg tended the vineyards with loving care. Thanks is still due to them for this today!

Even in the times of the Babenbergs Vienna was surrounded by a ring of green vineyards. In the 14th century, 18,000 candles per year were used in the Seitzerkeller, below the Tuchlauben. A chronicalist records at the beginning of the 15th century that gathering the vintage in Vienna lasted for fully forty days and that 300 carts laden with grapes were driven into the city daily. Even in those times new plantations were forbidden, in order to prevent a fall in prices. In the year 1448 Chancellor Aeneas, later Pope Pius II, wrote: "The wine cellars are so spacious and deep that people say the city has been built as much below ground as above it."

To the Vienna commercial fairs, held twice a year, it was possible to bring every type of commodity under the signed safe-conduct of the reigning prince, with the exception of beer and wine. In the 17th century, traders of Amsterdam and Gent showed a preference for Vienna "Nussberger". Before the irresistible tide of triumphs of the Turks was dammed at Vienna in 1683, they had already been quietly overcome by Vienna wine.

In 1872, peaceful progress in the vineyards was abruptly interrupted by the appearance of the phylloxera. Brought to Europe from overseas, this most dangerous of all vine parasites ruined nearly all the vineyards of the Continent. This meant bitter years for the Austrian wine-growing families, which numbered no less than 60,000, excluding all those whose livelihood depended indirectly on the vines, such as innkeepers, wine-dealers, cask-binders and the like. At last it became possible to revive the Austrian wine trade with the help of American vines, on to which the native high grades were grafted. Building in Vienna gladly and voluntarily halts at the vineyard districts. Well-known and honoured wine-names are here— Nussdorf, Heiligenstadt, Grinzing, Kahlenbergerdorf, Sievering, Neustift-am-Walde and Salmannsdorf. There, too, are to be found the wayside winegardens and taverns, the "Wiener Heurigen".

Of all the wine producing districts of Austria, the most important is Lower Austria. Wines of every type are to be found here, from the light and sparkling "Brünnerstrassler" to the heavy "Gumpoldskirchner"; from the noble and aromatic "Wachauer" to the pleasant and sweetish "Muskateller". It would involve a lesson in geography to name and locate all the places where the precious vines are grown and tended, starting with the southern slopes of the Wachau and continuing over the broad Krems vineyard area up to Langenlois, further on to Maissau or down towards the Bisamberg and vine-girdled Klosterneuburg, which is called the "Rinnende Zapfen"—"The Leaking Bung". The extensive vineyards around Retz produce that wine which the Viennese are fond of drinking in "Stehweinhallen" ("Standing Wine Bars") as "Special" or, abbreviated, as "Spezi".

In the south, beginning at Mauer and Perchtoldsdorf, lies the most famous Lower Austrian vineyard district, which includes the villages of Guntramsdorf, Gumpoldskirchen, Baden, Sooss, Vöslau and many others. The "Rotgipfler", the "Zierfandler" and the "Neuburger" are noted for their aromatic bouquet. The fragrant bouquet of Sooss Muscatel wines impresses every connoisseur. The red wines of Vöslau, especially the "Schlumberger Goldeck", have carried the renown of Austrian wines far beyond its frontiers.

The Styrian and South Styrian wines have an entirely different flavour. Here one again meets famous names—Schilcher, Portugieser, Sylvaner, Welschriesling, Weissburgunder, Traminer, Muskatsylvaner and Weissklevner.

The colours of the Burgenland provincial banner, red and gold, stand for the wine of the Province. Some fine vintages flourish in the mild climate of the Neusiedlersee. Heavy and golden lies Ruster wine in the glass, a king among wines. Mild and sweet, with an exquisite bouquet, it delights every experienced winebibber.

Sip it reflectively and with moderation! There is a secret about the wine which should only be unveiled with caution. In wine lies power, reality and truth. Let us hope that you, good friend, are a seeker after truth—at least you will become one through the local wines!

Although Austria has always been a wine country, the com-

petition of beer was felt even in the Middle Ages. The right to brew beer lay in the gift of the ruler. In 1430 there was already a "Bierglocke" ("Beer Bell") in the left Heidenturm (Heathen's Tower) of the Stephansdom which rang for working men to cease their labours. At the same time, the tolling of the bell forbade the further sale of beer, and meant that the taverns had to be closed.

A glass of beer on the way home during the warmer months is still the most popular drink. Any genuine Wiener would sooner risk getting the round paunch of a beer-drinker than deny himself this pleasure.

HE WHO WAS NEVER IN HIS CUPS

He who was never
in his cups is truth

a sorry swain forsooth
a very sorry swain. And he

who only "achteln" sups were wiser
to abstain indeed were wiser to

abstain. Then everything spins
"um und um" in this our

capitolium in this
our capitolium.

WENZEL
MÜLLER
1793

APRÈS SOUPER: The Austrian has thought out variations and combinations of food and drink and developed his own customs and habits. The first principle of the Vienna cuisine is that only the best ingredients should be used, and never substitutes. Although the rural inhabitants of the Provinces may conservatively adhere to the saying "What the peasant does not know he does not eat", the Viennese always was and still is willing to accept all good things which come from any part of the world, altering and adapting some of them to his own tastes. This chimes with their motto "Live and let live".

Even during the hard times of the war, the Viennese woman spent a commendable amount of trouble on the kitchen. Love of cooking and good taste enabled her continually to ring the changes at table, even when raw materials were most sadly lacking. Even though it seemed as though the days of éclairs with whipped cream, the cream fingers, the "baisers" and the cream horns had never been, there was still some kind of sweet on Sundays.

The Viennese housewife decks her board with artistry and good taste. It speaks of light-hearted friendliness and smiling festivity. The menu is free from the sort of vulgarity which rattles the money bags even at mealtimes. New ideas come to enliven the meal, and consideration for each individual guest creates the right atmosphere. Sensitive tact is the maître d'hotel, and tact is a quality which the Viennese woman enjoys instinctively from birth. A guest in a Viennese house feels himself surrounded by comfort and well-being and there is nothing to make him consider how much trouble work and thought have been employed to produce this apparently effortless result.

The Viennese woman of yesterday, of today and of tomorrow provides the right framework for the popular saying: "Food keeps body and soul together."

Dear friends, before you travel to Italy to see Naples and die, come first to Vienna to enjoy life happily and comfortably a little longer.

SPAS·
SPORT AND
HUNTING

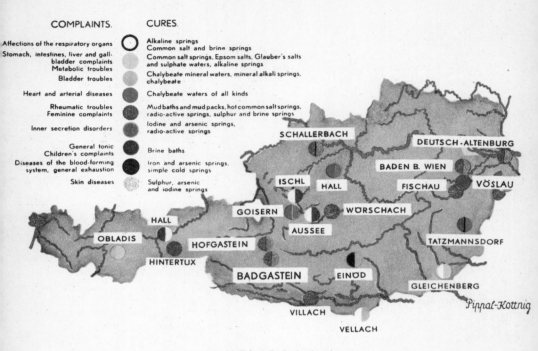

COMPLAINTS.

CURES.

Affections of the respiratory organs — Alkaline springs
Common salt and brine springs

Stomach, intestines, liver and gall-bladder complaints
Metabolic troubles — Common salt springs, Epsom salts, Glauber's salts and sulphate waters, alkaline springs

Bladder troubles — Chalybeate mineral waters, mineral alkali springs, chalybeate

Heart and arterial diseases — Chalybeate waters of all kinds

Rheumatic troubles
Feminine complaints — Mud baths and mud packs, hot common salt springs, radio-active springs, sulphur and brine springs

Inner secretion disorders — Iodine and arsenic springs, radio-active springs

General tonic
Children's complaints — Brine baths

Diseases of the blood-forming system, general exhaustion — Iron and arsenic springs, simple cold springs

Skin diseases — Sulphur, arsenic and iodine springs

SCHALLERBACH

DEUTSCH-ALTENBURG

BADEN B. WIEN

ISCHL HALL FISCHAU VÖSLAU

GOISERN WÖRSCHACH

AUSSEE

HALL

OBLADIS HOFGASTEIN TATZMANNSDORF

HINTERTUX

BADGASTEIN EINÖD

GLEICHENBERG

Pippal-Kottnig

VILLACH

VELLACH

Medicinal Baths in Austria.

HEALTH RESORTS AND SPAS.

Nature in Austria attracts not only through variety and charm, but also through a healthy climate which is bracing for mind and body. Situated between the oceanic West and the continental East, the graduated heights, the mountain ranges, lakes, rivers and forests provide many variations of climate, capable of satisfying a wide range of demands for a mild or bracing resort, and a variety of choice which enables every individual to select just what he wishes for himself.

There are over 200 health resorts in Austria, 110 of them being medicinal spas. Some of them are world-famous, attracting and retaining an international public. Others are quiet and remote, lying in gently rolling hill country, and others again call one to the invigorating heights of the mountains.

Along the long-known thermal line which skirts the eastern edge of the Alps and runs from the Danube through Lower Austria and the Burgenland down to

Styria, is a long succession of spas. Another group benefits by the mountain riches of salts and volcanic springs. There is a succession of healing health resorts extending from Bad Hall in Upper Austria across the Salzkammergut and the magnificent valley of the Gasteiner Ache to Solbad Hall-in-Tyrol.

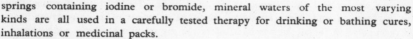

Chalybeate waters, radio-active springs, mineral-saline waters, sulphur springs containing iodine or bromide, mineral waters of the most varying kinds are all used in a carefully tested therapy for drinking or bathing cures, inhalations or medicinal packs.

Whatever could be done by man to add to the gifts of generous nature has been done in Austria. The health resorts and baths themselves are as diverse and manifold as the healing springs. Baden-bei-Wien lies in a specially favoured corner of the Wienerwald, with its sulphur springs which were valued by the Romans, amidst very lovely scenery. Nestling among forested hills and extensive vineyards, the town with its well-kept avenues, its park, its promenade, theatre and charmingly built villas is like a great hospitable garden. Baden has been a favourite resort for statesmen, men of science and artists from time immemorial when they have sought peace and recuperation to enable them to face new tasks.

Badgastein, situated amidst the impressive panorama of the Salzburg Tauern, has become Austria's most famous medicinal spa. Mountain sun, absence of fog and the purity of the air all help to increase the effect of the radioactive thermal waters. This place, with its varied profusion of pump rooms, fine houses and modern hotel residences towers above and around the rushing, foaming, cascading Gasteiner Ache like an enormous amphitheatre, a picture of elegance and comfort combined with nature in her most overpowering and impressive mood. The shady and well-kept paths hold memorials to many famous personages, to rulers, statesmen, diplomats and artists. An international public from all over the world gathers here in the hope of postponing old age and recovering youth.

One thing is common to all Austrian spas—to Tatzmannsdorf, Schallerbach, Vöslau, Gleichenberg, Warmbad Villach, Aussee and

Ischl. That is the atmosphere and feeling of comfort. There is a healthy optimism in the air of each, a natural and effervescent joy in living which knows no artifice.

SPORT.

The idea of sport in a modern sense—Athens in 1896, Coubertin, memories of Olympia—has fallen on fruitful soil in Austria, as her sportsmen have proved in the prizes which they have carried off at various international competitions. There is no need to concern ourselves here with gold and silver medals, nor with records, distances covered, split seconds and points. Let us leave aside champions and their tabulated achievements, the "wonder-teams" of former years, world-famous ski-ers and the "strong men" of Vienna. Here let us consider sport in its natural and most attractive shape, as a means of gaining strength and of recuperation for all, to whom it offers the joy in living which comes from a healthy body.

Expressions frequently heard such as the daily grind, the dull jogtrot of life are not applicable to Austria and its inhabitants in a literal sense. Whoever sets a wandering foot on the ground anywhere between the Bodensee and Neusiedlersee can be sure of a constantly changing view, of a world twisting and turning up hill and down dale in mountain and valley. Anyone wanting to go from one town to another, or even from village to village feels his senses quicken in the freedom of the lovely countryside. The air, fresh with the dew on the grass or heavy with the scent of flowers, so bathes the skin, the lungs, that it seems as though burdens had been cast away.

Living and working in this atmosphere throughout the centuries has given the men broad shoulders and sinewy figures; the women are high-waisted, with narrow hips, graceful necks and shoulders and slender, well-shaped feet. The

Austrian has a passion for "wandern"—for hiking—deeply engrained within him. His mouth demands to breathe in the air of the great mountains, his foot the soft carpet of mossy slopes and his eye continual change, now drinking in the green of near-by forests, now reaching out to the distant lines which the silent horizon has etched against the bright sunshine. The driving force behind all sport in Austria is the need to be with and to experience nature, the delight in the light of day, the need to grasp the earth as one's own possession. In her intensification of this harmony of man and nature and quickening of his joy of living, Austria cannot easily be excelled. From the highest point of the Tauern range down to the warm, sailcovered lakes of Carinthia, sport is being enjoyed in one form or another and is adding to Austria's sporting reputation as a whole.

There is something to suit everyone, no matter what his age or capability, which will help him to preserve his youth and pleasure in life as long as possible. Four types of sport predominate: Ski-ing, mountaineering, water sports and hunting game.

The Arlberg School of ski-ing is famous even beyond the Continent of Europe and is practised alongside glaciers and on mountains even in midsummer. But in winter more people make the shadowy tracks in the powdery snow according to rules of their own devising than there are ski-ing pupils in the whole country. Slalom on the steep slopes, the jump, skijöring, ski-elevator and overhead railway all crowd together within a small space.

Mountaineering is no less attractive. Climbing at the end of a rope or alone up through a narrow cleft in the side of a mountain, over precipices and crags, mountain trips, ascents along secured or dangerous pathways, the rest at the summit, life in the huts and tours along the mountain saddles. To reach the mountains has been made almost easy, for car roads, elevators and overhead railways do away with the toil of the ascent. But there is still room for both types, for the mountaineer of the old school who carries rucksack, pick and rope up to the heights himself and for the others who are in a hurry and who are saved half the trouble of climbing by making use of modern facilities.

On the lakes sport can be combined with pleasant holidays. There is rowing, swimming, sailing, diving and—the beach. In winter sleighs glide swift as the wind over the grey surface; skates carry one from shore to shore almost without effort, past clean-swept rinks where many an hour is spent in keen competition in the Austrian version of curling.

On the rivers, on the wildly foaming waters, paddlers guide the kajak and the light canoe boldly over dangerous snags and eddies. Golf, tennis, motor-boating, country riding, motoring, free gymnastic exercises with gymnasium apparatus and every kind of indoor sport are all

34

equally cultivated in Austria. Everything arouses enthusiasm which tends to bring man closer to nature.

HUNTING.

Everyone passing through Austria who looks at it with the eye of a hunter will immediately get an idea of the country's hunting possibilities from the variations of nature alone. There are ice-covered mountain peaks with rocky gorges and belts of meadows, dark mountain forests, open stretches covered with undergrowth, reed-surrounded lakes and ponds, fields lined by hedges and the unending ploughed fields of the eastern plains., From a huntsman's point of view this all affords ideal living conditions for furred and feathered game. This widely varying countryside provides plentiful food supplies for the many kinds of wild creatures who stock it.

The chamois, a species of game which is typical for Austria, can be found anywhere in the Alps. Hunting this mountain antelope, either the red summer chamois or the dark rutting chamois, is considered to be one of the most fascinating experiences. In well-stocked preserves made easily accessible by the narrow mountain paths that are to be found in North Tyrol, it often calls for no special exertion or knowledge of climbing to get the chance of a shot under the expert guidance of a gillie. Hunting on the slopes of the higher mountains where there is rough going among the rocks can be an altogether different business. The hunting tracks often follow difficult ascents with alarmingly steep precipices, the shooting hut may be close to a glacier. The exertion is well repaid on such difficult trips by the excitement of the chase.

A scarcely less thrilling experience—at rutting time it affords even more excitement—is deer-stalking in the mountains. Deer can be hunted in summer in the high alps, but the stalking of the rutting stag is the supreme experience for the sportsman. Anyone who has heard the rutting call of the stag amid the pastures and crags of our mountains, has watched the mating of the noble red deer among the lovely shades of autumn forests and has finally given proof of his hunting prowess by shooting a correctly stalked buck will record such hours in Austria in his golden book of the chase.

HEAD OF GAME SHOT IN 1935

Red Deer
14,390

Fallow Deer
457

Roebuck
76,416

Chamois
7,279

Black Game
157

Hares
528,766

Rabbits
32,611

Marmot
1,543

Foxes
11,707

Martens
1,265

Weasels
7,128

Polecats
4,235

Badgers
1,076

Vienna; Freudenau.

The stalking of blackcock and grouse is another form of hunting in the mountains. Spring is the time for shooting the cock. When the "Föhn" (south wind) gently caresses the Alps, shaking the snow from the evergreens, and the pastures begin to grow verdant, the capercailye struts and the black cock dances.

In the lower mountains, deer replace the chamois. You will find them everywhere in Austria, above all where forests are interspersed with rocky slopes. Thus the alpine foot-hills to the north and south of the main alpine chain, inclusive of the Wald- and Mühlviertel, are well stocked with this type of game.

Where you find deer, you may well find the heath-cock also. Epicures among sportsmen find themselves well repaid for the trouble of hunting this smallest type of cock. It only frequents the wooded countryside where deciduous trees and bushes mingle with the conifers. Martens, foxes, badgers, wood pigeons, woodcock and fieldfares can be found everywhere in the Austrian forests.

Descending into the valleys we reach the fields and flat-lying meadows, the habitat of the hare. The steppe-like plains and fields are its favourite haunt, although it may often be encountered in forest and mountain country. In ploughed land, however, hares spring everywhere from the furrows and the stubble. The pursuit of the hare, especially if you are aided by a good dog, provides a change and excellent sport.

Shooting waterfowl can be indulged in among the fields bordering the rivers, in the bog and moor districts of the great Alpine valleys and beside Alpine lakes as well as on the pools of the Wald- and Mühlviertel. The Danube, the Mur, the Drau, the Inn, the Salzach, the Enns and other rivers all have backwaters full of waterfowl. The Neusiedlersee with its vast forests of reeds is an eldorado for those who enjoy this sport. Wild-goose shooting is considered to be the most exciting.

Austria's extensive game-stocked countryside provides unusually good shooting. Stags near the Danube, deer, hare, rabbits, pheasants, snipe, quail, wild duck and wild turkey afford sport almost all the year round.

Finally let us mention that boar can be hunted in the preserves of the Wienerwald and the Leithagebirge, and that the uncommonly shy bustard is met with in the plains to the east and south-east

Otters
37

Squirrels
19,026

Musk Rats
3,490

Capercailye and Black Cock
2,859

Grouse
2,210

Heath-Cock
1,410

Woodcock
3,986

Snipe
105

Quail
402

Pheasants
180,314

Partridges
300,824

Bald Coot
216

Ptarmigan
163

Wild Geese
1,038

Wild Duck
11,228

Wood Pigeons
2,995

From the rushing Book for Tyrol and Görz of the Emperor Maximilian I (National Library, Vienna).

of Vienna. The importance of hunting in Austria and what it offers is shown in the accompanying figures for game killed in the year 1935.

The fisherman is just as well served as the hunter, for in the lakes of the Salzkammergut and those of Carinthia he can find pike, shad, lake trout and many varieties of coarse fish. The same is true of the Danube and its great tributaries which even in their upper reaches are rich in all kinds of sporting fish such as Huchen (the land-locked salmon of the Danube), grayling and trout. Trout of course are met with in the smallest streams high up in the Alps. Even in lakes lying at great altitudes there is fly-fishing for black char. Many memorable delightful days can thus be spent in Austria shooting and fishing.

Crested Duck
144

Owls
70

Hawks and Sparrow-hawks
12,343

Crows and Magpies
98,537

THE AUSTRIAN NOCTURNE

Vienna, the Stephansdom, April 1945.

In those ominous days of March, 1938, when the armies of the Third Reich were crossing the Austrian frontier, a poster appeared on walls and the shuttered windows of shops, showing Hitler and Bismarck together. The former, of course, stood obtrusively in the foreground, while the Iron Chancellor was placed modestly behind as a forerunner who had long been overtaken.

Probably the designer of the poster had forgotten—if he ever heard of them—the words which Bismarck had spoken to Maurus Jokai in 1874: "Any German statesman who dreamed of conquering something in Austria would deserve hanging."

The State Opera, Vienna, March 12th, 1945.

Nevertheless, Austria was annexed, and the prophetic words of another statesman, Prince Talleyrand, became bloodstained history: "To destroy Austria would be to replace order by chaos."

These words of the Frenchman, spoken of the great Austrian Empire, proved true enough as a political axiom applied to the small Republic. As long as Europe exists the peace of the Continent will stand or fall with Austria's independence as a State, whether the latter throws the weight of her own strength into the scale, or can only appeal to a higher law and the conscience of the world as she has done during the last decades.

When Austria was wiped off the map the great nocturne of heartless killing and soulless dying began. Hecatombs of victims have brought home unforgettably to the world what may result when the right and the liberty of the weak are trampled into the dust. Whoever instigated violence in Austria has always plunged the whole of Europe—this time it proved to be the entire world—into destruction as well. The further development of man, according to a writer's pessimistic words—from

537

PLAN OF WAR DAMAGE
IN AND AROUND THE FIRST DISTRICT OF VIENNA

(Design by Fred Hennings)

(Section)

AIR RAID OF 10th SEPTEMBER 1944
  "   "   "   5th NOVEMBER 1944
  "   "   " 15th JANUARY 1945
  "   "   "   7th FEBRUARY 1945
  "   "   " 12th MARCH 1945
  "   "   "   8th APRIL 1945
SHELL DAMAGE
BURNT-OUT BUILDINGS

humanity to bestiality through nationality—was in full progress. The proclamation of total war by the Nazi Propaganda Minister introduced the last stage of madness. There had to be annihilation one way or the other—if not of the enemy, then of his own people.

Vienna's bitterest days had dawned. Above the city which had been forcibly embodied in Hitler's armament machinery circled the bombers. Those who were our enemies in the front line and in their hearts our friends, were obliged to destroy in order to liberate. Cruel twentieth century!

As the seventh anniversary of Austria's annexation approached, Vienna was in flames from end to end. Transport was at a standstill. The streets were filled with dust, smoke, haze and people who were feverishly digging in the debris. Suddenly a rumour ran through the city which nobody would believe: "The Opera burns!"

People forgot their own fate and rushed on to the Ring. An endless procession of spectators a day and a night long and still another day and night. So long did it take for the building to burn down.

Vienna has two hearts. This first tragedy was followed a few weeks later by a senseless piece of brutality. The SS troops fleeing before the victorious Red Army started to fire on the venerable Cathedral of St. Stephen's with artillery posted in Leopoldau. A few hours later this landmark of the city was in flames, and with it the Kärntnerstrasse, the Rotenturmstrasse and the entire length of the Kai.

Destruction through denial of the Creator, the day of the great anti-Christ. Oh you men in uniform, what have you done to Vienna?—Slowly the night fades over Austria. The flames leaping from the high roof of the Cathedral silently ring in the dawn of freedom.

AUSTRIA–
EUROPES LAND OF
EVERYMAN

In the summer in Salzburg, the play of the wealthy Jedermann (Everyman) moves the feelings and senses of a public drawn from the whole world every year afresh. Many a stranger standing before the spacious Residence and its fountains, may think not only of the life and the death of this particular Jedermann but rather of all mankind and its works. Perhaps he may ponder over the fate of Austria as well. Under the spell of brilliant acting, evening serenades and solemn Cathedral concerts he may well pose the question with newly quickened senses—wherein lies value or worthlessness? He may try to read the impenetrable laws governing an unknown eternity.

What has remained to Austria of faith, of sound achievement, from the days when her frontiers encircled the earth and the sun never set on her Empire, when the peoples of the Old World and of the barely discovered New World alike bowed before her sceptre and her judgement? What has remained to Austria from all the battles and victories, the marriages and congresses, the royal pacts which she signed and the coalitions which she joined? What has she still left of pomp and dignity, of the conflicts of the mind in pulpits and university, of the gold-embroidered cloak of her matchless history?

All you foreigners and visitors, you trusted friends who come to Austria to see this land and get to know it, and who, once you know it, return again and again to see it afresh—it is you who answer, and do so most completely through your interest in her—to Austria remains her imperishable humanity.

To put it differently, Austria survives as a great meeting-place for peoples as well as for individuals. Conversation, the interchange of ideas, above all else. So long as the great nation-families of Europe exist, so long as these children bearing the same name carry on the royal dramas of occidental history in bloody episodes of wars and policies of revenge, so long will Austria continue undaunted to urge reconciliation, and will not hesitate to plead for peace.

For Austria is in a way the first attempt to create a European citizen—a world-citizen. What is elsewhere so often but a vague longing, an illusion or the unrealised dream of isolated individuals, has long been anchored in Austria among a wide circle of people. Though without the inclination or the possibility of breathing any other air than that of Austria, they yet feel mysteriously at home in another world which lies beyond their fellow citizens—beyond the world which ordinarily is theirs. This citizenship of another, a vaster world—the word "international" does not express it properly—this sharing in and understanding of the affairs of that great world is perhaps the biggest thing which the foreigner feels and realises in Austria.

We may consider this will and this ability to live humanly among other human beings as the call of Austria to the whole world. It is a part of that great

542

Everyman.

conversation which has been carried on in this country from its very beginnings through all the changing conditions of history. The song of the "silent night, holy night" is its Christmas thought, music its eternal content which all can understand.

Austria, country of the drama of "Everyman".

Austria, drama of everyman's country.

ILLUSTRATIONS.

A. Plates

B. Illustrations

The various illustrations were executed by:

Eugenie Pippal-Kottnig:

on pages 5, 11, 12/13, 31, 85 top picture, 85 bottom picture, 138/139, 142, 163, 173, 174 t. p., 174 b. p., 175 t. p., 175 b. p., 184/185, 187, 192 t. p., 192 b. p., 195 t. p., 195 b. p., 200 t. p., 200 middle picture, 200 b. p., 202, 204 t. p., 205, 208/209, 217 b. p., 221, 222, 229, 234/235, 244 t. p., 244 b. p., 246 t. p., 248 t. p., 252, 255, 258/259, 264 t. p., 264 b. p., 267, 270 b. p., 284/285, 288 t. p., 288 b. p., 295, 296 t. p., 297, 301, 305 t. p., 305 b. p., 308/309, 314 t. p., 314 b. p., 318, 321, 325, 335, 339, 342 b. p., 343, 344 t. p., 344 m. p., 344 b. p., 346 t. p., 346 m. p., 346 b. p., 353, 356/357, 414, 416, 420/421, 429, 436/437, 446/447, 473, 526, 538/539;

Hans Robert Pippal:

on pages 74, 89, 165, 166, 170, 172, 179, 180, 181 b. p., 182 b. p., 194, 196 t. p., 203, 204 b. p., 214, 216, 220, 223 t. p., 226, 227 t. p., 228, 237, 239, 242, 247, 248 b. p., 249, 261, 268, 270 t. p., 273, 276, 279, 281, 282, 289, 298, 299, 300, 302, 304, 316, 320, 323, 324, 327, 328, 330 b. p., 331, 336, 337 t. p., 340, 347, 352, 354, 358, 362 t. p., 362 b. p., 363, 366, 367 t. p., 367 b. p., 370, 373, 375, 386, 387, 389, 392 t. p., 392 b. p., 394, 396, 397, 398 t. p., 398 b. p., 399, 402, 403, 404, 419, 422, 423 t. p., 423 b. p., 440, 442, 443, 444, 445, 448, 471 t. p., 471 b. p., 473 b. p., 474 t. p., 474 b. p., 481, 482, 483, 484, 485, 486, 487, 488, 495, 498, 518, 523, 524, 527 t. p., 527 b. p., 528, 529, 531, 534, 540, 543, 544;

Elli Rolf:

on pages 6 t. p., 10, 16, 17, 18, 19, 20/21, 22 t. p., 23, 25, 29, 35, 36/37, 38, 58, 61, 72/73, 79, 82, 86/87, 91 t. p., 91 b. p., 96, 97, 101, 102/103, 104, 106, 108, 109, 110, 115, 120, 122, 125, 126, 132, 133, 136, 137, 140/141 t. p., 141 b. .p, 156, 167, 168 b. p., 176, 177, 181 t. p., 188/189, 193, 198, 201, 212 b. p., 215, 218, 225, 227 b. p., 230/231, 240 b. p., 245, 246 b. p., 250, 256, 263, 265, 266, 269, 272, 277, 280, 290, 294, 296 b. p., 306, 313, 315, 319, 329, 332, 337 b. p., 338, 341, 345, 348, 349, 350 t. p., 350 b. p., 361 t. p., 361 b. p., 371, 372, 374 t. p., 374 b. p., 378, 379, 381, 390/391, 393, 395, 449, 450/451, 452/453, 454/455, 456/457, 458/459, 460, 461, 462/463, 464/465, 466/467, 468/469, 470, 475, 478, 508, 509, 510, 511, 512, 516 t. p., 516 b. p., 517 t. p., 517 b. p., 519 t. p., 519 b. p.;

Epi Schlüsselberger:

on pages III, IV, V, VII, XV, 1, 3, 13, 15, 20/21, 27, 36/37, 51, 65, 66, 75, 93, 107, 127, 143, 153, 157, 159, 161, 162, 183, 186, 206, 207, 210, 217 t. p., 217 m. p., 219 m. p., 223 m. p., 223 b. p., 230/231, 232, 233, 236, 257, 260, 283, 286, 307, 310, 333, 334, 351, 355, 390/391, 405, 409, 415, 429, 441, 449, 476, 477, 479, 489, 499, 518, 521, 522, 525, 535, 541, Tafel VI, VII, VIII.

Design for Jacket: Hans Robert Pippal (Lettering Epi Schlüsselberger)
Design for Cover and End-papers: Epi Schlüsselberger.

C. Reproductions.

Illustrations on the following pages are reproduced from originals in the possession of:

Österreichische Nationalbibliothek, Bildarchiv: 7, 8, 11, 24, 30, 34, 39, 44/45, 54, 70/71, 78, 88, 98, 99, 112, 114, 117, 119, 123, 124, 128/129, 148, 150, 151, 164, 168 t. p., 169, 178, 190, 191, 196 b. p., 197 t. p., 197 b. p., 199, 211, 212 t.p., 213, 219 t. p., 224, 238, 240 t. p., 241, 250 t. p., 251, 262, 274, 287, 303, 311, 330 t. p., 342 t. p., 360, 364, 365, 368, 369, 376, 377, 380, 382, 383, 384, 388, 400, 401, 409 (Anton Hanak: "The Last Human Being", Österreichische Galerie, Vienna) 476 t. p., 477 t. p., 515, 541, Plate I.

Österreichische Nationalbibliothek, Manuscript Collection: 501, 505, 533, Plate III, Plate IV.

Österreichische Nationalbibliothek, Theatrical Collection: 28, 50, 77.

Haus-, Hof- und Staatsarchiv, Vienna: 14 (Seal of the Emperor Heinrich IV, 1074), 26 (Oldest surviving of the City of Vienna, 1288) 40, 48/49, 69, 100.

Kunsthistorisches Museum, Vienna: 4 (Youth of Helenenberg, circa 450 B. C., Provincial Roman Art), 22 (Vienna Pfennig, thin sheet of silver, 1192), 502.

Naturhistorisches Museum, Vienna: 3 (Venus of Willendorf, sandstone figure).

Städtische Sammlungen, Vienna: 94, 130/131, 134/135, Plate IX.

Bildstelle des Magistrates Vienna: 479.

Österreichisches Museum für angewandte Kunst: 499.

Universitätsbibliothek, Vienna: 52, 56, 57, 64 (all from the "Pietas victrice" of Nikolaus Avancinus).

Bundesdenkmalamt, Vienna: 90.

Albertina, Vienna: 412.

D. The following publishing houses or individuals

have placed blocks, reproduction rights, reproductions or maps at the disposal of the Publisher:

Friedl Goldschmid, Vienna, 522, Plate V.

Burgschauspieler Fred Hennings, Vienna, Bombing Map, 538/539.

Richard Larkens, Photo-Atelier, Vienna, Colour-diapositivs for 76, 81, 84, 92.

Dr. Eva Kraft, Vienna, 83.

Verlag Joh. Leon sen., Klagenfurt-Vienna, 253, 254.

Bruno Reiffenstein, Photo-Atelier, Vienna, 535, 536, 537.

Verlag Rudolf M. Rohrer, Brünn-München-Vienna, 292, 293.

Phot. J. Scherb, Vienna, 441.

Kunstverlag Anton Schroll & Co., Block for Plate X.

Photo W. Wagner, Vienna, 415, 435, 439.

Photo Maria Borik Wölfl, Vienna, 496.

Kunstverlag Wolfrum, Vienna, Blocks for Plates II, XI, XII, XIII, XIV, XV, XVI.

English version: Hedge-roses, Plate V by permission of Augener Ltd., Music Publishers, London.

Silent Night, Plates VI/VII by permission of Simon and Schuster, Inc., New-York.

English translation of the two Grillparzer Dramas in Chapter 3, pages 28 to 49, by permission of The Register Press, Yarmouth Port, Mass.

BIBLIOGRAPHY.

Arzt Leopold, Allgemeine Dermatologie, 1946 (General Dermatology)

Biach-Schiffmann Flora, Giovanni und Ludovica Burnacini, 1931 (Giovanni and Ludovica Burnacini)

Bourgoing Jean, Vom Wiener Kongreß, 1943 (About the Vienna Congress)

Diem Karl, Österreichisches Bäderbuch, 1914 (Austrian Spas)

Doerrer Anton, Das Schemenlaufen in Tirol, 1938 (Masked Festivals in Tyrol)

Frieberger Kurt, Die Spanische Hofreitschule, 1927 (The Spanish Riding School)

Fuchs-Hartmann Werner, Gastmahl der Völker, 1941 (Banquet of the Peoples)

Handbuch der Wiener internationalen Messe, 1937 (Handbook of the Vienna International Fair)

Handbuch für österreichische Ärzte, 1935 (Handbook for Austrian Doctors)

Hantsch Hugo, Die Geschichte Österreichs, 1947 (History of Austria)

Huber Alfons — Redlich Oswald, Geschichte Österreichs, 1885—1938 (History of Austria)

Koller Rudolf, Heimatkundliche Sammlungen, 1935 (Collections of Austrian Folklore)

Kunschak Leopold, Österreich 1918—1934; 1935 (Austria 1918—1934)

Leitich Ann Tizia, Die Wienerin, 1939 (The Vienna Woman)

— Verklungenes Wien, 1942 (Echoes of Vanished Vienna)

Lux P. T., Österreich 1918—1938 eine Demokratie? Betrachtungen eines Neutralen, 1947 (Austria from 1918—1938 a Democracy? Views of a Neutral)

Mayer Franz Martin, Geschichte Österreichs, 1900/1901 (History of Austria)

Morton Friedrich, Wirtschaftsraum Hallstatt, 1934 (The Economic Zone of Hallstatt)

Neuburger Max, Die Bedeutung des alten Österreich für die Entwicklung der Medizin, 1937 (The Importance of Former Austria to Medical Progress)

Österreichisches Institut für Wirtschaftsforschung, 21. Jahrg., Heft 6/48 (Austrian Institute of Economic Research)

Pirchan Emil, Moritz Michael Daffinger, 1943

Rauers Friedrich, Kulturgeschichte der Gaststätte, 1941 (Cultural History of Inns)

Renner Karl, Österreichs Erneuerung, I. bis III. Band, 1917 (Austria's Renewal)

— Denkschrift über die Geschichte der Unabhängigkeitserklärung und die Einsetzung der provisorischen Regierung der Republik, 1945 (Memorandum on the History of the Declaration of Independence and the Setting-up of a Provisional Republican Government)

— Drei Monate Aufbauarbeit der provisorischen Regierung der Republik Österreich, 1945 (Three Months' Reconstructional Work by the Provisional Government of Austria)

Riehl Hans, Barocke Baukunst in Österreich, 1930 (Baroque Architecture in Austria)

Sassmann Hans, Kulturgeschichte Österreichs, 1935 (Cultural History of Austria)

Schönbauer Leopold, Das medizinische Wien, 1947 (Medical Vienna)

Schraml Karl, Das oberösterreichische Salinenwesen, 1932 (Upper Austrian Salines)

Steiner Hugo, 950 Jahre Österreich, 1946 (950 Years of Austria)

Tenschert Roland, Salzburg und seine Festspiele, 1947 (Salzburg and its Festivals)

Uhlirz Karl und Mathilde, Handbuch der Geschichte Österreichs und seiner Nachbarländer Böhmen und Ungarn, 1927 (Manual of the History of Austria and her Neighbours, Bohemia and Hungary)

Wallis Alfons, Österreichs große Musiker, 1935 (Austria's Great Musicians)

Winkler Arnold, Geschichte Österreichs 1918—1945; 1946 (History of Austria)

INDEX.